MICHIGAN TREES

MICHIGAN

BURTON V. BARNES AND WARREN H. WAGNER, JR.

MICHIGAN TREES

A GUIDE TO THE TREES OF MICHIGAN AND THE GREAT LAKES REGION

Ann Arbor   The University of Michigan Press

1992   12

Originally published in 1913 as *Michigan Trees: A Handbook of the Native
and Most Important Introduced Species* by Charles Herbert Otis. Original art-
work by Sarah Phelps provided by courtesy of the Bentley Historical Library
at the University of Michigan.

Library of Congress Cataloging in Publication Data
Barnes, Burton Verne, 1930–
    Michigan trees.

    Bibliography: p.
    Includes index.
    1. Trees—Michigan—Identification.   2. Trees—Great
Lakes region—Identification.   I. Wagner, Warren
Herbert, 1920–   joint author. II. Otis, Charles
Herbert, 1886–   Michigan trees. III. Title.
QK484.M507 1981   582.1609774   80–39717
ISBN 0–472–08018–0

Cover photographs of *Corylus* and *Liriodendron* courtesy of T. Lawrence Mellichamp.

Michigan county map adapted from Wilbert B. Hinsdale, *Archaeological Atlas of
Michigan,* University of Michigan Press, 1931.

Preface

Michigan is fortunate to have a great diversity of trees and shrubs due to its geographical location, variety of climate, and multitude of different habitats. Many southern species occur in the bottom counties of the Lower Peninsula. In the top of the Lower Peninsula and in the Upper Peninsula we find a number of boreal species. In the past, disturbances of the native presettlement forests, especially by agriculture, lumbering, and postlogging fires, have caused profound changes in many localities, so that hardly a hectare remains untouched by human influences. Nevertheless, vigorous woody plant reproduction and reestablishment have revegetated our landscapes. The succession in forest composition provides historical lessons and ecological insights for every field biologist.

To assist you in relating each of the tree species to their physical and biotic surroundings, we have provided a chapter on Michigan's habitats and communities. In addition, there are sections on rare plants and pollination. Special natural history features, as well as landscaping or horticultural applications of each species, are also included.

We consider smaller woody plants, shrubs and vines, also to be important and deserving of study on their own merits. For this reason we have selected and described some of Michigan's more frequently encountered and noteworthy shrub species.

This book is designed for use by a wide audience—students in high schools and colleges, lifelong learners among the senior citizens, land administrators, amateur and professional field biologists, botanists, ecologists, foresters, and conservationists—all of whom have curiosity and a sense of wonder for the world of living things and the role of woody plants.

We wish to acknowledge the following individuals for their contributions: Frances G. Barnes, Janice G. Lacy, Terry L. Sharik, Paul W. Thompson, and Edward G. Voss. Above all we acknowledge the inspiration of our numerous students over the past two decades. Without their interest and encouragement we doubt whether this book would have come into being.

Contents

Woody Plant Identification

Successful identification of woody plants depends on knowing what to look for. Most species can be determined by a few distinguishing characteristics. We have presented in the main body of the book both a detailed description of each species and a concise list of its major or key characters for field use. In addition to dichotomous keys to genera and closely related species, we specifically contrast pairs of species that are difficult to separate. In the sections below, we discuss each of the useful identifying features, such as size and form, bark, and leaves in the order in which they appear in the description of each species. Drawings are added to the species descriptions to clarify the nomenclature and to illustrate different features. Following the detailed description of the trees, brief descriptions of selected shrubs and small trees are presented. A glossary is provided at the end of the book.

Kinds of Trees

Modern trees may be grouped as *gymnosperms* and *angiosperms*. The major gymnospermous trees in Michigan are the conifers, and 10 species of coniferous trees are native. Conifers are sometimes termed "softwoods" due to the soft, light, easily workable wood of some species. The conifers evolved long before the angiosperms and in Mesozoic times achieved great abundance. Most conifers have leaves that remain on the tree several years; the one exception in Michigan is the tamarack or eastern larch. Angiosperms or flowering plants arose later than the conifers, became abundant and widely distributed by the Tertiary period, and today far outnumber the conifers in number and diversity of species. Angiospermous trees typically shed their leaves during winter in the North Temperate Zone. Hence they are termed *deciduous*. Many angiospermous trees in subtropical and tropical climates retain their leaves for several years and are referred to as *evergreen*. No evergreen angiospermous tree is native in Michigan. Deciduous angiosperms are also termed *hardwoods* throughout much of the woody plant literature because their wood is often hard and tough compared to that of the gymnosperms.

Name

Common or colloquial names for each kind of tree have been passed down from generation to generation. We use here the most widely applied and appropriate common name for each species. Common names often designate some prominent feature (bitternut hickory), product (sugar maple), or, more rarely, habitat or place of origin (mountain maple, swamp white oak, Norway maple) or a famous botanist (Douglas-fir, Engelmann spruce). Because most trees have wide geographic ranges, several or many different common names may be used for the same species. In addition, different trade names are applied. Therefore, the scientific name in Latin is the one applied worldwide to maintain clear communication about each species.

The scientific name of a species always consists of two parts, as *Quercus alba,* in English, white oak. The genus name is a noun; it comes first and is always written with a capital letter. The second name, the species epithet, is usually an adjective, and is usually written with a small letter. It is customary to add to these the name (usually abbreviated) of the person or persons who first gave the name to the plant, as *Quercus alba* Linnaeus (*Q. alba* L.). When certain variants of a tree species are propagated for ornamental use, they may be given a garden variety or cultivar (cv.) name which is written as follows: *Populus nigra* cv. Italica or simply *P. nigra* 'Italica'. The cultivar name is always enclosed in single quotation marks or designated cv.; it is not italicized.

Hybrids between two species are designated by the multiplication sign × (meaning hybrid) which is placed before the species epithet if a binomial is used: *Betula ×purpusii,* the hybrid between *Betula alleghaniensis* and *B. pumila,* or a formula is used, for example, *Betula alleghaniensis × pumila.*

Meanings of the scientific names for tree species are available in dendrology books by Hosie (1969) and Harlow et al. (1979). Short biographical sketches of many botanical authors are given by Hosie (1969). A more detailed discussion of the taxonomy and nomenclature of plants is presented by Voss (1972) and Harlow et al. (1979).

Size and Form

Size and form or *habit* refer to the general appearance of the species. A tree is a woody perennial plant with a single trunk (typically unbranched near the base), usually exceeding 5 meters in height. A shrub is a woody perennial plant usually branched several times at or near the base, giving it a bushy appearance, usually less than 5 meters tall.

These are definitions of convenience because in some species many individuals may have a tall single trunk, whereas others may be short and repeatedly branched near the base, due to environmental conditions or damage at some time in their lives. Usually the distinction is clear, but some species have individuals that are small trees and others that are tall shrubs; these species are so indicated in the description.

Because specimens are variable, size and form may be of limited use in identification. Because of the great interference in Michigan forests and other habitats by humans, today we observe trees in a greater variety of stand and site conditions, densities, and associated species than was typical in the presettlement forest. Thus a consistent habit or shape may not be spotted. Tree size and form are strongly influenced by age too, as well as by soils and the level of the water table. Young trees are often narrow and conical in crown form and broaden out as they become older. Trees on moist, fertile soils grow faster than those of the same species on dry, infertile or wet, poorly aerated sites. Trees may be injured by storm, fire, or insects at some period in their growth, and their characteristic outline and symmetry altered. Finally, each specimen has an individuality of its own, controlled by genetic factors, and, as also in people, does not have exactly the same form or growth rate as other individuals of that species. Thus tree habit varies within a species and may not be initially as useful in identification as less variable features. However, in spite of the variation, with experience one soon can distinguish the characteristic stem form and branching pattern of each species. Certain trees may have such a distinctive form that they can be identified immediately, even from a moving vehicle; for example, eastern white pine with its long, upswept branches, American elm with its spreading branches, and Lombardy poplar with its sharply ascending branches.

In the description, each species is given a general size class—small, medium, or large—based primarily on average mature height (which is strongly correlated with trunk diameter). We recognize small trees as those up to about 10 meters, medium-sized trees averaging up to 20 meters, and large trees usually over 20 meters at maturity. Obviously these classes must be arbitrary because of the many factors influencing height and diameter. Thus only approximate ranges of the size a mature tree would attain can be given. The average mature diameter and height are often markedly smaller than that of the largest recorded tree of a given species in the state (Michigan Big Tree; see discussion following). The dimensions of the big trees, especially diameter, represent the maximal size attainable and may be abnormally large or uncharacteristic for the species.

Trunk and crown features are strongly influenced by whether the

3

tree has grown in the open or in a forest stand. Open-grown trees tend to have stout, low-forking trunks, often crooked trunks, and a large, wide-spreading crown. Forest-grown trees usually have long, slender, straight trunks, often well-pruned of lower branches, and a shorter, narrower crown. The diameter of the trunk is measured at breast height, 1.3 meters or 4.5 feet above the ground.

In considering tree form, structure, and the various morphological characters used in identification, it is important to stress the annual *shoot* as the unit of tree construction. Woody plants are constructed of repeating units, the annual shoots, which are made up of *leaves* and *buds* (vegetative and reproductive) attached to a *stem*. The stem portion of the shoot soon becomes woody and is termed a *twig*. The collection of twigs plus older stems makes up the branch system of the tree.

The branching pattern of the woody plant is controlled by the interacting combination of internal genetic factors and the plant's physical environment of soil and atmosphere. In northern and alpine environments, trees (primarily conifers) are adapted to grow in a much more conical or spirelike form than at more southerly latitudes because of the especially rigorous snow, ice, and wind conditions. In these species, especially spruces and firs, the terminal shoot or leader grows faster than the lateral branches below it. This occurs in such a symmetrical way that a strong central stem and a conical crown form are the result. This tree form is termed *excurrent*. It is typical of most conifers and a few deciduous trees such as tuliptree and white ash.

In many deciduous species, the lateral branches grow nearly as fast as or faster than the terminal shoot, and the main stem may fork repeatedly giving rise to a spreading form. This tree form is termed *decurrent* or *deliquescent*. It is typical of oaks, maples, some elms, and many other groups. For a concise treatment of woody plant form and structure see Spurr and Barnes (1980); for a detailed treatment see Kramer and Kozlowski (1979).

Most trees and shrubs reproduce vegetatively by stems or roots. In some species, many stems arise from the root system of a single individual that has been cut or killed by fire. Such a group of genetically identical stems is termed a *clone*. Large clones, growing in the open (as in aspens and some dogwoods) have a symmetrical, rounded profile; in Michigan they may spread up to 0.4 hectare (1 acre) but usually are much smaller. In the literature, terms such as colonies and thickets often indicate the clonal nature of a species.

The girth, diameter, height (to the nearest meter), and county of occurrence are presented for Michigan's largest tree of each species. Although the girth alone of a tree determines the Michigan Big Tree,

4

the national champion for each species is determined on a point system by adding the girth (inches), the height (feet), and one fourth of the average crown spread (feet). The big trees represent the maximum size attainable because they have grown under extremely favorable site conditions and for an unusually long time. Many of them are not found in natural stands but are planted specimens in parks, landscaped grounds, residential yards, and sometimes, in fact, are beyond the natural range of the species. Not surprisingly the dimensions of such open-grown trees are much larger than those of the typical mature tree of a given species in its typical habitat.

Michigan has over 90 national champion trees, second only to Florida. This impressive record is largely due to the dedication of Paul W. Thompson and Harold Nett of Birmingham who together have located 140 of the 167 state and national champions. Lists of the state champions are available in publications by Thompson (1975, 1977) and McKee (1979); the national register of big trees was published by Pardo (1978), and updated lists may be repeated at frequent intervals.

Bark

Characteristics of the bark are probably best for distinguishing species during the late fall and winter. Bark is readily accessible (unlike buds and twigs), and with experience one can distinguish nearly all Michigan species at a distance by their bark. However these characters often change markedly within a given species due to age and growth rate. Bark characters are difficult to describe and illustrate by drawings, but good bark photographs are available in several publications (Hosie 1969; Smith 1978; Harlow et al. 1979).

Bark is a term given to multilayered tissue on the outside of the tree (fig. 1). It consists of various combinations of cell types, but especially cork cells. Epidermis is present only on the youngest stems and is quickly replaced by bark tissues. Cork cambium begins to grow on older twigs leading most commonly to scaly, furrowed bark on old branches and trunks. All trees have smooth bark when young, but most trees soon form roughened bark layers that first show up at the bottom of the trunk. The color, nature, and size of soft, corky spots and lines called *lenticels* are the most important diagnostic features of smooth bark. Only a few trees maintain their smooth, nonexfoliating bark well into maturity. These include beech, downy serviceberry, bigtooth and trembling aspens, and pin cherry.

The main mature bark characters to look for are thickness, degree and nature of roughness (smooth, scaly, exfoliating, furrowed, etc.), color of outer and inner bark, depth and breadth of fissures, width of

5

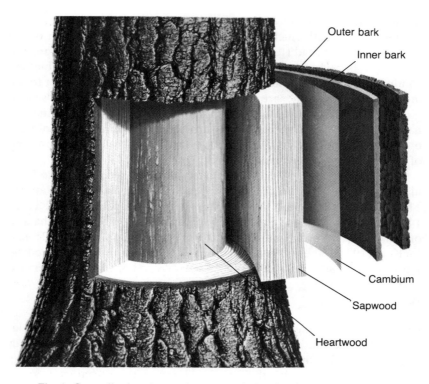

Outer bark

Inner bark

Cambium

Sapwood

Heartwood

Fig. 1. Generalized structure of a tree trunk showing the position of major tissues including the outer bark, inner bark, cambium, sapwood, and heartwood. (*Photo courtesy St. Regis Paper Company.*)

the plates or ridges between the fissures, length of the plates (for example, those of red oak are long, whereas those of black oak are short and blocky), and the degree of interlacing of the ridges (parallel and rarely interlacing in basswood and red oak, interlacing frequently in white ash and larger individuals of sassafras). The manner and rate of radial growth of the tree often determines the breadth of the fissures and whether paler bark layers are visible or not. Within a given species, the faster a tree grows the more likely it will be that the lighter layers are visible between the ridges. In addition, in mature individuals of certain species the inner bark layers are almost always visible, whereas in other species they are rarely visible. For example, mature red oak trees exhibit relatively wide fissures and visible paler inner layers. They are readily distinguished from similar-sized trees of black oak whose fissures are narrow so that lighter colored inner layers are not visible.

Leaves

Leaves are important means of discriminating between species because of their many distinctive features and the convenience of using them. However leaves are variable, occasionally inaccessible, and in our climate present on deciduous trees for only about six months of the year. Nevertheless, they can be used to distinguish all but the most closely related species. During winter the brown fallen leaves of deciduous trees almost always can be found on the ground under the crown.

One can be confused by leaves that are abnormally large or small. Leaf size is influenced by age, size, and vigor of the tree, the length and kind of shoot on which the leaves are borne, and habitat. When comparing leaves between two or more trees it is best to use leaves from the same position in the crown and from the same kind and size of shoot. Conifer leaves are less variable than those of deciduous trees and with one exception are persistent on the branches throughout the year.

Sun leaves are those in the upper and outer crown that are exposed to full sun. They are typically smaller, thicker, more lustrous, and more dissected (having deeper sinuses) than *shade leaves* of the lower and interior crown. Oak leaves in particular show major differences in sun and shade leaves on the same tree such that they are sometimes mistakenly identified as different species.

In winter, leaves of trees are preformed and tightly packed inside the terminal and lateral buds of the last season's shoots. These *early* leaves (so named because they develop early in the growing season) are the best ones to use in identification during the following growing season. Most useful are early leaves borne on *determinate* shoots (shoots that extend and then set buds early in the growing season). Shoots that continue to grow during the entire season (*indeterminate* shoots) have the early leaves along their base and then give rise to new *late* leaves as the shoot develops during the latter part of the season. These late leaves may be markedly different from the typical, preformed early leaves. Late leaves are hard to use in making identifications because they are so different. The long shoots with both types of leaves are usually the terminal shoot of the tree and the dominant laterals. They are found most frequently in the upper crown. Early and late leaves in conifers are not greatly different and create no problems in identification.

Some genera (*Ginkgo, Larix, Prunus, Betula, Malus*) have short, spurlike shoots, bearing leaves more or less clustered, in addition to long shoots. These leaves are good for identification purposes.

Under certain conditions shoots issue directly from the trunk of

7

species in various genera (*Quercus, Prunus, Ulmus,* among others) and are termed *epicormic branches.* They often produce leaves markedly different from the typical early leaves of the species. These leaves are confusing and should be avoided in identification.

Leaves exhibit many characters that are good for identification. However, not every possible character is given for each species, just those of particular importance. For each species the pertinent characters are described in a systematic way in the following sequence:

Leaf arrangement on the stem (alternate, opposite, or whorled)
Blade division (simple or compound)
Blade size and shape for simple leaves, leaf length and leaflet size and shape for compound leaves
Blade tip and base
Blade margin (entire, lobed, serrate, etc.)
Blade texture
Blade color of both sides in the growing season and in autumn
Blade pubescence
Venation (number, pattern, branching)
Petiole (size, shape, color, presence of glands)

Examples of leaf shapes or outlines are illustrated in figure 2; kinds of leaf tips and bases are shown in figure 3; and the most common margin types are pictured in figure 4.

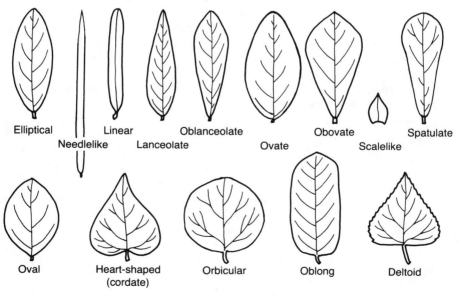

Elliptical   Linear   Oblanceolate   Obovate   Spatulate
Needlelike   Lanceolate   Ovate   Scalelike

Oval   Heart-shaped   Orbicular   Oblong   Deltoid
(cordate)

Fig. 2. Leaf shapes

8

Leaf size and shape are important characters for many species. However, leaf dimensions are highly variable, even within a single tree, and so the dimensions presented serve only as a relative guide to leaf and blade size. For simple leaves the blade length of representa-

Leaf Tips

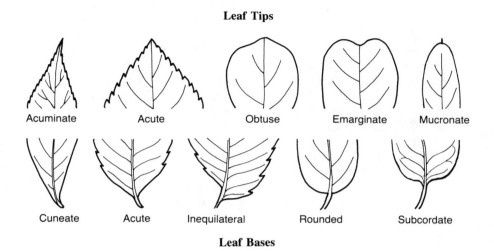

Leaf Bases

Fig. 3. Selected leaf tips and bases

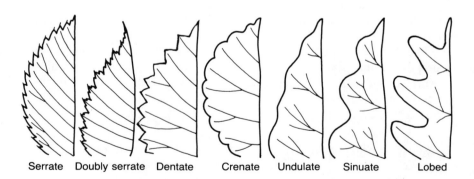

Fig. 4. Leaf margins

9

tive leaves is given and the width is usually expressed as a proportion of the length. The relative petiole length is also sometimes useful and is mentioned separately from blade dimensions. For compound leaves, total length and the dimensions of the leaflets are given.

It is best to examine the most striking characters first, i.e., whether leaf arrangement is alternate or opposite and whether leaves are simple or compound. Most tree species have alternate arrangement (in a spiral along the shoot). Therefore, when one finds leaf arrangement to be opposite, identification is greatly simplified. Because buds arise in the axils of leaves, species with opposite leaf arrangement also have opposite branch arrangement (if both branches develop). Thus if leaves are absent or too high to reach, the branching pattern can indicate the leaf arrangement. Most trees have simple leaves; therefore the presence of compound leaves narrows the task of identification considerably.

Leaves of some deciduous trees are persistent in a brown and withered form over winter. Leaf retention occurs primarily in the Fagaceae and in some Aceraceae. It is characteristic especially of young, open-grown trees but may also occur on the lower, inner branches of large trees.

Twigs

We define a twig or branchlet as the woody terminal portion of a branch. It is distinguished from a shoot in that it consists of stem and buds, whereas a shoot consists of a stem plus its leaves and buds, i.e., the current year's growth. Twigs are not only the stem of current annual shoots, but may include the stem portions of recent years' shoots that have become woody. These woody twig sections of a branch no longer bear leaves and young buds but have leaf scars and undeveloped old buds.

The annual shoot is the repeating unit of which woody plants are composed, and patterns of shoot growth give each species its peculiar form and structure. We have identified three kinds of shoots in the section on leaves, and two of these often occur on the same plant. The shoot types are:

Short, spurlike or dwarf shoots (fig. 5). They are preformed inside certain lateral vegetative buds, and make little growth in length because there is little or no interleaf elongation. They bear only early leaves (and sometimes flowers), and are found in *Ginkgo, Larix, Prunus, Malus,* and *Sorbus.*

10

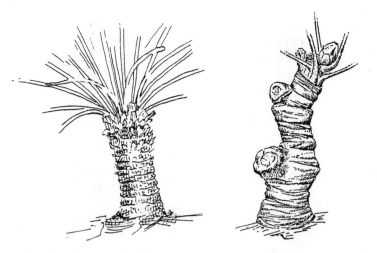

Fig. 5. Short, spurlike or dwarf shoot of larix and apple. (*Apple shoot after Core and Ammons 1973.*)

Seasonally determinate long shoots (fig. 6). These are totally preformed within the terminal buds and vegetative lateral buds,
make substantial growth in length, bear only early leaves, and are
found in all species.

Seasonally indeterminate long shoots. The basal portion is predeter-
mined in terminal buds. After this portion (bearing early leaves)
elongates in the spring, a new section of shoot continues to grow
in the late spring and summer (often 25 centimeters or more),
and gives rise to late leaves. This shoot type may stop growth
temporarily during summer drought, but only ceases growth entirely as the shortening days of late summer and autumn signal
the approach of winter. Such shoots are found in *Betula, Larix,
Pinus, Prunus, Populus,* and *Salix.*

If in reach, twigs provide good identifying characteristics for the
keen observer throughout the year. In the spring, the stems of new
annual shoots are green and herbaceous. They change color rapidly
during the growing season and the same twig the following year takes
on a different color and becomes woody. The position of the twigs in
the crown markedly affects their exposure and hence their color and
size.

The principal twig characters for identification are diameter (slender
or stout); color; form (straight, drooping, zigzag); pubescence (often
deciduous); prickles, spines, and thorns; leaf scars and bundle scars;

11

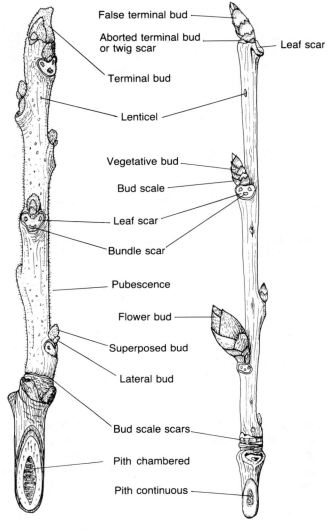

False terminal bud

Aborted terminal bud
or twig scar

Leaf scar

Terminal bud

Lenticel

Vegetative bud

Bud scale

Leaf scar

Bundle scar

Pubescence

Flower bud

Superposed bud

Lateral bud

Bud scale scars

Pith chambered

Pith continuous

Black Walnut (× 1⅓)   **American Elm (× 2)**

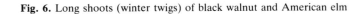

Fig. 6. Long shoots (winter twigs) of black walnut and American elm

pith (color, shape, whether continuous, diaphragmed, or chambered); lenticels; other characters such as peeling epidermis, corky ridges, etc. Figure 6 illustrates shoots of black walnut and American elm with various twig characters as well as winter buds.

Prickles, spines, and thorns

Sharp-pointed structures, such as prickles, spines, and thorns, are good identification features. They serve to protect the shoot, especially in the juvenile stage, from herbivores. *Prickles* are an outgrowth of the epidermis or cortex and are relatively easily dislodged from the twig (as in roses, or Hercules-club). They lack vascular strands. *Spines* are specialized leaves or parts of leaves; the stipular spines of black locust are one example. *Thorns* are probably more common than prickles or spines and are specialized stems. Both spines and thorns have vascular bundles just as in typical leaf and stem tissues. In hawthorns and Osage-orange, the thorns are unbranched, whereas in honeylocust they are typically branched.

Leaf scars and bundle scars

The arrangement, size, and shape of leaf scars and the number and arrangement of bundle scars within the leaf scar are excellent diagnostic traits. In balsam fir, the round, nonelevated leaf scar is distinctive. In contrast, leaves of all spruce species are borne on small projections or pegs raised above the twig surface; these are termed *sterigmata* (singular *sterigma*). Deciduous trees shed their leaves in autumn through the action of a corky *abscission layer*. This layer causes the leaf to snap off and then seals the living tissues of the stem for protection. The scar of the leaf attachment or *leaf scar* varies greatly in size and shape depending on features of the petiole. Furthermore, within the leaf scars are one or more small raised or depressed spots or dots, which though sometimes quite inconspicuous, are often very prominent. These scars are left by the vascular strands, bundles, or traces that pass through the stem into the petiole and leaf blade (fig. 7A) and that carry water and nutrients into and from the veins of the leaves. They are termed *bundle scars* and have a characteristic number and arrangement (fig. 7B,C,D,E). There may be only one, as in sassafras, hackberry, and privet; two, as in ginkgo; three, as in poplars, aspens, cherries, and maples; or many, as in oaks and ashes. They may be arranged in a curved group (fig. 7B), sometimes referred to as a U- or V-shaped line, or rarely they appear to be without definite order (fig. 7C). Their number may vary from many (fig. 7B and C), to a few (fig. 7D), or even one (fig. 7E).

Pith

In the center of the twig, a mass of soft-walled parenchyma cells, termed *pith,* provides important distinguishing features. Usually it is white, but it may be brown, green, yellow, or pink. In cross section, the pith is usually circular, but it may be triangular as in the alders, or

13

star-shaped as in oaks. When cut longitudinally, the pith is typically *continuous* and homogeneous (fig. 8*A*). However, it may also be *diaphragmed,* i.e., having at regular intervals plates of heavier-walled, horizontally arranged cells (fig. 8*B*). Rarely, empty spaces are formed between the diaphragms resulting in small spaces or chambers, hence the term *chambered pith* (fig. 8*C*). Diaphragmed pith is found in tuliptree and blackgum and chambered pith in butternut and black walnut.

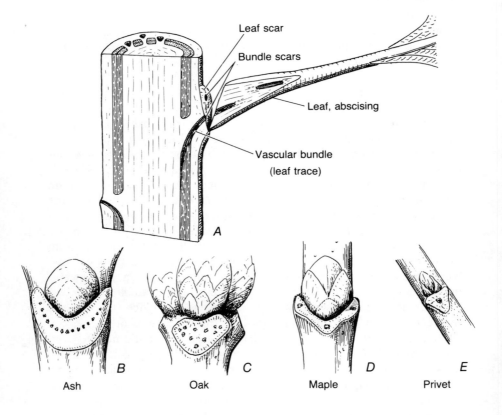

Fig. 7. *A:* Longitudinal section of twig and petiole illustrating the position of vascular tissues. *B–E:* Leaf scars of woody plants illustrating the number and arrangement of bundle scars. *B:* Ash; *C:* Oak; *D:* Maple; *E:* Privet. (*After Core and Ammons 1973.*)

Lenticels

The small, corky, wartlike prominences in the form of bumps or lines irregularly scattered over the surface of twigs are called *lenticels*. They function to admit oxygen and other gases needed in respiration and other physiological processes. In extreme cases, as when flooded for prolonged periods, trees like willows and cottonwoods can obtain oxygen for respiration of their roots through lenticels on the stems above water. The shape of lenticels may help in identification; most are round or oval, but they may be elongated horizontally in the cherries and birches. In *Sambucus* species, the abundance and large size of wartlike lenticels are a striking feature.

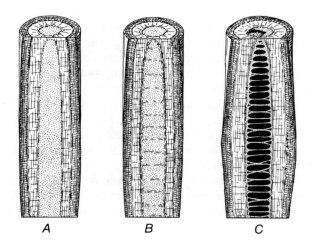

Fig. 8. Longitudinal stem sections illustrating pith types. *A*, continuous pith; *B*, diaphragmed pith; *C*, chambered pith. (*After Core and Ammons 1973.*)

Stipule scars
Stipules are small leafy flaps that occur at each side of the petiole base where it attaches to the stem. When they fall off they leave tiny scars called *stipule scars*. They are not present in all species and when present usually appear as little, inconspicuous lines or dots.

Winter Buds

Buds are like tiny cocoons. They are the dormant undeveloped young shoots usually protected by special, hard flaps called *bud scales*. The majority of buds, especially laterals, remain quiescent and never form shoots unless induced to do so by growth regulators or injury. Buds are formed of protective outer bud scales that are exposed, additional but softer inner bud scales, embryonic leaves, and in the very center, the delicate embryonic growing point. The formation of a new shoot, as in

15

the spring of the year, is accomplished by shedding the bud scales, enlarging the leaves, and (except in short or spurlike shoots) elongating the stem axis. Some buds produce flowers.

Buds are important identification characteristics in autumn and winter. Their arrangement, size, shape, color, the presence or absence of pubescence, and the number, kind, and arrangement of bud scales are major identification features. All species have lateral buds, situated on the sides of the shoot in the axils of the leaves (in winter the leaf scars). The buds may be closely appressed to the stem or may diverge from it in varying degrees. All species have buds at the end of the current shoot, *terminal* or *end buds,* but not all species have true terminal buds since the end bud in many species is actually a lateral bud. In birches, elms, willows, basswood, and many other groups, the tip of the twig dies back or aborts, leaving a small bump or scar at the end of the twig. The closest lateral bud then takes the place of the true terminal bud and is termed a *false terminal bud, pseudoterminal bud,* or simply *end bud.* The presence of the aborted tip and a leaf scar immediately below and to one side of the end bud indicates that the true terminal bud is absent (see fig. 6).

Lateral buds are typically similar to the terminal buds, but they are usually smaller. In the species descriptions, it is the terminal or end buds that are described unless otherwise indicated. Lateral buds are either vegetative (containing the embryonic lateral shoots and their leaves) or reproductive (containing embryonic flowers or cones). In some hardwood groups, the walnuts for example, the lateral vegetative and flower buds are positioned one above the other, termed *superposed.* The flower bud is typically located below the vegetative bud on the stem. Flower buds and cone buds are often somewhat larger and more globose than vegetative lateral buds.

Wood

Being a less accessible character than the other traits for the naturalist and field biologist, wood is not used as a major distinguishing feature. However, we have maintained the basic description of wood characters and have included the major uses of the wood for most species.

The general view of the structure of a tree trunk, figure 1, illustrates the position of the bark, cambium, sapwood, and heartwood. The *cambium* is the living meristematic sheath of cells that surrounds the trunk, branches, shoots, and roots. Toward the outside of the tree the cambium gives rise to the *phloem,* part of the inner bark, through which food materials and other substances (especially growth regulators) are transported, mainly from the crown to stem and root tissues. Toward

16

the inside of the tree the cambium gives rise to the water-conducting tissue or *xylem* that forms the *sapwood.* As the tree ages, the dead cells of the xylem become filled with resins and other compounds giving the *heartwood* a harder texture and a darker color than the sapwood.

The radial or diameter growth of trees is primarily due to the periodic formation of layers of xylem cells. In species of the temperate zones, the annual growth rings are more or less distinguishable and enable one to determine the age of the tree. This radial growth of trees is termed *secondary growth,* whereas the extension growth of shoots is termed *primary growth.* For details of the structure and physiological relations of wood consult Kramer and Kozlowski (1979). For those interested in the properties of wood and its uses, the book by Panshin and de Zeeuw (1970) is recommended.

Uses of Woody Plants

Today many of the traditional uses of trees and shrubs have been supplanted by other sources. For example, plastics are often used in place of wood in many instances. Nevertheless, we have included in our species descriptions under the heading "Wood" many of the traditional uses, even though some of these are no longer of primary importance.

We should emphasize that all woody plants can be used for firewood, although some species are better than others. All woods per unit of weight yield approximately the same amount of heat energy when burned, approximately 8,500 to 9,000 Btu.'s per oven dry pound. Thus, dense hardwoods (such as oaks, hickories, sugar maple, beech, birches) yield more heat *per unit volume* than such woods as aspens, spruces, and northern white-cedar. In general, conifers have a higher heat value per unit of weight than do hardwoods. In addition, resins present in conifers, such as the pines, provide additional heat. However, the conifers are usually less dense than most hardwoods, tend to burn faster, and require more volume for a given amount of heat (more trips to the woodbox!). All wood contains some moisture, and the higher the moisture content (for example, freshly cut, living trees) the greater amount of heat required to evaporate the moisture in the wood; as a consequence a lower amount of heat is available. Thus, well-dried or seasoned wood is desirable.

Flowers and Pollination

Flowers are almost always excellent features for plant classification and identification because they tend to vary less than leaf, twig, and habit characters. They are especially useful for recognizing genera. The ma-

17

jor drawbacks of tree flowers for identification are that they are often borne in the upper crown, and they last for only a brief time. They are unavailable to most people (except those who are 45 feet tall). Therefore although we have described the floral features, we have not used them to distinguish species.

The young reproductive structures of conifers are termed *strobili, conelets,* or *cones.* They are not technically flowers because the seed is not enclosed in an ovary nor are other floral parts (stamens, pistils, calyx, or corolla) ever present. The seed or ovule enclosing the embryo is borne naked on the scale of the cone.

Individual tree flowers are usually unisexual, small, and inconspicuous. They are commonly borne in catkins or aments. Many tree species have male and female flowers or cones on the same individual; this is termed the *monoecious* condition. Certain genera (*Populus, Fraxinus, Ailanthus, Ginkgo, Acer*) have species in which male and female flowers are borne separately on unisexual trees; this is termed the *dioecious* condition. Rarely do trees bear perfect flowers having both stamens and pistils as well as showy petals. Species in *Prunus, Tilia,* and *Robinia* do have perfect flowers, and these are insect-pollinated groups. The parts of a perfect flower are shown in figure 9. All conifers and the majority of deciduous tree species in Michigan are wind-pollinated. Some wind-dispersed tree pollens cause allergies to some people in the spring.

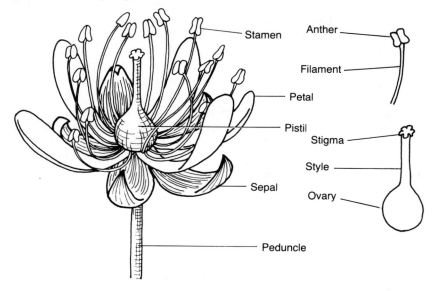

Fig. 9. Parts of a perfect flower

The different ways the flowers are borne on deciduous trees are shown in figure 10. The flower clusters are called *inflorescences*. The fruits develop from the fertilized female flowers and therefore are borne in the same way. The fruit clusters are sometimes termed *infructescences*.

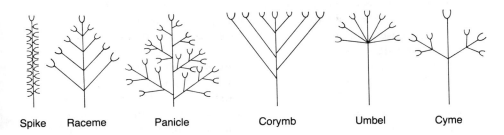

| Spike | Raceme | Panicle | Corymb | Umbel | Cyme |

Fig. 10. Types of inflorescences of flowering trees

Juvenile trees do not normally flower and fruit. The age and size at which each species begins flower and seed production are closely associated with its growth rate. Fast-growing species (willows, white birch, aspens, jack pine) typically become reproductively active much earlier chronologically than slow-growing trees (beech, hemlock, sugar maple). Although some fruits or cones are usually produced each year, especially by fast-growing, shade-intolerant species, abundant crops are produced at irregular intervals. The age of seed bearing and the periodicity of fruiting for most tree species are available from the U.S. Department of Agriculture (1974).

Pollination

The transfer of pollen from the male organs to the appropriate receptors in the female organs is called pollination. The actual fertilization is accomplished later inside the primordial seed. Pollen as seen en masse is generally a yellowish powder, the individual grains microscopic, averaging 0.02–0.04 millimeters in diameter. The most conspicuous "pollen rains" in Michigan are seen in the coniferous forests of the north, where at the proper time, usually late May or early June, enormous quantities of yellow pollen are released into the air. These so-called sulfur showers may actually coat the surfaces of ponds and lakes so as to make them bright yellow. Most pollen, however, is unnoticed (except by individuals who are allergic to it), though during the proper seasons the air, even in downtown Detroit or Lansing, contains sizable quantities.

The two major means of pollination in our area are wind and insects. All of the gymnosperms are pollinated by wind. The flowering plants may be pollinated one way or the other, depending on the species. A few, like certain willows, may be pollinated both ways. Because there is much chance involved in wind pollination and only a few pollen grains reach their goal by this means, wind-pollinated plants produce relatively large amounts of pollen. In contrast, insect-pollinated plants need to produce only small amounts of pollen, because the insect tends to visit other flowers of the same kind, and thus usually transfers the pollen with considerable precision.

Wind-pollinated cones and flowers are generally very simple. They lack or have only slightly developed petals or attractive structures, and they are usually unisexual, having either only male organs or only female organs. Insect-pollinated flowers can be recognized because they are more or less showy, the petals well developed and usually white or brightly colored. They tend to be fragrant, and they usually produce nectar which the insects use as food. The nectaries often appear as shiny swellings in the flower, and at the time of pollination they secrete sugary liquid. Insect-pollinated flowers tend to have both sex organs present at the same time in the same flower, even though they may not necessarily function at exactly the same time. A complete flower with sepals, petals, stamens, nectaries, and ovaries all present is practically always pollinated by insects. In the tropics other animals commonly participate in pollination, notably bats and birds. Among warm-blooded animals in Michigan, only hummingbirds carry out pollination. Trees and shrubs in our area are pollinated by a variety of insects, including flies, bees and wasps, butterflies and moths, and beetles. In general, the bees and wasps are most efficient.

Interestingly the incidence of wind pollination is much greater in trees than in shrubs. In Michigan practically all of our large forest trees are wind-pollinated, some prominent exceptions being tuliptree, sassafras, and black cherry. Conversely, practically all of our shrubs are insect-pollinated, some exceptions being dwarf birch, sweet-fern, and American hazelnut. The bulk of pollination takes place between the middle of April and the middle of June (or later farther north) in our woody plants. Certain closely related species may pollinate at different times; for example, dwarf hackberry and northern hackberry are separated by as much as 8–10 days, and the same is true of trembling aspen and bigtooth aspen.

The season of maximum production of wind-borne tree pollen is around the first of May in southern Michigan. Certain individuals develop allergic reactions to pollens of such trees as elms, oaks, and birches. A few species flower in late summer and fall. The latest flowering woody plant in the Great Lakes area is the witch-hazel (*Hamamelis virginiana*) which flowers as late as November. The shrubby cinquefoil is unusual in blooming throughout late spring and summer until fall; its beautiful yellow flowers may be seen practically any time during the warm·seasons.

Fruits and Cones

The seed-bearing products of the plant, termed *fruits* in angiosperms and *cones* in conifers, are extremely important in identifying species. One or more fruit or cone characters are almost always among the key characters of each species. Fruits and cones are more accessible than flowers because they stay on the tree for a longer time, and often they may be found under or near the tree. Fruits and cones, like flowers, are also usually less variable than leaves, twigs, and habit.

In conifers, the seeds are borne in cones, which may be woody or, rarely, fleshy. In angiospermous trees seeds are borne in fruits, which differ markedly in morphology due to the many ways in which the ovary walls, which contain the seeds, develop: a thin, papery outgrowth or wing in the *samara,* a stony inner wall and an outer fleshy covering in the *drupe,* and the all or mostly fleshy tissue of the *berry* and *pome.* The major fruit types are illustrated in figure 11.

Dry fruits that split open along suture lines include the *capsule, legume,* and *follicle.* Dry fruits that do not split are the *nut, samara,* and *achene.* Many of the dry fruits that split open enclose seeds that have tufts of cottony hairs attached to them (willows, poplars, and aspens) or wings, as in catalpa. These seeds are primarily wind disseminated. Fleshy fruits, the *berry, drupe,* and *pome,* are primarily dispersed by birds and mammals which eat them.

Simple fruits are sometimes more or less permanently clustered together as compound fruits. They are termed either aggregate or multiple depending on whether the fruits are derived from a single flower with many pistils (*aggregate*) or many, separate flowers (*multiple*). The tuliptree has an aggregate of samaras, red and white mulberry a multiple of drupes, and sycamore a multiple of achenes.

Distribution

A general statement of the present natural occurrence of each species is given. It is based on the range maps of Little (1971, 1977), specimens at the University of Michigan Herbarium, and personal observations by the authors. In addition, an estimate of the abundance of each species is given based on a continuously grading five-part scale modified from Voss (1972):

21

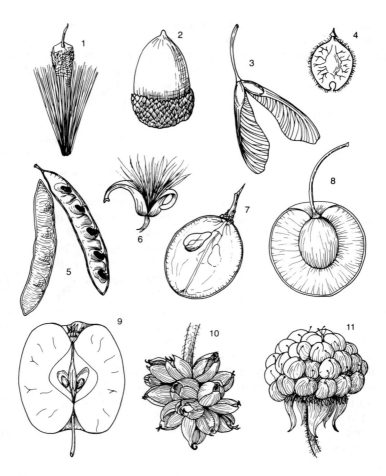

Fig. 11. Selected fruit types of woody plants: (1) *achene* of sycamore (*Platanus*); (2) *acorn* of oak (*Quercus*); (3) double *samara* of maple (*Acer*); (4) single *samara* of elm (*Ulmus*); (5) *legume* of black locust (*Robinia*), open; (6) *capsule* of willow (*Salix*); (7) *berry* of grape (*Vitis*), cut open; (8) *drupe* of cherry (*Prunus*), cut open; (9) *pome* of apple (*Malus*), cut open; (10) multiple of *drupes* of mulberry (*Morus*); (11) aggregate of *drupes* of black raspberry (*Rubus*).

Rare	Very seldom encountered, occurring singly or in small numbers wherever found, often absent in the expected habitats.
Occasional	Infrequent in the habitats and areas where it grows.
Frequent	Usually found if one looks for it, but not commonly occurring.

Common	Usually and easily found, widespread and reasonably plentiful throughout its range and expected habitats.
Abundant	Very common to always present in its expected range and habitats.

The distribution and abundance statements given by us will vary in their accuracy and should be used and interpreted with care. Significant occurrences of a species outside the range indicated should be reported to the authors.

Habitat

We have attempted to describe briefly the natural, presettlement forest habitat of each species as well as other habitats in which the species occurs today. What we call simply a forest is actually a complex ecological system, or *ecosystem*, of many interrelated parts. A forest ecosystem is composed of the living organisms, plants and animals of all sizes and descriptions, and its nonliving physical environment, termed its *habitat* or *site*. Habitat, or site, is defined as the sum total of atmospheric and soil factors available and surrounding the plant. The biotic component of plants and animals constantly interacts with these physical factors such that the microclimate and the soil are influenced and changed by the plants and animals occupying the habitat. Therefore, there never can be a completely clear and sharp distinction between the habitat and the biota—they are intimately interrelated, each changing the other in a continually changing and dynamic process.

Most tree species have very wide habitat tolerances. If planted they will grow over a surprising range of climatic and soil conditions, often markedly different from their natural habitat. This is observed in the success of many introduced trees, such as Norway spruce, Norway maple, and Lombardy poplar. The European white poplar apparently has a greater geographic range than any native species of North America. Native trees such as American elm and silver maple, whose natural habitats are flooded, alluvial stream banks, fertile bottomlands, and swamps, thrive on upland city streets when planted. Thus where there is no or little competition and they are established by planting, trees are able to grow in a wide variety of climates and soils, far outside their geographic ranges.

All tree species grow best on moist, fertile sites that are not too hot or cold and not too wet or dry, i.e., a *mesic* site condition. Jack pine, occurring naturally on hot, dry sites with deep, infertile, sandy soils, would thrive on moister, more fertile sites. However, it cannot compete with the species better adapted to these sites (sugar maple, beech, basswood, yellow birch) under natural conditions.

23

Under presettlement forest conditions, competition for light, soil moisture, and nutrients was keen, and the various species tended to be restricted to habitats where they were genetically adapted to reproduce and establish. For certain trees this meant severe restriction to extreme sites (usually wet or dry habitats). Tamarack was relegated to swamps, and jack pine to the driest, most infertile, sandy soils. Other species had traits enabling them to compete, reproduce, and establish on a much wider spectrum of sites.

Disturbances by fire, wind, flooding, ice storms, etc., were common occurrences in presettlement forests, and the forests were in a constant state of changing species composition. The concept of the completely stable, unchanging, virgin, or pristine forest is a myth. All species are more or less adapted to colonize sites where natural disturbances remove competing vegetation and provide light, moisture, or a suitable seedbed for establishment and growth. Some species, such as pines, aspens, birches, and elms are much more adapted to disturbances than others. Therefore, as far as we understand these complex relationships, we present the presettlement forest habitat of each species. The tree species that are most likely to be associated with the described species in its presettlement habitat are also listed. For introduced species we give the site conditions in which they will grow.

Habitat is less of a distinguishing characteristic today than it would have been in presettlement times. The enormous disturbance by humans, much of it quite unlike natural disturbances, pine logging and subsequent hot slash fires, land clearing, draining of lowlands, and highway construction, have caused many site changes. Thus site distinctions and resultant communities that were once relatively clear are today often blurred and sometimes totally gone. With natural competition reduced, many species that are well equipped for rapid colonization have become established on sites that would not have been available to them under presettlement conditions or in numbers that would have previously been unlikely. The small-seeded, wind-dispersed deciduous trees (aspens, elms, white birch, ashes) benefited most, and bird-dispersed species such as the cherries, junipers, and hawthorns, have also apparently increased in abundance.

Fire exclusion is a particularly important practice that was introduced by humans. It is slowly changing the composition of Michigan communities, and in some places creating situations that rarely occurred in presettlement times. Fire was always periodically present in the presettlement forest, and lack of fire has allowed many stands of fire-dependent species (pines, oaks) to be invaded by species (such as red maple, sugar maple, ashes) that would have been killed by fire.

The habitat conditions of the species are described primarily in relation to soil moisture, water table levels, and nutrient status (fertile, infertile). Light relations are described briefly in the notes. Soil moisture conditions are rated on an arbitrary but widely used five-part scale from very dry to very wet: xeric, dry-mesic, mesic, wet-mesic, and hydric. The level of the water table is estimated on a scale from low (far below the root zone) to high (at the surface): excessively drained, somewhat excessively drained, well drained, moderately well drained, somewhat poorly drained, poorly drained, and undrained. Sandy sites where jack pine typically grows would be characterized as xeric and excessively drained; the swamp conditions where black spruce is dominant would be classed as hydric and poorly drained or undrained.

Habitat relations of forest trees are very complex, and the descriptions presented are necessarily oversimplified. This is especially true because optimum conditions for one factor may compensate for less than adequate conditions for one or more other factors. Nevertheless, for the keen and understanding observer, habitat is still a powerful means of discriminating between species, despite human disturbances. For a detailed description of species in relation to site and community factors, the reader may consult Spurr and Barnes (1980) and the U.S. Department of Agriculture (1965).

Notes

Pertinent information about the species not presented in earlier sections is included in the notes. This includes the ability of individuals of a species to establish and survive in the forest understory, estimated using several arbitrary *shade tolerance* classes: very shade-tolerant, shade-tolerant, moderately shade-tolerant, shade-intolerant, and very shade-intolerant. The establishment of a seedling is the single most critical period in the plant's life. The ability of a tree seedling to establish in the forest understory is therefore highly significant. Those trees capable of surviving in the understory and responding to release to reach the overstory will inevitably form a major part of the evolving forest community. The ability of a woody plant to survive and prosper in the understory depends on its tolerance of several factors of the understory environment that may be limiting. Shade, reduced light intensity, is one major factor. Some species are able to survive and grow in the deeply shaded understory (beech, hemlock, sugar maple), whereas shade-intolerant species (willows, eastern cottonwood, aspens, white birch, sycamore, jack pine, tamarack, etc.) would soon die. They require high light intensities to survive and prosper. However, shade is not the only limiting factor of the understory. Moisture is often even more important due to the intense competition for soil moisture in mid-summer by the roots of trees already present. Nutrients, microclimate, browsing animals, insects, and disease are other factors that also may limit a plant's establishment in the understory. Although we use the term shade tolerance to indicate the ability of a species to become established under unfavorable understory conditions, one must always keep in mind that many other interacting factors besides light are involved. The estimates of understory tolerance given here are based on the observations and experience of field biologists as well as on the results of controlled light-intensity experiments with many species. Tolerance to shade and understory conditions varies considerably within a species, and so such estimates must be interpreted with great care. In almost all species, seedlings (juvenile plants) are more tolerant of shade and the understory environment than older individuals of the same species, i.e., tolerance decreases with increasing age. Estimates of understory tolerance have been published by forest ecologists, and detailed discussions about the nature of understory tolerance as well as tables giving tolerance ratings are presented by Daniel et al. (1979) and Spurr and Barnes (1980).

Although the growth rate of a species varies greatly due to age and site conditions, we have estimated a height growth rate that young to middle-aged trees would achieve in their representative forest habitat. These approximate rates are: slow-growing, less than 30 centimeters (1 foot) per year; moderately slow-growing, 30–60 centimeters (1–2 feet) per year; moderately fast-growing, 60–90 centimeters (2–3 feet) per year; fast-growing, greater than 90 centimeters (3 feet) per year.

The longevity of each species in its natural habitat is estimated as either short-lived (less than 100 years), moderately short-lived (100–150 years), moderately long-lived (150–250 years), and long-lived (over 250 years).

Other kinds of information presented include sprouting ability, uses of the plant, origin of the name, and hybrids with other species. Brief descriptions of closely related species are also given where appropriate.

Key Characters

Rapid and accurate identification is accomplished by knowing what characters to examine. We have therefore ranked in rough order of importance and convenience the major distinguishing features of each species. In addition, the specific features of species that are easily confused and difficult to distinguish are contrasted. This is a supplement to the key, which because of its brevity, may not give all the useful characters.

26

Rare Trees and Shrubs

In this book we leave out or only mention a number of trees and shrubs that are so rare they are unlikely to be encountered by the average person. Among them is the remarkable devil's-club, *Oplopanax horridus* (Sm.) Miq., of Isle Royale, where it is disjoined from the metropolis of its range in western North America (Montana, westward and northward) by roughly 3200 kilometers. *Rare* species are those that are so uncommon that they should be monitored to determine whether their populations are becoming threatened. *Threatened* species are so uncommon or likely to be exploited that they may become endangered. An *endangered* species is one that is so precarious that it may become extinct. Approximately twenty woody plants, half trees and half shrubs, are considered rare or threatened in Michigan (Wagner et al. 1977).

In addition to these species, some of our rarest trees are actually interspecific hybrids; these are often single individuals, usually growing with or near their parents. They are usually not listed together with threatened or endangered species because if the parents are common and grow in the same habitats, occasional hybrids will be expected to form. Also, hybrids tend to be reduced in fertility, or unable to compete and form viable populations.

Many of our rare plants are considered so because the edge of their natural range barely enters Michigan. A case in point is the swamp cottonwood, *Populus heterophylla,* which reaches its northernmost limit in a few localities in southern Michigan. Users of this book are urged to inform authorities in research centers (e.g., Michigan State University, University of Michigan, Cranbrook Institute of Science) of any unusual finds. Usually a carefully pressed shoot with its leaves (and fruits if present) can be identified by an expert.

27

Michigan Habitats and Communities

The distribution of woody plants is closely related to climate, geological features, and soils. We consider briefly the physical setting of Michigan forests before discussing the forest species and communities in relation to their environments.

Climate

Climate is the primary factor determining the occurrence of trees on a regional level (Great Lakes region or state of Michigan). On the local level, physiography (elevation, aspect, slope position, water table conditions, etc.) and soils (particle size, nutrient availability, etc.), together with local climate and other factors combine to determine occurrence.

The most important climatic factor is temperature. In Michigan, decreasing temperatures from south to north, a mean annual change from 50° F (10° C) to 40° F (4.4° C) (fig. 12). The average minimum and maximum temperatures (figs. 13 and 14) also show a marked decrease from south to north. These temperature variations cause major changes in the distribution of trees. For example, southern Michigan is the northern limit of continuous distribution for many species. Temperature is strongly modified by large bodies of water, especially Lakes Michigan and Superior. The minima of the northern Lower Peninsula and Upper Peninsula are from 4 to 10° F warmer along the lake margins than in the interior (fig. 13).

Temperature effects are best assayed and understood in terms of plant growth, which is strongly related to the number of days in the growing season—the number of days between the last frost in spring and the first frost in autumn (fig. 15). In the southernmost part of the Lower Peninsula there are 160 to 170 days of growing season, whereas in the high plains of the northern Lower Peninsula there is a progressive decline to about 70 days. There is also a marked difference in minimum temperatures, about 10° F (5.6 C) from south to north. One would expect a major difference in forest composition, and there is. The striking moderating effects of Lake Michigan are noted in figure 15. In the Upper Peninsula the pattern of growing season length is

28

Fig. 12. Michigan annual mean temperature (°F), 1940–69. (*From Michigan Department of Agriculture, Michigan Weather Service. 1975.* Mean temperature maps for the period 1940–1969. *Supp. to* The climate of Michigan by stations. *East Lansing, Mich.: State of Michigan, Department of Agriculture.*)

Fig. 13. Michigan January average daily minimum temperature (°F), 1940–69. (*From Michigan Department of Agriculture, Michigan Weather Service. 1976. Average daily minimum temperature maps for the period 1940–1969. Supp. to* The climate of Michigan by stations. *East Lansing, Mich.: State of Michigan, Department of Agriculture.*)

Fig. 14. Michigan July average daily maximum temperature (°F), 1940–69. (*From Michigan Department of Agriculture, Michigan Weather Service. 1976. Average maximum temperature maps for the period 1940–1969. Supp. to* The climate of Michigan by stations. *East Lansing, Mich.: State of Michigan, Department of Agriculture.*)

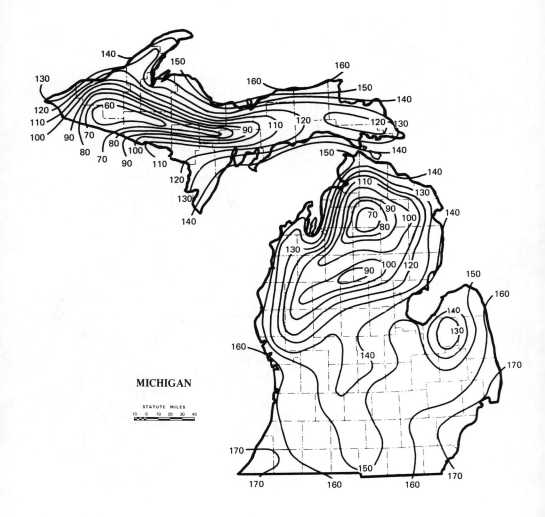

Fig. 15. Average length of growing season (32°F freeze-free period) in days, state of Michigan. (*After Van Den Brink et al. 1971.*)

similar to that of the northern Lower Peninsula—relatively long adjacent to the lakes and decreasing toward the interior.

Compared to the strong differentiation in temperatures, which tends to limit the development and diversity of vegetation northward, precipitation is more uniform over the state (fig. 16). In the Lower Peninsula, there is a gradual decrease from southwest to northeast. In the Upper Peninsula, precipitation increases somewhat from east to west, primarily due to the high precipitation (much of it as snow) that reaches the west coast from winds blowing across Lake Superior. Precipitation occurs relatively evenly throughout the year. Most importantly, there is considerable precipitation (10–15 inches; 250–380 millimeters), mostly from frontal activity during the growing season of May through August. Although no particular part of Michigan has a major deficiency of water, physiographic and soil features bring about major differences in soil water availability during the spring and summer, and account for marked local modifications of species occurrence and community composition (from prairie and savanna to bog and swamp forest).

Geology and Soils

Michigan's surface features were strongly influenced by the great ice sheets of the Pleistocene glaciation, the last period of which, the Wisconsinan, ended about 10,000 years ago. Glacial moraines, till plains, outwash plains, and lake plains dominate the landscape (fig. 17). Whereas geological features do not usually control the distribution of vegetation over wide regions as strongly as climate, they have a significant effect within a climatic zone. Glacial till soils are typically composed of a mixture of large and fine soil particles. These hold enough moisture during the summer growing season and have enough nutrients that hardwood trees, rather than pines, can dominate the forest. However, where outwash sands occur, such as over large areas of central and northern lower Michigan, pines dominate (or once dominated) the forests. These sandy soils are porous, and moisture from summer rains percolates rapidly through them. The resulting drought conditions favor jack and red pines whose deep tap roots and wide-spreading lateral roots obtain enough water to support a crown whose thick needles are designed to minimize water loss. Furthermore, ever-present lightning storms initiate wildfires, which, fueled by extremely flammable pine needles, help maintain the dominance of the native pines for generations.

In many parts of the state the terrain is low-lying, largely due to the many glacial lake basins that were at one time or another filled with

33

Fig. 16. Michigan annual mean precipitation in inches, 1940–69 (one inch = 25.4 millimeters). (*From Michigan Department of Agriculture, Michigan Weather Service. 1975.* Mean precipitation maps for the period 1940–1969. *Supp. to* The climate of Michigan by stations. *East Lansing, Mich.: State of Michigan, Department of Agriculture.*)

34

EXPLANATION

Wisconsin end moraines

Ground moraines and outwash plains

Lake sediments

Ice-contact stratified drift

No glacial deposits

1 Watersmeet moraine
2 Munising moraine
3 Kalamazoo moraine
4 Tekonsha moraine
5 Lake Border moraine
6 Tinley moraine
7 Valparaiso moraine
8 Defiance moraine
9 Ft. Wayne moraine

Fig. 17. Glacial features of Michigan. (*From Dorr and Eschman 1970.*)

35

water as the ice receded (in southeastern Michigan, the Thumb and Saginaw Bay area, and much of the eastern part of the Upper Peninsula). Here the water table is high, and swamp forests and bogs are typical. Furthermore, as glacial ice melted in place, ice blocks were often buried in glacial deposits or surrounded by waterlaid sediments from the melting glaciers, and depressions of various sizes and depths were formed. The depth and areas of these depressions largely determined whether lakes, bogs, marshes (wet treeless areas), swamps (forested wet areas), or lowland forests developed. Thus the glacial features that dominate Michigan's landscape form a mosaic of repeating topographic patterns that determine species occurrence and community composition within a climatic region.

Habitat Regions

To aid in understanding the occurrence of species and the composition of communities, Michigan may be divided into four major landscapes or habitat (site) regions that exhibit different climate, physiography, and soils (fig. 18). In the Lower Peninsula, the warm southern half is more or less separated from the cooler northern part by a transition or tension zone. In describing the distribution of many of the species, we have typically related occurrence to the southern or northern half of the Lower Peninsula. The solid line across the approximate center of the Lower Peninsula indicates this division. This arbitrary line approximates the 47° F isotherm of mean annual temperature. The dashed lines on either side show the relatively broad transition zone. Here local factors are more important than climate in determining forest composition. The position of these lines is based on length of the growing season, average annual daily minimum temperature, mean annual temperature, and physiographic features. Many tree and shrub species are found primarily in the warmer southern Lower Peninsula region; thus the forests of the southern tiers of counties are quite different in species composition and are much more diverse than the forests of the northern moraines and plains.

In the Upper Peninsula, geological, physiographic, and climatic conditions provide the basis for recognizing western and eastern habitat regions (fig. 18). The line dividing the regions is based primarily on the geological division of Cambrian and Precambrian bedrock to the west and the younger Ordovician and Silurian bedrock to the east, and the 305 meter (1,000 foot) altitudinal line. The eastern region is characterized by low elevation above sea level; relatively young bedrock, often limestones and dolomites; and lake basins that were once filled by water from melting ice. The growing season is mostly between 120 and

36

Fig. 18. Habitat regions of Michigan. *Lower Peninsula.* The solid line indicates the division between the southern half, Region I, and the northern half, Region II, of the peninsula. East-to-west dotted lines indicate the boundary of the transition zone between the southern Region I and the northern Region II. The north-to-south dashed line indicates the division between the Lake Michigan watershed (west) and the Lake Huron watershed (east). *Upper Peninsula.* The solid line indicates the division between the eastern half, Region III, and the western half, Region IV, of the peninsula. The east-to-west dashed line indicates the division between the Lake Michigan watershed (south) and the Lake Superior watershed (north). *(Adapted from Hudgins 1961.)*

37

140 days and thus is similar to that of Region II of the northern Lower Peninsula, to which the vegetation is similar in many respects. However, the northern Lower Peninsula region has distinctive, high outwash plains near its center which are dominated largely by pines and oaks. In contrast, the eastern Upper Peninsula region has no comparable high plains, but has a considerable expanse of lowland swamps. In addition, the Upper Peninsula was virtually cut off from plant migration from the south and was reforested primarily by the advances of species from the east (from New England and Canada).

The western Upper Peninsula is distinguished by its extremely ancient bedrock, of Precambrian and Cambrian origin. Bedrock outcrops are common, especially in the Michigamme Highlands (Marquette and Baraga counties), the Porcupine Mountains, and the mountains of late Precambrian age, the Keweenawans of the Keweenaw Peninsula. These outcrops locally control the composition of the vegetation. The climate is more continental than in the eastern Upper Peninsula. The growing seasons are as brief as 60 days. The western and northern shorelines, however, are strongly moderated by the influence of Lake Superior.

Not only are there differences in species occurrence between the habitat regions, but growth rates within species also differ. For example, conifers (red pine, eastern white pine, jack pine, tamarack, balsam fir) originating from the Upper Peninsula are genetically fixed to grow more slowly than those from the Lower Peninsula when planted in the Lower Peninsula (Wright 1972). Similar differences have been shown for yellow birch seedlings (Wearstler and Barnes 1977).

For those wishing to delve deeper into the physical environment of Michigan we recommend *Geology of Michigan* (Dorr and Eschman 1970), *Atlas of Michigan* (Sommers 1977), and *Climate of Michigan by Stations* (Michigan Department of Agriculture—Michigan Weather Service 1974).

Forest Communities

A forest community is a distinctive assemblage of plants and animals, dominated by one or more tree species, living together in a common habitat. The biotic community interacting together with its nonliving habitat is the *forest ecosystem*. The nature of a given forest community is determined by the interaction of three groups of factors: first, the site or habitat available for plant growth; second, the plants and animals available to occupy the habitat; and third, changes in site and biota over a period of time as influenced by climate, soils, vegetation, and animals, as well as human beings.

An understanding of Michigan forest communities is put into historical perspective by a look at post-Pleistocene tree migrations. Michigan communities are relatively young; only about 18,000 years ago ice, up to a few thousands of meters thick, covered the state. Michigan is one of the more recently uncovered areas of the world. As the ice retreated, tree species migrated into Michigan from the east and south. Boreal Forest species, dominated by spruces, but also including balsam fir, tamarack, northern white-cedar, and associated hardwoods, reinvaded as the ice retreated approximately 14,000 years before the present (B.P.) in southern Michigan and about 9,500 years B.P. in northern Michigan. The spruce-dominated Boreal Forest reached its maximum abundance about 11,000 to 10,000 years ago and then declined quickly (moving farther northward) as the climate rapidly became drier and warmer. This past vegetational history is deciphered primarily by analyzing the pollen composition in successive layers of the sediments taken chiefly from the bottoms of lakes.

Different tree species migrated at different rates, and some still may be advancing westward. The pines came rapidly from the east, first jack and red pines, followed about 1,000 years later by eastern white pine. Pines, already present 11,000 years ago, dominated central and northern Michigan 10,000 to 9,000 years ago when oaks and associated dry-mesic and xeric hardwoods rapidly invaded southern Michigan from the south. Warming and drying continued, and with it a shift to the oak–dry-mesic forest, which advanced northward to replace pines in the central and northern parts of the Lower Peninsula. This dominance by the dry oak forest probably reached its peak about 7,000 years ago when the prairie reached its maximum eastward extent in the Midwest.

By 7,000 years ago the climatic influence of the continental ice sheet had declined markedly, and the vegetational changes from 7,000 to 2,000 B.P. were much smaller than before. The climate slowly became moister and cooler, the prairie retreated to the west, and the pines and oaks moved southward. Mesophytic species, such as yellow birch, maples, beech, and hemlock, which had initially migrated into Michigan from the east 8,000 years ago, increased markedly in abundance from 7,000 to 2,000 B.P. with the cooler and moister climatic trend. Some of these species have moved much less toward the west than others, for example the beech has reached only as far as Marquette County in the Upper Peninsula.

From 500 B.P. to the present, and especially during the past century, humans have had a profound impact on the landscape, due primarily to agriculture and lumbering. This is evident by the marked decrease in pine and oak pollen and the sharp increase in herbaceous pollen found in sediment analyses.

Although the spruce-fir forest, the pines, and the dry oak forests were apparently in past times much more widespread over the Lower Peninsula than they are today, they still remain in local environments that are suited to their particular requirements. Relict pockets of black spruce, tamarack, and other boreal plants remain in cold, wet bogs and swamps of southern Michigan. Oaks keep their foothold in the north on warm, south-facing slopes, rocky sites, and near lakes—microsites where the climate is milder than elsewhere. The postglacial history is thus a complex sequence of events with species migrating from different directions, at different times, at different rates, and forming communities—sometimes quite similar to those of today and sometimes markedly different. For details of this fascinating history the reader is directed to papers by Davis (1976), Bernabo and Webb (1977), and Kapp (1977).

A general appreciation of the state's forest communities is given by the Michigan portion of Küchler's (1964) map of the potential vegetation of the United States (fig. 19). Küchler defines potential vegetation as

> the vegetation that would exist today if man were removed from the scene and if the resulting plant succession were telescoped into a single moment. The latter point eliminates the effects of future climatic fluctuations while the effects of man's earlier activities are permitted to stand.

Obviously, this vegetation would not necessarily be the same as that of presettlement times (1500–1600) because humans have caused some significant changes to the physical environment (by severe burning, draining of lands, and cultivation). Nevertheless, the potential communities give a reasonable overview of what the major presettlement communities were probably like.

The communities shown in figure 19 are termed *climax* communities, those that terminate a successional sequence. Natural disturbances are always occurring in the forest and they initiate a series of changes in species composition on a given site. Shade-intolerant or *pioneer species* that establish following disturbances are replaced by longer-lived and understory-tolerant species. This vegetational development or *biological succession* is dependent first on the regional climate and second on soils, physiography, and other local site factors. Succession is not necessarily an entirely orderly and predictable process. Succession and climax are complex concepts, and the reader is referred to Spurr and Barnes (1980) for a detailed discussion.

We have slightly modified Küchler's climax communities of Michigan because they were developed for the entire United States and

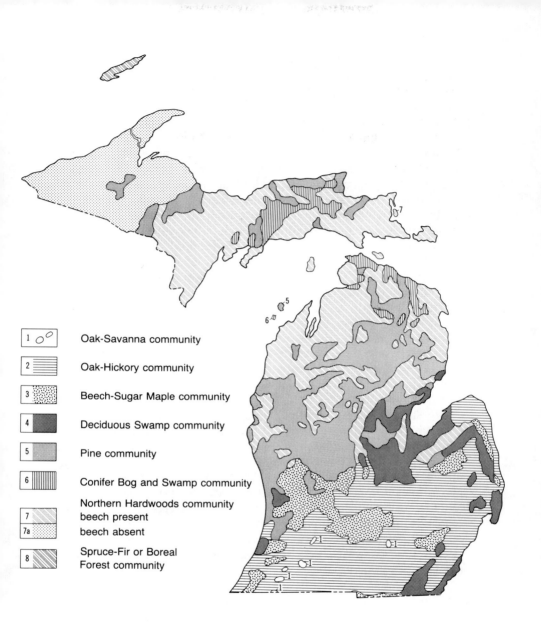

Fig. 19. Potential forest communities of Michigan. (*Modified from Map of Potential Natural Vegetation of the Conterminous United States by A. W. Küchler 1964. Reprinted by permission of the American Geographical Society.*)

Legend:

1	Oak-Savanna community
2	Oak-Hickory community
3	Beech-Sugar Maple community
4	Deciduous Swamp community
5	Pine community
6	Conifer Bog and Swamp community
7	Northern Hardwoods community beech present
7a	beech absent
8	Spruce-Fir or Boreal Forest community

41

therefore are not entirely appropriate for a close look at Michigan. We have listed and described below nine different communities (eight of which are shown on Küchler's map). In addition we have presented a list of early-successional, pioneer species that may be found at an early stage in one or more of these communities. Following the description of all communities, we list the tree species that typically would be mature dominant trees in each of the communities. Although one species might occur in several communities, a species was put in the one or two communities in which it would be most characteristic.

Spatially, community types may change gradually from one to another along a transect, or abruptly from one to another, as from a deciduous swamp to an oak-hickory forest in less than 10 meters. The rapidity of change of vegetation depends primarily on the steepness of the gradient in the site conditions, i.e., the more abruptly the site conditions change, the more abruptly the vegetation changes.

Although the map shows a large continuous area for many of the communities, for example the Oak-Hickory Community, there is actually a mosaic of different communities within each one. For example, swamps, stream floodplains, and moist flats occur in the area mapped as Oak-Hickory. Each supports a different forest community (not Oak-Hickory), but these are simply too small to be shown on the map. The large expanse of Oak-Hickory on the map indicates that much or most of this geographic area would typically support oak-hickory forests.

We strongly emphasize that there is great variation within any one of the major communities named. Within each, through detailed ecological study, many different ecosystems could be identified which would vary slightly but significantly in species composition, soils, and physiography. For example, in the natural area of the Cyrus H. McCormick Experimental Forest (near Marquette) we have classified and mapped eight different northern hardwoods ecosystems. Each has a slightly different combination of overstory tree dominants, shrubs, herbaceous plants, soils, and physiography.

Presented below is a brief description of each of the climax communities shown in figure 19.

[1] **Oak-Savanna Community.** In southern Michigan, many small pockets of Oak-Savanna mark the interface between prairie and forest. The habitat is characterized by the hot, dry summers, conducive to frequent fires that favor grasses over trees. These areas are often wet in the spring so that plants persisting there are adapted to both wet and dry conditions. Oaks, such as bur and northern pin, are dominant trees. Since settlement, oak-savanna communities (oak openings) have sometimes appeared as a result of fire along railroad lines.

2 **Oak-Hickory Community.** Occurring in our area only in the southern part of the state, the habitat is characterized by a relatively warm climate, long growing season, and xeric to dry-mesic, well-drained, soil moisture conditions. Drought, causing trees to be stressed by lack of moisture, is a major habitat factor. The warm and dry conditions lead to periodic fires, which together with the moisture stress, favor oaks and hickories. These species sprout vigorously following fire, hence assuring their persistence, often for several generations. Exclusion of fire favors invasion by species of the Beech–Sugar Maple Community.

3 **Beech–Sugar Maple Community.** Occurring mainly in the southern half of the Lower Peninsula, the habitat is characterized by a relatively warm climate, long growing season, and mesic soil moisture conditions (soils adequately supplied with moisture during the growing season). It is similar in many respects to the Northern Hardwoods Community, but includes several species (the walnuts, bitternut hickory, tuliptree, among others) that are not hardy in northern Michigan. This community is a dominant one throughout much of Indiana and Ohio, and much of the present farmland in southern Michigan was once forested by this community.

4 **Deciduous Swamp Community.** Occurring mainly in the southern half of the Lower Peninsula, the habitat is wet and cool. Water tables are high, fluctuate only slightly, and water and nutrients are available to tree roots much if not all of the year. Although areas of this community are shown in the central and southern parts of the state, deciduous swamps also occur in the north, and these two components are described separately.

Swamps in the southern and central Lower Peninsula, shown on the map, occupy the major postglacial lake basins adjacent to Lake Erie and Lake Huron. These habitats are typically flat, low-lying ground with high water tables, abundant nutrients, and usually circumneutral or basic soil reactions (pH 6.5–7.5). In addition, this community is often found in the small depressions (kettle holes) that are located throughout most of the area mapped as Oak-Hickory forest. Besides being wet and nutrient-rich, kettle holes have organic soil and are cool because of cold air drainage from surrounding higher terrain.

Not shown on the map are small areas in the northern half of the Lower Peninsula and in the Upper Peninsula that have a very similar species composition to the deciduous swamp communities in southern Michigan. However, they differ from the foregoing in their simpler composition; they lack blue-beech, pin oak, swamp white oak, and various other trees and shrubs, but have balsam poplar and speckled alder. The habitats are colder than surrounding terrain, have high water tables during the year, and are acid to circumneutral in soil reaction.

5 **Pine Community.** Occupying large areas in the central Lower Peninsula and small areas in the Upper Peninsula, the habitat is characterized by sandy (sometimes rocky), droughty, acid, nutrient-poor soils, and a relatively high frequency of wildfires. Jack pine is most frequent in the extreme habitats, whereas eastern white pine predominates on the dry-mesic sites and competes with hardwoods on more mesic and nutrient-rich habitats adjacent to the sandy pine lands. Today oaks, aspens, and other hardwoods, in addition to jack pine, predominate on the pine lands, due to logging and to postlogging fires. The large pines (primarily eastern white pine) were cut, and an immense logging industry established in the era 1850–1900. Although clear-cutting was practiced where the trees were all large, in many places the smaller trees were not cut and would have replaced the giant pines and reseeded the open areas. However, the widespread fires in the logging slash (highly flammable tree tops and branches) that inevitably followed logging killed most of the smaller trees. The hardwoods that were present sprouted, and light-seeded, wind-dispersed aspens, white birch, and red maple colonized great portions of the former white pine–red pine forest.

6 **Conifer Bog and Swamp Community.** Occurring in the northern tip of the Lower Peninsula and in the eastern Upper Peninsula, the habitat is characterized by flat, low-lying terrain of former glacial lake basins. The consistently high water table favors certain conifers and bog shrubs. In addition, there are hundreds or thousands of small pockets of this community scattered throughout the state which are too small to appear on the map. Many of these form part of the classic bog: a pond surrounded by an open marshlike floating mat, a shrubby area, and then the acidic, conifer-dominated swamp forest. Often ridges, supporting pines and hardwoods, are interspersed throughout the bog-muskeg habitat, especially in the eastern Upper Peninsula. Where limestone influence is strong, northern white-cedar is abundant, particularly when moving, aerated water also occurs. Where water movement is severely restricted, as in stagnant swamps, black spruce, tamarack, and bog shrubs predominate. As aeration and nutrients increase, northern white-cedar, speckled alder, and other hardwoods such as red maple and yellow birch increase in abundance. Thus the conifer bog and swamp community may grade into a northern deciduous-conifer swamp community and to the circumneutral northern deciduous swamp.

7 **Northern Hardwoods Community.** This is a widespread community in the northern United States. It occurs from Minnesota to Maine, south to North Carolina and Tennessee in the Appalachian Mountains. We divide this community into two parts, the major part that contains beech (7), and the part in the western Upper Peninsula from which beech is absent (7a). The habitat of both parts is characterized by cool, mesic, nutrient-rich or nutrient-poor conditions, and mainly acid, mineral soils. It is essentially a northern, less-diverse version of the Beech–Sugar Maple Community that in the western Upper Peninsula lacks beech as a major dominant. Because of the moist conditions fire is not frequent, and this enables the fire-susceptible hardwoods to reproduce and control the habitat for long periods. However, fire is frequent enough to maintain eastern white pine as an important component. In addition, stands of white pine and red pine are interspersed on the drier and rockier sites (often south and west aspects). The large area mapped as Northern Hardwoods is actually a mosaic of communities—pine forest, conifer bogs, stream floodplain forest, deciduous swamps—that are individually too small to show on the map.

8 **Spruce-Fir or Boreal Forest Community.** Mapped as occurring only on Isle Royale, this community is scattered throughout the Upper Peninsula but reaches the height of its development in Canada. The north shore of Lake Superior is a good example. The habitat is characterized by cold, wet conditions and shallow, rocky, acid soils; fire is also a very important site factor.

9 **River Floodplain and Bottomland Hardwood Community.** Not shown specifically on the map is a very important community along rivers and streams throughout the state. The habitat is characterized by periodic flooding, siltation, nutrient-rich alluvial soils, and low fire incidence. The local climate is warmer and more humid in the summer and cooler in the spring than that of the surrounding upland terrain. Unlike the deciduous swamp, more marked changes in water level occur nearly every year due to flooding. In addition, sand and silt may accumulate around the bases of the trees. The habitat is characterized by different zones (determined primarily by the frequency of flooding and the height of the water table), and different species typically occupy these zones. The species composition differs in the southern and northern parts of the state. The southern and northern parts are drastically different in diversity of species. In the list (p. 48), species characteristic of south or north are identified either with an *S* or an *N*.

In the southern third or half of the state, the bottomland forest is an extremely rich woody plant community. Some species with predominantly a southern geographic distribution in the United States occur in southern Michigan and there only along rivers and streams (redbud, honeylocust, Kentucky coffeetree, sycamore, butternut, northern hackberry, shingle oak, among others). These southern species thrive only in the river bottomlands because of the hotter and more humid summer environment compared to that of the surrounding terrain and because colder spring conditions act to retard the leafing-out of trees, enabling them to avoid spring frosts. The slow warming of the river water and cold air drainage into the river basin combine to bring about the colder conditions of the floodplain compared to that of adjacent upland sites.

Similar site conditions exist in the northern half of the Lower Peninsula and the Upper Peninsula, but climate is markedly colder and the communities conspicuously lack the diversity of tree species found in southern floodplains.

Pioneer Species

An assorted group of early-successional, short-lived, pioneer species rarely or never provide the dominant species of the climax communities described above. However, many, such as aspens, may occur in early stages in most of the above communities, and all occur in the beginning of at least one. Such species are not indicated on the map but are listed in this section. Pioneer species colonize disturbed habitats rapidly; seeds of many of these species are disseminated widely every year by wind, water, mammals, and birds. Seeds of some species, cherries in particular, may lie dormant in the forest floor for several years and are stimulated to germinate following a disturbance. In addition, many angiospermous species sprout from roots or the base of the stem and thereby quickly revegetate and dominate a burned or cutover area. Pioneer species usually require full sunlight and an open, competition-free site for establishment and vigorous growth. These short-lived species are rapidly or gradually replaced in the absence of fire or other disturbances by more long-lived and shade-tolerant species. They are the initiators of our forest world, but they have extremely important functions in the ecosystem. They protect the habitat from erosion and excessive drying; absorb mineral nutrients that might be removed by percolating water; offer food, shelter, and hiding places for wildlife; and provide suitable conditions for herbs, shrubs, and the next generation of trees.

List of Tree Species of the Potential Forest Communities of Michigan[1] (including small tree species that may occur as shrubs)

1 Oak-Savanna Community
Bur oak, *Quercus macrocarpa*
Black oak, *Quercus velutina*
Northern pin oak, *Quercus ellip-soidalis*

2 Oak-Hickory Community
White oak, *Quercus alba*
Black oak, *Quercus velutina*
Red oak, *Quercus rubra*
Pignut hickory, *Carya glabra*
Shagbark hickory, *Carya ovata*
Black cherry, *Prunus serotina*
Hop-hornbeam, *Ostrya virginiana*
White ash, *Fraxinus americana*
Witch-hazel, *Hamamelis virginiana*
Downy serviceberry, *Amelanchier arborea*
Flowering dogwood, *Cornus florida*
Eastern redcedar, *Juniperus virginiana*
Chinkapin oak, *Quercus muehlenbergii*
Dwarf chinkapin oak, *Quercus prinoides*
American chestnut, *Castanea dentata*
Dwarf hackberry, *Celtis tenuifolia*

3 Beech–Sugar Maple Community
Beech, *Fagus grandifolia*
Sugar maple, *Acer saccharum*
Red oak, *Quercus rubra*
Basswood, *Tilia americana*
White ash, *Fraxinus americana*
Black walnut, *Juglans nigra*
Tuliptree, *Liriodendron tulipifera*
Bitternut hickory, *Carya cordiformis*
Shagbark hickory, *Carya ovata*
Slippery elm, *Ulmus rubra*
Rock elm, *Ulmus thomasii*
Alternate-leaf dogwood, *Cornus alternifolia*
Blue ash, *Fraxinus quadrangulata*
Downy serviceberry, *Amelanchier arborea*

4 Deciduous Swamp Community
Red maple, *Acer rubrum*
Black ash, *Fraxinus nigra*
Yellow birch, *Betula alleghaniensis*
American elm, *Ulmus americana*
Silver maple, *Acer saccharinum*
Blue-beech, *Carpinus caroliniana*
Alternate-leaf dogwood, *Cornus alternifolia*

---

1. See figure 19 for map of the forest communities, p. 41; modified from Küchler (1964). Plants are ranked more or less in order of their abundance in the community.

Nannyberry, *Viburnum lentago*
Pin oak, *Quercus palustris*
Swamp white oak, *Quercus bico-
lor*

5 Pine Community
Jack pine, *Pinus banksiana*
Red pine, *Pinus resinosa*
Eastern white pine, *Pinus strobus*
White oak, *Quercus alba*
Northern pin oak, *Quercus ellip-
soidalis*
Black oak, *Quercus velutina*
Pin cherry, *Prunus pensylvanica*
Scarlet oak, *Quercus coccinea*

6 Conifer Bog-Swamp Commu-
nity
Black spruce, *Picea mariana*
Tamarack, *Larix laricina*
Northern white-cedar, *Thuja oc-
cidentalis*
White spruce, *Picea glauca*
American mountain-ash, *Sorbus
americana*

7 Northern Hardwoods Com-
munity
Sugar maple, *Acer saccharum*
Beech, *Fagus grandifolia*
Yellow birch, *Betula alleghanien-
sis*
Eastern hemlock, *Tsuga canaden-
sis*
Red maple, *Acer rubrum*
Basswood, *Tilia americana*
Balsam fir, *Abies balsamea*
Eastern white pine, *Pinus strobus*
Striped maple, *Acer pensylvani-
cum*

8 Spruce-Fir Community
White spruce, *Picea glauca*

Black spruce, *Picea mariana*
Speckled alder, *Alnus rugosa*
Trembling aspen, *Populus tremu-
loides*
Balsam fir, *Abies balsamea*
White birch, *Betula papyrifera*
Tamarack, *Larix laricina*
American mountain-ash, *Sorbus
americana*

9 River Floodplain and Bottom-
land Community (not on map)
Speckled alder, *Alnus rugosa* (N)
Black willow, *Salix nigra* (S)
Eastern cottonwood, *Populus
deltoides* (S)
Balsam poplar, *Populus balsamif-
era* (N)
Silver maple, *Acer saccharinum*
(S)
Red ash, *Fraxinus pennsylvanica*
American elm, *Ulmus americana*
Slippery elm, *Ulmus rubra*
Mountain maple, *Acer spicatum*
(N)
Black walnut, *Juglans nigra* (S)
Tuliptree, *Liriodendron tulipifera*
(S)
Black maple, *Acer nigrum* (S)
Black ash, *Fraxinus nigra* (N)
Boxelder, *Acer negundo* (S,
rarely N)
Butternut, *Juglans cinerea* (S,
rarely N)
Rock elm, *Ulmus thomasii*
Swamp white oak, *Quercus bico-
lor* (S)
Red mulberry, *Morus rubra* (S)
Pin oak, *Quercus palustris* (S)
Northern hackberry, *Celtis occi-
dentalis* (S)
Peachleaf willow, *Salix amygda-
loides* (S)

Sycamore, *Platanus occidentalis*
(S)
Redbud, *Cercis canadensis* (S)
Chinkapin oak, *Quercus muehlenbergii* (S)
Honeylocust, *Gleditsia triacanthos* (S)
Kentucky coffeetree, *Gymnocladus dioicus* (S)
Pawpaw, *Asimina triloba* (S)
Blue ash, *Fraxinus quadrangulata*
(S)
Shellbark hickory, *Carya laciniosa* (S)
Shingle oak, *Quercus imbricaria*
(S)
Ohio buckeye, *Aesculus glabra*
(S)

List of Pioneer Species (not on
map)
White birch, *Betula papyrifera*
Sassafras, *Sassafras albidum*
Trembling aspen, *Populus tremuloides*
Bigtooth aspen, *Populus grandidentata*
Black cherry, *Prunus serotina*
Chokecherry, *Prunus virginiana*
Hawthorns, *Crataegus* spp.
Eastern redcedar, *Juniperus virginiana*
Pin cherry, *Prunus pensylvanica*
Black willow, *Salix nigra*
Peachleaf willow, *Salix amygdaloides*
Nannyberry, *Viburnum lentago*
Wild crab apple, *Malus coronaria*
Canada plum, *Prunus nigra*

Introduction to Summer and Winter Keys to the Tree Genera

A key is a device for identifying any unknown object under considera-
tion easily and quickly. In this book the keys are intended to make it
possible for any person, even one with meager botanical training, to
determine the native or introduced trees that grow around or near his
or her home, in a city park, or in forest communities of Michigan.
Within limitations they will prove useful for common or conspicuous
species throughout the western Great Lakes region and for much of
northeastern North America. If your plant does not key out in this
book, it may be a species or hybrid so rare that it is only mentioned in
the text, or is not included at all.

Keys are based on the most striking differences and similarities of
the various parts of a tree—habit, leaves, twigs, buds, etc. The keys
used here are modeled after the type described by Voss, and for a
detailed discussion about the use of this kind of key see Voss (1972).
The key is characterized by paired statements called *couplets*. Each
statement is called a *lead* and the two leads of each couplet have the
same number and the same indentation on the page. At each couplet,
select the lead that best describes the specimen. This statement may
direct you to a genus name. If a name is not given, go on to the next
couplet and again examine each lead very carefully. Follow this sequence until you reach the genus name. Then turn to the genus description and study other characters to make sure you have correctly
identified the genus. A similar key to species is provided for genera
having more than one species.

If there is any question as to whether the plant you are identifying is
classified as a tree or a shrub, use the tree key first. If your plant does
not key out there, then use the shrub key (p. 310).

Arrangement

We have tried to place related species together. It would be easy
merely to arrange all the species according to the alphabet, but this
would lead to a highly artificial sequence. We do separate the shrubs

and vines from the trees, which is also an artificial arrangement, but the difference between shrub and tree is usually so dependable and biologically significant that it is a convenient one for identification purposes. However, several small trees that may also occur as shrubs, such as *Acer pensylvanicum, Acer spicatum, Alnus rugosa, Asimina triloba, Cornus alternifolia, Cornus florida, Prunus virginiana,* and *Viburnum lentago* are arbitrarily placed with the trees. Some large shrubs that may also occur as small trees are arbitrarily placed with the shrubs and vines (see p. 309).

We have grouped the species in seven major groups, and these accord with present-day thinking about relationships. Within genera we have arranged the species alphabetically except where there are obvious subgeneric groups, as in maples, oaks, pines, and poplars.

The first several families are very ancient plants that go back in the fossil record to at least the Coal Age. The Ginkgo Group is known mainly from fossils, but one species still exists on earth, although its presence depends apparently on cultivation by humans; it does not grow and reproduce any more in the wild. The Pine Group is more successful, and includes what we usually call *conifers,* cone-bearing plants. In addition to the pines themselves, there are numerous other genera in the group, including spruces, hemlocks, cedars, and yews— all plants with needle or scalelike leaves.

The remaining five groups are all flowering plants and are much more recent in the fossil record. These groups correspond to the subclasses of Cronquist (1968). Flowering plants or angiosperms dominate the earth today; their species number in the hundreds of thousands. In addition to flowers, they have closed containers (ovaries) in which the seeds develop—the cavities of the so-called pistils. Most botanists today regard the Magnolia Group (Magnoliidae) as the closest to the original flowering plant. In this book such plants as pawpaw, barberry, and sassafras represent the Magnolia Group. The Basswood Group (Dilleniidae) is more advanced, and it includes such trees and shrubs as blueberries, and possibly willows and poplars as well. The actual status of the latter (Salicaceae) is still in considerable question, but most botanists classify them in the Basswood Group. The Rose Group (Rosidae) is one of our largest groups, including several different subgroups: the apples, cherries, gooseberries, and locusts in one; the bittersweets, grapes, and hollies in another; and the sumacs, maples, buckeyes, and walnuts in another. The Rose Group, like the foregoing groups, is held together by numerous resemblances, some of which, it is unfortunately true, are highly technical, having to do with such things as flower anatomy, types of pollen grains, and other characteristics that we do not need to use for routine study and identification.

51

An extremely important group is that of the witch-hazel and its apparent relatives (Hamamelidae), because it includes a number of our major forest hardwoods. Examples are birches, beeches, chestnuts (American chestnut, once a major tree, is now because of a blight reduced to planted individuals or to a few sprouts), mulberries, hackberries, elms, and sycamores. Much less important in Michigan's tree flora is the Aster Group (named after the common fall-blooming herbs with beautiful white or blue flowers). In the Aster Group (Asteridae) we find elderberries, buttonbushes, and viburnums, mainly shrubs, but there are a few trees, such as catalpa.

Summer Key to the Tree Genera

1. Leaves compound.
   2. Leaves alternate.
      3. Leaves once-pinnately compound.
         4. Branches armed with paired, short, sharp spines .... ROBINIA, p. 162
         4. Branches not armed with short, paired spines.
            5. Leaflets nearly entire, with the exception of 2 or more coarse glandular
               teeth on the basal margins .... AILANTHUS, p. 178
            5. Leaflets serrate or crenate-serrate almost the entire length.
               6. Upper leaflets less than 2.5 cm wide.
                  7. Leaflets 2–4 cm long; trunk and large branches usually armed with
                     stout, branched or unbranched thorns .... GLEDITSIA, p. 166
                  7. Leaflets 5–7 cm long; trunk and large branches
                     unarmed .... SORBUS, p. 136
               6. Upper leaflets 3–5 cm wide.
                  8. Leaflets 5–9; pith continuous .... CARYA, p. 212
                  8. Leaflets 11–23; pith chambered .... JUGLANS, p. 206
      3. Leaves twice-pinnately compound.
         9. Leaflets 2–4 cm long; trunk and large branches usually armed with stout,
            branched or unbranched thorns .... GLEDITSIA, p. 166
         9. Leaflets 5–6 cm long; trunk and branches
            unarmed .... GYMNOCLADUS, p. 164
   2. Leaves opposite.
      10. Leaves palmately compound; fruit a large prickly, 1-
          or 2-seeded capsule .... AESCULUS, p. 180
      10. Leaves pinnately compound; fruit a samara.
          11. Leaflets 3–5 (rarely 7–9); samaras fused in pairs .... ACER, p. 187
          11. Leaflets 7–11, exceptionally 5; samaras not paired .... FRAXINUS, p. 298
1. Leaves simple.
   12. Leaves needle-shaped, strap-shaped, or scalelike (conifers).
      13. Leaves in clusters of 2–many.
         14. Leaves in clusters of 2–5, persistent for several years .... PINUS, p. 80
         14. Leaves mostly in clusters of 10–many, on short, lateral shoots, or scattered
             singly along leading shoots, deciduous in autumn .... LARIX, p. 68
      13. Leaves solitary, not clustered.
         15. Leaves opposite, scalelike or needlelike.
            16. Twigs flattened; leaves all scalelike; cone small and
                woody, pale brown .... THUJA, p. 100
            16. Twigs essentially round; leaves of two kinds, either scalelike or needle-
                shaped, often both kinds on the same branch;
                cone berrylike, bluish .... JUNIPERUS, p. 98
         15. Leaves alternate or in a tight spiral, mostly needlelike.
            17. Leaves 4-sided, relatively rigid and not flexible .... PICEA, p. 70
            17. Leaves flattened, soft and flexible.

53

18. Leaves of two types, spreading lateral leaves and small appressed leaves; cones short, 1.3–2 cm long .... TSUGA, p. 96

18. Leaves all of one type; cones 5–10 cm long.

    19. Cone scales deciduous at maturity; terminal buds small, globose, greenish, containing resin .... ABIES, p. 64

    19. Cone scales not deciduous, cones remaining intact at maturity; terminal buds moderately large, conical, reddish brown .... PSEUDOTSUGA, p. 94

12. Leaves broad and flat (hardwoods).

  20. Leaves opposite or whorled.

    21. Margin of leaf blades entire or only slightly undulate.

      22. Leaves opposite, lanceolate-ovate, 7–12 cm long; fruit an ovoid, scarlet drupe .... CORNUS, p. 170

      22. Leaves whorled or nearly so, heart-shaped, 12–30 cm long; fruit a long, slender-cylindrical capsule .... CATALPA, p. 291

    21. Margin of leaf blades serrate to lobed.

      23. Main veins pinnate; margin of leaf blades finely serrate .... VIBURNUM, p. 296

      23. Main veins palmate; margin of leaves strongly lobed, lobes toothed or entire .... ACER, p. 187

  20. Leaves alternate or clustered, never opposite or whorled.

    24. Margin of leaf blades entire or only slightly undulate.

      25. Leaf blades heart-shaped; fruit a flat pod (legume) ..... CERCIS, p. 168

      25. Leaf blades ovate to lanceolate, not heart-shaped; fruit not a flat pod.

        26. Leaf blades oblanceolate, 10–25 cm long; fruit a large, big-seeded berry .... ASIMINA, p. 102

        26. Leaf blades ovate or obovate, 5–20 cm long; fruit not a large berry.

          27. Branches armed with stout, straight spines; fruit a large, green multiple of drupes .... MACLURA, p. 252

          27. Branches without spines; fruit small, not as above.

            28. Fruit an acorn; leaves mostly leathery .... QUERCUS, p. 262

            28. Fruit a drupe or berry, leaves thinner.

              29. Twigs spicy-aromatic when bruised; leaves of several shapes on the same shoot .... SASSAFRAS, p. 104

              29. Twigs not spicy-aromatic; leaves of similar shape on the same shoot.

                30. Leaf blades thick, abruptly pointed, very lustrous above, not clustered at the ends of the shoots; veins divergent, inconspicuous .... NYSSA, p. 176

                30. Leaf blades thin, long-pointed, not lustrous above, clustered at the ends of the shoots; veins parallel to blade margin, conspicuous .... CORNUS, p. 170

    24. Margin of leaf blades serrate, toothed, or lobed.

      31. Margin of leaf blades lobed.

        32. Leaves fan-shaped with dichotomous veins, usually bilobed .... GINKGO, p. 62

      32. Leaves not fan-shaped, main veins arising from a midrib.

        33. Buds at shoot tip usually in clusters; fruit an acorn .. QUERCUS, p. 262

        33. Buds at shoot tip usually solitary; fruit otherwise.

          34. Leaf lobes entire.

35. Leaf blade 4-lobed, the lobes angular; blades lustrous above; twigs not spicy-aromatic when bruised ... LIRIODENDRON, p. 106
35. Leaf blade 1- to 3-lobed, the lobes rounded; blades dull above; twigs spicy-aromatic when bruised .... SASSAFRAS, p. 104
34. Leaf lobes sinuate-toothed to serrate.
   36. Underside of leaf blades densely white-tomentose .... POPULUS, p. 110
   36. Underside of leaf blades glabrous to somewhat tomentose.
      37. Veins palmate; leaf lobes coarsely sinuate-toothed .... PLATANUS, p. 288
      37. Veins pinnate; leaf lobes serrate.
         38. Branches unarmed; sap milky .... MORUS, p. 254
         38. Branches armed with stiff, sharp thorns; sap clear.
            39. Fruits with hard pits; thorns smooth on sides .... CRATAEGUS, p. 149
            39. Fruits with papery core; thorns rough on sides .... MALUS, p. 136
31. Margin of leaf blades serrate to coarsely toothed.
  40. Branches armed with thorns.
    41. Fruits with hard pits; thorns smooth on sides . CRATAEGUS, p. 149
    41. Fruits with papery core; thorns rough on sides ..... MALUS, p. 136
  40. Branches not armed.
    42. Base of leaves inequilateral or asymmetrical.
      43. Leaf margin coarsely crenate or wavy; blades obovate .... HAMAMELIS, p. 222
      43. Leaf margin finely serrate to toothed; blades not obovate.
         44. Leaf blades about as long as wide, heart-shaped . TILIA, p. 108
         44. Leaf blades 1½–2½ times as long as wide, not heart-shaped.
            45. Leaf blades thin, coarsely but singly serrate; fruit a globular drupe, ripe in autumn; pith chambered ..... CELTIS, p. 236
            45. Leaf blades thick, coarsely and doubly serrate; fruit a samara, ripe in spring; pith continuous .... ULMUS, p. 241
    42. Base of leaf blades essentially symmetrical.
      46. Blade margin teeth coarse, 1–2 per cm of margin.
         47. Mature leaves glabrous both sides; fruit a prickly bur with 1 or more nuts.
            48. Leaf blades 7–12 cm long, very lustrous beneath, teeth with points only; bark tight, smooth, light bluish gray .... FAGUS, p. 260
            48. Leaf blades 15–21 cm long, not lustrous beneath, teeth with long bristles; bark fissured, brownish .. CASTANEA, p. 258
         47. Mature leaves pubescent or white-tomentose, at least beneath; fruit lacking a prickly bur.
            49. Leaf blades 5–13 cm long, long-petiolate, broadly ovate to suborbicular; fruit a small capsule, shedding seeds in spring .... POPULUS, p. 110
            49. Leaf blades 10–25 cm long, short-petiolate, oblong-lanceolate to obovate; fruit an acorn, falling in autumn .... QUERCUS, p. 262
      46. Blade margin teeth fine, 3–many per cm of margin.

50. Leaf petioles laterally compressed; leaves trembling .... POPULUS, p. 110
50. Leaf petioles round, not laterally compressed; leaves not trembling.
   51. Leaf blades at least 3 times as long as wide.
      52. Twigs brittle at base; fruit a small capsule, shedding seeds in spring; twigs lacking bitter almond taste and smell when crushed .... SALIX, p. 125
      52. Twigs flexible at base; fruit a fleshy drupe, falling in late summer; twigs with a bitter almond taste and smell when crushed .... PRUNUS, p. 152
   51. Leaf blades 2 times or less as long as wide.
      53. Leaf blades 1½ times or less as long as wide (nearly as wide as long).
         54. Sap milky; leaves not crowded on short, spurlike shoots; fruit an ovoid, cylindrical cluster of little drupes, white, red, or purple in color .... MORUS, p. 254
         54. Sap clear; leaves crowded on short, spurlike shoots; fruit a large green, yellow, or red pome or apple . MALUS, p. 136
      53. Leaf blades about 2 times as long as wide.
         55. Underside of leaf blades usually stained with rusty brown resin; terminal buds long, 1.5–2 cm, covered with sticky, aromatic resin .... POPULUS, p. 110
         55. Underside of leaf blades without resin stain; terminal buds shorter, lacking aromatic resin.
            56. Margin of leaf blades singly serrate; fruit fleshy.
               57. Lenticels conspicuous; pith whitish or brownish; bark easily peeled off in papery layers; buds ovoid, not curved .... PRUNUS, p. 152
               57. Lenticels inconspicuous; pith greenish; bark not separable into papery layers; buds narrow-conical, curved .... AMELANCHIER, p. 145
            56. Margin of leaf blades doubly serrate; fruit not fleshy.
               58. Trunk rough, furrowed or exfoliating.
                  59. Bark of trunk grayish brown, broken into vertically narrow, flattish pieces loose at the ends; fruit enclosed in ovoid bladders, arranged in hoplike catkins .... OSTRYA, p. 234
                  59. Bark of trunk white, yellow, or gray, exfoliating or cleaving off in papery layers; fruit tiny, borne on 3-lobed bracts in tight catkins . BETULA, p. 224
               58. Trunk smooth, bark not furrowed or exfoliating.
                  60. Trunk not round in cross section, fluted with musclelike ridges; fruit borne on a narrow, 3-lobed bract about 2 cm long, falling in autumn; major leaf veins usually not branching near the margin .... CARPINUS, p. 232
                  60. Trunk round in cross section, not fluted; fruit a woody catkin, persisting into following growing season; major leaf veins commonly branching near the margin .... ALNUS, p. 230

Winter Key to the Tree Genera

1. Leaves persistent and green throughout the winter, needle-shaped or scalelike. (The following genera can be keyed using the summer key as well as this one.)
  2. Leaves in clusters of 2–5 .... PINUS, p. 80
  2. Leaves solitary, or only overlapping, not clustered.
    3. Leaves opposite; needles scalelike or short.
      4. Twigs flattened; leaves all scalelike; cone small, woody, pale brown .... THUJA, p. 100
      4. Twigs rounded; leaves of two kinds, either scalelike or needle-shaped, often both kinds on the same branch; cone berrylike, bluish .. JUNIPERUS, p. 98
    3. Leaves alternate or in a tight spiral; mostly needlelike.
      5. Leaves 4-sided, relatively rigid and not flexible, sharp-pointed .... PICEA, p. 70
      5. Leaves flattened, soft and flexible.
        6. Leaves seldom over 1.3 cm long; cones short, 1.3–2 cm long .... TSUGA, p. 96
        6. Leaves 1.3–7 cm long; cones 5–10 cm long.
          7. Cones disintegrating at maturity; terminal buds small, globose, greenish .... ABIES, p. 64
          7. Cones remaining intact at maturity; terminal buds large, conical, reddish brown .... PSEUDOTSUGA, p. 94
1. Leaves not persistent and green throughout the winter but deciduous in early autumn or turning brown.
  8. Twigs, branches, or trunk armed with spines or thorns.
    9. Thorns or spines not exceeding 2.5 cm.
      10.Spines in pairs at each node; buds rusty-hairy, 3–4 superposed; fruit a flat pod (legume) .... ROBINIA, p. 162
      10.Spines never in pairs; buds otherwise; fruit fleshy.
        11.Twigs slender, dark brown to black with short thornlike twigs; bark thin, splitting vertically into large plates; fruit a yellow to red drupe, 2–3 cm in diameter .... PRUNUS, p. 152
        11.Twigs stout, orange brown with stout, straight spines; bark thick, deeply furrowed with interlacing ridges; fruit a pale green multiple of drupes, 10–14 cm in diameter .... MACLURA, p. 252
    9. Thorns or spines exceeding 2.5 cm.
      12. Thorns often branched; lateral buds superposed, the lower covered by bark; fruit a flat pod (legume) .... GLEDITSIA, p. 166
      12. Thorns unbranched; lateral buds not as above; fruit a pome.
        13. Thorns smooth on sides; fruits with hard pits .... CRATAEGUS, p. 149
        13. Thorns rough on sides; fruit with papery core .... MALUS, p. 136
  8. Twigs, branches, and trunk not armed with spines or thorns.
    14. Twigs with a bitter almond smell and taste when crushed .. PRUNUS, p. 152
    14. Twigs lacking a bitter almond smell and taste when crushed.
      15. Leaf scars mainly or often on short, lateral shoots.

16. Lateral shoots stubby with leaf scars contiguous; seeds if present naked on stalks or in cones.
   17. Bundle scar 1; seeds borne in small cones, usually present .... LARIX, p. 68
   17. Bundle scars 2; seeds large and fleshy, falling in autumn .... GINKGO, p. 62
16. Lateral shoots narrow with leaf scars more or less separated; seeds if present contained within an ovary.
   18. Bark white or silvery yellowish gray, exfoliating in strips or thin papery layers; lenticels horizontally elongated .... BETULA, p. 224
   18. Bark dark gray, not exfoliating; lenticels not horizontally elongated .... MALUS, p. 136
15. Leaf scars distributed along the main twigs.
  19. True bud scales absent (buds naked) or scales valvate (not overlapping).
    20. Terminal buds stalked.
      21. Leaf scars and lateral buds opposite .... ACER, p. 187
      21. Leaf scars and lateral buds alternate.
        22. Fruit a tiny nut in a persistent conelike structure; twigs glabrous .... ALNUS, p. 230
        22. Fruit a capsule, usually present in winter; twigs usually scurfy-pubescent .... HAMAMELIS, p. 222
    20. Terminal or end buds sessile.
      23. Leaf scars and lateral buds opposite.
        24. Flower buds swollen at base, apex spirelike; fruit a bluish black drupe .... VIBURNUM, p. 296
        24. Flower buds spherical or vertically flattened; fruit a scarlet drupe .... CORNUS, p. 170
      23. Leaf scars and lateral buds alternate.
        25. Buds dark red with a glaucous bloom, glabrous; fruit a conelike cluster of samaras, fruit axis and basal samaras persistent in winter .... LIRIODENDRON, p. 106
        25. Buds yellow or dark brown, hairy or powdery; fruit a berry or nut, falling in autumn.
          26. Buds rusty brown or blackish, hairy .... ASIMINA, p. 102
          26. Buds sulfur yellow, scurfy or powdery .... CARYA, p. 212
  19. True bud scales present, overlapping or solitary.
    27. Leaf scars mostly 3 at a node (whorled) .... CATALPA, p. 291
    27. Leaf scars 1–2 at a node (not whorled).
      28. Leaf scars 2 at a node (opposite).
        29. Terminal buds 1.5–4 cm long; twigs very stout; fruit a large capsule containing 1–3 large, smooth seeds .... AESCULUS, p. 180
        29. Terminal buds rarely exceeding 1.5 cm; twigs not conspicuously stout; fruit a samara.
          30. Bundle scars usually 3, distinct, separated ...... ACER, p. 187
          30. Bundle scars many, minute, forming a U-shaped line .... FRAXINUS, p. 298
      28. Leaf scars 1 at a node (alternate).
        31. Leaf scars crowded at the ends of slender, upswept twigs .... CORNUS, p. 170
        31. Leaf scars not crowded at ends of slender, upswept twigs.
          32. Bundle scars 4–many.

33. Bundle scars in a single U-shaped line or curved group.
    34. Terminal bud present; fruit a pome; small tree or
        shrub .... SORBUS, p. 136
    34. Terminal bud absent; fruit not a pome; large tree.
        35. Leaf scar surrounding the bud; bark peeling in thin plates,
            expressing different ages and colors of different
            layers .... PLATANUS, p. 288
        35. Leaf scar not surrounding the bud; bark otherwise.
            36. Twigs slender .... ULMUS, p. 241
            36. Twigs very stout.
                37. Bundle scars not more than 5; buds in hairy
                    pits .... GYMNOCLADUS, p. 164
                37. Bundle scars 9 or more; buds not in
                    pits .... AILANTHUS, p. 178
33. Bundle scars variously grouped or scattered, but not in a single
    line.
    38. Buds cigar-shaped or narrowly elongated, at least 4 times as
        long as wide; bark smooth, light bluish
        gray .... FAGUS, p. 260
    38. Buds shorter and broader, ovoid, only 1.5–2.5 times as long
        as wide; bark rough or, if smooth, black.
        39. True terminal bud absent (occasionally present in *Casta-*
            nea), replaced by the uppermost lateral bud.
            40. Buds at end of twig inequilaterally ovoid (lopsided),
                obliquely sessile; bud scales usually 2, lustrous, green or
                red .... TILIA, p. 108
            40. Buds otherwise.
                41. Bud scales 2–3 visible; pith star-shaped in cross sec-
                    tion; sap clear .... CASTANEA, p. 258
                41. Bud scales 4–8; pith not star-shaped in cross sec-
                    tion; sap milky .... MORUS, p. 254
        39. True terminal bud present.
            42. Buds at the tips of shoots clustered; bud scales tightly
                appressed .... QUERCUS, p. 262
            42. Buds single; bud scales looser, more
                spreading .... CARYA, p. 212
32. Bundle scars usually 1–3.
    43. Pith chambered.
        44 Twigs stout, hairy or pubescent; bark ridged or furrowed;
            fruit a large nut .... JUGLANS, p. 206
        44. Twigs slender, glabrous; bark smooth with warty excres-
            cences; fruit a small drupe .... CELTIS, p. 236
    43. Pith continuous, lacking chambers.
        45. Bundle scar appearing as 1 (a horizontal line); twigs green,
            spicy aromatic .... SASSAFRAS, p. 104
        45. Bundle scars 3 or in 3 compound but distinct groups.
            46. True terminal bud present.
                47. Pith with firmer diaphragms at intervals; main branches
                    conspicuously at right angles to the trunk
                    (horizontal) .... NYSSA, p. 176
                47. Pith without firmer diaphragms; branches otherwise.

48. Buds cylindrically elongated, linear, scales twisted; twigs very slender; bark smooth with longitudinal stripes .... AMELANCHIER, p. 145
48. Buds narrowly to broadly ovoid or conical; twigs moderately thick; bark smooth with horizontal lenticels or ridged .... POPULUS, p. 110
46. True terminal bud absent (sometimes present on short shoots of *Betula*), replaced by the uppermost lateral bud.
  49. Bud scale 1; twigs usually brittle at base .... SALIX, p. 125
  49. Bud scales 2 or more; twigs flexible at base.
    50. Buds in hairy pits; twigs very stout .... GYMNOCLADUS, p. 164
    50. Buds not in hairy pits; twigs slender.
      51. Bark smooth, with musclelike ridges .... CARPINUS, p. 232
      51. Bark rough, peeling, furrowed, or shreddy.
        52. Fruits or catkins not present in winter; bundle scars depressed; leaf scars covered with a corky layer .... ULMUS, p. 241
        52. Fruits or male catkins usually present in winter in mature plants; bundle scars not depressed; leaf scars not corky.
          53. Fruit a flat pod (legume); catkins not present .... CERCIS, p. 168
          53. Fruit otherwise; catkins present, male catkins visible in winter.
            54. Bark of trunk white, yellow, or gray, exfoliating or cleaving off in papery layers; fruit tiny, borne on 3-lobed bracts in tight catkins .... BETULA, p. 224
            54. Bark of trunk grayish brown, broken into vertically narrow, flattish pieces loose at the ends, shreddy; fruit enclosed in ovoid bladders, arranged in hoplike catkins .... OSTRYA, p. 234

Tree Descriptions

GINKGOACEAE

Ginkgo biloba Linnaeus

Ginkgo   Maidenhair Tree

Size and Form. Large tree, 15–25 m high and 50–100 cm in diameter. Slender, spire-like tree in youth, excurrent form with a straight, strongly tapering trunk and short lateral branches; with age the lower branches grow out horizontally and the crown becomes more spreading. Michigan Big Tree: girth 3.3 m, diameter 103 cm, height 27 m, Hillsdale Co.

Bark. Thick, ash gray and somewhat roughened; becoming fissured with age.

Leaves. Clusters of 3–5 at the ends of short spur shoots or separated alternately on long terminal branches; simple; 5–10 cm broad; fan-shaped, closely ribbed, usually bilobed and irregularly crenate at the upper extremity; thin and leathery; glabrous; flushing bright yellow green, becoming dark green, turning a clear, golden yellow in autumn; veins fanlike, fine veins dichotomous, forking many times from the base of the blade; petioles long, slender.

Twigs. Stout, gray brown, smooth; leaf scars with 2 bundle scars.

Winter Buds. Terminal bud about 3 mm long, flat-conic, smooth, light red brown; lateral buds divergent, usually only on rapid-growing shoots.

Wood. Light, soft, weak, close-grained, yellow white to light red brown, with thin, lighter-colored sapwood.

Male Organs. May, with the leaves; catkins short-stalked, pendulous, 3–6 cm long, thick, and yellow. Trees dioecious.

Female Organs. May; like tiny, long-stalked acorns, 1–2 cm on 4 cm pedicels, consisting of 2 naked ovules, one of which usually aborts. Wind-pollinated. Ripening in autumn, a globose drupelike structure (actually a seed covered by a pulpy outer coat), orange yellow to green, 25–30 cm in diameter, consisting of an acrid, putrid-smelling pulp enclosing a smooth, whitish, somewhat flattened, almond-flavored seed.

Distribution. Native in the mountains of eastern China, Anhwei Province; introduced from England into Philadelphia in 1784. Fre-quently planted in city parks and on lawns. Hardy in the southern half of the Lower Peninsula.

Habitat. Well drained soils.

Notes. The sole surviving genus of an ancient order of plants having characters of both ferns and conifers. Extensively cultivated in temperate countries. The drupelike structure is esteemed as a delicacy in China and Japan. The fleshy covering of the seed is slippery and malodorous when it falls, and thus only male trees are recommended for planting. Slow-growing; long-lived; almost free of insect pests and diseases; little-harmed by pollutants. Easily propagated from seed. Early Chinese names were duck's feet (because of the leaf shape) and silver apricot (because of the whitish seed). The name ginkgo is a transliteration of the Chinese ideograph of yin hsing (silver apricot). See Li (1963) for historical considerations.

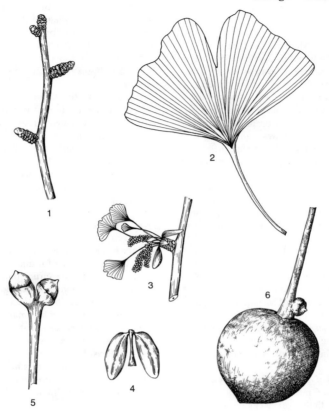

1. Winter twig, with short shoots × ½.
2. Leaf, × ½.
3. Pollen-bearing twig, × ½.
4. Pollen sacs, enlarged.
5. Unfertilized seed twig, enlarged.
6. Mature fleshy seed, × 1.

**Key
Characters**
• fan-shaped leaves borne in clusters on short, spur shoots
• strongly excurrent form with straight trunk and horizontal lateral branches
• female trees with malodorous pulpy covering of the seed
• planted in urban environments

PINACEAE
Abies balsamea (Linnaeus) Miller

Balsam Fir

Size and Form. Medium-sized tree, 10–25 m high and 20–40 cm in diameter. Slender, symmetrical, excurrent form with a narrow, spire-topped pyramidal crown; in closed stands dead branches persist below the live crown. Root system shallow on heavy-textured soils and poorly drained sites, moderately deep on more porous and better-drained soils. Michigan Big Tree: girth 2.1 m, diameter 68 cm, height 35 m, Ontonagon Co.

Bark. Thin and smooth on young trunks, pale grayish brown and marked by raised resin blisters; reddish brown on old trunks and somewhat roughened by small irregular scaly plates.

Leaves. Spiral, but often appearing 2-ranked; 1.3–3 cm long, sessile; narrowly linear, soft; apex rounded or notched; lustrous, dark green above, pale beneath due to numerous white lines of stomata; aromatic; persistent 8–10 years.

Twigs. Slender, at first grayish and pubescent, becoming grayish brown and smooth; leaf scars distinctive, flush with surface, roundish.

Winter Buds. Globose, orange green, resinous, small, 3–6 mm in diameter.

Wood. Very light, soft, weak, coarse-grained, perishable, pale brown, with thick, lighter-colored sapwood. Uses include pulpwood, boxes, crates, sashes, general construction lumber, woodenware.

Pollen Cones. May; oblong-cylindrical, 6 mm long, composed of yellow pollen scales. Trees monoecious.

Seed Cones. Young cones in May; wind-pollinated; oblong-cylindrical, located on the topmost branches of the crown, 2.5 cm long, composed of orbicular, purple ovule scales (subtended by yellowish green bracts) spirally arranged upon a central axis. Ripening in autumn of first season; oblong-cylindrical, erect, finely hairy, dark purple, 5–10 cm long and 2.5 cm in diameter; very resinous; woody scales deciduous in autumn, only the woody cone axis persistent on uppermost branches in winter; seeds 6 mm long, much shorter than their light brown wings.

Distribution. Abundant in the Upper Peninsula; common in the northern half of the Lower Peninsula; absent in the southern half of the Lower Peninsula except for a sphagnum bog in Ingham Co. and ornamental plantings.

Habitat. Characteristic of the cold, wet Boreal Forest of Canada, but occurring in a variety of sites in Michigan from cold, poorly drained swamps to well drained uplands. Less tolerant of poorly drained conditions, less tolerant of fire, and more tolerant of warmer and drier climate than the spruces. Frequent associates include white spruce, black spruce, trembling aspen, red maple, yellow and white birches.

Notes. Highly shade-tolerant; slow-growing; short-lived. Seedlings often found in the understory of disturbed forests where they grow slowly and may persist for many years. Severely attacked by the spruce budworm (*Choristoneura fumiferana*), especially mature and overmature trees; susceptible to heart rots. A popular Christmas tree because of long-persistent needles that are not shed readily. Aromatic needles prized for making balsam pillows. Medium-aged trunks are characterized by rounded blisters under the bark; these are full of clear, aromatic resin and may be broken with the fingernail.

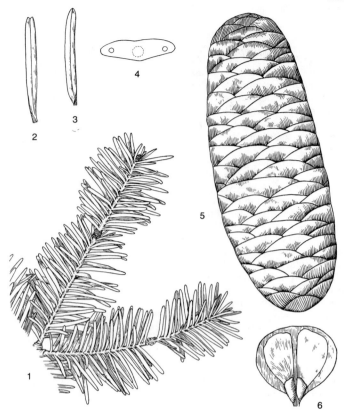

1. Winter shoot, × 1.
2–3. Leaves, × 2.
4. Cross section of leaf, enlarged.
5. Unopened cone, × 1.
6. Cone scale with seeds, × 1.

Key Characters
• 2-ranked needles, soft, apex rounded or notched; needles leaving a flush, roundish leaf scar
• bark smooth, gray, with resin blisters
• seed cones erect, scales deciduous, woody cone axis persistent

PINACEAE

Abies concolor (Gordon and Glendinning)
Lindley

White Fir

Size and Form. Medium-sized tree, 12–20
m high and 30–60 cm in diameter. Trunk
straight, crown oval or cylindrical, rather
open; branches tend to bend downward and
may reach the ground when tree is open-
grown. Roots shallow. Michigan Big Tree:
girth 112 cm, diameter 36 cm, height 21 m,
Oakland Co.

Bark. Thin, smooth, dark gray, many resin
blisters; becoming scaly and finally broken
into fissures with flat, dark gray ridges.

Leaves. Spirally arranged in rows extending
nearly horizontally from all sides of the
branch, more or less 2-ranked; 4–7 cm long,
sessile; linear, flattened, thick, leathery, apex
rounded or acute; uniformly silvery blue gray
both sides; persistent 8–10 years.

Twigs. Moderately stout, grayish and pubescent, becoming grayish brown and
smooth, leaf scars distinctive, flush with surface, roundish.

Winter Buds. Globose, yellowish brown,
very resinous.

Seed Cones. Young cones in May; wind-
pollinated; ripening in autumn of first season; oblong, domed, erect, smooth, bracts
shorter than scales, olive green tinged with
purple, 8–12 cm long; very resinous; at top
of tree only; woody scales deciduous, woody
cone axis persistent on uppermost branches
in winter. Trees monoecious.

Distribution. Native in Rocky Mountains
and Sierra Nevada of California. Occasionally planted as a park or lawn tree.

Habitat. Grows well on most upland soils;
hardy.

Notes. Shade-tolerant, slow-growing, long-
lived. An important ornamental tree because
of its graceful form and large sprays of glaucous, bluish gray foliage.

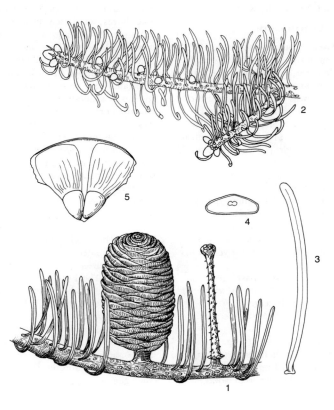

1. Winter shoot with leaves, cone, and cone axis, × ½.
2. Winter shoot with buds, × ½.
3. Leaf, × 1.
4. Cross section of leaf, × 5.
5. Cone scale with seeds, × 1.

Key Characters
- leaves silvery bluish gray both sides
- leaves long, 4–7 cm, thick-leathery
- leaf scars flush with twig, roundish
- seed cone scales deciduous, woody cone axis persistent on top branches

PINACEAE
Larix laricina (Du Roi) K. Koch

Tamarack   Eastern Larch

Size and Form. Medium-sized tree, 12–20 m high and 30–60 cm in diameter. Straight trunk of little taper, forming an open, pyramidal crown of horizontal branches. In closed stands crowns small, narrow, conical; when open-grown crown broad, irregular, and appearing ragged. Shallow and wide-spreading root system; moderately windfirm. Michigan Big Tree: girth 2.7 m, diameter 85 cm, height 21 m, Lake Co.

Bark. Thin, reddish brown, scaly; inner bark dark reddish purple.

Leaves. Singly along the leading shoots but mainly in clusters of 10–20 on short, spur shoots; 2–2.5 cm long, sessile; linear, soft, flexible, rounded above, keeled beneath, apex blunt; bright green, turning yellow in autumn; deciduous.

Twigs. Slender, at first grayish, glaucous, later light orange brown, finally dark brown; leaf scars with 1 bundle scar.

Winter Buds. Small, globose, lustrous, dark red.

Wood. Heavy, hard, very strong, coarse-grained, very durable, light brown, with thin, nearly white sapwood. Uses include poles, posts, piling, rough lumber, pulpwood, boxes, crates.

Pollen Cones. May; in sessile, subglobose, yellow clusters composed of many short-stalked pollen scales spirally arranged about a central axis. Trees monoecious.

Seed Cones. Young cones in May; wind-pollinated; issuing from short shoots along branches of the upper crown, each cone a short-stalked cluster of orbicular, green seed scales (subtended by red bracts) spirally arranged about a central axis. Ripening in autumn of first season, but persistent on the tree for a year longer; ovoid, obtuse, light brown, shiny; erect on stout, short, curved stalks, 1–2 cm long; scales glabrous and striated outside; bracts ¼ as long as the scales; seeds 3 mm long, with pale brown wings, 6 mm long, widest near the middle.

Distribution. Common throughout the state.

Habitat. Primarily relegated to cold, wet, poorly drained sites (including swamps, bogs, lake shores, wet beach thickets) because other species are more vigorous and better competitors on the drier, more nutrient-rich upland sites. Common along the forest edge of sphagnum bogs and invading the bog mat; associated here most commonly with black spruce. A shade-intolerant pioneer species, it colonizes drier sites when competition is lacking; here it is an associate of trembling aspen, balsam fir, white birch. In southern Michigan bogs and swamps associated almost always with poison sumac, yellow birch, and sometimes black spruce; many orchids also grow with it.

Notes. Shade-intolerant; fast-growing; short-lived. Grows slowly in swamps but much more rapidly on well drained soils. Tolerates both acid and basic lowlands. Severely decimated by the larch sawfly (*Pristiphora erichsonii*), few old-growth individuals remain. The European larch, *Larix decidua* Miller, has been planted because of its very rapid early growth. It has stouter, yellower twigs, more abundant and somewhat longer leaves, and markedly larger cones (with pubescent scales) than the native larch. The Japanese larch, *Larix leptolepis* (Siebold and Zuccarini) Gordon, is also planted in Michigan as an ornamental and in forest plantations. It has distinctly reddish twigs, longer branches, and large cones with wavy scales.

68

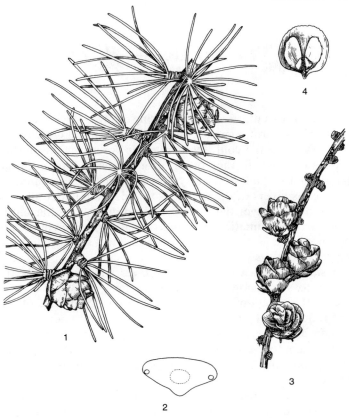

1. Autumn shoot, with leaves on short shoots, and cones, × 1.
2. Cross section of leaf, enlarged.
3. Cone-bearing twig in winter, × 1.
4. Cone scale with seeds, × 2.

Key Characters
- needles mainly borne on short, spur shoots, 10–20 in a group; short, soft, flexible, giving the crown a feathery appearance
- needles turning yellow in autumn, deciduous
- seed cones small, less than 2 cm long, with lustrous brown, striated scales
- typically found in swamps, bogs, and other lowland areas

69

The Spruces—*Picea*

The spruces have tall, gradually tapering trunks, thickly covered with branches, which form compact, pyramidal or conical crowns. They are confined wholly to the cold, temperate, or boreal regions of the northern hemisphere, where they often form extensive forests. Spruces are characterized by shallow root systems, often largely confined to the organic humus layers of the acid soils that develop under all spruces. It is this shallow top layer that warms up and dries out sufficiently under arctic or northern climatic conditions to make tree growth possible. On light-textured and warmer soils, however, most spruces develop moderately deep root systems.

Their sharply conical crowns make them well suited to bear winter snows and to shed snow when slight warming or winds occur. Partly because of their shallow root systems and partly because of their low nutrient requirements, spruces are tolerant of acid, undrained soil conditions and are able to survive and even grow in northern bogs and in cold, wet, rain forest or cloud forest conditions. It is therefore the northern plains and cold swamps of Michigan that furnish conditions suitable for their best development.

The minutely stalked leaves are for the most part 4-sided, spirally arranged on the branches, and persist for 5–10 years. The leaves are borne on woody, peglike bases (sterigmata). All spruces are monoecious and wind-pollinated. The seeds are light, with rather large wings that enable them to be widely disseminated by the wind.

Seven species of spruces are found in North America, of which 2, white spruce and black spruce, are native to Michigan. White spruce is an important timber and pulpwood tree, besides being planted for ornamental purposes. The black spruce is a smaller tree, is short-lived, and is not recommended for ornamental planting because other species far surpass it for this purpose.

Besides the native spruces, several introduced species are planted. Norway spruce and Colorado blue spruce are probably the best known of these. Norway spruce originates in central and northern Europe. It has been planted mostly for ornamental purposes and for windbreaks, but in the future it may also be planted as a timber and pulpwood species.

The Colorado blue spruce, a native of the Rocky Mountains, is commonly planted as an ornamental tree on lawns and in parks. The foliage of its most popular cultivars is striking; the branchlets are in horizontal layers and the leaves of each new season are pale blue or silvery, contrasting with the darker blue green of the older foliage.

The Engelmann spruce, *Picea engelmannii* Parry, also from the Rocky Mountains, resembles the native white spruce but is more beautiful in the color and texture of its foliage, the leaves being blue green or silvery blue. In general habit and other characters it resembles the Colorado blue spruce and is difficult to distinguish from it. Engelmann spruce has cones about 5 cm long, with thin flexible scales, toothed on the margin, whereas those of Colorado blue spruce are much larger, usually twice as long and lighter in color. Engelmann spruce is hardy, but should be planted in cool, moist habitats for the best development.

Summer and Winter Key to Species of *Picea*

1. Leaves usually 0.5–1.2 cm long, blunt; twigs rusty-pubescent; cones ovoid, less than 2 times as long as wide when open .... *P. mariana*, p. 76
1. Leaves usually 1–2 cm long, sharp-pointed; twigs glabrous; cones elongated, greater than 2 times as long as wide.
  2. Cones 2.5–5 cm long, scales with entire or nearly entire margins .. *P. glauca*, p. 74
  2. Cones 6–15 cm long, scales with finely toothed margins.
    3. Cone scales papery, flexible; leaves bluish green; terminal buds brownish yellow .... *P. pungens*, p. 78
    3. Cone scales woody, stiff; leaves green; terminal buds orange brown .... *P. abies*, p. 72

PINACEAE
Picea abies (Linnaeus) Karsten

Norway Spruce

Size and Form. Large tree, 15–25 m high and 30–100 cm in diameter. Forming a dense, conical, spire-topped crown, mature trees with numerous, vertically drooping branchlets on branches that persist nearly to the ground; crown thins greatly with old age. Root system very shallow on clay or poorly drained soils, moderately deep in more porous, well drained soils. Michigan Big Tree: girth 3.6 m, diameter 113 cm, height 25 m, Oakland Co.

Bark. Thin, reddish brown, shredding finely into small papery scales; on old trunks becoming grayish brown or dark purplish and cracked into small, hard, smooth, rounded plates.

Leaves. Spirally arranged along the shoot, crowded; 1.5–2.2 cm long; rigid, curved, acute, sharp-pointed; lustrous dark green; persistent 5–7 years.

Twigs. Moderately stout, reddish or orange brown, smooth or corrugated.

Winter Buds. Ovoid, acute, reddish or orange brown, not resinous, 0.5–1 cm long; bud scales often with spreading tips.

Wood. Light, strong, tough, elastic, soft, fine-grained, white, with thick sapwood, indistinguishable from heartwood.

Pollen Cones. May; in ovoid to subglobose, long-stalked clusters in the upper crown, 2–2.5 cm long, composed of crimson to yellowish pollen scales.

Seed Cones. Young cones in May; wind-pollinated; cylindrical, sessile, erect clusters, 4–5 cm long, composed of many scarlet seed scales. Ripening in autumn of first season, falling in spring or summer of second season; rarely present as squirrels cut them in summer (as early as July) or autumn and eat the seeds. Sessile, cylindrical, apex broadly rounded, 12–15 cm long, pendent from tips of uppermost branches; cone scales woody and stiff with finely toothed margin; seeds reddish brown, rough, 3 mm long, with long wings.

Distribution. Introduced from central and northern Europe where it is very widely distributed in montane and Boreal forests.

Habitat. Grows well on mesic sites of acid, moist, fertile soil; does not thrive on dry, excessively drained, sandy-gravelly soils; intolerant of lime in the topsoil; grows well on heavy clay soils if kept well watered; sensitive to late frost.

Notes. Shade-tolerant; moderately fast-growing; long-lived in its native habitats, short-lived in urban environments. The major timber species in central Europe; important throughout central and northern Europe and Asia, reaching heights of 45 m. Hardy in Michigan although susceptible to drought, drying winds, ice and glaze, calcareous soils, and late frost. Easily transplanted. Desirable for ornamental planting, hedges, and windbreaks, loses much of its beauty in old age. Many horticultural varieties and forms, including dwarf, compact, and creeping snake-like forms.

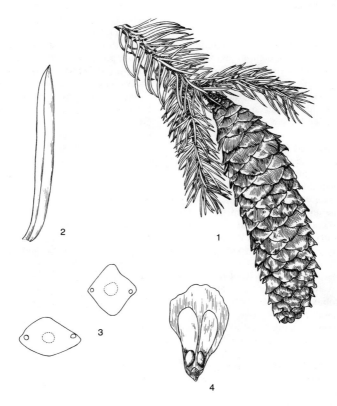

1. Shoot with partly opened cone, × ½.
2. Leaf, × 3.
3. Cross sections of leaves, enlarged.
4. Cone scale with seeds, × 1.

Key Characters

- seed cones large, long, cylindrical; scales woody
- needles stiff, curved, sharp-pointed; lustrous dark green
- twigs and buds orange brown
- mature trees with numerous vertically drooping branchlets

73

PINACEAE
Picea glauca (Moench) A. Voss

White Spruce

Size and Form. Medium-sized to large tree, 15–25 m high and 30–60 cm in diameter. Trunk straight, excurrent form; densely foliated, narrow conical crown. Roots shallow on poorly drained soils, moderately deep on well drained soils. Michigan Big Tree: girth 3.3 m, diameter 106 cm, height 31 m, Luce Co.

Bark. Thin, light grayish brown, separating into thin, platelike scales; inner bark cinnamon or reddish brown.

Leaves. Spirally arranged, but crowded on the upper side of branches by the twisting of those on the under side; 1–2 cm long but as short as 0.5 cm; needle-shaped, blunt, stiff, 4-sided, incurved, apex acute; dark bluish green; disagreeable odor when crushed; persistent for 7–10 years.

Twigs. Slender, smooth except for peglike leaf bases, usually without hairs, grayish green, becoming orange brown, finally dark grayish brown.

Winter Buds. Broadly ovoid, obtuse, light brown, 3–6 mm long; outer bud scales pointed, not projecting beyond tip of bud.

Wood. Light, soft, weak, straight-grained, light yellow, with sapwood of same color. Uses include pulpwood, construction lumber, furniture, interior trim, musical instruments, sounding boards, paddles, boxes, crates.

Pollen Cones. May-early June; oblong-cylindrical, long-stalked, 1.3–2 cm long, comprised of many spirally arranged, red pollen scales.

Seed Cones. Young cones in May-early June; wind-pollinated; oblong-cylindrical clusters of broad, reddish seed scales (subtended by orbicular bracts) spirally arranged upon a central axis. Ripening in autumn of first season, falling soon after discharging the seeds; pendent, slender, oblong-cylindrical, nearly sessile, glossy green before maturity, pale brown at maturity, 2.5–5 cm long; cone scales with nearly entire margins; seeds 2–3 mm long with large wings oblique at apex, 0.6–1 cm long.

Distribution. Common throughout the Upper Peninsula and in the northern tip of the Lower Peninsula; outliers in Wexford, Isabella, and Macomb Co.

Habitat. Characteristic of mesic and wet-mesic sites in the cold, moist Boreal Forest region, primarily to the north of Michigan; occurring as individuals in upland, hardwood-conifer stands; associates include balsam fir, red maple, black spruce, yellow birch, trembling aspen, balsam poplar, eastern white pine, tamarack, paper birch; found in aerated (nonstagnant) conifer swamps, bogs, upland edges of swamps and bogs, stream borders, lake shores.

Notes. Shade-tolerant, slow-growing, long-lived. Able to establish in the shade of other species on moist or wet sites and, unless fire kills the young trees, gradually able to grow into the forest overstory. Indians used the pliable roots for lacing birch bark on canoes. Major insect pest is the spruce budworm (*Choristoneura fumiferana*) which mainly damages mature and overmature trees.

74

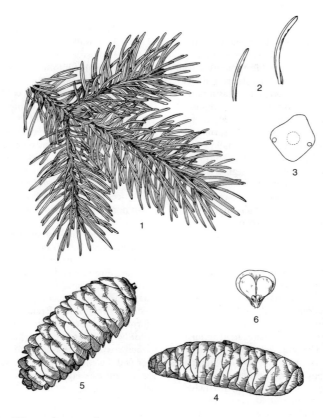

1. Winter shoot, × 1.
2. Leaves, × 1.
3. Cross section of leaf, enlarged.
4. Unopened cone, × 1.
5. Partly opened cone, × 1.
6. Cone scale with seeds, × 1.

Key Characters

- slender cylindrical seed cones with close-fitting scales and smooth cone-scale margin
- twigs essentially without hairs
- inner bark layers cinnamon or reddish brown

Easily distinguished from black spruce by the longer, narrower, more cylindrical seed cones whose scales have smooth, not rough or toothed, margins; cones not persistent in top of crown; inner bark cinnamon brown not olive green. Less easily distinguished by needles and twigs; needles usually longer, twigs glabrous. White spruce more typical of upland sites, rarely in pure stands, whereas black spruce typically occurs in stagnant swamps and sphagnum bogs, often in pure stands.

PINACEAE
Picea mariana (Miller) BSP.

Black Spruce

Size and Form. Small to medium-sized tree, 5–15 m high and 10–25 cm in diameter. Slender, with a straight, little-tapering trunk; often small and stunted. In stands the stem self-pruned of lower branches, has a narrow, irregular, conical, spirelike crown of short, slender branches. Top of crown often club-shaped. Branches drooping and turning up at the tips. Root system flat and shallow regardless of soil or water table condition; not windfirm. Michigan Big Tree: girth 1.4 m, diameter 46 cm, height 19 m, Isabella Co.

Bark. Thin, scaly, grayish brown, separating into thin, appressed scales; inner bark layers yellowish to olive green.

Leaves. Spirally arranged, spreading in all directions; 0.5–1.2 cm long; needle-shaped, more or less incurved, 4-sided, stiff, apex blunt; dark bluish green and glaucous; persistent 7–10 years.

Twigs. Slender, at first green and whitish-pubescent, becoming dull reddish brown and rusty-pubescent.

Winter Buds. Ovoid, acute, light reddish brown, 3–6 mm long; outer bud scales grayish, finely hairy, with long slender points that project well beyond tip of bud.

Wood. Light, soft, weak, pale yellowish white, with thin pure white sapwood. Uses include pulpwood, poles, furniture, interior trim, paddles and oars, musical instruments, ladder rails.

Pollen Cones. May-early June; in subglobose clusters, about 1.2 cm long, composed of many spirally arranged, dark red pollen scales.

Seed Cones. Young cones in May-early June; wind-pollinated; oblong-cylindrical clusters, composed of broad, purple seed scales (subtended by rounded, toothed, purple bracts), spirally arranged upon a central axis, about 1.2 cm long. Ripening in autumn of first season, persisting on branches at top of crown many years, opening intermittently during drying and releasing seeds for 1–2 years; pendent, short-stalked, ovoid, egg-shaped, 2–3 cm long; with close-fitting scales, margins roughly toothed; seeds about 3 mm long, with pale brown wings, 0.8–1.2 cm long.

Distribution. Common throughout the Upper Peninsula and the northern half of the Lower Peninsula; rare in southern Michigan (only in bogs), south to Calhoun and Washtenaw Co.

Habitat. Characteristic of cold, highly acid, sphagnum bogs, poorly drained and undrained swamps; frequent in swamps and bogs where water movement is very slow, hence low in oxygen; associated with tamarack, balsam fir, red maple, yellow birch; less frequent in swamps with moving, aerated water and high lime content where northern white-cedar, black ash, and alders thrive; also northward on dune ridges and lake shores.

Notes. Moderately shade-tolerant; very slow-growing; moderately long-lived. Regenerated naturally by wild fires, forming dense stands. Fire opens the cones but does not destroy them, prepares the seedbed for germinating seeds, and provides nutrients in the ash of burned litter. Branches often deformed by dwarf mistletoe, *Arceuthobium pusillum*. Lower live branches take root when covered by mosses and litter (process termed *layering*) or when pressed into organic soil by weight of snow. Weight of the tree may cause it to sink into sphagnum moss and this may lead to layering of branches. These branches eventually become new trees, and a small colony or clone of trees is formed around the parent tree. Undesirable for Christmas trees because needles fall off rapidly after tree is cut. Undesirable for ornamental planting because lower branches die early and persist as dead branches on trunk.

76

1. Winter shoot, × 1.
2. Leaves, × 2.
3. Cross sections of leaves, enlarged.
4–5. Opened cones, × 1.
6. Cone scale with seeds, × 1.

Key Characters

- seed cones short and nearly spherical when scales are open; cones persistent in tree top
- seed cone-scale margin roughly toothed
- twigs with short, dense dull reddish brown pubescence
- inner bark layers olive green
- crown slender, spirelike, sometimes with clublike top
- dense pure stands in undrained swamps and bog margins

Easily distinguished from white spruce if the small, rounded seed cones with roughly toothed scale margins are present on or under the tree. Also distinguished from white spruce by its olive green inner bark rather than cinnamon brown bark, shorter needles with presence of dense reddish brown pubescence, and occurrence in pure stands in stagnant swamps and bogs, whereas white spruce is usually scattered in slightly drier and more upland sites.

PINACEAE
Picea pungens Engelmann

Colorado Blue Spruce

Size and Form. Medium-sized tree, 10–15
m high and 25–50 cm in diameter. Trunk
straight, crown narrowly conic, branches in a
layered arrangement, rather dense, often
downswept in large trees; crowns of open-
grown trees reaching the ground. Roots shallow. Michigan Big Tree: no record.

Bark. Thin and smooth on young trees;
forming large, thin, purplish or grayish
brown, loosely attached scales, coarsely
flaky, some flakes ash gray.

Leaves. Spirally arranged, spreading in all
directions at right angles to the shoot, the
majority on the upper side and upswept;
1.5–2 cm long; linear, stiff, extremely sharp-
pointed; new foliage bright bluish gray or
bluish green, turning grayish green; covered
with a powdery bloom.

Twigs. Moderately stout, tan to light
orange brown when young, becoming grayish
brown.

Winter Buds. Ovoid-conic, brownish yellow, 5–6 mm long; brown bud scales curving
out in a rosette.

Seed Cones. Young cones in May-June;
wind-pollinated; ripening autumn of first season; cylindrical-oblong, often curved, 8–15
cm long, light brown; scales thin, papery,
pale wavy margin finely toothed.

Distribution. Native in the central and
southern Rocky Mountains. Commonly
planted as an ornamental.

Habitat. Grows well on almost any upland
soil; drought resistant.

Notes. Shade-tolerant; slow-growing; long-
lived. Highly prized ornamental because of
its bright bluish gray foliage. Trees in the
Rocky Mountains vary greatly in foliage
color; many cultivars have been selected for
their bluish foliage and are propagated by
grafting. Widely planted cultivars include
'Koster', 'Bakeri', 'Hoopsii', 'Moerheimii',
and 'Thompsonii'. Root system very shallow
on heavy-textured or wet soils and exposed
trees prone to wind-throw.

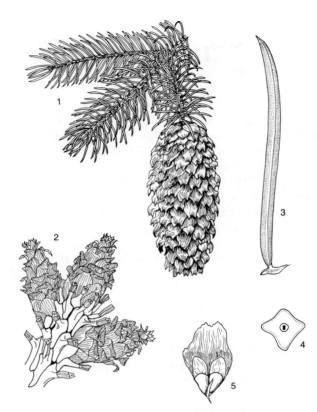

1. Winter shoot, with leaves and cone, × ½.
2. Shoot with winter buds, leaves cut off, × 2.
3. Leaf, × 2½.
4. Cross section of leaf, × 7½.
5. Cone scale with seeds, × 1.

Key Characters

- foliage bluish gray or bluish green, needles extremely sharp-pointed
- seed cones long, light brown; scales thin and papery with wavy, finely toothed margins
- crown narrowly conic; branches of biggest trees usually downswept

79

The Pines—*Pinus*

The pines are the largest genus of trees included in the great cone-bearing family, Pinaceae. Of the 36 species found in the United States, only 3 are native in Michigan. Formerly much of the northern part of the state was a vast forest of white pine and red pine intermixed with hardwoods. The exploitation of these great timber stands played an important role in the economic and industrial development of Michigan. However, the character of the northern forest has been profoundly changed by the logging and the many, uncontrolled fires that followed.

The genus *Pinus* is one of the most important of all tree genera. About 100 species exist, and most of them are locally or nationally important in the timber or fiber economy. They occur from the Boreal Forest to south of the equator in the mountains of Sumatra and Java. Pines, despite their taxonomic variety, have a great deal in common in their ecological place in the world's forests. Virtually all are characteristic of coarse dry soils, especially sands, gravels, and rock outcrops, and most owe their dominance to frequent burning and their ability to regenerate abundantly in the ashes of the blackened site. As a group, the pines have a deep root system, with the growing tips requiring large soil spaces for penetration. Because of the deep root system, they do not grow well on frozen or poorly drained soils. They have a high ability to withstand hot, dry conditions, whether in the tropics or in northern continental climates as in the interior of Canada and Siberia. An excellent monograph of the genus is available (Mirov, 1967).

The pines, like the other members of the family, produce their seeds in cones. They are peculiar, however, in that their cones require 2 years for maturation. The young reproductive structures also take the form of cones, the male pollen-bearing and the female ovule-bearing clusters being separated, although both may be found on the same tree, i.e., monoecious. The pollen matures in May or June, is yellow, and is wind-disseminated in great abundance. Most of the seed-bearing cones develop on the upper branches, and the seeds are disseminated during the second autumn. The empty cones with opened, woody scales may fall soon or may cling to the tree for some time (many years in jack pine).

The leaves of all the evergreens persist on the branches several years. The leaves of eastern white pine, for example, drop when they are 2 or 3 years old. The arrangement of the leaves, or needles, in clusters of from 2 to 5 offers a simple means of distinguishing the species. Species of the *soft pine* group, eastern white pine in Michigan, have 5 leaves in a cluster, whereas those of the *hard pine* group, red and jack pines in Michigan, have 2 to 3 needles in a cluster with the base of each cluster encased in a persistent, membranous sheath. The names of these groups come from the relatively soft and hard textures of their wood.

Besides the native pines, a number of introduced species have been planted, either for ornamental or for forest production purposes. Of these, 2 European pines, Scots and black, were among the first to be so used, and large trees of these species are seen frequently. The mugo pine is also from Europe and is noted for its dwarf or shrublike forms. It is among the most important of the low pines for parks and gardens.

Summer and Winter Key to Species of *Pinus*

1. Leaves 5 in a cluster; cones cylindrical, 10–25 cm long; scales
   flexible . . . . *P. strobus*, p. 82
1. Leaves 2 in a cluster; cones less than 10 cm long; scales rigid.
   2. Leaves 2.5–10 cm long.
      3. Cones (open or closed) persistent on the branches . . . . *P. banksiana*, p. 84
      3. Cones not persistent on the branches.
         4. Bark of the upper trunk orange brown, flaking off in thin plates; medium-sized tree; needles silvery blue green; cones stout-stalked, light gray
            brown . . . . *P. sylvestris*, p. 86
         4. Bark of the trunk gray black, not as above; shrublike or a small tree; needles dark green; cones sessile, brown . . . . *P. mugo*, p. 88
   2. Leaves 10–15 cm long.
      5. Leaves snap cleanly when bent sharply; bark of trunk red brown; cones egg-shaped, brown, about 5 cm long; cone scales thickened at the apex, but
         unarmed . . . . *P. resinosa*, p. 90
      5. Leaves not snapping cleanly when bent sharply; bark of trunk pinkish gray to nearly black; cones 5–8 cm long, yellowish brown; cone scales thickened at the apex and topped at first with a short spine, which is soon
         deciduous . . . . *P. nigra*, p. 92

PINACEAE
Pinus strobus Linnaeus

Eastern White Pine

Size and Form. Large tree, 20–30 m high and 60–100 cm in diameter. Open-grown trees exhibit a wide-spreading pyramidal crown, excurrent form. Branches in mid-crown spread at nearly right angles to the stem, upper branches ascend and often grow irregularly away from the prevailing wind direction giving the tree a wind-swept appearance that is distinctive at a distance. Branches spaced in annual, false whorls at intervals of 0.3–1 m along the trunk; tree age can be determined by counting the number of whorls. Wide-spreading lateral root system, sinker roots but no distinct taproot; very windfirm. Michigan Big Tree: girth 6.0 m, diameter 192 cm, height 34 m, Keweenaw Co. (tree 48 m tall in Ontonagon Co.).

Bark. Thin, smooth, greenish on young trees; becoming thick, dark gray, and deeply fissured longitudinally into broad scaly ridges.

Leaves. In clusters of 5; 7–12 cm long; slender, straight, needle-shaped, 3-sided, edges finely toothed, flexible and soft; pale blue green; sheath at base of needle cluster deciduous; clusters persistent about 2 years.

Twigs. Slender, at first rusty-tomentose, later smooth and light brown, finally thin, smooth, greenish.

Winter Buds. Oblong-ovoid, slender, sharp-pointed, yellow brown, 0.6–1.3 cm long.

Wood. Light, soft, weak, compact, straight-grained, easily worked, light brown, with thin, whitish sapwood. Used for doors, sashes, interior finish, cabinetwork, construction timber, pulpwood, matches, boxes; one of the most generally useful of all American woods.

Pollen Cones. June; clustered at the base of last year's shoots, concentrated in mid-crown, ovoid, about 8 mm long, composed of many sessile, yellow pollen scales arranged on a central axis. Trees monoecious.

Seed Cones. Young cones in June; wind-pollinated; cylindrical, 1–5 at tips of new growth in the upper crown, long-stalked, 0.6–1 cm long, composed of many pinkish purple scales spirally arranged upon a central axis. Ripening in autumn of the second season, falling during the winter and succeeding spring; pendent, short-stalked, narrow-cylindrical, often curved, greenish, 10–25 cm long; scales flexible, slightly thickened at the apex; seeds reddish brown, 6 mm long, with wings 2 cm long.

Distribution. Abundant in the Upper Peninsula and the northern half of the Lower Peninsula; south to Berrien, St. Joseph, Oakland, and formerly Wayne Co.; often-planted and vigorous as an ornamental tree.

Habitat. Grows well on a wide variety of sites; moraines of moderately well drained loams and silt loams (associated with sugar maple, yellow birch, beech, basswood, hemlock); well drained, dry, highly acid, infertile, sandy soils and dunes (associated with red pine, jack pine, red oak, black oak, white birch, trembling aspen); small ridges or mounds in swamps and poorly drained sites (associated with spruces, balsam fir, northern white-cedar, yellow birch, red maple); floodplains; rock ridges and outcrops.

Notes. Moderately shade-tolerant; moderately fast-growing, long-lived. A fire-dependent species, regenerating following fire on a variety of habitats. Because of its long life it is the only native pine that can compete with and replace (following fire) stands of northern hardwoods on the better sites. It is also shade-tolerant enough to establish without aid of fire in the understory of stands of red pine, jack pine, and red, white, and black oaks and gradually to replace them in the overstory. Severely restricted in commercial planting, except for ornamental use, by its susceptibility to the white pine blister rust fungus (*Cronartium ribicola*) and the white pine weevil (*Pissoides strobi*). The major species of the lumber industry in Michigan from about 1850–1900, enormous stands and volumes were harvested in the upper part of the Lower Peninsula. State tree of Michigan.

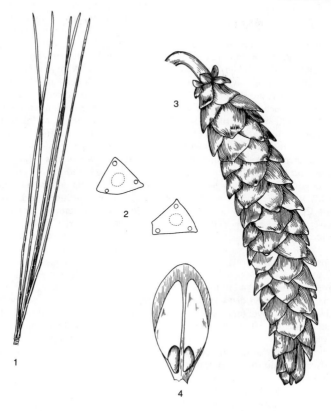

1. Cluster of leaves, × 1.
2. Cross sections of leaves, enlarged.
3. Partly opened cone, × ¾.
4. Cone scale with seeds, × 1.

Key Characters

- needles 5 per cluster
- cylindrical seed cone at least twice as long as wide; flexible cone scales
- wide-spreading horizontal branches in mid-crown and wind-swept branches in upper crown

PINACEAE
Pinus banksiana Lambert

Jack Pine

Size and Form. Small to medium-sized tree, 10–17 m high and 40–60 cm in diameter on good sites, usually small, 8–15 m high and 20–30 cm in diameter. Highly variable in form from short, bushy, crooked or distorted, open-grown trees on dry, sandy soils and rocky sites to tall, straight trunks of little taper and a short conical crown on better sites. Trees often with a scraggly, branchy, unkempt appearance. Wide-spreading root system reaching far beyond the crown, tap root distinct in young trees. Michigan Big Tree: girth 2.2 m, diameter 70 cm, height 19 m, Marquette Co. Trees over 30 m tall reported to have occurred on the Yellow Dog Plains, Marquette Co.

Bark. Thin, dark reddish brown to dark gray, with shallow, rounded ridges, rough-scaly on the surface.

Leaves. In clusters of 2; 2–4 cm long; narrow-linear; stout, curved or twisted, apex acute, relatively blunt; divergent from a short, persistent sheath; yellowish green; persistent 2–3 years.

Twigs. Slender, yellowish green, becoming purple, finally dark reddish brown and rough with persistent scales.

Winter Buds. Terminal bud ovoid, with rounded apex, pale brown, 6 mm long; lateral buds smaller.

Wood. Light, soft, weak, close-grained, light brown, with thick, whitish sapwood. Uses include pulpwood, posts, and boxes.

Pollen Cones. May-June; in dense cylindrical clusters, 1–2 cm long, at the base of current year's shoots, occurring throughout the crown, composed of many sessile, yellow pollen scales attached to a central axis.

Seed Cones. Young cones May-June; wind-pollinated; small, rounded, at ends of last year's shoots in upper and mid-crown, each cone a subglobose cluster of many purple scales (subtended by small bracts) spirally arranged upon a central axis. Ripening in autumn of the second season, may open and discharge seeds or remain closed (*serotinous* condition) and persistent on the branches 10–20 years or more, open cones also persistent; erect, usually incurved and often pointing forward, oblong-conical, sessile, 4–7 cm long; scales thickened at the apex, unarmed; seeds triangular, small, nearly black, 3 mm long, with wings about 10 mm long.

Distribution. A Boreal Forest tree but common in the Upper Peninsula and the northern half of the Lower Peninsula; occurs sparingly along the Lake Michigan shore as far south as Berrien Co. and into Indiana; in eastern Lower Peninsula as far south as Huron, Tuscola, and Saginaw Co. Extensive forests and woodlands located on the Yellow Dog, Baraga, and Panola Plains of the Upper Peninsula and in the high outwash plains of the north-central Lower Peninsula.

Habitat. Characteristic of excessively drained, dry, sterile, highly acid soils (common on sands of the Grayling and Rubicon soil series) where they grow slowly, often in woodlands or savannas; associated with northern pin oak, red pine, black oak, bigtooth aspen. Capable of growing well on better soils, but limited by competition from white and red pines and many deciduous trees. Sometimes found in swamps or on sand ridges in swamps.

Notes. Shade-intolerant; fast-growing; short-lived. Fire-dependent species par excellence; fire opens the closed cones whose scales are bonded with resin. The degree of cone serotiny varies geographically and with fire frequency (Schoenike 1976); Michigan trees have a lower percentage of closed cones than those of the Boreal Forest of Canada. Thousands of seeds are stored on each tree until fire occurs. Besides promoting seed dispersal, fire prepares a suitable seedbed by reducing the humus of the forest floor or by baring mineral soil, thus reducing competition from grasses and other plants and providing available nutrients in the ash. Seeds germinate readily following post-fire rains. Parklike or savanna stands in north-central Michigan are prime habitat for the rare Kirtland's or jack pine warbler that breeds nowhere else in the world. Jack pine may be damaged by major outbreaks of an insect defoliator, the jack pine budworm (*Choristoneura pinus*).

1. Cluster of leaves, × 1.
2. Cross section of leaf, enlarged.
3. Twig with closed (serotinous) cone, × 1.
4. Twig with opened cone, × 1.
5. Cone scale with seeds, × 1.

**Key
Characters**
- closed and open seed cones persistent on branches, closed cones incurved
- needles short and stout, slightly twisted
- bushy open-grown form or slender, little-tapering trunks in dense, closed stands

PINACEAE
Pinus sylvestris Linnaeus

Scots Pine   Scotch Pine

Size and Form. Medium-sized tree, 10–18 m high and 20–50 cm in diameter. Highly variable in form, from short crooked stems with wide-spreading limby crowns (southern European origin) to tall straight stems with good natural branch pruning (northern European and mountain origins). Wide-spreading lateral root system and a distinct tap root in youth. Michigan Big Tree: girth 4.5 m, diameter 143 cm, height 19 m, Lenawee Co.

Bark. Thin, pale gray with scaly ridges on young trees; moderately thick on older trees, orange brown and finely scaly or flaky in the mid and upper trunk, becoming shallowly or deeply fissured into dark red, scaly plates.

Leaves. In clusters of 2; 5–10 cm long; stiff, thick, broad, more or less twisted, spreading slightly from a short sheath; bluish or often glaucous green, sometimes silvery; persistent 3–4 years.

Twigs. Slender, reddish to orange brown, becoming grayish; strong shoots finely ribbed.

Winter Buds. Oblong-ovoid, sharp-pointed, reddish brown, some with white resin, about 6 mm long.

Wood. Light, stiff, straight-grained, strong, hard, resinous, reddish brown, with thick, yellow to reddish white sapwood.

Pollen Cones. May-June; at the base of new shoots, in ovoid, short-stalked clusters, about 6 mm long, composed of many sessile, yellowish pollen scales attached to a central axis. Trees monoecious.

Seed Cones. Young cones in May-June; wind-pollinated; 1–5 at tips of new shoots in upper crown, short-stalked, reddish, about 6 mm long. Ripening in autumn or winter of second season, falling as soon as ripe; pendent, stout-stalked, ovoid-conical, 5–8 cm long; scales dull grayish brown, apex thickened into 4-sided, recurved points; seeds reddish brown, 5–6 mm long, with wings 1.3–2 cm long.

Distribution. Introduced from Europe where it has the widest geographic range of any pine species. Many races and varieties are recognized (Wright et al. 1966). Planted throughout the state; hardy throughout Michigan and the western Great Lakes region.

Habitat. Grows on virtually any upland soil when planted. Thrives on sandy loam soils; similar in habitat to red pine.

Notes. Shade-intolerant; fast-growing; moderately long-lived. Highly variable genetically in form, growth rate, winter foliage color, and many other characters as a consequence of marked racial differences in populations throughout its wide distribution. Southern European races happened to be introduced early into the United States and Michigan. These races exhibited such a crooked stem form and limby growth habit that the species was essentially given up for reforestation and timber purposes. Exceptionally straight-stemmed races from northern Europe are generally slower growing. Nevertheless, considerable potential for use in forest production exists. Planted widely as an ornamental, especially for Christmas trees; varieties for Christmas tree use are described by Wright et al. (1976). Some races are highly susceptible to the European pine shoot moth (*Rhyacionia buoliana*).

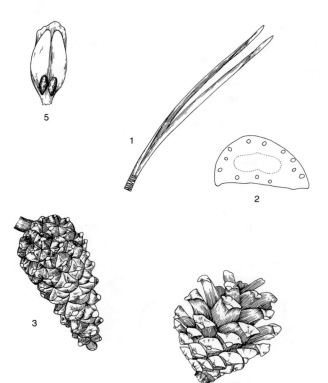

1. Cluster of leaves, × 1.
2. Cross section of leaf, enlarged.
3. Unopened cone, × 1.
4. Partly opened cone, × 1.
5. Cone scale with seeds, × 1.

Key
Characters
- needles glaucous green, slightly twisted, in 2s
- bark of upper trunk orange brown, flaky
- seed cone scales grayish, apex thickened into 4-sided recurved points, no prickles
- usually planted, often in sizable plantations

PINACEAE
Pinus mugo Turra

Mugo Pine   Mountain Pine

Size and Form. Small tree to prostrate shrub, 1–8 m high and 2–10 cm in diameter. Tree form with pyramidal crown, lower branches horizontal then upcurved; more often a low, many-stemmed shrub. Michigan Big Tree: no record.

Bark. Thin, smooth, dark gray; becoming blackish with curling scales.

Leaves. In clusters of 2, in very dense, spiral arrangement, appearing whorled; 3–6 cm long; narrow, linear, rigid, grooved inside; basal sheath broad, recurved, persistent; dark green; persistent 3–4 years.

Twigs. Slender to moderately stout, reddish to orange brown, becoming gray.

Winter Buds. Ovoid, reddish brown, 6–8 mm long.

Pollen Cones. May-June; similar to those of Scots pine only smaller. Trees monoecious.

Seed Cones. Young cones May-June, wind-pollinated, ripening in autumn of second season; sessile, ovoid-conic, 3–5 cm long; scales with reddish brown or purple inner lip, basal scales curved downward, tan or dark brown; apex bordered by a dark ring bearing a mucro or a remnant of a mucro.

Distribution. Native in the Alps of Austria, Switzerland, and southern France. Commonly planted as a low shrub.

Habitat. Grows well on almost any upland soil.

Notes. Shade-intolerant; slow-growing; moderately long-lived. A highly variable species in form, from a prostrate shrub to a tree 25 m tall that closely resembles Scots pine in its native habitat. Important ornamentally for its dwarf forms of dark green foliage.

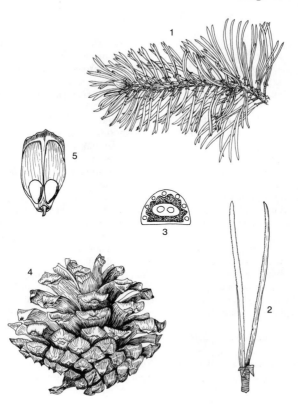

1. Winter shoot, × ½.
2. Cluster of leaves, × 1.
3. Cross section of leaf, × 10.
4. Cone, × 1.
5. Cone scale with seeds, × 1½.

Key Characters
- dwarf tree or tall shrub with dark green needles
- seed cones small, armed; scales with reddish brown or purple inner lip
- planted near homes and buildings

PINACEAE
Pinus resinosa Aiton

Red Pine

Size and Form. Large tree, 20–30 m high and 60–100 cm in diameter. Stout, horizontal branches form a broad, rounded, rather open crown; excurrent form. In closed stands, trunks are long and limbless, crowns short and oval. Branches spaced in annual false-whorls at intervals of 0.3–1 m along the trunk; tree age can be determined by counting the number of these whorls. Wide-spreading lateral roots and a distinct tap root in youth. Michigan Big Tree: girth 3.0 m, diameter 97 cm, height 35 m, Gogebic Co. (tree 43 m tall in Ontonagon Co.)

Bark. Thick and reddish, flaky; on old trees shallowly fissured with broad, flat, flaky ridges; fire-resistant.

Leaves. In clusters of 2; 10–17 cm long; slender, straight, needle-shaped, sharp-pointed, flexible but snapping apart when bent sharply, issuing from elongated persistent sheaths; semicircular in cross section; lustrous dark green; tufted on branch tips; persistent 4–5 years.

Twigs. Orange brown, becoming rough with persistent scales.

Winter Buds. Ovoid or conical, acute, reddish brown, with rather loose scales, about 2 cm long.

Wood. Light, hard, very close-grained, pale red, with thin, yellow to white sapwood. Uses include general construction, pulpwood, ladders, piling, poles, interior and exterior trim.

Pollen Cones. April-May; wind-pollinated; in dense cylindrical clusters, 1.3–2 cm long, at the base of last year's shoots, predominantly in mid-crown, composed of many sessile, purple pollen scales attached to a central axis. Trees monoecious.

Seed Cones. Young cones in April-May; small, rounded, at ends of the new shoots in upper crown, each cone a subglobose cluster of scarlet scales spirally arranged upon a central axis, borne on stout peduncles covered with pale brown bracts. Ripening in autumn of the second season, falling the next summer; egg-shaped, nearly sessile, brown, only about 5 cm long; scales thickened at the apex, unarmed; seeds oval, compressed, light, mottled brown, with wings 1–1.5 cm long.

Distribution. Common to frequent in the Upper Peninsula and the northern half of the Lower Peninsula, south to Ottawa Co. on the west and St. Clair Co. on the east. Vigorous as an ornamental tree farther south.

Habitat. Characteristic of well drained, dry, highly acid, sandy soils of outwash plains and gravelly ridges; associated with jack pine, white pine, oaks, aspens, white birch. Also common on rock outcrops and sand dunes. Not competitive with hardwoods on the better (heavier textured) soils; does not tolerate a high water table or frost pockets.

Notes. Shade-intolerant; fast-growing; long-lived; fire-dependent for establishment. Easily cultivated in nurseries and easily raised in plantations; the most extensively planted of any Michigan species. Gremmeniella (or Scleroderris) canker, caused by *Gremmeniella abietina*, is an important disease of young trees especially in frost pockets and depressions. European pine shoot moth (*Rhyacionia buolinana*) is an important insect pest. Sometimes called Norway pine, it does not grow in Norway or elsewhere in Europe; it is said to have received the name from the town of Norway, Maine.

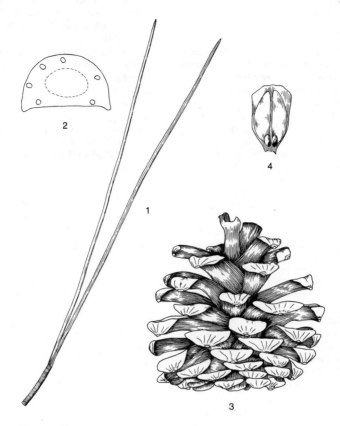

1. Cluster of leaves, × 1.
2. Cross section of leaf, enlarged.
3. Opened cone, × 1.
4. Cone scale with seeds, × 1.

**Key
Characters**
- long needles in 2s giving the tree a tufted appearance from a distance; needles snapping cleanly in two when bent double
- moderately large, egg-shaped, unarmed brown seed cones
- flaky reddish to pinkish brown bark

91

PINACEAE
Pinus nigra Arnold

Black Pine

Size and Form. Large tree, 15–24 m high and 60–100 cm in diameter. Forming a massive, spreading, open crown of stiff, large branches; excurrent form. Long needles in dense clusters give the crown a tufted appearance. Old trees broadly flat-topped. Very wide-spreading lateral roots, extending many meters beyond the crown; tap root strongly developed. Michigan Big Tree: girth 2.5 m, diameter 81 cm, height 26 m, Lenawee Co.

Bark. Thick, pinkish gray to nearly black; on old trunks coarsely and deeply fissured, flaking coarsely.

Leaves. In clusters of 2; 8–16 cm long; slender, stiff but flexible, not snapping apart when bent sharply, curved toward the twig, sharp-pointed; dark green on both sides; persistent 3–6 years.

Twigs. Stout, yellowish brown to olive brown and smooth, becoming darker with age.

Winter Buds. Oblong-conical, abruptly sharp-pointed, reddish brown, often white with resin, 1.2–1.6 cm long.

Wood. Moderately heavy, strong, very resinous, reddish brown, with thick yellowish to reddish white sapwood.

Pollen Cones. May-June; wind-pollinated; at the base of new shoots in cylindrical, sub-sessile clusters, about 2 cm long, composed of many bright yellow pollen scales attached to a central axis. Trees monoecious.

Seed Cones. Young cones in May-June; 1–5, at tips of new shoots, each cone a small, rounded cluster of bright red scales arranged on a central axis. Ripening in autumn of second season, opening 2 years after full size is attained and remaining on the tree several years; erect, sessile, long-ovoid, 5–8 cm long; scales smooth, yellowish brown, lustrous, apex thickened and topped with a short prickle in the center, prickle deciduous; seeds reddish brown, 6 mm long, with wings 1.5–2 cm long.

Distribution. Native in central and southern Europe. Frequently cultivated as an ornamental tree. Hardy.

Habitat. Grows on any well to moderately well drained soil when planted. High tolerance for rocky, gravelly, and drought-prone soils and those with a high lime content.

Notes. Shade-intolerant; fast-growing; moderately long-lived. A variable species with several geographic varieties; sometimes known as Austrian or Corsican pine. Hardy and easily transplanted when small. A popular ornamental because of its bushy, dark green foliage, compact growth when young, and its high survival ability on a variety of soils. Well adapted for screens and windbreaks.

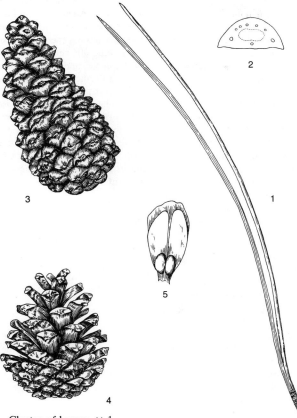

1. Cluster of leaves, × 1.
2. Cross section of leaf, enlarged.
3. Unopened cone, × 1.
4. Partly opened cone, × ½.
5. Cone scale with seeds, × 1.

Key Characters
- long, stiff needles in 2s; not brittle, do not break when bent sharply
- large, long-ovoid seed cones appearing unarmed when mature
- bark pinkish gray
- usually open-grown trees, young trees dense and compact, old trees with massive spreading crowns, often flat-topped

Distinguished from red pine by needles that do not snap when bent sharply and by the larger, yellowish brown, armed cones.

93

PINACEAE
Pseudotsuga menziesii (Mirbel) Franco

Douglas-fir

Size and Form. Medium-sized tree, 12–20 m high and 30–60 cm in diameter. Open-grown trees with straight stems and conical crowns, extending to the ground. Michigan Big Tree: no record.

Bark. Thin, gray, smooth except for resin blisters; becoming thick and deeply furrowed into gray or reddish brown ridges.

Leaves. Spirally arranged, spreading from all sides of the shoot but appearing somewhat 2-ranked; 2–2.5 cm long; linear, soft, apex rounded or sharp-pointed, base constricted; yellowish green to dark bluish green, glaucous above; persistent 5–8 years.

Twigs. Moderately stout, at first pale brown to reddish brown and pubescent, becoming grayish brown, glabrous, and roughened.

Winter Buds. Conical or fusiform, sharp-pointed, lustrous, reddish brown.

Pollen Cones. May-June; composed of a number of spirally arranged, short-stalked, subglobose pollen scales. Trees monoecious.

Seed Cones. Young cones in May-June; wind-pollinated; conical, at ends of shoots or in axils of upper leaves, composed of several spirally arranged, overlapping, 3-lobed bracts each subtending a small ovate seed scale with 2 basal ovules. Ripening in autumn of first season, ovoid-cylindrical, pendent, green becoming dull brown, 5–8 cm long; 3-lobed appressed or reflexed bracts extending beyond the scales; seeds triangular, with large wings.

Distribution. Native in the Rocky Mountains from Mexico to British Columbia, Canada, and along the west coast of North America from California to British Columbia. Occasionally planted as a park or lawn tree or in Christmas tree plantations.

Habitat. Grows well on most upland soils except those with high lime content in the topsoil.

Notes. Moderately shade-tolerant; moderately fast-growing; long-lived. Old-growth trees in the Pacific Northwest average 55–76 m high and 1.2–1.8 m in diameter. They form part of the Pacific Northwest conifer forest which is among the tallest and most massive in the world (Waring and Franklin 1979). Many races exist, and morphological features, especially leaf and cone traits, vary markedly among races. The Rocky Mountain race is generally shorter, exhibits a grayish green foliage, and is more drought resistant than the Pacific Coast race. One of the world's most important commercial species; widely planted in Europe for timber as well as for ornament. Planted by many commercial growers in Michigan for Christmas trees; popular as a Christmas tree because it is naturally more bushy in habit than balsam fir, and its needles persist long after the tree has been cut.

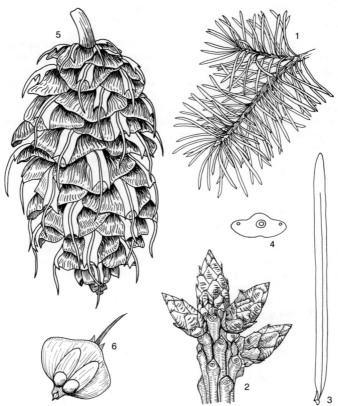

1. Winter shoot, × ½.
2. Winter buds, (leaves removed), × 2.
3. Leaf, × 2.
4. Cross section of leaf, × 10.
5. Opened cone, × 1.
6. Cone scale with seeds, × 1.

**Key
Characters**
• seed cones with 3-lobed bracts extending beyond the scales
• terminal buds conical or fusiform, lustrous, reddish brown
• needles spreading from all sides of the shoot, only slightly 2-ranked; usually bluish green with a glaucous coating.

PINACEAE
Tsuga canadensis (Linnaeus) Carrière

Eastern Hemlock

Size and Form. Large tree, 20–30 m high and 60–120 cm in diameter. Young trees with a straight trunk and slender flexible branches that form flat sprays, drooping at their ends; the leader shoot droops slightly. Mature trees forming a massive, pyramidal, ragged crown of densely foliated branches; trunk with marked taper. Root system widespreading and shallow, very fibrous; not windfirm. Michigan Big Tree: girth 4.2 m, diameter 133 cm, height 39 m, Marquette Co.

Bark. Thick, reddish brown or gray, deeply divided into broad, flat-topped scaly ridges; reddish purple when freshly cut; inner bark layers purple.

Leaves. Spirally arranged around the shoot, but appearing 2-ranked by the twisting of the petioles; 0.6–1.4 cm long; linear, flat, apex rounded, minutely toothed near apex, blade narrows abruptly at the base to a short, threadlike petiole; tiny needles lying upside down and appressed to the top of the shoot; dark yellowish green and shining above, a whitish band on either side of the midrib below; persistent about 3 years.

Twigs. At first pale brown and pubescent, becoming glabrous, grayish brown.

Winter Buds. Ovoid, blunt, reddish brown, slightly puberulent, 2 mm long.

Wood. Light, soft, weak, brittle, coarse- and crooked-grained, not durable, ill-smelling, light reddish brown, with thin, darker-colored sapwood. Uses include pulpwood, general construction, boxes, crates, sashes, doors, and cabinets.

Pollen Cones. April-May; in axils of the previous season's leaves, short-stalked, light yellow, subglobose clusters of pollen scales, about 1 cm long. Trees monoecious.

Seed Cones. Young cones in April-May; wind-pollinated; at ends of new shoots, oblong-cylindrical, pale green clusters of short, pinkish seed scales, 3 mm long. Ripening in autumn of first season, gradually losing seeds during winter and falling the next spring; oblong-ovoid, pointed, short-stalked, reddish brown, margin of scales smooth or faintly toothed, 1.3–2 cm long; seeds triangular, 3 mm long, with wings about twice as long.

Distribution. Common throughout the state with the exception of the southeastern part; more common on the western than the eastern side. Abundant in the western half of the Upper Peninsula.

Habitat. Characteristic of cool, moist, highly acid sites where it is typically associated with yellow birch. Occurs singly or in groups in stands of northern hardwoods (sugar maple, beech, basswood, yellow birch, red maple); rarely found in pure stands; often occurs in groups along lake shores and streams, in ravines, on wooded dunes, and at the edges of conifer swamps. Typically requires moist, cool sites to establish. Characteristic of (1) low-lying areas with relatively high water table, (2) upland areas where heavy-textured soils impede downward water movement, and (3) low ridges with sand soils that are too infertile for hardwoods. In the southern half of the Lower Peninsula found in moist, cool microsites. Seedlings typically found on rotting logs and growing in the moss on rocks and logs.

Notes. Highly shade-tolerant; very slow-growing; very long-lived (600+ years). May exist 50–100 years or more in the shaded forest understory and gradually reach the overstory. Once established it creates its own microenvironment. Its needles decay slowly in the forest floor, yielding strong acids that leach soil of minerals, humus and clay particles, and nutrients. Virtually no tree seedlings survive under large hemlock trees or stands because of the deep shade they cast and the dry (hemlock roots take the moisture) and highly acidic soil. Thick bark is fire resistant, but shallow roots with thin bark may be killed and cause the tree to die. Mature trees extremely sensitive to opening of the forest (as for roads); mortality highly likely. A useful ornamental for shaded places. Bark was the main source of natural tannin for the leather industry. Not the hemlock Socrates drank, the Socratic potion was from an herb, *Conium maculatum* L. in the Umbelliferae.

96

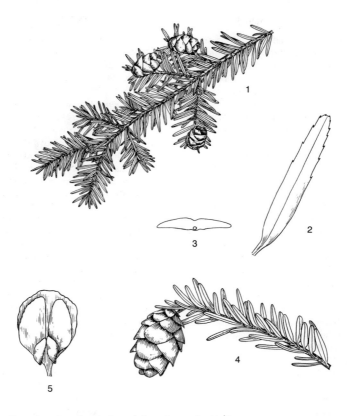

1. Cone-bearing shoot viewed from beneath, × ½.
2. Leaf, × 3.
3. Cross section of leaf, enlarged.
4. Shoot with partly opened cone, × 1.
5. Cone scale with seeds, × 3.

Key Characters

- short needles, appearing 2-ranked; also tiny needles appressed upside down to the top of the shoots
- reddish purple inner bark layers
- drooping leader and branchlets, foliage in flat sprays
- seed cones very small, scale margin appearing smooth

97

CUPRESSACEAE
Juniperus virginiana Linnaeus

Eastern Redcedar   Juniper

Size and Form. Small to medium-sized tree, 10–15 m high and 30–60 cm in diameter. Forming an irregular, pyramidal, columnar, or pear-shaped crown. Trunk rapidly tapering and irregular (not round) in cross section. Roots deep and extremely fibrous; windfirm. Michigan Big Tree: girth 2.3 m, diameter 73 cm, height 15 m, Grand Traverse Co.

Bark. Thin, fibrous, light reddish brown, exfoliating lengthwise into long, narrow, persistent, shreddy strips, exposing the smooth, brown inner bark layers.

Leaves. Opposite, of two kinds: (1) sessile, scalelike, closely appressed, overlapping, 4-ranked; 2 mm long; ovate, acute, without glandular pits; found only on older trees; (2) sessile, needle-shaped, loosely arranged in whorls of 2–3; 0.6–1.3 mm long; found on young trees and vigorous shoots of older trees; persistent 5–6 years.

Twigs. Slender, bluish green to reddish brown, smooth, not forming flat sprays.

Winter Buds. Appearing naked, minute, covered by the leaves.

Wood. Light, soft, close-grained, brittle, weak, durable, very fragrant, dull red, with thin, whitish sapwood. Uses include posts, pencils, cedar chests, woodenware, veneers, interior finish.

Pollen Cones. April-May; minute, oblong-ovoid, composed of 4–6 shieldlike pollen scales, each bearing 4–5 yellow, globose pollen sacs. Trees usually dioecious.

Seed Cones. Young cones in April-May; wind-pollinated; ovoid, composed of about 3 pairs of fleshy, bluish scales, united at the base, with each pair bearing 2 ovules. Ripening in autumn of first or second season; nearly circular, berrylike, 3–6 mm in diameter, dark blue and glaucous; flesh sweet and resinous; seeds 1–3, not winged.

Distribution. Abundant in the southern half of the Lower Peninsula.

Habitat. Characteristic of well drained, calcareous, sandy or gravelly soils in open areas including old fields and pastures, open hillsides, fence rows, rocky slopes, sand dunes, and borders of lakes, streams, and swamps. Often found as a small tree in the understory of oak-hickory forests; occasionally found on mounds in deciduous swamps; sometimes forming open juniper savannas with the dwarf juniper, *Juniperus communis* var. *depressa* Pursh.

Notes. Shade-intolerant; drought-resistant; very slow-growing; long-lived (200–300 years). Seeds disseminated widely by birds so that junipers are typically found under large trees in many different forests and adjacent to boulders. The abundance of the tree has increased markedly due to the widespread disturbance and in some cases elimination by humans of old-growth forests in southern Michigan. Susceptible to the cedar-apple rust (*Gymnosporangium juniperi-virginianae*). Many cultivars of *Juniperus* have been developed and used in landscaping. The fleshy cones of junipers (this and other species) are used in the preparation of gin to give it a distinctive flavor. This species was called "baton rouge" or "red stick" by French settlers; the capital city of Louisiana was named for it.

The juvenile foliage of this species resembles that of the typical foliage of *J. communis* var. *depressa* (see p. 318). The needle-like leaves of this species are shorter and straighter than those of *J. communis* var. *depressa,* and it has two white bands of stomata on the upper surface instead of one. Cones of eastern redcedar are borne on more or less straight, ascending peduncles, whereas those of the ground juniper are borne on more or less arched or recurved peduncles.

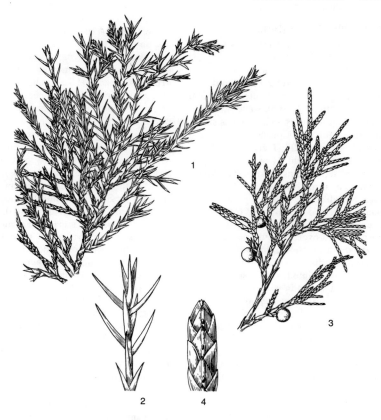

1. Shoot with needle-shaped leaves, × 1.
2. Tip of shoot, showing needle-shaped leaves, enlarged.
3. Cone-bearing shoot with scalelike leaves, × 1.
4. Tip of shoot, showing scalelike leaves, enlarged.

Key Characters
- needle-shaped leaves on young trees and scalelike, closely appressed, overlapping leaves on older trees
- cones globose, berrylike, dark blue with a glaucous bloom
- tree upright, crown pyramidal or pear-shaped
- bark fibrous, forming long, narrow, shreddy strips

CUPRESSACEAE
Thuja occidentalis Linnaeus

Northern White-cedar   Arborvitae

Size and Form. Small to medium-sized tree, 10–15 m high and 30–60 cm in diameter. Open-grown trees exhibit a dense, wide-based, conic-columnar crown reaching the ground; trunk much-tapered, often twisted or leaning and buttressed; trunk sometimes divided into 2–3 secondary stems. Roots shallow and spreading, often protruding above the ground. Michigan Big Tree: girth 5.5 m, diameter 175 cm, height 34 m, Leelanau Co.

Bark. Thin, light reddish brown, breaking into long, thin, shreddy strips.

Leaves. Scalelike in 2 pairs, opposite, 4-ranked, appressed, the rows of overlapping leaves covering the stem, the side pair keeled and partly folded over, clasping the pair on the upper and lower sides, the latter flat with conspicuous glandular spots; 3–6 mm long; ovate; obtuse or pointed; yellowish green, often becoming brown in winter; strongly aromatic when crushed; persistent for 1–2 years.

Twigs. Slender, yellowish green, flattened, forming broad, fernlike sprays, becoming light red, finally smooth, lustrous, dark orange brown.

Winter Buds. Appearing naked, minute.

Wood. Light, soft, brittle, rather coarse-grained, durable, fragrant, pale yellowish brown, with thin, whitish sapwood. Uses include poles, posts, shingles, cabin logs, rustic furniture, interior paneling, woodenware.

Pollen Cones. April-May; obscure at ends of new shoots, minute, globose, yellowish with black scales, composed of 4–6 pollen scales arranged oppositely on a short axis. Trees monoecious.

Seed Cones. Young cones in April-May; wind-pollinated; small oblong-cylindrical, reddish, composed of 8–12 seed scales arranged oppositely on a short axis. Ripening in early autumn of first season but persistent on the branch throughout the winter; erect, short-stalked, oval, pale brown, small, 0.8–1.3 cm long; composed of 8–12 scales, only the middle scales bear seeds; seeds 3 mm long, oblong, acute.

Distribution. Abundant throughout the Upper Peninsula; common in the Lower Peninsula and as far south as Berrien and Cass Co. on the west and Washtenaw and Jackson Co. on the east.

Habitat. Characteristic of cold, poorly drained swamps with moving water and a neutral or basic (pH 7 and above) substrate of organic matter; forming nearly impenetrable, pure stands in such swamps (associated with black ash, balsam poplar, speckled alder, trembling aspen, red maple); very common on low stream borders (associated with balsam fir, black spruce, eastern hemlock, white spruce, and hardwoods). Not found in the center of acid, stagnant (poorly aerated) swamps where black spruce dominates but sometimes occurs along the edge where aeration and nutrients are more favorable. Also occurs on upland sites of dry, calcareous soils often over limestone bedrock. In northern Michigan it is abundant on sites with calcareous soils and high water tables—the gravelly shores, dunes, and ridges of Lakes Michigan and Huron. Not found in upland areas with deep, acid soils.

Notes. Shade-tolerant; very slow-growing; relatively short-lived. Often found in pure stands that were established following fire. The most important winter food for deer; swamp stands provide shelter for deer during winter. Reproduces vegetatively by layering and tipping (as trees tip over and lie flat in the swamp, branches grow upright, take root, and form a row of live trees along the buried trunk). Widely planted as an ornamental for screens and hedges. Many cultivars.

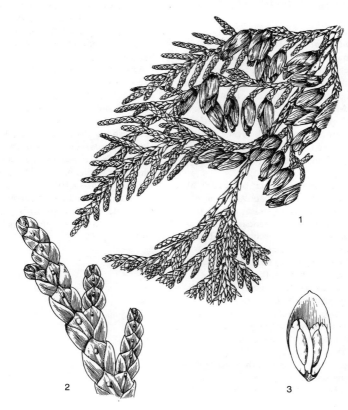

1. Cone-bearing shoot, × 1.
2. Tip of shoot enlarged.
3. Cone scale with seeds, × 3.

Key Characters

• flat, scalelike, yellowish green leaves with conspicuous glandular spots appressed to and hiding the stem; leafy shoots flat, in fan-shaped sprays
• bark in shreddy, linear strips
• seed cones small, oblong, with few, dull brown scales
• found in circumneutral or basic swamps, along streams and lake shores with calcareous soils

101

ANNONACEAE
Asimina triloba (Linnaeus) Dunal

Pawpaw

Size and Form. Tall shrub or low tree, 3–5 m high and 5–10 cm in diameter. Trunk short, slender; crown broad, round-topped, with horizontal-spreading branches. Forms small groups or dense thickets from root sprouts. Michigan Big Tree: girth 0.9 m, diameter 28 cm, height 14 m, Macomb Co.

Bark. Thin, smooth, dark brown with whitish blotches and small wartlike protuberances; becoming rough, scaly, and slightly fissured.

Leaves. Alternate; simple; blades 10–30 cm long, about half as wide; obovate-lanceolate, gradually tapering to the base; entire; thin; light green above, paler beneath; rusty-pubescent when young becoming glabrous both sides; veins prominent; aromatic or odorous when bruised (smelling like motor oil); petioles short and stout, 0.5–2 cm long.

Twigs. Slender, slightly hairy to glabrous, brownish, enlarged at the nodes.

Winter Buds. Terminal buds naked, flat, rusty brown, tomentose, 6–9 mm long; lateral buds similar but very small, sessile, appressed; flower buds globose; leaf scars broadly crescent-shaped, with 5 (or 7) bundle scars, sometimes compound.

Wood. Light, soft, coarse-grained, weak, pale yellow.

Flowers. Late May-June, with the leaves, solitary, showy, 3–4 cm across, borne on short, stout, hairy pedicels on twigs of the previous year; perfect; sepals 3; petals 6, overlapping, dark reddish purple, 1–2 cm across; stamens very numerous, small; ovaries 3–5. Insect-pollinated.

Fruit. Berry; September-October; greenish yellow becoming dark brown or black; ellipsoid to oblong, drooping, 5–12 cm long, 2–6 cm thick; seeds many, dark brown, lustrous, flattened, embedded in a sweet pulp, 2–3 cm long, 1–1.5 cm across.

Distribution. Rare in the southern 2–3 tiers of counties of the Lower Peninsula, north to Muskegon, Genesee, and Kent Co. Species of southern distribution reaching a part of its northernmost range in southern Michigan.

Habitat. Characteristic of river valleys and bottomlands with moist, fertile, alluvial soil. Also in Lake Michigan dunes. An understory species; associated with butternut, elms, red ash, basswood, northern hackberry, red mulberry, redbud.

Notes. Shade-tolerant; slow-growing; short-lived. Fruits may be made into desserts or eaten raw with cream. Taste must be cultivated as the pulp is considered nauseating by some. Handling fruit is reported to cause a skin rash on some people. Seeds contain an alkaloid, *asiminine,* a French word (derived from the Native American *Arsimin*) for which the tree is named. The name *triloba* was derived from the petals, borne in sets of 3. Bark once used as a medicine, contains the alkaloid *analobine*. Birds and mammals often eat the fruit before it ripens enough for humans to eat.

102

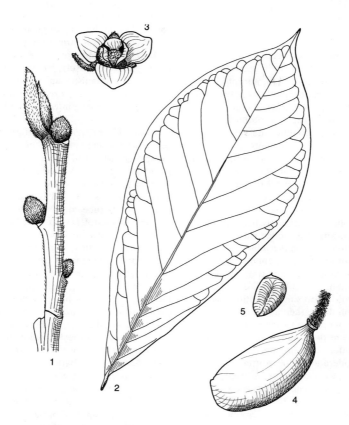

1. Winter twig, × 2½.
2. Leaf, × ½.
3. Flower, × ½.
4. Fruit, berry, × ½.
5. Seed, × ½.

Key Characters
- leaf blades large, obovate, thin
- terminal bud naked, flat, rusty brown, tomentose
- bark smooth, dark brown with white splotches
- fruit bananalike; seeds large, dark brown, flattened, embedded in sweet pulp
- small understory tree of bottomland sites

103

LAURACEAE
Sassafras albidum (Nuttall) Nees

Sassafras

Size and Form. Small to medium-sized tree, 6–15 m high and 20–60 cm in diameter. Trunk stout, often contorted, abruptly spreading branches form a flat-topped, rather open, columnar crown; ends of branches markedly upswept. Tap root prominent in youth; lateral roots shallow and very wide-spreading; in open-grown plants, root suckers arise spontaneously along the lateral root system forming a multistemmed clone. Michigan Big Tree: girth 4.2 m, diameter 133 cm, height 27 m, Berrien Co.

Bark. Thick, aromatic, dark reddish brown, deeply and irregularly fissured into broad, interlacing, flat-topped ridges.

Leaves. Alternate, simple, blades 8–15 cm long, 5–10 cm wide; oval to oblong or obovate, 3 distinct forms on the same tree: unlobed, 2-lobed "mitten," and 3-lobed (rarely 5), lobes fingerlike with broad sinuses; entire; thin, glabrous, dull dark green above, paler and glabrous or pubescent beneath, turning pink, red, or brilliant orange in autumn; aromatic; petioles slender, 2–3 cm long.

Twigs. Moderately stout, brittle, glabrous or pubescent, spicy-aromatic, lustrous, yellowish green, becoming reddish brown and shallowly fissured when 2–3 years old, upswept at ends. Unlike most trees, shoots of the current year may branch.

Winter Buds. Terminal bud 0.8–1.2 cm long, ovoid, acute, greenish, soft-pubescent, flower-bearing; lateral buds much smaller. Aromatic.

Wood. Soft, weak, brittle, coarse-grained, very durable in the soil, aromatic, dull orange brown, with thin, light yellow sapwood. Uses include furniture, lumber, fence posts, rails, wooden pails.

Flowers. May, with the young leaves; greenish yellow, on slender pedicels, in loose, drooping, few-flowered racemes 5 cm long; calyx of 6 sepals, yellowish green; corolla 0; stamens of male flower 9, in 3 rows, of female flower 6, in 1 row; ovary 1-celled; glistening nectaries present in both types of flowers. Trees dioecious. Insect-pollinated.

Fruit. Drupe, September-October; oblong-globose, lustrous dark blue, 1 cm long, surrounded at the base by the scarlet calyx, borne on a narrow, bright red pedicel.

Distribution. Common in the southern half of the Lower Peninsula, becoming rare northward to Manistee and Grand Traverse Co. A southern species reaching the northern limit of its range in the Lower Peninsula of Michigan.

Habitat. Characteristic of disturbed sites in dry-mesic and mesic forests; most abundant along fence rows and in old fields where it forms small clones. Associates include black, white, and red oaks, white ash, black cherry, black walnut, aspens, red and sugar maples, beech, hop-hornbeam.

Notes. Shade-tolerant as a seedling, becoming intolerant; fast-growing; short-lived. Disseminated by birds and mammals, existing in the shaded understory of dry-mesic oak forests until a disturbance provides an opening for it to quickly colonize the space. Disturbance by humans has provided the opportunity for it to colonize fence rows, old fields and pastures, drainage ditches, and roadsides. Sprouts vigorously from its wide-spreading lateral root system. Oil of sassafras is distilled from the bark of the roots and trunk. It is used to flavor medicines, candy, root beer, tobacco, and soap. Sassafras tea was used as a spring tonic to "thin the blood" but is suspected of being carcinogenic. Difficult to transplant as a sapling but easily propagated from seeds.

104

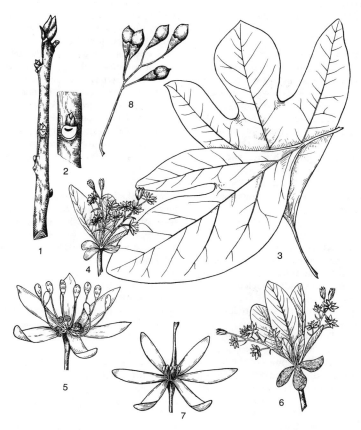

1. Winter twig, × 1.
2. Portion of twig, enlarged.
3. Leaves, × ½.
4. Male flowering shoot, × ½.
5. Male flower (ovary aborted), enlarged.
6. Female flowering shoot, × ½.
7. Female flower (stamens aborted), enlarged.
8. Fruit, drupes, × ½.

Key Characters	• leaf blades of 3 distinct forms present on the same tree: unlobed, 2-lobed, 3-lobed; margins entire; turning pink, red, or orange in autumn
	• spicy-aromatic twigs, buds, bark, leaves, and roots
	• fruit a shiny, dark blue drupe, borne on a bright red, narrow pedicel
	• clone-forming in the open

105

MAGNOLIACEAE
Liriodendron tulipifera Linnaeus

Tuliptree   Yellow-poplar

Size and Form. Large tree, 15–30 m high and 60–150 cm in diameter. Trunk columnar with a long, branch-free bole forming a compact, rather open, conical crown of slender branches. Roots deep, wide-spreading; juvenile tap root deep, penetrating. Michigan Big Tree: girth 7.2 m, diameter 230 cm, height 60 m, Cass Co.

Bark. Thin, scaly, greenish gray, with conspicuous vertical white lenticels on young stems; becoming thick, brownish, and deeply furrowed with rounded, interlacing ridges and grayish crevices.

Leaves. Alternate, simple, blades 8–15 cm long, wider than long; symmetrical, 4-lobed with a broad notch at the tip; lobes entire; lustrous dark green above, pale or glaucous beneath, turning clear yellow in autumn; glabrous; petioles long, slender, angled, 12–16 cm long.

Twigs. Stout, smooth, lustrous, reddish, becoming brownish and finally gray.

Winter Buds. Terminal bud 1.3–2 cm long, somewhat stalked, obtuse, flattened, with 2 valvate scales (actually stipules of the topmost leaf), dark red, covered with a glaucous bloom; lateral buds small, sessile.

Wood. Light, soft, brittle, weak, easily worked, light yellow or brown, with thin, cream white sapwood. Uses include interior and exterior trim, core stock for furniture and veneer, boxes, crates, pulpwood, excelsior.

Flowers. May-June, after the leaves; perfect; terminal; solitary on stout peduncles, tulip-shaped, very showy, greenish yellow, 5 cm or more across; sepals 3, greenish, early deciduous; petals 6, in 2 rows, greenish yellow with a bright orange spot at the base; stamens numerous, somewhat shorter than the petals; pistils numerous, clinging together around a central axis; each ovary 1-celled. Insect-pollinated.

Fruit. Aggregate of samaras; September-October; samaras borne in a narrow, light brown, conelike cluster, 5–8 cm long; samara long, flat, with a small, angled seed case at the base bearing 1–2 seeds; samaras separating from the slender, persistent stalk at maturity, some conelike clusters often persistent in the tree top in winter.

Distribution. Occasional in the lower three tiers of counties of the Lower Peninsula, north to Kent, Saginaw, and Sanilac Co. A southern species reaching the northern limit of its range in southern Michigan.

Habitat. Characteristic of bottomland and beech-maple forests with moist, fertile, sheltered conditions; also margins of swamps. Associates include sugar maple, beech, blue-beech, basswood, flowering dogwood, red oak.

Notes. Shade-intolerant; very fast-growing; moderately long-lived. Sprouts readily from root collar or stump when injured by fire, cutting, or browsing. Lacking serious insect and disease pests; sensitive to frost damage. An important ornamental tree for lawns and parks.

The magnolias, which belong to the same family as the tuliptree, are extensively planted in their cultivar and hybrid forms, especially the *Magnolia* ×*soulangiana* Soul., the saucer magnolia. Magnolias are valued for their large, showy, and mostly fragrant flowers, which appear in early spring, and for their large leaves.

The hardiest magnolia is the cucumber tree, *Magnolia acuminata* (L.) L., a native of Ohio and adjacent regions to the south and east. Its leaf blades are 10–24 cm long, about half as wide, entire, tip acute, base mostly rounded. The fruit is an aggregate of follicles, borne in a conelike cluster, 5–7 cm long; individual follicles are red, 1.2 cm long. The winter buds are densely covered with pale, silky hairs and are nearly surrounded by the leaf scars. Hardy in southern Michigan.

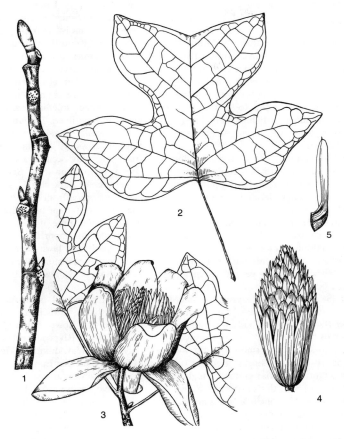

1. Winter twig, × 1.
2. Leaf, × ½.
3. Flowering shoot, × ½.

4. Fruit, aggregate of samaras, × ½.
5. Single samara, × ½.

Key Characters

- leaf blades symmetrical, 4-lobed with a broad notch at the tip; margins entire
- terminal bud flattened, with 2 large, valvate, dark red scales, appearing like a duck's bill
- fruit an aggregate of samaras borne in an erect, conelike cluster, some clusters persistent in the tree top; individual samaras long, with angled seed case at base
- bark of mature trees deeply furrowed with rounded ridges and grayish crevices

TILIACEAE
Tilia americana Linnaeus

Basswood   Linden

Size and Form. Large tree, 18–24 m high and 40–120 cm in diameter. Trunk straight, extending well into the upper crown; numerous slender branches forming a dense, ovoid or rounded crown. Sprouts arise at the base of living trees or stumps. Roots deep, widespreading; windfirm. Michigan Big Tree: girth 6.8 m, diameter 216 cm, height 35 m, Grand Traverse Co.

Bark. Thin, smooth, dark gray on young stems; on old trunks thick, deeply furrowed into many, long, narrow, flat-topped, scaly ridges; ridges nearly parallel, sometimes interlacing.

Leaves. Alternate, simple, blades 12–15 cm long, 7–10 cm wide; obliquely heart-shaped, with unequal lobes, base decidedly inequilateral; coarsely serrate; thin and firm; dull dark yellowish green above, paler beneath; glabrous; petioles slender, 2.5–5 cm long.

Twigs. Stout, somewhat zigzagged, smooth reddish gray, becoming dark gray or brown.

Winter Buds. Terminal bud absent; end and lateral buds inequilaterally ovoid (lopsided), obliquely sessile, acute, smooth, 6 mm long; bud scales usually 2, lustrous, green or red.

Wood. Light, soft, close-grained, tough, light reddish brown, with thick sapwood of nearly the same color. Uses include boxes and crates for food products, interior trim, veneer, plywood, furniture parts, excelsior, woodenware. Highly valued for hand carving.

Flowers. June-July, after the leaves; perfect, regular; yellowish white, downy, fragrant, borne on slender pedicels in loose, drooping cymes, the peduncle attached for half its length to a narrow, oblong, yellowish, leaflike bract; sepals 5, downy; petals 5, creamy white; stamens numerous, in 5 clusters; ovary 5-celled; stigma 5-lobed. Insect-pollinated.

Fruit. Nut; October; globose, woody, thick-shelled, gray, tomentose, 6 mm across, about the size of a pea, attached to a leafy bract, some usually remaining on the tree far into the winter.

Distribution. Common in deciduous forests of the Lower Peninsula; frequent in deciduous forests of the Upper Peninsula.

Habitat. Characteristic of mesic deciduous forests with moist, nutrient-rich, well drained to somewhat poorly drained soils; lake and stream borders, bottomlands. Associates include sugar maple, beech, yellow birch, red maple, American elm, white ash, black walnut, butternut, red and white oaks.

Notes. Shade-tolerant; moderately slow-growing; long-lived. Sprouts prolifically at the root collar following injury by fire, cutting, or browsing; circular clumps of several trunks typically occur around decaying stumps on cutover areas. Seeds very difficult to germinate. Bark fibrous; Native Americans made rope from bark of young stems. A source of nectar for bees; basswood honey is highly valued. Free of serious insect and disease pests. An important ornamental for street, park, and lawn planting, but European species are more frequently used. Also called lime or whitewood. Bois Blanc (literally white wood), the early French explorer's name for basswood, is the name of 2 well known islands in Michigan (one just east of the tip of the Lower Peninsula and the other in the Detroit River just east of Detroit).

The small-leaved linden, *Tilia cordata* Miller, is native in Europe and has long been planted as an ornamental. It is smaller than the native basswood (5–15 m high) and has a compact, densely branching, conical crown. The leaves are much smaller, 4–6 cm long, but are similar in shape; they are dark lustrous green above, often glaucous beneath. The fruit is a small nut and differs from our species in being thin shelled. It is hardy throughout the state and is excellent for lawn, garden, and street plantings as it can withstand urban air pollution.

Related species of lesser ornamental value include the large-leaved linden, *T. platyphyllos* Scopoli and the European linden, *T. ×europaea* L., a hybrid between *T. cordata* and *T. platyphyllos*. The large-leaved linden has big leaves, 6–12 cm long, light green and pubescent beneath; fruit is tomentose, hard-shelled, and pear-shaped. The European linden is intermediate in most characters between those of the parents.

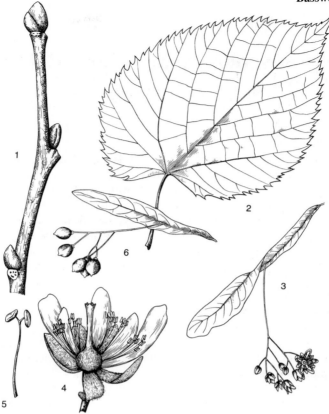

1. Winter twig, × 1.
2. Leaf, × ½.
3. Bract with cluster of flowers, × ½.
4. Flower, partly dissected to show parts, enlarged.
5. Stamen, enlarged.
6. Bract bearing cluster of fruit, × ½.

Key Characters

- leaf blades large, obliquely heart-shaped with one side lower than the other, singly toothed
- buds broad, obliquely sessile, lopsided, lustrous green or red
- fruit a globose, woody nut, borne on a long, leafy bract
- bark thick, with many long, narrow, nearly parallel ridges
- sprouts usually found at the base of living trees or stumps

The Cottonwoods, Aspens, and Balsam Poplar—*Populus*

The genus *Populus* belongs to the willow family, and the aspens, cottonwoods, and poplars resemble the willows, especially in flower and fruit characters. The pendulous catkins of flowers are borne upon different trees (dioecious condition), and, expanding before the leaves appear, are conspicuous objects in early spring. The flowers are wind-pollinated. As in the willows, the seeds are very light, and they are produced in great abundance. Each seed has attached to it a tuft of long, white hairs or "cotton" which aids in its dispersal. Seeds are disseminated early in the season by the wind. Because of this, several species are known as "cottonwoods."

Species of the genus are distributed widely, extending from the Arctic Circle to Mexico and from the Atlantic to the Pacific. Ten species occur in North America, of which 5 are native to Michigan. Two introduced plants are commonly cultivated, the European white or silver poplar and a cultivar of the European black cottonwood (termed black poplar in Europe), the Lombardy poplar.

The three major groups of *Populus* species, the aspens, balsam poplars, and cottonwoods, are markedly different in the habitats they occupy. The aspens are boreal and northern species, adapted to a cold climate and either moist or dry soils. They reproduce abundantly by seeds under the right site conditions. Aspens are also adapted to fire and sprout profusely from roots when their trunks are scorched and killed. The colonies or groups of stems so formed from a single individual are termed *clones*. The balsam poplars are also northern species, inhabiting wet streamsides and swamps. Like the aspens they are also natural clone formers, sprouting from roots when fire kills the parent stem. Cottonwoods are more southern, warm and humid climate species that grow along rivers and in floodplains. They are adapted to prolonged flooding. Besides prolific reproduction by seeds, they may also reproduce vegetatively when live branches, broken from their crowns, take root in the moist soil along the river or in the floodplain.

Summer Key to Species of *Populus*

1. Petioles essentially round; undersurface of leaves usually stained with rusty brown resin .... *P. balsamifera*, p. 122
1. Petioles strongly flattened; undersurface of leaves not stained with resin.
   2. Petioles and lower sides of leaves tomentose .... *P. alba*, p. 116
   2. Petioles and lower sides of leaves glabrous.
      3. Leaves distinctly deltoid in shape.
         4. Leaf blades longer than they are wide, apex more or less taper-pointed; marginal teeth rather conspicuously incurved; branches spreading, forming a broad crown .... *P. deltoides*, p. 112
         4. Leaf blades broader than they are long, apex abruptly acuminate; marginal teeth not conspicuously incurved; branches erect and more or less appressed to the main stem, forming a narrow, spirelike crown .. *P. nigra 'Italica'*, p. 114
      3. Leaves ovate to nearly orbicular in shape.
         5. Margin of leaves very coarsely sinuate-toothed; leaves 7–13 cm long .... *P. grandidentata*, p. 118
         5. Margin of leaves finely serrate; leaves less than 7 cm long .... *P. tremuloides*, p. 120

Winter Key to Species of *Populus*

1. Branches erect, more or less appressed to the main stem, forming a narrow, spirelike crown .... *P. nigra 'Italica'*, p. 114
1. Branches spreading, forming a broad crown.
   2. Terminal buds 0.4–1 cm long; not resinous.
      3. Buds and twigs conspicuously white-downy; twigs green .... *P. alba*, p. 116
      3. Buds and twigs not conspicuously white-downy; twigs usually reddish brown or gray.
         4. Terminal buds puberulent, dusty looking; lateral buds widely divergent; twigs coarse .... *P. grandidentata*, p. 118
         4. Terminal buds glabrous, lustrous; lateral buds more or less appressed; twigs slender .... *P. tremuloides*, p. 120
   2. Terminal buds 1.3–2 cm long, sticky-resinous.
      5. Terminal buds not aromatic; twigs usually yellowish green, more or less strongly angled .... *P. deltoides*, p. 112
      5. Terminal buds aromatic; twigs usually reddish brown and seldom strongly angled .... *P. balsamifera*, p. 122

SALICACEAE
Populus deltoides Marshall

Eastern Cottonwood

Size and Form. Large tree, 18–25 m high
and 100–150 cm in diameter. In stands, trees
develop slender, smooth trunks and relatively short, open, symmetrical crowns;
trunks of open-grown trees often divide into
two or more stems that form a wide, spreading, open, often irregular crown of massive
branches. Roots wide-spreading; generally
shallow-rooted, but deep where water table
permits. Not forming natural clones by root
suckering. Michigan Big Tree: girth 8.0 m,
diameter 255 cm, height 42 m, Wayne Co.

Bark. Thin and smooth on young stems,
yellowish gray, soon developing rough, furrowed bark at the base; becoming thick on
old trunks, ashy gray, deeply divided into
straight furrows with broad, flat-topped
ridges.

Leaves. Alternate, simple, blades 6–12 cm
long, nearly as wide, broadly triangular;
coarsely toothed above the entire base, teeth
conspicuously incurved, gland-tipped; thick
and firm; very lustrous, dark green above,
paler beneath; glabrous except for the finely
hairy margins of juvenile leaves; petioles
slender, compressed laterally, 5–8 cm long.

Twigs. Stout, smooth, yellowish green, angled in cross section, vigorous shoots with
corky linear ridges.

Winter buds. Terminal bud 1.3–2 cm long,
slender, angled, long-pointed, very resinous,
shining, yellowish brown.

Wood. Light, soft, weak, close-grained,
dark brown, with thick, whitish sapwood;
warps badly, difficult to season. Uses include
pulpwood, excelsior, boxes, crates, plywood,
furniture core stock, woodenware.

Flowers. April-May, before the leaves in
hairy-bracted catkins; male catkins short-
stalked, densely flowered, 8–10 cm long;
calyx 0; corolla 0; stamens 40–60 with red
anthers; female catkins short-stalked, few-
flowered, elongating to 15–20 cm; stigmas 3–
4, spreading. Wind-pollinated.

Fruit. Capsule; late May-June; 2–4 valved,
short-stalked, borne in drooping catkins, 15–
20 cm long; seeds whitish to light brown, a
tuft of white hairs ("cotton") attached.

Distribution. Common in the southern half
of the Lower Peninsula; rare in the northern
half of the Lower Peninsula; very rare in the
Upper Peninsula, known from Menominee
Co.

Habitat. Characteristic of warm, humid,
river floodplains; associated with black willow, sandbar willow, silver maple, red ash,
American elm, northern hackberry, boxelder. A pioneer species colonizing open
areas, including wet fields and ditches far
from streams. Not hardy in cold climates;
present in northern Michigan locally where
the climate is moderated by Lake Michigan
or Lake Huron. Tolerates flooding, silting,
and high water tables.

Notes. Very shade-intolerant; fast-growing;
short-lived. Propagated vegetatively by
woody stem-cuttings. Not favored as a city or
lawn tree because of great amounts of "cotton" shed in spring with seeds by female
trees and roots which clog drains. Subject to
many insect pests.

The tree known as swamp cottonwood,
Populus heterophylla L., is actually not a
true cottonwood at all; it belongs to a distinctive group of poplars in which the leaf
petioles are not laterally flattened but are cylindrical. The leaf blades are much larger
than those of cottonwood, averaging about
15 cm long and 10 cm wide; the blade outline is ovate (not deltoid) either rounded or
cordate at the base, and the leaf tip is
rounded or merely acute (not acuminate).
Both the leaves and the twigs are tomentose
when young. One of Michigan's rarest trees,
the swamp cottonwood is known only from
two small colonies in swampy habitats in the
southern part of the state. A full discussion
of this species in Michigan, including leaf
forms, in comparison with true cottonwood is
given by Wagner et al. (1980).

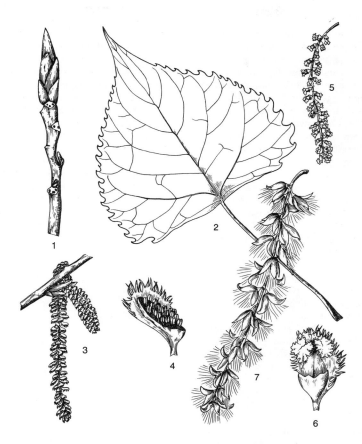

1. Winter twig, × 1.
2. Leaf, × ½.
3. Male flowering catkin, × ½.
4. Male flower, enlarged.

5. Female catkin, × ½.
6. Female flower, enlarged.
7. Fruiting catkin with open capsules, × ½.

Key Characters

- leaves with deltoid shape; upper surface bright, shiny, yellowish green; coarsely toothed, teeth gland-tipped
- buds long-pointed, angled, resinous
- vigorous shoots with corky linear ridges
- grows along banks of streams, river floodplains; colonizes wet, disturbed sites

SALICACEAE
Populus nigra Linnaeus 'Italica'

Lombardy Poplar

Size and Form. Medium-sized tree, 12–20 m high and 30–80 cm in diameter. Trunk straight, slender, with ascending branches forming a narrow, columnar (fastigiate) crown to a tapered apex; trunk covered with branch sprouts (epicormic sprouts). Michigan Big Tree: girth 4.7 m, diameter 150 cm, height 22 m, Chippewa Co.

Bark. Thin and smooth on young stems; thick and grayish brown on lower portion of old trunks, deeply and irregularly furrowed; large trunks buttressed.

Leaves. Alternate; simple; blades 5–7 cm long, usually somewhat wider than long; broad-deltoid, apex abruptly acuminate; many, small curved teeth; thick and firm; dark green and shiny above, lighter and rather lustrous beneath; glabrous; petioles slender, laterally compressed, 2–5 cm long.

Twigs. Slender, glabrous, lustrous, yellowish brown, becoming gray.

Winter Buds. Terminal bud conical, slightly angled, very slender.

Wood. Light, soft, easily worked, not liable to splinter, weak, not durable, light reddish brown, with thick, nearly white, sapwood.

Flowers. April-May, before the leaves in hairy-bracted catkins; male clone, catkins about 8 cm long, stamens 8–10, with white filaments and purple anthers.

Fruit. None; no female flowers.

Distribution. Origin unknown, earliest trees possibly from northern Italy. Commonly planted throughout the state.

Habitat. As a cultivar of *Populus nigra* (European cottonwood or European black poplar) it is adapted to a warm, humid climate and alluvial soils. Planted trees in Michigan grow on a variety of upland soils from clay to loamy sand. Not hardy except in sheltered sites or areas where climatic extremes are moderated.

Notes. Shade-intolerant; fast-growing; usually short-lived. Usually dies within 15 years of planting; longer-lived individuals found in such places as the western Michigan shoreline of Lake Michigan (on Leelanau Peninsula, for example). Easily propagated from woody stem-cuttings.

Apparently spontaneously derived from the European black poplar and repeatedly propagated by stem cuttings for over 300 years. Planted in the early 1600s along the Po River in the Lombardy region of northern Italy, hence the common and cultivar names. Several fastigiate-crowned clones of *P. nigra* exist, the most important for ornamental purposes being the male clone 'Italica'. Several female clones also exist in Europe, but are not reported from Michigan. Widely planted throughout the United States as an ornamental because of its striking form. Often reaches much larger sizes (1.5 m in diameter and over 30 m high) than found in Michigan. For details of origin and cultivation see Li (1963). Sometimes confused with the fastigiate form of the European white poplar.

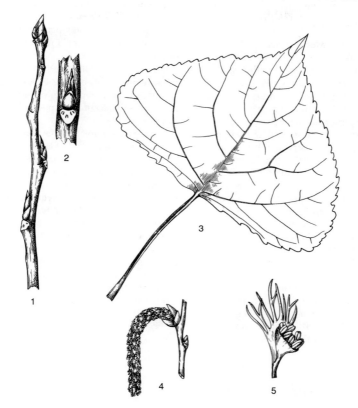

1. Winter twig, × 1.
2. Portion of twig, enlarged.
3. Leaf, × ¾.
4. Male flowering catkin, × ½.
5. Male flower, enlarged.

Key Characters
- spirelike, narrow-columnar or fastigiate form, with ascending branches
- leaves deltoid in shape, wider than long
- male flowers only

115

SALICACEAE
Populus alba Linnaeus

European White Poplar

Size and Form. Medium-sized to large tree, 16–24 m high and 60–120 cm in diameter. Trunk crooked, often forked; forming a large, spreading, rounded or irregular crown of large, crooked branches and sparse, stout branchlets; trunk often leaning. Wide-spreading lateral roots giving rise to deep sinker roots; lateral roots near the surface may send up root suckers that form a clone. Michigan Big Tree: girth 5.8 m, diameter 184 cm, height 26 m, Charlevoix Co.

Bark. Thin on young trees with open crowns, creamy white or gray, smooth or with small diamond-shaped pits; thick on old trunks, dark grayish green, fissured at the base and becoming black and deeply pitted up to 3–5 m above the base.

Leaves. Alternate, simple, blades 5–10 cm long and almost as broad; broadly ovate to suborbicular; irregularly sinuate-toothed; glabrous, dark green above, white-tomentose becoming glabrous beneath; leaves at the ends of long shoots in the upper crown palmately 3–5 lobed, with triangular, coarsely toothed lobes, white-tomentose beneath; petioles long, slender, flattened, tomentose.

Twigs. Stout, green, covered with white down, becoming greenish gray or pale brown the second year and marked with darker blotches.

Winter Buds. Terminal bud 4–6 mm long, ovoid, pointed, not viscid, downy-white.

Wood. Light, soft, weak, difficult to split, reddish yellow, with thick, whitish sapwood.

Flowers. April-May, before the leaves in hairy-bracted catkins; male catkins thick, cylindrical, 4–8 cm long; calyx 0; corolla 0; stamens 6–16 with purple anthers; female catkins slender, 2–5 cm long; stigmas 2, branched, yellow. Only female trees (perhaps one clone) known in Michigan and the western Great Lakes region. Wind-pollinated.

Fruit. Capsule; May-June; ovoid, 2-valved, 3–6 mm long, borne in drooping catkins, 4–8 cm long; seeds whitish or light brown, pubescent, a tuft of white hairs attached.

Distribution. Native in Europe and western Asia along rivers and in bottomlands; introduced into North America as a female clone or clones and commonly planted by settlers for shade and ornament. Frequent throughout the state.

Habitat. Adapted for best growth to warm, moist, alluvial soils of river banks and bottomlands. Grows rapidly in open areas on almost any soil except cold, poorly drained swamps. Hardy.

Notes. Shade-intolerant; fast-growing; individual stems short-lived. Also known as European silver poplar. Surface lateral roots produce numerous suckers for a considerable distance from the tree. Hybridizing locally with bigtooth aspen, less frequently with trembling aspen. Although termed a poplar, it is more closely related to the native aspens than to eastern cottonwood. Occasionally planted is *P. alba* 'Pyramidalis' or 'Bolleana' Bolle's poplar. It has a narrow, spirelike crown of erect branches, thus resembling the Lombardy poplar in form. Bolle's poplar is attractive for its fastigiate form, but it is not very hardy.

116

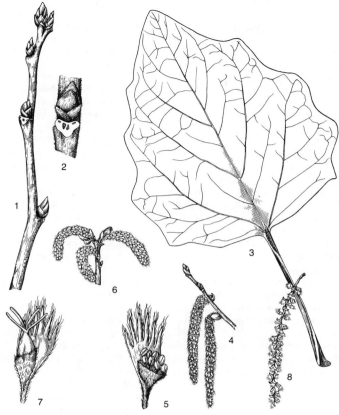

1. Winter twig, × 1.
2. Portion of twig, enlarged.
3. Leaf, × 1.
4. Male flowering catkins, × ½.
5. Male flower, enlarged.
6. Female flowering catkins, × ½.
7. Female flower, enlarged.
8. Fruiting catkin with open capsules, × ½.

Key Characters

- leaves dark green above, white-tomentose beneath, becoming glabrous; leaves at ends of long shoots in upper crown white-tomentose on undersurface, palmately 3–5 lobed
- petioles, new shoots, and buds downy-white with pubescence
- trunk crooked, with diamond-shaped pits in bark

117

SALICACEAE
Populus grandidentata Michaux

Bigtooth Aspen

Size and Form. Medium-sized tree, 15–20 m high and 30–60 cm in diameter. Trunk slender, supporting a loose, open, ovoid or rounded crown of a few, coarse, spreading branches. Trunk little-tapered, branchless and smooth for much of its length. Forms multistemmed clones. Very wide-spreading lateral root system; roots larger and fewer than in trembling aspen; sinker roots to 3 m. Michigan Big Tree: girth 3.4 m, diameter 107 cm, height 22 m, Manistee Co.

Bark. Thin, smooth, yellowish gray to tan, sometimes with greenish or orange cast; becoming dark gray, irregularly fissured, with broad, flat-topped ridges at the base of old trunks or trees in deep shade.

Leaves. Alternate, simple, blades 7–13 cm long, 5–9 cm wide; ovate-orbicular; coarsely and irregularly sinuate-toothed, about 10 (6–15) teeth per side; thin and firm; densely white-tomentose beneath when young, becoming dark green above, paler beneath, glabrous both sides; petioles long, slender, laterally compressed.

Twigs. Moderately stout, greenish gray and at first white-tomentose, becoming lustrous, orange or reddish brown, and finally greenish gray.

Winter Buds. Terminal bud 0.8–1 cm long, ovoid to conical, acute, midportion of light chestnut scales covered with light gray pubescence, not gummy or fragrant, dusty looking; lateral buds widely divergent.

Flowers. April, before the leaves in hairy-bracted catkins, 7–10 days following trembling aspen; male catkins 3–8 cm long, pubescent; calyx 0; corolla 0; stamens 6–12 with red anthers; female catkins loose-flowered, pubescent, 3–8 cm long, gradually elongating; stigmas 2, 2-lobed, scarlet. Wind-pollinated.

Fruit. Capsule; May-June; 2-valved, conical, acute, hairy, 6 mm long, borne in drooping catkins, 8–15 cm long; seeds minute, smaller than in trembling aspen, brown, a tuft of white hairs attached.

Wood. Light, soft, weak, close-grained, light brown, with thin, whitish sapwood, durable if kept dry. Uses include plywood, boxes, crates, matches, excelsior, veneer, furniture stock, interior trim, but pulpwood is of major economic importance.

Distribution. Throughout the state; abundant in the northern half of the Lower Peninsula where it reaches the maximum abundance of its limited North American range; frequent in the southern half of the Lower Peninsula; occasional in the Upper Peninsula.

Habitat. Mesic to dry-mesic forests; associated primarily with pines and oaks, often with many other upland hardwoods. Grows well on dry, sandy soils; does not tolerate wet, poorly drained sites.

Notes. Shade-intolerant; fast-growing; individual stems short-lived. Seedlings established with difficulty, but once established root suckers arise readily following death of parent stem by fire, cutting, or browsing. Suckers may grow 2 m or more the first year. Clones may be perpetuated indefinitely by fire; largest known clone in Michigan occupies 0.4 ha. Logging and subsequent fires have vastly increased its abundance in former pine areas. Formerly a weed species, now a major pulpwood species.

Highly variable in morphological and phenological traits. Hybridizes readily with trembling aspen in southeastern Michigan (Barnes 1961; Wagner 1970); hybrids rare in northern lower Michigan and the Upper Peninsula. Unlike willows and cottonwoods, it does not propagate from woody stem-cuttings. Attacked by many insects; resistant to hypoxylon canker. Major source of food for beaver and white-tailed deer. For details on clonal habit and variation see Barnes (1966, 1969), for general ecology and insect and mammal relations see Graham et al. (1963).

118

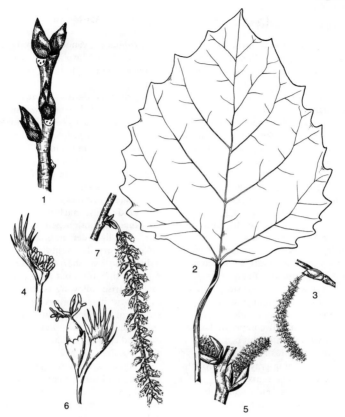

1. Winter twig, × 2.
2. Leaf, × 1.
3. Male flowering catkin, × ½.
4. Male flower, enlarged.
5. Female flowering catkin, × ½.
6. Female flower, enlarged.
7. Fruiting catkin with open capsules, × ½.

Key Characters
- leaves with large teeth, about 10 per side
- bud scales tomentose, bud dusty looking
- bark smooth, tan with greenish or orange cast
- grows in clones of many genetically identical stems, with similar leaf morphology, stem and crown form, flushing time, and fall coloration

119

SALICACEAE
Populus tremuloides Michaux

Trembling Aspen   Quaking Aspen

Size and Form. Medium to large tree, 12–22 m high and 25–60 cm in diameter. Trunk straight or crooked, supporting an open, rounded crown of slender branches; slender trunk with little taper, branchless and smooth for much of its length. Typically grows in multistemmed clones formed by the development of many suckers from the roots of trees killed by fire, cutting, or browsing. Roots extensive, very wide-spreading, shallow. Michigan Big Tree: girth 2.7 m, diameter 87 cm, height 33 m, Ontonagon Co.

Bark. Thin, creamy white to yellowish green, smooth; becoming fissured and gray with long, flat-topped ridges at the base of old trees or trees in deep shade.

Leaves. Alternate, simple, blades 4–6 cm long and nearly as wide; ovate to orbicular; base cuneate to subcordate; finely serrate, about 30 (25–40) serrations per side; thin and firm; lustrous, dark green above, dull and pale beneath; glabrous; petioles slender, typically longer than blade, laterally compressed so that leaves tremble with slightest breeze.

Twigs. Slender, very lustrous, glabrous, reddish brown, becoming grayish and roughened by the elevated leaf scars.

Winter Buds. Terminal bud 6–8 mm long, slender, angled, acute, reddish brown, lustrous, resinous but not gummy or fragrant; basal scales sometimes with minute pubescence, otherwise glabrous; lateral buds often appressed, tips turning inward.

Wood. Light, soft, weak, close-grained, not durable, light brown, with thin, whitish sapwood. Uses include pulpwood, boxes, crates, matches, excelsior, furniture stock, interior trim. As for bigtooth aspen pulpwood has great economic importance.

Flowers. March-April, before the leaves in hairy-bracted catkins; male catkins 4–8 cm long, pubescent; calyx 0; corolla 0, stamens 6–12 with red anthers; female catkins 4–8 cm long, becoming gradually longer, pubescent; stigmas 2, 2-lobed, scarlet. Wind-pollinated.

Fruit. Capsule; May-June; 2-valved, oblong-cylindrical, short-pedicelled, 6 mm long; seeds light brown, a tuft of white hairs attached.

Distribution. Abundant throughout the state. A Boreal Forest tree, approaching the southern limit of its range in southern Michigan.

Habitat. In old-growth forests, relegated mostly to open, lowland sites such as streams and swamp margins because of competition with other species; from there it colonizes openings in upland stands following wildfires. Associates include balsam poplar, red maple, bigtooth aspen, white birch, pines, oaks, and many other species. Thrives on wet-mesic, fertile sites; survives but grows slowly on dry, sandy soils; much less vigorous on dry sites than bigtooth aspen. Nutrient-, moisture-, and light-demanding.

Notes. Very shade-intolerant; fast-growing; individual stems short-lived. Seedlings establish with difficulty, but once established root suckers arise following death of parent stem by fire, cutting, or browsing. Suckers may grow 2 m or more the first year. Clones may be perpetuated indefinitely by fire; largest reported clone in Michigan is 0.2 ha; some clones in the central Rocky Mountains exceed 40 ha (Kemperman and Barnes 1976). Logging and subsequent fires have greatly increased its abundance in pine and hardwood areas. Formerly a weed species, now a major pulpwood species.

Highly variable in morphological and phenological traits. Hybridizes readily with bigtooth aspen in southeastern Michigan (Barnes 1961; Wagner 1970); hybrids rare in northern lower Michigan and the Upper Peninsula. Unlike willows and cottonwoods, it does not propagate from woody stem-cuttings. Hypoxylon canker (*Hypoxylon mammatum*) the major disease; attacked by many insects, especially the forest tent caterpillar (*Malacosoma disstria*). Major source of food for beaver and white-tailed deer. For details on clonal habit and variation see Barnes (1966, 1969), for general ecology and insect and mammal relations see Graham et al. (1963).

120

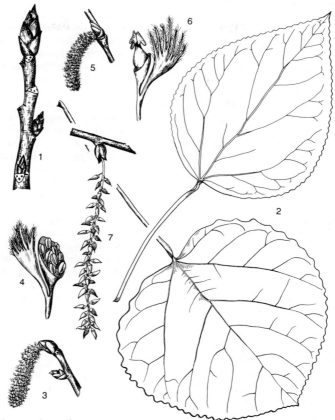

1. Winter twig, × 2.
2. Leaves, × 1.
3. Male flowering catkin, × ½.
4. Male flower, enlarged.
5. Female flowering catkin, × ½.
6. Female flower, enlarged.
7. Fruiting catkin with capsules, × ½.

Key Characters

- leaves with flattened petioles, tremble in slightest breeze; many fine teeth, about 30 per side
- bark smooth, creamy white to yellowish green
- grows in clones of many genetically identical stems, with similar leaf morphology, stem and crown form, flushing time, and fall coloration

Distinguished from eastern cottonwood by smaller leaf and many more fine serrations, buds lustrous but not gummy, twigs without linear ridges.

121

SALICACEAE
Populus balsamifera Linnaeus

Balsam Poplar

Size and Form. Medium-sized to large tree, 16–24 m high and 30–60 cm in diameter. Trunk slender, crown rather narrow, open, with a few stout ascending branches. Forms multistemmed clones. Wide-spreading root system, shallow-rooted. Michigan Big Tree: girth 3.9 m, diameter 125 cm, height 39 m, Marquette Co.

Bark. Thin, relatively smooth on young trees, often with many small branches and branch scars; thick, grayish on old trunks and deeply fissured into broad, flat-topped ridges separated by irregular V-shaped crevices.

Leaves. Alternate, simple, blades 8–13 cm long, about half as wide; ovate to ovate-lanceolate, apex long-tapering; many small, low-rounded teeth; thin and firm; lustrous, dark green above, whitish green or silvery beneath and often stained rusty brown with resin; glabrous; young leaves oily with balsam, aromatic and fragrant; petioles slender, round, smooth, 3–4 cm long.

Twigs. Stout, smooth, reddish brown, becoming dark orange, finally greenish gray.

Winter Buds. Terminal bud 1.5–2 cm long, ovoid, long-pointed, reddish brown, very resinous, sticky, aromatic and fragrant.

Wood. Light, soft, weak, close-grained, light reddish brown, with thick, nearly white sapwood. Uses include excelsior, furniture stock, boxes, pulpwood.

Flowers. April-May, before the leaves in hairy-bracted catkins; male catkins long-stalked, 8–10 cm long; calyx 0; corolla 0; stamens 20–30 with red anthers; female catkins long-stalked, loose-flowered, 10–13 cm long; ovary short-stalked; stigmas 2, wavy-margined. Wind-pollinated.

Fruit. Capsule; May-June; 2-valved, ovoid, short-pedicelled, 6–8 mm long, borne in drooping catkins, 10–15 cm long; seeds light brown, a tuft of white hairs attached.

Distribution. Common in the Upper Peninsula and northern half of the Lower Peninsula, rare in the southern half of the Lower Peninsula. A Boreal Forest species that approaches its southern limit in southern Michigan.

Habitat. Wet, cool, lowland sites such as swamps, stream banks and floodplains, borders of lakes, and other wet depressions; associated with swamp conifers, black ash, red maple, trembling aspen, white birch, speckled alder. Found on dry sands such as dunes where water table is near the surface.

Notes. Shade-intolerant; fast-growing; individual stems short-lived. Forming natural clones by the development of many suckers from the roots of trees killed by fire, cutting, or browsing. Not colonizing dry, sandy pine sites like the aspens. Easily propagated from woody stem-cuttings. Sometimes called balm-of-Gilead (also called Taccamahac and Bam) referring to the alleged healing properties of the fragrant balsam or resin on buds and young leaves. The plant known as balm-of-Gilead (*P. candicans* Aiton) is probably a single female clone, derived from cuttings from a form of balsam poplar with heart-shaped leaves, *P. balsamifera* var. *subcordata* Hylander (Hosie 1969).

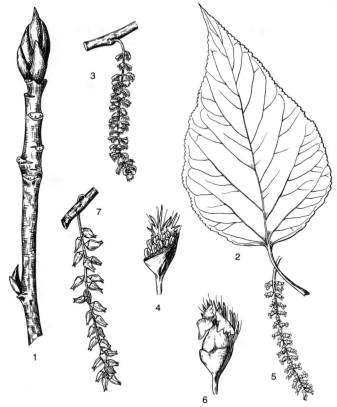

1. Winter twig, × 1.
2. Leaf, × ¾.
3. Male flowering catkin, × ½.
4. Male flower, enlarged.
5. Catkin of female flowers, × ½.
6. Female flower, enlarged.
7. Fruiting catkin with capsules, × ½.

Key Characters

- large leaf blade with a long-tapering tip; dark green above, whitish green or silvery beneath, usually stained rusty brown with resin; many low-rounded teeth; fragrant
- terminal buds long-pointed, very resinous, fragrant
- forming many-stemmed clones in wet, cool, lowland sites

123

The Willows—*Salix*

The genus *Salix* is represented in Michigan by 25 or more species, and there may be many hybrids. The majority of willows are shrubs, only a few becoming truly arborescent. All willows are characterized by one exposed bud scale, the dioecious flowering condition, and a shallow root system. The flowers are drastically reduced, the male flower merely composed of 2–10 stamens, the female with one compound ovary. Each flower has a tiny yellow nectary at its base and is subtended by a small hairy scale or bract. The flowers are insect- and wind-pollinated. Because of the similarity of their botanical characters, the variation they exhibit in response to their environment, and the apparent frequency with which they hybridize, willows are considered a difficult group. The scope of this book being necessarily limited, we describe only two of our native willows and two species introduced from Europe and Asia.

Summer Key to Species of *Salix*

1. Petioles without glands.
   2. Leaves 0.6–2 cm wide, leaves green, not glaucous beneath, petioles short (0.3–0.6 cm); stipules persistent .... *S. nigra*, p. 132
   2. Leaves 2–5 cm wide, leaves glaucous beneath, petioles long (0.7–3 cm); stipules early deciduous .... *S. amygdaloides*, p. 126
1. Petioles glandular above.
   3. Leaf blades 0.6–1.3 cm wide, sharp-serrate; tree with weeping habit, twigs markedly pendent; buds small, 2–5 mm long .... *S. babylonica*, p. 128
   3. Leaf blades 1.5–3.5 cm wide, blunt-serrate; tree with upright habit, twigs not markedly pendent; buds medium-sized, 3–7+ mm long .... *S. fragilis*, p. 130

SALICACEAE
Salix amygdaloides Andersson

Peachleaf Willow

Size and Form. Small tree, 8–12 m high and 30–40 cm in diameter. Trunk straight or leaning; ascending branches form a rather narrow, rounded crown. Often a shrub. Michigan Big Tree: girth 1.5 m, diameter 49 cm, height 34 m, Macomb Co.

Bark. Thin; becoming thick and brown on old trunks, irregularly fissured into flat, connected ridges.

Leaves. Alternate, simple, 5–15 cm long, 2–5 cm wide; lanceolate to ovate-lanceolate, long-pointed; finely serrate; thin and firm; light green and shining above, pale and glaucous beneath; glabrous; petioles long, slender, twisted, round, 0.7–3 cm long, glandless; stipules semicordate, early deciduous.

Twigs. Slender, glabrous, lustrous, yellow, orange, or reddish brown, becoming darker orange brown.

Winter Buds. Terminal bud absent; lateral buds broadly ovoid, swollen on one side, lustrous, dark brown, 3 mm long.

Wood. Light, soft, weak, close-grained, light brown, with thick, whitish sapwood.

Flowers. April, with the leaves; borne in crowded, slender, pubescent catkins, 5–8 mm long; calyx 0; corolla 0; bracts villous both sides; stamens 5–9; ovary oblong-conical, with stigmas nearly sessile. Insect- and wind-pollinated.

Fruit. Capsule; May; 1-celled, globose, 6 mm long, containing many minute seeds with long, silky, white hairs.

Distribution. Frequent in the southern half of the Lower Peninsula; infrequent in the northern half of the Lower Peninsula; rare in the Upper Peninsula (known only from Menominee Co.); sometimes planted.

Habitat. Banks of streams and wet, open sites free of competition.

Notes. Shade-intolerant; fast-growing; short-lived.

126

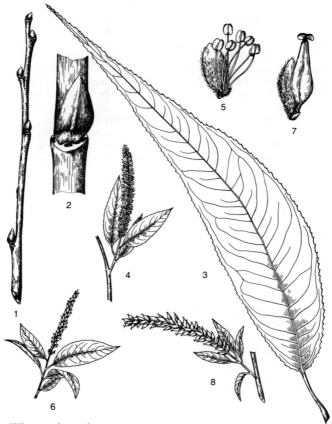

1. Winter twig, × 1.
2. Portion of twig, enlarged.
3. Leaf, × 1.
4. Male flowering shoot with catkin, × ½.
5. Male flower, enlarged.
6. Female flowering shoot with catkin, × ½.
7. Female flower, enlarged.
8. Fruiting shoot with catkin, × ½.

Key Characters

• leaves long, yet relatively wide; light green, lustrous above, pale and glaucous beneath
• petioles glandless, relatively long, slender, round
Distinguished from black willow by wider leaves, longer, rounder petioles, and smaller, early deciduous stipules.

127

SALICACEAE
Salix babylonica Linnaeus

Weeping Willow

Size and Form. Medium-sized to large tree, 15–25 m high and 80–120 cm in diameter. Trunk short and stout; long, slender branchlets, often a meter or more long, droop gracefully, giving the tree a weeping habit. Michigan Big Tree: girth 6.9 m, diameter 219 cm, height 36 m, Wayne Co.

Bark. Thick and gray on old trunks, rather smooth or irregularly fissured into shallow, firm interlacing ridges; light orange inner bark layer often visible.

Leaves. Alternate, simple, blades 8–18 cm long, 0.6–1.3 cm wide; linear to linear-lanceolate, long-pointed; finely sharp-serrate; thin and firm; dark green above, paler beneath; glabrous; petioles 1 cm or less long, glandular above, often hairy; stipules lanceolate, usually absent.

Twigs. Slender, glabrous, olive green, long pendulous.

Winter Buds. Terminal bud absent; lateral buds narrow-conical, sharp-pointed, somewhat flattened, brownish, 2–5 mm long.

Wood. Light, soft, weak, close-grained, light brown, with thick, whitish sapwood.

Flowers. April-May, with the leaves; borne in slender, nearly glabrous catkins, 2–5 cm long; calyx 0; corolla 0; bracts ovate-lanceolate, slightly hairy; ovary ovoid-conical, very short-stalked, with stigmas longer than the style. Female trees apparently rare. Insect- and wind-pollinated.

Fruit. Capsule; May-June; 1-celled, narrow-ovoid, sessile, about 5 mm long, containing many minute seeds with long, silky, white hairs.

Distribution. Native in the mountains of western China on the upper reaches of the Yangtze River (Li 1963). Clone(s) introduced into California from Japan; other clone(s) introduced into eastern North America from Europe. Widely cultivated in North America; male clone(s) common throughout Michigan.

Habitat. Requires much light and moisture; thrives in any open, moist or wet habitat, such as along streams, near lakes and ponds. Not hardy in very cold, dry climates.

Notes. Very shade-intolerant; fast-growing; short-lived. Much planted for ornament and shade in cemeteries, parks, lawns, and in moist places, such as near streams, lakes, and ponds. Undesirable to many as a lawn tree because it sheds branchlets profusely; suffers ice damage. Easily propagated from woody shoot-cuttings. Hybridizes with both crack willow and white willow, *Salix alba* L. The name "willow of Babylon" was mistakenly given; the "willow" in Psalms, growing by the river of Babylon, is a poplar, *Populus euphratica,* not a willow. See Li (1963) for details of origin and cultivation.

128

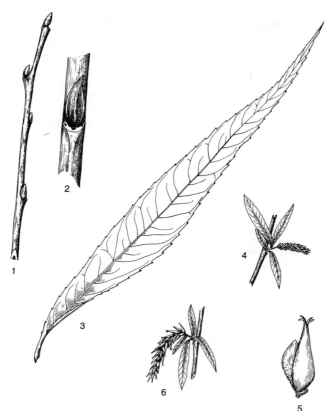

1. Winter twig, × 1.
2. Portion of twig, enlarged.
3. Leaf, × 1.
4. Female flowering shoot with catkin, × ½.
5. Female flower, enlarged.
6. Fruiting shoot with catkin, × ½.

Key Characters
- drooping branches and shoots give a distinctive weeping form
- leaf petioles short, glandular on upper surface

129

SALICACEAE
Salix fragilis Linnaeus

Crack Willow   Brittle Willow

Size and Form. Medium-sized to large tree, 15–25 m high and 100–200 cm in diameter. Large spreading branches form a broadly conical, open crown; branches long, up-swept. Michigan Big Tree: girth 7.7 m, diameter 247 cm, height 37 m, Macomb Co.

Bark. Thick, dull, dark gray; smooth on young trees, very rough and irregularly scaly ridged on old trees.

Leaves. Alternate, simple, blades 8–16 cm long, 1.5–3.5 cm wide; lanceolate to a long-pointed, often twisted point, base acute; finely glandular-serrate; thin and firm; rich glossy green above, grayish green or glaucous beneath; usually slightly silky at first, soon glabrous both sides; petioles short, stout, usually with 2 glands at the junction of blade and petiole, 1–2 cm long; stipules small, early deciduous.

Twigs. Slender, yellow, becoming greenish brown, glabrous, lustrous, spreading very straight from larger shoots and snapping off very readily and cleanly at the base; shoots pale orange in March before leaves appear.

Winter Buds. Terminal bud absent; lateral buds long-conical, pointed, closely appressed, glabrous, bright reddish brown, 3–7+ mm long.

Wood. Light, soft, tough, close-grained, reddish brown, with thick, whitish sapwood. Uses same as for black willow.

Flowers. April-May, with the leaves; borne in slender, pubescent catkins, 2–5 cm long; calyx 0; corolla 0; bracts blunt, somewhat pubescent; stamens 2; ovary narrowly conical, stigmas nearly sessile. Insect- and wind-pollinated.

Fruit. Capsule; May-June; 1-celled, long-conical, short-stalked, about 6 mm long, containing many minute seeds with long, silky, white hairs.

Distribution. Native in Europe and western Asia, introduced in North America and has become naturalized in many places. In Michigan found primarily in the southeastern part; also known from Gladwin and Grand Traverse Co. in the northern Lower Peninsula and in Mackinac, Menominee, and Marquette Co. in the Upper Peninsula.

Habitat. Grows rapidly in open, wet or moist sites.

Notes. Very shade-intolerant; fast-growing; short-lived. Hardy throughout the state. Easily grown from stem cuttings. The shoots may be used in the manufacture of baskets and furniture. The shoots are very brittle at the base and are easily broken by the wind, hence the names crack and brittle willow.

1. Winter twig, × 1.
2. Portion of twig, enlarged.
3. Leaf, × 1.
4. Male flowering shoot with catkin, × ½.
5. Male flower, enlarged.
6. Female flowering shoot with catkin, × ½.
7. Female flower, enlarged.
8. Fruiting shoot with catkin, × ½.

Key Characters

• leaves usually with 2 glands at the junction of blade and petiole
• leaves rich, glossy green above, grayish green or glaucous beneath
• shoots very brittle at the base, snapping off very readily and cleanly

Distinguished from black willow by 2 rather than 3–6 stamens on male trees, glands on the petiole, longer buds, more glaucous color of the undersurface of leaves, and early deciduous stipules.

131

SALICACEAE
Salix nigra Marshall

Black Willow

Size and Form. A medium-sized tree, 12–15 m high and 50–100 cm in diameter. Stout spreading branches form a broadly rounded, irregular, open crown. Trunks single, or often forking near the base into two or more stems; trunks crooked and leaning. Michigan Big Tree: girth 8.6 m, diameter 272 cm, height 27 m, Grand Traverse Co.

Bark. Thick, dark brown or nearly black on old trunks, deeply divided into long, broad, flat-topped, connecting ridges, often becoming shaggy or stringy.

Leaves. Alternate, simple, blades 8–15 cm long, 0.6–2 cm wide; linear-lanceolate, very long-pointed, often curved at the tip; finely serrate; thin; green both sides, rather lustrous above, paler and often hairy on veins beneath; petioles short, 3–6 mm long, more or less pubescent; stipules semicordate, persistent, especially on sprouts.

Twigs. Slender, glabrous or pubescent, bright reddish brown, becoming darker with age; young branches flexible but brittle at base.

Winter Buds. Terminal bud absent; lateral buds narrow-conical, acute, lustrous, reddish brown, small to medium-sized, 2–5 mm long.

Wood. Light, soft, weak, close-grained, light reddish brown with thin, whitish sapwood. Uses include boxes and crates, artificial limbs, polo balls, pulpwood, veneer, and furniture.

Flowers. April-May, with the leaves; borne in crowded, slender hairy catkins, 3–8 cm long; calyx 0; corolla 0; bracts villous; stamens 3–6; ovary ovoid-conical, short-stalked, with stigmas nearly sessile. Insect- and wind-pollinated.

Fruit. Capsule; June; 1-celled, ovoid-conical, 3–4 mm long, containing many minute seeds with long, silky, white hairs; seeds disseminated in June and germinate shortly thereafter.

Distribution. Common in the southern half of the Lower Peninsula; rare or absent in the northern half of the Lower Peninsula and in the Upper Peninsula (known from Iron and Houghton Co.).

Habitat. Characteristic of river and stream banks, also lake shores and wet depressions. Because of its high shade-intolerance and high moisture requirement throughout the growing season, it is most competitive along the water's edge; associated with sandbar willow, eastern cottonwood, silver maple, red ash. It typically forms, together with eastern cottonwood, the first or river-front zone of the bottomland forest. Thrives at or slightly above water level; tolerates flooding and silting.

Notes. Very shade-intolerant; fast-growing; short-lived (less than 85 years, mature by 55 years). Branchlets brittle at the base; if broken off by wind they may be carried downstream, catch in a muddy bank, and take root there. Very easily propagated by stem cuttings. Individuals in younger stands may appear as shrubs rather than trees.

132

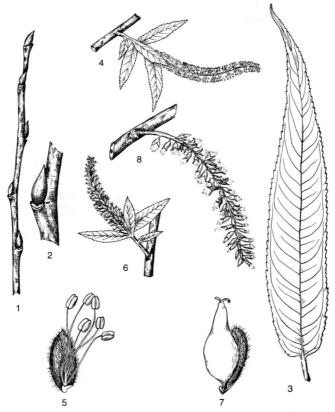

1. Winter twig, × 1.
2. Portion of twig, enlarged.
3. Leaf, × 1.
4. Male flowering shoot with catkin, × 1.
5. Male flower, enlarged.
6. Female flowering shoot with catkin, × 1.
7. Female flower, enlarged.
8. Fruiting catkin with capsules, × 1.

Key Characters

- usually large tree, found along streams, lakes, and wet depressions
- bark dark gray to black, deeply fissured with broad, flat-topped ridges in mature trees
- leaves green both sides; petiole short, flat, glandless, stipules large and persistent, especially on sprouts

Distinguished from peachleaf willow by narrower leaves and shorter, flatter petioles; from crack willow by petioles without glands and smaller buds; and from both by the tendency toward persistent stipules.

THE ROSE FAMILY—*ROSACEAE*

The Rosaceae are one of the largest families of plants. They comprise trees, shrubs, and herbs which are widely distributed throughout the temperate regions of the world. Their flowers are showy and insect-pollinated. Of the 90 or more genera, 5 are represented in Michigan by native treelike forms: *Malus, Sorbus, Amelanchier, Crataegus,* and *Prunus.* The generic interpretation is not agreed upon with different authorities segregating or uniting genera.

The Apples,
Pears, and Mountain-Ashes
Malus—Pyrus—Sorbus

The trees in the genera *Malus, Pyrus,* and *Sorbus* are small. Their flowers, abundant and showy, are borne in loose cymelike clusters that terminate the leafy branches or spurlike shoots. They are perfect, with the calyx, corolla, and stamens borne on the margins of a fleshy receptacle that encloses the ovary. It is largely this ovary and surrounding receptacle that develop later into the fruit, termed a *pome.* The leaves are arranged alternately and may be either simple or compound.

Only 4 species of *Malus* and *Sorbus* are native to Michigan, the wild crab apple, prairie crab apple, American mountain-ash, and showy mountain-ash. Many introduced species have been cultivated since early times, but have been improved by humans from their primitive and often less attractive forms. Among these are our well-known domestic fruit trees, the cultivated pear, *Pyrus communis* L., the apple, *Malus pumila* Mill., and the quince, *Cydonia oblonga* Mill. Through the work of horticulturists there has been a continuous development of these forms and countless varieties and cultivars have been originated. These are adapted to a great variety of conditions throughout the temperate regions of the world.

There are many flowering crabs that are widely planted among the 400 to 600 found in the United States. At least 100 to 200 kinds of crab apples are grown in North American nurseries and at least an additional 300 to 400 types can be found in botanical gardens and arboretums. A description of many of the important types is given by Wyman (1965) and Dirr (1977).

The native American mountain-ash is one of the beautiful small trees of the north. Its distribution is limited; the tree so commonly planted in Michigan is the European mountain-ash or rowan tree, *Sorbus aucuparia* L.

Summer Key to Species of *Malus* and *Sorbus*

1. Leaves compound; pomes small (5–7 mm in diameter) .... *S. americana,* p. 142
1. Leaves simple; pomes large (5–9 cm in diameter).
    2. Branches unarmed; leaves and twigs mostly pubescent; plants
    solitary .... *M. pumila,* p. 140
    2. Branches armed with rough thorns or sharp-pointed twigs; leaves and twigs mostly
    glabrous; plants clustered in large shrubby clones .... *M. coronaria,* p. 138

Winter Key to Species of *Malus* and *Sorbus*

1. Branches armed with rough thorns or sharp-pointed twigs .... *M. coronaria,* p. 138
1. Branches unarmed.
    2. Twigs mostly glabrous; buds acute-oblong, gummy; pomes small (5–7 mm in di-
    ameter), in dense clusters .... *S. americana,* p. 142
    2. Twigs mostly pubescent; buds blunt-ovoid; not gummy; pomes large (5–9 cm in
    diameter), not in dense clusters .... *M. pumila,* p. 140

ROSACEAE
Malus coronaria (Linnaeus) Miller

Wild Crab Apple

Size and Form. Small tree, 4–7 m high and 20–30 cm in diameter. Trunk short and crooked; forming a broad, irregular, rounded crown of rigid, contorted branches bearing many short, thornlike shoots. Often a bushy shrub, forming thicketlike clones. Michigan Big Tree: girth 66 cm, diameter 21 cm, height 8 m, Wayne Co.

Bark. Thin, reddish brown, scaly, breaking into longitudinal fissures.

Leaves. Alternate, simple, blades 5–10 cm long, almost as wide; ovate to nearly triangular, widest below the middle; sharply, irregularly, and deeply serrate, sometimes lobed; membranous; bright green above, paler beneath, tomentose at first, becoming glabrous both sides; petioles long, slender, often with two dark glands near the middle.

Twigs. Slender, at first hoary-tomentose, becoming glabrous, reddish brown; abortive, needle-tipped, thornlike shoots numerous on the branches, thorns rough on the sides.

Winter Buds. Terminal bud 3–6 mm long, conical, obtuse, bright red, hairy; lateral buds smaller, conical-oblong, appressed; scales pubescent, acute.

Wood. Heavy, rather soft, close-grained, weak, reddish brown, with thick, yellow sapwood. Wood blocks used in carving.

Flowers. May, after the leaves; perfect; 3–5 cm across; very fragrant; borne on slender pedicels in 5–6-flowered umbels; calyx urn-shaped, 5-lobed, tomentose; petals 5, white-to-rose colored; stamens 10–20; ovary hairy; styles 5. Insect-pollinated.

Fruit. Pome; October; depressed-globose, 2–4 cm in diameter, pale green to yellowish, very fragrant, with a waxy surface, flesh very tart or sour, often hanging on the tree far into the winter, does not rot until following spring.

Distribution. Frequent in the southern half of the Lower Peninsula, north to Oscoda Co. Species with a midwestern range, reaching its northern limit in the Lower Peninsula.

Habitat. Most common in disturbed habitats such as old fields, clearings, pastures, fence rows, edges of woods, along streams; not soil-specific, occasionally found in the understory of open oak forests.

Notes. Shade-intolerant; slow-growing; individual stems short-lived. An excellent native ornamental tree or shrub for lawns and small gardens. The fruit is sometimes gathered for making preserves and jellies.

138

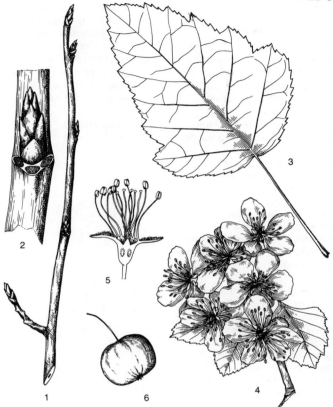

1. Winter twig, × 1.
2. Portion of twig, englarged.
3. Leaf, × ¾.
4. Flowering twig, × ½.
5. Vertical section of flower with petals removed, × ½.
6. Fruit, pome, × ½.

Key Characters
- branches bearing numerous thorns or sharp-pointed, thornlike shoots
- leaf blades widest below the middle, irregularly serrate or toothed
- pome moderately small, 2–4 cm long, pale green to yellowish, very tart or sour
- terminal bud bright red, hairy
- clone-forming shrub or small tree of open, disturbed habitats

139

ROSACEAE
Malus pumila Miller

Common Apple

Size and Form. A small to medium-sized tree, 5–12 m high and 20–60 cm in diameter; trunk usually short, branches low, supporting a dense, wide-spreading, rounded crown. Michigan Big Tree: girth 3.0 m, diameter 97 cm, height 12 m, Oakland Co.

Bark. Thin; becoming moderately thick, dark gray, breaking into numerous flat plates or scales.

Leaves. Alternate, simple, blades 4–10 cm long, 3–6 cm wide; mostly on short spur shoots; broad-elliptic to broad-ovate, short-pointed to rounded; finely crenate-serrate; moderately thick and firm; green above, paler green beneath; tomentose becoming almost glabrous above, tomentum somewhat persistent beneath; veins somewhat protruding below; petioles stout, 1–2.5 cm long, pubescent.

Twigs. Moderately stout, unarmed, brownish gray, tomentose, especially when young; short spur shoots conspicuous.

Winter Buds. Terminal bud blunt-ovoid, pubescent; scales more or less obtuse.

Wood. Heavy, strong, hard, tough, close-grained. Sought for firewood.

Flowers. May, with the leaves; perfect; borne in several-flowered clusters on short shoots, peduncles 1–2.5 cm long; calyx of 5 green, tomentose sepals; corolla of 5 pinkish white or white petals, 2.5–3 cm across; stamens very numerous; ovary usually 5-celled, inferior. Insect-pollinated.

Fruit. Pome; August-September; large, ovoid-globular, usually 7–10 cm long and 5–9 cm wide, surface green, usually becoming red at maturity; seeds borne in papery core of usually 5 partitions and surrounded by massive fleshy tissue; highly edible.

Distribution. Ancient cultivated fruit, derived originally from Europe and western Asia. Planted throughout humid regions of the Temperate Zone; naturalized and reproducing spontaneously in many areas.

Habitat. Grows well on upland soils not subject to severe drought; often persisting on old home sites; commonly found in old fields, at roadsides, and in second-growth woods, also in plantations. Widely planted as a fruit crop in the Lower Peninsula.

Notes. Moderately shade-tolerant; slow-growing; moderately long-lived. Often becoming unattractive and irregular in form if unattended. Numerous cultivars of major economic importance. Fruits of feral plants sometimes infested with worms.

140

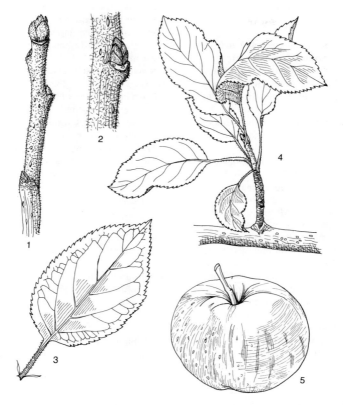

1. Winter twig, × 1½.
2. Portion of twig, × 2½.
3. Leaf, × ½.
4. Short shoot with leaves, × ½.
5. Fruit, pome, × ½.

Key Characters
- fruit a green, red, or yellow pome, tasty
- most leaves and all flowers and fruits borne on conspicuous short, spur shoots
- leaves, twigs, and buds tomentose or pubescent
- low-branching, open-grown tree planted in orchards and in home gardens

ROSACEAE
Sorbus americana Marshall

American Mountain-ash

Size and Form. Small tree, 4–7 m high and 10–25 cm in diameter. Trunk short; branches slender, spreading, forming a narrow, rounded crown. Michigan Big Tree: girth 1.1 m, diameter 36 cm, height 22 m, Leelanau Co.

Bark. Thin, light grayish brown, smooth or slightly roughened, scaly on old trees; inner bark fragrant.

Leaves. Alternate, pinnately compound, blades 15–25 cm long. Leaflets 9–17, 5–7 cm long, 1–2 cm wide; sessile or nearly so, except the terminal; lanceolate to oblong-lanceolate, taper-pointed; finely and sharply serrate above the entire base; membranous; dark yellowish green above, paler beneath, turning clear yellow in autumn, glabrous; petioles slender, grooved, enlarged at the base.

Twigs. Stout, at first reddish brown and hairy, becoming glabrous, dark brown.

Winter Buds. Terminal bud about 1.2 cm long, conical to oblong, acute, with curved apex; lateral buds smaller, appressed; scales rounded on the back, purplish red, slightly pilose above, lustrous, gummy.

Wood. Light, soft, close-grained, weak, pale brown, with thick, lighter colored sapwood.

Flowers. May–June, after the leaves; perfect; 6 mm across; borne on short pedicels in many-flowered flat cymes 7–20 cm across; calyx urn-shaped, 5-lobed, puberulent; petals 5, white; stamens numerous; styles 2–3. Insect-pollinated.

Fruit. Pome; October, but persistent in winter; subglobose, 5–7 mm in diameter, bright orange red, with thin, acid flesh; eaten readily by birds.

Distribution. Occasional in the northern third of the Lower Peninsula, increasingly rare southward. A Boreal, northern, and mountain species, reaching the southern limit of its midwestern range in northwestern lower Michigan.

Habitat. Characteristic of acid, northern white-cedar and black spruce swamps, bogs, swamp borders, and edges of streams; tolerates highly acid, purely organic soil; also on rocky hillsides and mountains of conifer and northern hardwoods forests. Associates include black spruce, larch, bog shrubs, balsam fir, white spruce, red maple, yellow birch, sugar maple.

Notes. Moderately shade-tolerant; slow-growing; short-lived. Easily transplanted. Often a shrub. One of the most beautiful flowering trees of the northern forest. The fruit and inner bark formerly were used for medicinal purposes.

The showy mountain-ash, *S. decora* (Sarg.) Schneid., is a boreal species and is occasional to rare in the Upper Peninsula and the northern half of the Lower Peninsula. It is distinguished from the American mountain-ash by its shorter leaves, 10–15 cm long, villous inner bud scales, and its larger fruit, often 1.2 cm in diameter.

The European mountain-ash or rowan tree, *S. aucuparia* L., is the most commonly planted mountain-ash due to its fast growth and profuse crops of showy white flowers and orange fruits. It is also small, 6–12 m high, with a slender, short trunk that separates 1–2 m above the ground into stout, spreading branches to form a rounded crown. The leaves are pinnately compound as in the American mountain-ash, but the leaflets are blunt, rounded or short-pointed at the apex, and they are more or less pubescent on both sides. Other distinguishing features are the fruit, which is somewhat larger, about 8 mm in diameter, and the twigs and winter buds. The twigs are pubescent; the buds are woolly and not gummy. A form with orange yellow fruit is typically planted.

142

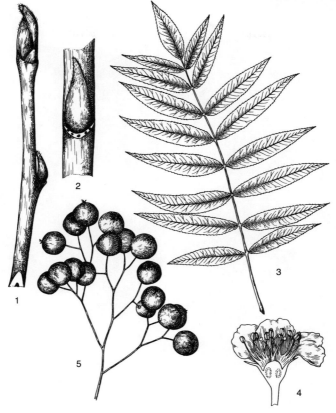

1. Winter twig, × 1.
2. Portion of twig, enlarged.
3. Leaf, × ⅓.
4. Vertical section of flower, enlarged.
5. Portion of a fruiting cyme, × 1.

**Key
Characters**
• leaves pinnately compound; leaflets sharply serrate
• buds purplish red, lustrous, gummy
• fruit bright orange red, spherical pomes
    Distinguished from the European mountain-ash by sharp-pointed, glabrous leaflets; glabrous twigs; gummy and only slightly hairy buds (not woolly).

The Serviceberries— *Amelanchier*

The name serviceberry is a corruption of the name sarvissberry. Sarviss is a transformation of the word *sorbus* given by the Romans to a related kind of fruit (Peattie 1950). Peattie notes: "Sarviss is a good Shakespearean English form of the most classic Latin, whereas Serviceberry is meaningless as a name, or is at least a genteel corruption of an older and more scholarly form." The name serviceberry has its own folklore dating back to pioneer days when the showy flowering, marking the end of winter, coincided with memorial services for people who died during the winter season. According to some, services were deferred because travel conditions in the mountains were too difficult for all those who wished to pay their respects. According to others, services were deferred until the blooming signaled the time when the soil could be turned and the bodies buried in the ground. The name Juneberry is derived from the early ripening of the fruit in some areas. The name Shadbush is also used; it is an eastern name which refers to the coincidence of the flowering time with the spawning runs of the shad fish.

The amelanchiers are a confusing group, including many hybrids. Two major tree species, as well as a number of shrubby species, have been described.

ROSACEAE
Amelanchier arborea (Michaux f.) Fernald

Downy Serviceberry   Juneberry

Size and Form. Small tree, 4–8 m high and 10–30 cm in diameter. Trunk tall and slender; forming a narrow, rounded crown of many small branches and slender twigs. Michigan Big Tree: girth 1.2. m, diameter 40 cm, height 16.2 m, Oakland Co.

Bark. Thin; pale, smooth on young trees; becoming grayish to reddish brown and divided by dark, shallow fissures into narrow, longitudinal ridges.

Leaves. Alternate, simple, blades 7–10 cm long, about half as wide; ovate to obovate; finely and sharply serrate; downy-pubescent when young, becoming glabrous and dark green above, paler beneath with pubescent midrib and main veins; petioles slender, 2–3 cm long.

Twigs. Very slender, smooth, light green, becoming reddish brown.

Winter Buds. Yellowish brown to reddish brown, narrow-ovoid to conical, sharp-pointed, 0.6–1.3 cm long; bud scales apiculate, often twisted, slightly pubescent.

Wood. Heavy, very hard, strong, close-grained, dark reddish brown, with thick, lighter-colored sapwood.

Flowers. April-May, when the leaves are small, downy, and folded; perfect; large, white, borne in erect or lax racemes 7–12 cm long; calyx 5-cleft, campanulate, villous on the inner surface; petals 5, narrow, strap-shaped, white, 2–3 cm long; stamens numerous; styles 5, united below. Insect-pollinated.

Fruit. Pome; June-August; globular, 0.8–1.2 cm long; the lowest in a cluster borne on a pedicel about 1.2 cm long; turning from bright red to dark purple with slight bloom, dry and tasteless.

Distribution. Common to occasional throughout the state.

Habitat. An understory tree with wide site tolerances, including xeric sandy pine or oak forests and cutover lands, dry-mesic oak-hickory forests, and mesic beech-maple or northern hardwood forests. Intolerant of wet soils.

Notes. Shade-tolerant; slow-growing; mod-erately long-lived. Warm, moist late autumn weather of some years causes the bud scales to swell and sometimes causes the leaves to flush out. Besides the downy serviceberry described above, one may also recognize the related Allegheny or smooth serviceberry, *A. laevis* Wieg. It is distinguished from downy serviceberry by (1) leaves glabrous or only slightly pubescent in the bud, (2) leaves at least half-grown at flowering time, (3) pedicel of the lowest fruit in a cluster 2.5–5 cm long, (4) fruit juicy and sweet. The difficulties in distinguishing distinct species arise from the lack of knowledge of variation within each species, hybridization between the two tree species, and hybridization between the tree species and related shrub species.

146

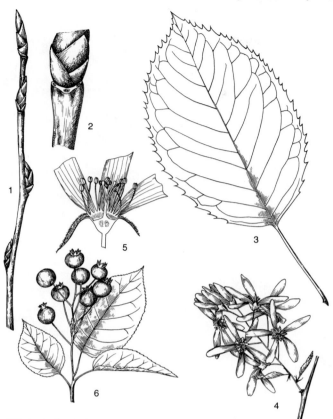

1. Winter twig, × 1.
2. Portion of twig, enlarged.
3. Leaf, × 1.
4. Flowering shoot, × ½.
5. Vertical section of flower, enlarged.
6. Fruiting shoot, × ½.

Key   • bark smooth, grayish, thin
Characters • winter buds long and narrow, sharp-pointed, scales often twisted
             • leaf blades finely and sharply serrate
             • small tree

147

The Hawthorns, Haws, Thorns, or Thorn-apples—*Crataegus*

Owing to the complexity of the various forms in this genus, the present state of uncertainty as to the value of certain characters, and the questionable validity of many of the so-called species, it is beyond the scope of this book to give more than a general description of the group as a whole.

The hawthorns are generally low, wide-spreading trees or shrubs, 1–8 m high. The largest hawthorn in Michigan, in Oakland Co., has a girth of 1.3 m, a diameter of 40 cm, and a height of 11.9 m. Hawthorns have strong, tortuous branches and more or less zigzag branchlets usually armed with stiff, sharp thorns. The bark varies from dark red to gray and is scaly or shallowly fissured with narrow, shreddy vertical plates that sometimes become loose at both ends.

The leaves are alternate, simple, serrate, often lobed, with short or long petioles. The leaves are highly variable even on the same plant depending on whether they are borne on vegetative or floral shoots.

The winter buds are small, nearly globose, lustrous brown. Two buds often occur side by side on the twigs, one of which develops into a new shoot and the other into a thorn. The thorns are smooth, lustrous, rigid, and sharp-pointed. They do not produce the buds that are sometimes found on the thornlike shoots of the plums and crab apples, but they may occasionally bear a vestigial leaf. The wood is heavy, hard, tough, close-grained, reddish brown, with thick, pale sapwood.

The flowers, whitish or pinkish, perfect, appear in May or June, with or after the leaves, in simple or compound corymbs. They are insect-pollinated. The fruit is a red to yellow (in one species blue or black) pome, subglobose to pear-shaped, with 1–5 hard pits containing the seeds. The flesh is usually dry and mealy, but may be sweet and succulent. The fruits are eaten by birds and mammals and thus widely dispersed.

The hawthorns are abundant in the southern Lower Peninsula and occasional in the Upper Peninsula. They are characteristic of open, disturbed sites, being intolerant of shade. They are found in old fields, pastures, open woodlands, cutover forests, and along roads and streams. Some species are desirable for ornamental planting in parks and gardens by virtue of their showy and abundant flowers and attractive fruits.

The variation in the hawthorns is probably due above all to the massive disturbance of original forest lands that provided the opportunity for their hybridization, colonization, and spread in many areas previously densely forested and unavailable to them. The asexual reproduction of hybrids by seeds also has undoubtedly increased the variation spectrum.

The dotted haw (*Crataegus punctata* Jacquin), illustrated here, is characteristic of one of the many groups within the hawthorns. It has obovate, very shallowly lobed leaf blades. The fruit is a dull red.

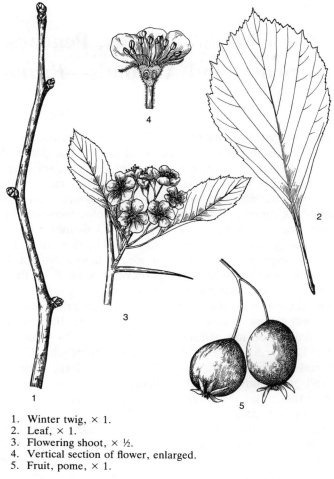

1. Winter twig, × 1.
2. Leaf, × 1.
3. Flowering shoot, × ½.
4. Vertical section of flower, enlarged.
5. Fruit, pome, × 1.

The Cherries, Plums, Peaches, Apricots, and Almonds—*Prunus*

The species of *Prunus* number over 400, well distributed over the North Temperate Zone and occurring locally in the tropics. Some 25 species occur in North America, 18 of which are of tree size. Seven species are native to Michigan. They are all shrubs or small or medium-sized trees with conspicuous white or pink flowers which are insect-pollinated. One, the black cherry, in more southern latitudes becomes a large tree, sometimes attaining a height of 35 m, with a diameter of 1.5 m. All species of the genus *Prunus* are distinguished by their stone fruits, i.e., drupes. The twigs and leaves of many species have a distinctive chemistry including benzaldehyde and hydrocyanic acid, from the latter of which poisoning occurs in cattle and humans.

Among the introduced species that have been cultivated extensively are the sweet cherry or mazzard, *P. avium* (L.) L.; the sour cherry, *P. cerasus* L.; the perfume cherry, *P. mahaleb* L.; the garden plum, *P. domestica* L.; the apricot, *P. armeniaca* L.; the peach, *P. persica* (L.) Batsch; and the almond, *P. dulcis* (Mill.) D. A. Webb. These, like the apples and pears, have been the subject of continual improvement by humans so that today there are many cultivars and forms adapted to a great range of climates.

The ornamental flowering almond of American gardens is *P. triloba* Lindl. It is a small tree not more than 3–5 m high, and more often it is shrublike. Its native home is China, but it has been grown in this country for a long time for its showy blossoms which appear just before the leaves. The flowers are solitary, short-pedicelled, 2–4 cm across, clear pink or sometimes white.

Summer Key to Species of *Prunus*

1. Leaves oblong-ovate to obovate, apex abruptly acuminate; marginal teeth not incurved.
    2. Margin of leaves sharp-serrate with spreading teeth; leaves not rugose, veins not prominent; fruit 7–9 mm in diameter, red to purple, racemose; bark of trunk brown, smooth or only slightly fissured; usually a large clonal shrub; unarmed . . . . *P. virginiana*, p. 160

2. Margin of leaves coarsely, doubly crenate-serrate; leaves more or less rugose, veins prominent; fruit 2–3 cm in diameter, orange red, umbellate; bark of trunk grayish brown, early splitting off in large, thick plates; a small tree; armed with thornlike twigs .... *P. nigra*, p. 154
1. Leaves narrowly ovate to oblong-lanceolate, apex gradually taper-pointed; marginal teeth incurved.
   3. Fruit bright red, umbellate; twigs usually less than 2 mm thick, pith of twigs brown; more common northward .... *P. pensylvanica*, p. 156
   3. Fruit purple black, racemose; twigs usually more than 2 mm thick; pith of twigs white; more common southward .... *P. serotina*, p. 158

Winter Key to Species of *Prunus*

1. Terminal bud deciduous; some twigs thornlike; bark of young trunks early splitting off in large, thick plates; twigs lacking bitter almond smell and taste when crushed .... *P. nigra*, p. 154
1. Terminal bud present; twigs not thornlike; bark of young trunks smooth; twigs having bitter almond smell and taste when crushed.
   2. Buds clustered at the tips of all shoots; twigs usually less than 2 mm thick; pith of twigs brown; bark light reddish brown, lustrous .... *P. pensylvanica*, p. 156
   2. Buds not clustered, or clustered only on short, spurlike shoots; twigs usually more than 2 mm thick; pith of twigs white; young bark dark purplish brown.
      3. Buds usually 6 mm or less in length; bud scales uniform in color, not pale brown on the margins, apex apiculate; bark on mature trunks blackish, rough-scaly; small to large solitary tree .... *P. serotina*, p. 158
      3. Buds usually 6–9 mm long; bud scales pale brown on the margins, apex rounded; bark on mature trunks brown, smooth or only slightly fissured; usually a large clonal shrub; unarmed .... *P. virginiana*, p. 160

ROSACEAE
Prunus nigra Aiton

Canada Plum

Size and Form. A small tree, 6–8 m high and 12–20 cm in diameter. Trunk short, crooked, usually dividing 2 m or less above the ground into a number of stout, upright, crooked branches, forming a narrow, broad-topped, rigid crown of twisted, zigzag branches; sometimes forming low, broad clones. Michigan Big Tree: girth 1.3 m, diameter 40 cm, height 16 m, Macomb Co.

Bark. Thin, smooth, young trunks grayish brown, very soon splitting vertically into large, thick plates exposing darker inner bark.

Leaves. Alternate, simple, blades 6–12 cm long, half as wide; oblong-ovate to obovate, abruptly acuminate; coarsely and doubly crenate-serrate; relatively thin and firm, more or less rugose, veins prominent; light green above, paler beneath; glabrous; petioles short, stout, bearing 2 large, dark red glands near the blade.

Twigs. Slender, green, marked by numerous pale lenticels, later dark brown to black; thornlike twigs and short, spurlike shoots occur along the branches.

Winter Buds. Terminal bud deciduous, absent; end and lateral buds 3–6 mm long, ovoid, acute, glabrous, chestnut brown; lateral buds appressed.

Wood. Heavy, hard, strong, close-grained, light reddish brown, with thin, lighter-colored sapwood.

Flowers. April-May, before the leaves; perfect; slightly fragrant; 2–3 cm across; borne on slender, glabrous, red pedicels in 2–5-flowered umbels; calyx 5-lobed, dark red; petals 5, white fading to pink; stamens 15–20, with purple anthers; ovary 1-celled; style 1; stigma 1. Insect-pollinated.

Fruit. Drupe; August-September; 2–3 cm in diameter, oblong-ovoid, with a tough, thick, yellow to red skin mostly lacking bloom, and yellow, juicy, sour flesh adherent to the flat stone. Eaten raw or cooked.

Distribution. Occasional to rare throughout the state.

Habitat. Disturbed, open sites; edges of woods and particularly stream floodplains.

Notes. Shade-intolerant; relatively slow-growing; short-lived, but resprouting following fire. An attractive ornamental tree because of its leaves and showy flowers. The fruit is used for preserves and jellies. Species name refers to the dark branches.

The American wild plum, *P. americana* Marsh., is closely related to the Canada plum and resembles it in many respects. In contrast to the Canada plum, the American wild plum has a lanceolate blade shape, apex abruptly long-acuminate, marginal teeth sharply (sometimes doubly) serrate, nonglandular petiole (glands are on the margin of blade near petiole), and the calyx of the flower is glabrous along the margins. Both species occur more commonly in the southern half of the Lower Peninsula but are found sporadically in the northern Lower Peninsula and the Upper Peninsula. Habitat of the American wild plum is open, disturbed, dry hillsides, old fields, and edges of woods. Michigan Big Tree: girth 0.9 m, diameter 29 cm, height 10.7 m, Oakland Co.

154

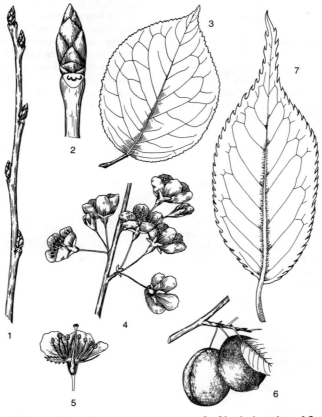

1. Winter twig, × 1.
2. Portion of twig, enlarged.
3. Leaf, × ½.
4. Flowering twig, × ½.

5. Vertical section of flower, × 1.
6. Fruiting shoot with drupes, × ½.
7. *Prunus americana,* leaf, lower surface, × 1.

Key Characters

- leaf blades coarsely, doubly crenate-serrate; petioles with large, dark red glands near the blade
- small tree, often in clonal thickets
- thornlike twigs present
- fruit large, with a tough, yellow to red skin; stone flattened

Distinguished from chokecherry by coarsely, doubly crenate-serrate leaves, thornlike twigs and short, spurlike shoots; fruits larger, with tough yellow to red skin, not in racemes.

Distinguished from pin cherry by broadly ovate or obovate leaf blades; coarsely, doubly crenate-serrate margins; twigs dark brown to black, not reddish; thornlike twigs; fruits larger, with tough, yellow to red skin, borne in umbels not racemes; bark grayish brown to black, not light reddish brown.

155

ROSACEAE
Prunus pensylvanica Linnaeus f.

Pin Cherry

Size and Form. Small tree, 5–10 m high and 20–25 cm in diameter. Trunk slender, relatively straight and extending well into the upper crown; crown rather open, narrow, rounded, with slender, regular branches. Small clones formed by suckers arising from roots. Michigan Big Tree: girth 1.0 m, diameter 31 cm, height 14 m, Huron Co. (tree 26.8 m high in Leelanau Co.).

Bark. Thin, smooth, light reddish brown, with large, conspicuous, widely-spaced, orange lenticels; peeling off horizontally into broad, papery plates; bitter, aromatic.

Leaves. Alternate, simple, blades 7–11 cm long, about ⅓ as wide; oblong-lanceolate, gradually tapering to a sharp tip; finely and sharply serrate with uneven, incurved teeth; thin and fragile; bright yellow green and shining, paler beneath, turning bright red in autumn; glabrous both sides; petioles slender, glandular near the blade, 1–2 cm long.

Twigs. Very slender, at first lustrous, red, marked by orange lenticels, becoming brownish, bitter almond smell and taste when crushed; pith brown.

Winter Buds. Terminal bud small, 2–3 mm long, broadly ovoid, rather blunt, brownish, smooth; lateral buds divergent, clustered near the tip of twig.

Wood. Light, soft, close-grained, light brown, with thin, yellow sapwood.

Flowers. May or early June, with the leaves; perfect; 1–1.2 cm across, on slender pedicels in 4–5-flowered umbels, usually 2 or 3 together; calyx 5-cleft, campanulate; petals 5, white, 6 mm long; stamens 15 or more. Insect-pollinated.

Fruit. Drupe; July-August; globular, 6 mm in diameter, bright red, with thick skin and sour flesh.

Distribution. Occasional throughout most of the state except the south-central portion, south to St. Joseph, Montcalm, Oakland, and Wayne Co.

Habitat. Characteristic of open, disturbed, upland areas such as roadsides and recently burned-over or cutover areas. Associates include sumacs, white birch, bigtooth and trembling aspens, red oak, pines.

Notes. Shade-intolerant; fast-growing; short-lived. Sprouts vigorously from roots following injury by fire or cutting. Not a component of the mature forest as it is rapidly over-topped by other species. Other common names include fire cherry, bird cherry, wild red cherry.

156

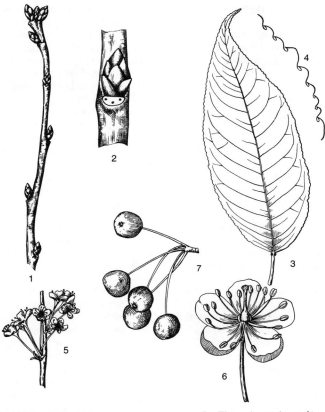

1. Winter twig, × 1.
2. Portion of twig, enlarged.
3. Leaf, × ¾.
4. Margin of leaf, enlarged.

5. Flowering twig, × ½.
6. Flower, enlarged.
7. Fruit, drupes, × 1.

Key Characters

- leaf blades long and gradually tapering to a sharp tip, broader below or near the middle; yellowish green
- bark smooth, light reddish brown, with widely spaced, conspicuous lenticels
- buds very small, several lateral buds clustered at the tip of each shoot
- fruits bright red, borne in umbels

Distinguished from black cherry by leaf blades lacking reddish brown pubescence along the midrib on lower side; smaller buds, laterals clustered at tip of the shoots; pith of twigs brown; fruits bright red, borne in umbels not racemes; small tree.

Distinguished from chokecherry by longer, yellowish green leaves; bark more reddish, with more conspicuous lenticels; smaller buds, laterals clustered at tip of the shoots; fruits bright red, borne in umbels, not racemes.

157

ROSACEAE
Prunus serotina Ehrhart

Black Cherry

Size and Form. Medium-sized tree, 12–20 m high and 25–80 cm in diameter. Trunk of open-grown trees usually crooked, low branching; trunk in forest stands slender, relatively straight, free of lower branches; branches few, large, crooked, forming a rather spreading, oblong or rounded crown. Taproot prominent in youth, giving way to a spreading lateral system. Michigan Big Tree: girth 7.2 m, diameter 230 cm, height 35 m, Van Buren Co.

Bark. Young trunks smooth, thin, dark reddish brown, with conspicuous, horizontal, gray lenticels; older trunks blackish and rough, broken into thick, irregular plates, giving a "burnt potato chip" appearance.

Leaves. Alternate, simple, 6–12 cm long, about ⅓ as wide; narrowly oval to oblong-lanceolate, acuminate or abruptly pointed; finely serrate, teeth incurved; moderately thick and leathery; dark green and very lustrous above, paler beneath, with dense, reddish brown (initially white) pubescence along both sides of the midrib near the blade base; petioles short, slender, usually bearing 2 red glands near the blade.

Twigs. Slender, smooth, green becoming red to reddish brown, spurlike shoots on older growth; bitter almond smell and taste when crushed; pith white.

Winter Buds. Terminal bud 4–6 mm long, ovoid, blunt to acute; scales keeled on the back, apiculate, reddish brown, darker at tip, greenish where not exposed.

Wood. Moderately heavy, rather hard, strong, close- and straight-grained, light brown or red, with thin, yellow sapwood. Highly valued for veneer and furniture. Other uses include interior trim, printers' blocks, scientific instruments, woodenware, gunstocks.

Flowers. May-June, when leaves are half- to full-grown; perfect; 6 mm across; borne on slender pedicels in many-flowered, loose racemes, 10–12 cm long; calyx cup-shaped, 5-lobed, persistent; petals 5, white; stamens 15 or more; stigma thick, club-shaped. Insect-pollinated.

Fruit. Drupe; August-September; globular, 8–9 mm in diameter, calyx conspicuous at base; nearly black, with dark purple, juicy flesh, slightly bitter, edible.

Distribution. Common in the southern half of the Lower Peninsula; occasional to rare in the northern half of the Lower Peninsula and in the Upper Peninsula.

Habitat. Characteristic of disturbance-caused openings in dry-mesic oak-hickory forests and mesic beech-maple forests of the Lower Peninsula; occasional in northern hardwoods forests of the Upper Peninsula. Common as an understory plant in many forest communities. Common in fence rows, old fields, and edges of woodlots; does not tolerate high water tables or poorly drained sites; resistant to frost. Associates include oaks, hickories, maples, ashes, walnuts, elms, basswood, white pine, among others.

Notes. Shade-tolerant in youth, becoming intolerant; fast-growing; moderately long-lived (150–200 years). Seeds may lie dormant 1–2 years in the soil before germinating. An opportunistic species colonizing various open sites, including forest edges and openings in the forest. Sprouts readily from the root collar or stump following injury by fire, cutting, or browsing. Leaves and twigs contain hydro-cyanic acid, poisonous to browsing livestock. Common pests include the eastern tent caterpillar (*Malacosoma americanum* forming "tents" or "bags" between branches and defoliating trees) and "black knot" (*Dibotryon morbosum*), a conspicuous disease of branches and small stems.

The introduced sweet cherry, *P. avium* L., is commonly planted and sometimes reproduces spontaneously. It differs from *P. serotina* in its broader, more ovate, coarsely doubly-toothed leaf blades with conspicuous veins, 2 large red glands at blade base, leaves borne on conspicuous short shoots, and its sweet, dark red cherries borne several per cluster.

158

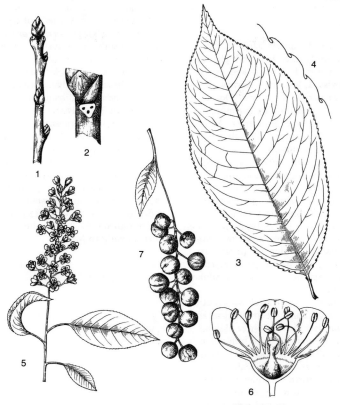

1. Winter twig, × 1.
2. Portion of twig, enlarged.
3. Leaf, × ¾.
4. Margin of leaf, enlarged.

5. Flowering shoot, × ½.
6. Vertical section of flower, enlarged.
7. Fruiting shoot with drupes, × ½.

Key Characters

- leaf blades long and narrowly ovate; finely serrate with incurved teeth; dense reddish brown pubescence on lower surface along the midrib; petioles with small red glands near the blade base
- bark broken into rough irregular plates resembling "burnt potato chips"
- fruit a small, globose drupe, nearly black, flower parts (calyx) conspicuous at base

Distinguished from chokecherry by solitary, medium-sized tree habit, not a clonal shrub; leaves longer, blades narrower with incurved teeth, dense pubescence along midrib of lower surfce; terminal buds smaller, reddish brown; fruit nearly black, flower parts conspicuous at base.

Distinguished from pin cherry by medium-sized tree habit; leaf blades darker green with dense reddish brown pubescence along midrib of lower surface; young trees with darker bark—reddish brown to black; pith of twigs white; fruits nearly black, not bright red, borne on long racemes, not in umbels.

159

ROSACEAE
Prunus virginiana Linnaeus

Choke Cherry

Size and Form. Usually a large shrub, sometimes a small tree, 4–10 m high and 10–15 cm in diameter. Trunk crooked, often leaning or twisted; forming a narrow, irregular or somewhat rounded crown. Dense clonal colonies are produced by sprouting from the root collar and suckering from rhizomes. Michigan Big Tree: girth 1.8 m, diameter 56 cm, height 20 m, Kent Co.

Bark. Thin, smooth, dark brown, slightly fissured or with fine scales; horizontal lenticels not noticeable.

Leaves. Alternate, simple, blades 5–10 cm long, half as wide; obovate to oblong-obovate or broadly oval, abruptly acuminate; finely and sharply serrate, teeth spreading, each tooth ending in a narrow point; very thin; dull dark green above, paler beneath; glabrous; petioles short, slender, glandular near the blade.

Twigs. Slender to moderately stout, at first light brown or greenish, becoming grayish brown, finally dark brown; bitter almond smell and taste when crushed; pith white.

Winter Buds. Terminal bud 0.6–1.2 cm long, conical, sharp-pointed; scales rounded at the tip, dark brown with pale brown edges, giving a two-tone appearance (dark brownish black at the tip and pale brown at the middle).

Wood. Heavy, hard, close-grained, weak, light brown, with thick, lighter-colored sapwood. Not commercially important.

Flowers. May-June, when the leaves are nearly grown; perfect; 0.8–1 cm across; borne on short, slender pedicels in many-flowered racemes, 7–15 cm long; calyx cup-shaped, 5-lobed; petals 5, white; stamens 15–20; stigma broad, on a short style. Insect-pollinated.

Fruit. Drupe; July-August; globular, 7–9 mm in diameter, calyx deciduous, varying from deep red to dark purple, with dark red flesh, astringent, but edible.

Distribution. Abundant in the southern half of the Lower Peninsula; common throughout the rest of the state.

Habitat. Characteristic of open areas and in the understory of many forests where light is sufficient for growth (particularly oak-hickory forests); grows on a great variety of sites and soils, from swamp margins and mounds in swamps to xeric, well drained upland soils. Associates include oaks, maples, ashes, black cherry, black walnut, sassafras, hop-hornbeam, and many others.

Notes. Moderately shade-tolerant; slow-growing; individual stems short-lived; re-sprouting vigorously following fire. An opportunistic species whose seeds are widely disseminated by birds and mammals. One of the most widely distributed native trees of North America, extending from the Atlantic all the way west to the Pacific Ocean, and from west central Canada (58° north latitude) south into the Rocky Mountains and in California nearly to Mexico.

160

1. Winter twig, × 1.
2. Portion of twig, enlarged.
3. Leaf, × 1.
4. Margin of blade, enlarged.

5. Flowering shoot, × ½.
6. Vertical section of flower, enlarged.
7. Fruiting shoot with drupes, × ½.

Key Characters

- leaf blade broadly ovate, abruptly acuminate; fine narrow teeth point away from the leaf; petioles with small glands near the blade base
- typically a clonal shrub
- terminal buds conical, sharp-pointed, appearing two-toned dark and pale brown with a conspicuous dark brown tip
- fruit a reddish purple drupe, borne on a raceme
- bark smooth, dark brown

Distinguished from black cherry by its shrub or small tree habit; smaller, broader leaves with sharp-pointed, nonincurved teeth; bark smooth; terminal buds more conical, sharp-pointed, scales two-toned dark and pale brown; fruit with barely noticeable calyx remains at base.

Distinguished from pin cherry by smaller and broader leaves; twigs grayish brown, not reddish; buds large, more sharp-pointed and conical, two-toned brown, not reddish; fruit deep red to purple, not bright red; borne in racemes not umbels.

161

FABACEAE (LEGUMINOSAE)
Robinia pseudoacacia Linnaeus

Black Locust

Size and Form. Medium-sized tree, 9–15 m high and 30–60 cm in diameter. Forming a narrow, oblong-cylindrical, open, irregular crown of more or less contorted branches. Roots shallow to moderately deep in a wide-spreading lateral system. Michigan Big Tree: girth 5.6 m, diameter 179 cm, height 29 m, Hillsdale Co.

Bark. Thick, deeply furrowed into rounded, interlacing scaly ridges.

Leaves. Alternate, pinnately compound, 20–35 cm long. Leaflets 7–21, short-petiolate, 2–5 cm long, about half as wide; ovate to oblong-oval; entire; very thin; dull dark green above, paler beneath; glabrous. Petioles slender, pubescent, covering the bud, slightly enlarged at the base.

Twigs. Moderately stout, rigid, zigzag, smooth, green, more or less rough-dotted at first, becoming reddish brown, usually armed with 2 stipular spines at each node.

Winter Buds. Terminal bud absent; lateral buds minute, naked, 3–4 superposed, partially sunken within the leaf scar, rusty-hairy.

Wood. Heavy, very strong and hard, close-grained, very durable in contact with the soil, brown, with very thin, pale yellow sapwood. Uses include fence posts, railroad ties, lumber, boxes, crates.

Flowers. May-June, after the leaves; perfect; showy and abundant; very fragrant; 10–25 on slender pedicels in drooping racemes 10–12 cm long; calyx short, bell-shaped, 5-lobed, hairy; corolla of sweet pea type, white, 5-petaled; stamens 10. Insect-pollinated.

Fruit. Legume; late autumn, but persistent through the winter; pods smooth, dark brown, flat, 7–10 cm long, containing 4–8 small, flattish, brown seeds.

Distribution. Native in the Appalachian Mountains and the Ozark Region; formerly much planted in Michigan for ornamental, erosion control, and commercial purposes.

Habitat. Cove forests and open, upland slopes in Appalachian and Ozark forests. Grows well in many soils except those of consistently high water tables. Grows better in lighter-textured soils (sandy loams, loams) than in heavy-textured soils (clay loams and clay). Thrives on limestone-derived soils.

Notes. Shade-intolerant; fast-growing; short-lived. Sprouts readily from roots and forms natural clones (often termed "thickets"); rapidly colonizes old fields and disturbed sites. Nitrogen-fixing bacteria occurring in nodules on the roots act to enrich the soil. It is the most common caterpillar food plant for our largest skipper butterfly, the showy silver-spotted skipper. Widely planted for erosion control because of vigorous, wide-spreading root system and sprouting habit; sometimes escaping along roads and in open areas. Often grown for fence posts because of its extremely durable wood. Plantations suffered greatly from the locust borer (*Megacyllene robiniae*), and widespread cultivation has been largely abandoned. Many cultivated varieties have been developed and are used in horticulture, especially in Europe due to the absence of the borer.

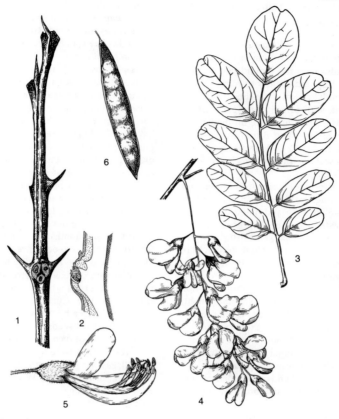

1. Winter twig, × 1.
2. Vertical section through lateral buds, enlarged.
3. Leaf, × ⅜.
4. Raceme of flowers, × ½.
5. Flower, with part of corolla removed, enlarged.
6. Fruit, legume, × ½.

Key Characters
- leaves pinnately compound
- twigs usually with pairs of stipular spines borne at each node
- bark deeply furrowed into rounded, interlacing, scaly ridges
- clusters of thin legume-pods containing 4–8, small, brown seeds

163

FABACEAE (LEGUMINOSAE)
Gymnocladus dioicus (Linnaeus) K. Koch

Kentucky Coffeetree

Size and Form. Medium-sized to large tree, 15–23 m high and 60–90 cm in diameter. Trunk divides near the ground into several stems which spread slightly to form a narrow, pyramidal crown; branches few, coarse, stout, blunt, with conspicuous leaf scars. Michigan Big Tree: girth 4.0 m, diameter 129 cm, height 33.5 m, Van Buren Co.

Bark. Thick, hard, dark gray, deeply fissured with scaly or sharp horny ridges curling out at their edges.

Leaves. Alternate, bipinnately compound, 30–90 cm long. Leaflets 40 or more, no endleaflets, 5–6 cm long and half as wide, shortstalked; ovate, acute; entire; thin and firm; light green above, pale yellowish green beneath; glabrous. Petioles stout, terete, glabrous. Appear late in spring; leaflets drop early in autumn.

Twigs. Very stout, rigid, blunt, with short, dense, reddish pubescence, becoming light brown, with orange lenticels, often coated with a crusty film; knobby from big, raised, concave leaf scars; bundle scars 3 or 5.

Winter Buds. Terminal bud absent; lateral and end buds minute, superposed, flatdomed, deeply sunken, surrounded by an incurved hairy ring of bark, bronze-brown, silky-pubescent.

Wood. Heavy, somewhat soft, strong, coarse-grained, very durable in contact with the soil, light reddish brown, with thin, lighter-colored sapwood. Uses include fence posts, rough construction, furniture, interior trim.

Flowers. June, after the leaves; greenish white; male flowers short-stalked, in racemose corymbs, 7–10 cm long; calyx tubular, hairy; petals 5, keeled, nearly white; stamens 10; female flowers long-stalked, in racemes 25–30 cm long; ovary hairy. Insectpollinated. Trees dioecious or polygamous.

Fruit. Legume; autumn, but persistent until late winter; short-stalked, thick, reddish brown, 15–25 cm long, 3–5 cm wide, containing 4–7 large, hard-shelled seeds imbedded in sweet, sticky pulp; seeds blackish brown, about 2 cm in diameter, rounded and somewhat flattened.

Distribution. Rare in southern Michigan as far north as the Grand River. A species of the midwestern states, reaching its northern limit in Michigan.

Habitat. Invariably found on alluvial soils of river floodplains and nearby terraces. Associates include silver maple, red ash, American elm, eastern cottonwood, red mulberry, basswood, northern hackberry.

Notes. Shade-intolerant; relatively fastgrowing; moderately long-lived. Formerly planted as an ornamental tree in parks and cemeteries; also planted as a street tree. Grows in a variety of soils; hardy in southern Michigan. Free from insects and diseases. Because of early shedding of its leaflets and late spring leafing-out it is barren of foliage for at least six months; the genus name refers to this naked appearance. Seeds, resembling coffee beans, apparently led to the common name, seeds were roasted and used by early settlers as a bitter, unpalatable substitute for coffee. Curtis (1959) reports cultivation of the tree by Native Americans: "The large, hard seeds of this species were used in a sort of dice game by various tribes. As a result, they were lost in the vicinity of the villages. At present, the species has a very local distribution in Wisconsin, with each locality at or near the site of an Indian village."

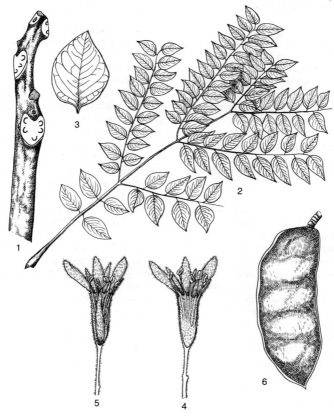

1. Winter twig, × 1.
2. Leaf, × ¼.
3. Leaflet, × ½.
4. Vertical section of male flower, enlarged.
5. Vertical section of female flower, enlarged.
6. Fruit, legume, × ¼.

Key Characters
- leaves very large, doubly compound
- twigs few, very stout, blunt
- buds minute, deeply sunken
- fruit a legume (pod) enclosing large, rounded seeds in a sticky pulp
- bark gray, scaly with the edges of ridges curling outward

165

FABACEAE (LEGUMINOSAE)
Gleditsia triacanthos Linnaeus

Honeylocust

Size and Form. Medium-sized tree, 15–23 m high and 60–90 cm in diameter. Trunk dividing near the ground into several large, upright branches which divide again into long, slender, horizontal branchlets; forming an open, broad, often flat-topped crown; both trunk and large branches armed with stout, rigid, simple or many-branched thorns. Michigan Big Tree: girth 5.2 m, diameter 165 cm, height 35 m, Wayne Co.

Bark. Moderately thin; smooth when young; on mature trees iron gray to blackish and deeply fissured into long, narrow ridges roughened by small scales; typically covered with dense clusters of stout, single or many-branched thorns, 6–10 cm long.

Leaves. Alternate, pinnately or bipinnately compound, 15–30 cm long. Leaflets 18 or more, no end-leaflets, nearly sessile, 2–4 cm long, ⅓ as wide; lanceolate-oblong; remotely crenulate-serrate, sometimes lacking serrations; thin; lustrous, dark green above, dull yellowish green beneath; glabrous. Petioles pubescent, enlarged at the base.

Twigs. Slender, zigzag, lustrous, reddish brown, becoming grayish brown; armed with simple or 3 or more branched, reddish brown thorns; leaf scar shield-shaped, bundle scars 3.

Winter Buds. Terminal bud absent; lateral buds minute, 3 or more superposed, glabrous, brownish, more or less covered by the torn margin of the leaf scars.

Wood. Hard, strong, coarse-grained, durable in contact with the soil, reddish brown, with thin, pale sapwood. Uses include fence posts, construction, furniture, interior trim, veneer.

Flowers. May-June, when the leaves are nearly full grown; male flowers in short, many-flowered, pubescent racemes; calyx campanulate, hairy, 3–5-lobed; petals 3–5, greenish; stamens 3–10; female flowers in slender, few-flowered racemes; on shoots of the preceding season; ovary 1-celled, woolly. Trees polygamodioecious. Insect-pollinated.

Fruit. Legume; autumn, falling in early winter; pendent, flat, twisted, reddish brown, aromatic pods, 25–45 cm long, short-stalked in short racemes; seeds 12–14, ovoid, flattened, lying in a sweet pulp.

Distribution. Rare in the southernmost two tiers of counties of Lower Michigan; planted as far north as Emmet Co. A species of midwestern and southern distribution, reaching its northern limit in southern Michigan.

Habitat. Characteristic of alluvial soils near streams and lakes, especially river floodplains, adjacent terraces, and limestone-derived soils; drought-hardy and tolerant of high lime concentrations. Associates include northern hackberry, black walnut, Kentucky coffeetree, American elm, red ash, bur oak.

Notes. Shade-intolerant; fast-growing; moderately long-lived. Sprouts readily and can be propagated from stem and root cuttings. Good growth on a variety of soils when planted. Trees of northern populations are relatively frost hardy. The rigid, branched thorns and long pods that litter the ground make the tree unsuitable for street planting. Various clones of the thornless cultivar *G. triacanthos* 'Inermis' are used extensively in landscape plantings. The cultivar 'Sunburst' is widely planted for its vivid yellow foliage in early spring and its yellowish green summer hue.

166

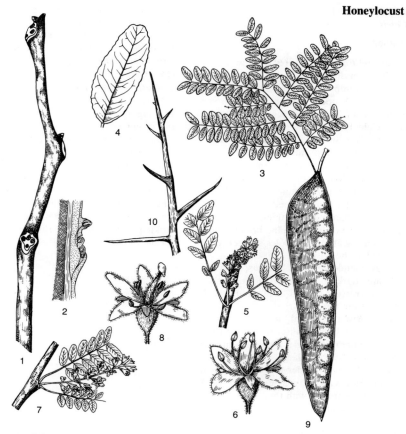

1. Winter twig, × 1.
2. Vertical section through lateral buds, enlarged.
3. Leaf, × ¼.
4. Leaflet, × 1.
5. Male flowering shoot, × ½.
6. Male flower, enlarged.
7. Female flowering shoot, × ½.
8. Female flower, enlarged.
9. Fruit, legume, × ¼.
10. Thorn from trunk, × ½.

Key Characters
- leaves pinnately or doubly pinnately compound
- bark with narrow ridges and dense clusters of single or many-branched thorns
- shoots armed with simple or branched thorns
- fruit pods long, twisted, aromatic, containing many seeds

167

FABACEAE (LEGUMINOSAE)
Cercis canadensis Linnaeus

Redbud

Size and Form. Small tree, 4–8 m high and 20–30 cm in diameter. Trunk divided near the ground into stout, spreading branches to form a broad, open, flat, or rounded crown. Michigan Big Tree: girth 1.6 m, diameter 50 cm, height 19 m, Wayne Co.

Bark. Thin, smooth, and gray on young stems; outer bark of mature trees reddish brown to black, furrowed, forming long, narrow, scaly ridges; inner bark reddish.

Leaves. Alternate, simple, blade 7–12 cm long and wide; heart-shaped or rounded; apex short, blunt; entire; thick; dark green above, paler beneath, turning bright yellow in autumn; glabrous; petioles slender, terete, enlarged at the base.

Twigs. Slender, zigzag, lustrous, brown, becoming dark or grayish brown to black; leaf scar crescent-shaped, somewhat raised, fringed at the top.

Winter Buds. Terminal bud absent; lateral buds 2–3 mm long, obtuse, somewhat flattened and appressed, glabrous, brownish to dark red; flower buds larger, stalked, rounded, borne on older twigs and branches.

Wood. Heavy, hard, coarse-grained, weak, dark reddish brown, with thin, lighter-colored sapwood.

Flowers. April-May, before or with the leaves, scattered along the branches; perfect; bilateral, about 1.2 cm long; borne on short, jointed pedicels in fascicles of 4–8; calyx campanulate, 5-toothed, dark red; petals 5, rose colored; stamens 10 in 2 rows. Insect-pollinated.

Fruit. Legume; June-July, persistent in winter; pods flat, short-stalked, 5–8 cm long, 1.2 cm wide, pointed at both ends, reddish brown, borne in small clusters along the branches; seeds 10–12, smooth, brownish, about 5 mm long.

Distribution. Rare in the southern tiers of counties to the valley of the Grand River on the west and the Raisin River on the east. Tree of widespread distribution south of Michigan, reaching its northernmost limit in the relatively mild and protected river valleys of southern Michigan.

Habitat. Characteristic understory tree of forests of stream borders and moist, fertile bottomlands. Associates include American elm, basswood, silver maple, red ash, red mulberry, northern hackberry.

Notes. Moderately shade-tolerant; slow-growing; relatively short-lived. Under full sun in summer leaf blades in upper crown often fold up nearly double (reduces amount of radiation received by leaf). Successfully transplanted only when very young. Grows well on many soils outside its native bottom-land habitat. Trees begin to flower freely when 4–5 years old. Highly prized and widely planted as an ornamental due to its striking beauty when flowering in early spring.

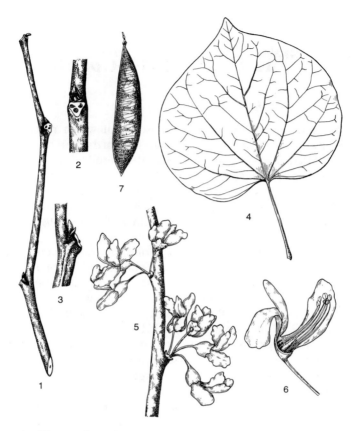

1. Winter twig, × 1.
2. Portion of twig, front view, enlarged.
3. Portion of twig, side view, enlarged.
4. Leaf, × ½.
5. Flowering twig, × 1.
6. Vertical section of flower, enlarged.
7. Fruit, legume, × ½.

Key Characters
- leaf blade heart-shaped or rounded; entire
- small tree with a flat or rounded crown
- fruit pods borne in small clusters along the branches; pods flat, pointed at both ends
- branches covered with rose-colored flowers in early spring

169

The Dogwoods—*Cornus*

The dogwoods are primarily shrubs, some of which reach small-tree size. Some 15 or more species occur in North America, and 7 are native to Michigan. One of these, the alternate-leaf dogwood, *Cornus alternifolia,* has its leaves arranged alternately; the others, in common with most of the members of the genus, have opposite leaf arrangement. The leaves are simple, with entire margins, and the lateral veins are parallel, extending along the margin well toward the apex of the leaves.

The flowering dogwood, *Cornus florida,* is a conspicuous feature of the landscape in May or early June when the blossoms occur. The flowers themselves are small, in dense clusters, surrounded by four large, petallike bracts, which commonly are mistaken for a corolla. The flowers are insect-pollinated. The fruit is a small drupe, with thin flesh enclosing a bony stone and seed. Dogwoods have a bitter, astringent bark. From early times the dogwoods have been planted around homes and in parks and places of recreation.

A foreign dogwood, which is a large shrub or small tree, 4–6 m high, is frequently planted in North America where it is quite hardy. A native of Europe and western Asia, it is called the Cornelian-cherry, *Cornus mas* L. It does not have the showy bracts of the flowering dogwood of North America. Its attractive features include yellowish flowers that appear in early spring before the leaves unfold. Individually these are small, but the umbellike clusters are borne in great profusion, clothing the plant with yellow. The leaf blades are 3–7 cm long, with 3–4 pairs of veins, and are more or less appressed-pubescent on both sides. The fruit is an oblong, scarlet drupe, about 1.2 cm long, ripe in summer, sweet and edible, taken by the birds before Labor Day. The twigs are appressed-hairy, greenish yellow, later turning brown. The lateral buds are very divergent, and the branchlets into which they develop are often short and nearly at right angles to the branch.

Summer Key to Species of *Cornus*

1. Leaves alternate, but crowded near the ends of the upswept shoots, appearing whorled; branches usually greenish or brownish; flowers not surrounded by large petallike bracts; fruit globular, blue, borne many in loose clusters .... *C. alternifolia,* p. 172
1. Leaves opposite; branches usually reddish or yellowish; flowers surrounded by large petallike bracts; fruit ovoid, scarlet, borne 3–6 in tight clusters ... *C. florida,* p. 174

Winter Key to Species of *Cornus*

1. Leaf scars alternate, but crowded near the ends of the upswept shoots, appearing whorled; buds light brown; branches usually greenish or brownish .... *C. alternifolia,* p. 172
1. Leaf scars opposite; buds greenish; branches usually reddish or yellowish .... *C. florida,* p. 174

CORNACEAE
Cornus alternifolia Linnaeus f.

Alternate-leaf Dogwood

Size and Form. Small tree, 4–8 m high and 5–15 cm in diameter. Trunk short, slender, straight; branches long, slender, upswept at the tips, arranged in irregular whorls, forming flat, horizontal tiers that give the tree a storied effect. Michigan Big Tree: girth 0.6 m, diameter 19 cm, height 12 m, St. Clair Co.

Bark. Thin, dark reddish brown, smooth, becoming shallowly fissured.

Leaves. Alternate, clustered at the ends of the shoots, shoots often so short that the clustered leaves appear to be opposite or whorled; simple, blades 7–12 cm long, 6–8 cm wide; oval or ovate, long-pointed, base wedge-shaped; entire, slightly undulate, or obscurely wavy-toothed; thin; dark green, nearly glabrous above, paler and covered with appressed hairs beneath, turning yellow and scarlet in autumn; veins parallel to the margin; petioles slender, grooved, hairy, with clasping bases, 2–5 cm long.

Twigs. Slender, greenish or reddish, becoming smooth, lustrous, dark green to dark purplish red; tips upswept; leaf scars crowded at tip.

Winter Buds. Vegetative buds small, acute, scales 2, light brown, valvate; flower buds spherical or vertically flattened.

Wood. Heavy, hard, close-grained, reddish brown, with thick, lighter-colored sapwood.

Flowers. May-June, after the leaves; perfect; borne on slender pedicels in many-flowered, irregular, open cymes from the season's shoots; calyx cup-shaped, obscurely 4-toothed, covered with fine, silky, white hairs; petals 4, cream colored; stamens 4; ovary 2-celled. Insect-pollinated.

Fruit. Drupe; October; globular, bluish black, 6–8 mm in diameter, borne in loose, red-stemmed clusters, flesh bitter.

Distribution. Occasional to locally common throughout the state.

Habitat. An understory species of mesic beech-maple forests (Lower Peninsula), mesic northern hardwood forests (Upper Peninsula), wet-mesic deciduous swamps and swamp borders, stream banks and floodplains, ravines and at bottoms of steep slopes. Requires shaded, cool, moist, fertile sites. Tolerates relatively high water tables and organic soils; not found on dry, drought-prone sites. Associates include blue-beech, spicebush, basswood, black ash, red maple, sugar maple, yellow birch, beech, red oak.

Notes. Shade-tolerant; slow-growing; relatively short-lived. Reproduces vegetatively by layering of branches; easily propagated. Shoots and leaves arranged to make the best use of low light conditions of the forest understory.

172

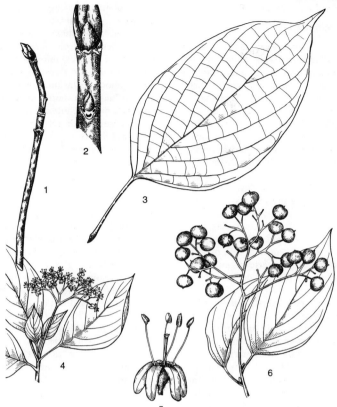

1. Winter twig, × 1.
2. Portion of twig, enlarged.
3. Leaf, × ¾.
4. Flowering shoot, × ½.
5. Flower, enlarged.
6. Fruiting shoot with drupes, × ½.

Key Characters

• leaves alternate, but crowded near the ends of the shoots, appearing whorled; blades long-pointed, entire, veins parallel to the margin
• small tree or shrub
• fruit a bluish black drupe

173

CORNACEAE
Cornus florida Linnaeus

Flowering Dogwood

Size and Form. Small tree, 5–10 m high and 15–30 cm in diameter. Trunk short, often crooked, dividing near the ground, forming a flat-topped crown of wide-spreading branches. Root system moderately deep. Michigan Big Tree: girth 1.4 m, diameter 44 cm, height 17 m, St. Joseph Co.

Bark. Thin, reddish brown or blackish; separating into quadrangular, blocky, plate-like scales and forming an alligator-hide pattern.

Leaves. Opposite, closely clustered at the ends of the twigs, simple, blades 7–12 cm long, 5–8 cm wide; ovate to elliptical; entire or obscurely wavy-toothed; thick and firm; bright green, covered with minute, appressed hairs above, pale and more or less pubescent beneath, turning bright scarlet in autumn; veins parallel to the margin; petioles short, grooved.

Twigs. Slender, pale green with whitish hairs, becoming red or yellowish green the first winter, later becoming light brown or reddish gray, glabrous.

Winter Buds. Terminal bud narrow-conical, acute, greenish to reddish, downy, with 1 pair of bud scales, valvate; lateral buds minute, appressed; flower buds stalked, spherical or vertically flattened, dome or pagoda-shaped, grayish.

Wood. Heavy, hard, strong, tough, close-grained, brownish, with thick, lighter-colored sapwood. Uses include shuttles, spools, mallet and golf club heads, bobbin pins.

Flowers. May or early June, with the leaves; perfect; greenish; in dense clusters surrounded by 4 very large white or pinkish, petallike bracts up to 5 cm long (often mistaken for a corolla), borne on short, stout peduncles; calyx 4-lobed, light green; petals 4, yellowish green; stamens 4, alternate with the petals; ovary 2-celled. Insect-pollinated.

Fruit. Drupe; October; ovoid, scarlet, borne in close clusters of 3–6; flesh bitter.

Distribution. Common in the southern half of the Lower Peninsula, north to Mason, Lake, and Saginaw Co. A species of south-erly distribution reaching its northern range limit in southern Michigan.

Habitat. A typical understory species of many forest communities; very wide site tolerances; dry-mesic oak forests to mesic beech-maple forests; intolerant of flooded sites and soils with a consistently high water table. Associates include oaks, sugar maple, beech, blue-beech, hop-hornbeam, white ash, black walnut, hickories, basswood.

Notes. Very shade-tolerant; very slow-growing; long-lived. Easily injured by fire, but sprouts vigorously from the root collar, stump, and rhizomes. Also reproduces vegetatively by layering of stems; easily propagated by layering the branches. Epicormic branches frequent on the stem. Sensitive to drought but tolerant of high and low temperatures. The leaves concentrate particularly high amounts of calcium which permits rapid decomposition; among the fastest decomposing leaves of any forest tree, thus rapidly releasing important mineral nutrients in the soil. Various clones have been propagated and are used ornamentally; among these are plants having red- or pink-flowering bracts, pendulous branches, and yellow fruits. A solution made from the bark and flowers was used in the past to treat jaundice, cholera, and malaria and as a substitute for quinine in the Civil War.

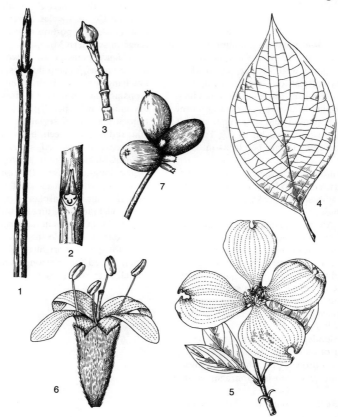

1. Winter twig, with leaf buds, × 1.
2. Portion of twig, enlarged.
3. Winter twig, with flower bud, × 1.
4. Leaf, × ½.
5. Flowering shoot, × ½.
6. Flower, enlarged.
7. Fruit, drupes, × 1.

Key Characters
- leaves opposite; blades entire; veins parallel to the margin
- bark blocky, resembling alligator hide
- flower buds dome or pagoda-shaped
- fruit a scarlet drupe

NYSSACEAE
Nyssa sylvatica Marshall

Blackgum

Size and Form. Small to medium-sized tree, 10–15 m high and 20–40 cm in diameter. Trunk extending well into the crown which is conic or cylindrical, often flat-topped; formed by crooked, horizontally spreading, often drooping branches that turn up at the ends. Roots shallow and spreading; sprouts develop from roots. Michigan Big Tree: girth 3.6 m, diameter 113 cm, height 24 m, Cass Co.

Bark. Thick, dark gray to reddish brown, deeply furrowed into long, irregular blocky ridges or with short, blocky plates resembling alligator hide.

Leaves. Alternate, simple, 5–12 cm long, half as wide; oblong-obovate to oval; entire, or sometimes wavy-margined especially near the tip; thick and firm; very lustrous, glabrous, and dark green above, pale and often hairy beneath, turning bright scarlet, deep red, or sometimes purplish in autumn on the upper surface only; veins divergent not arcuate; petioles short.

Twigs. Slender, greenish or light brown, smooth or often downy, becoming smooth, dark reddish brown; pith white, continuous, but with firmer greenish diaphragms at intervals.

Winter Buds. Terminal bud 3–6 mm long, ovoid, obtuse, often hairy, dark red; lateral buds smaller, widely divergent.

Wood. Heavy, soft, strong, very tough, difficult to split, not durable in contact with the soil, pale yellow, with thick, whitish sapwood. Uses include furniture, veneer, plywood, tool handles, shipping crates, boxes.

Flowers. May-June, with the leaves; greenish; borne on slender, downy peduncles; male flowers slender-pedicelled, in many-flowered heads; calyx cup-shaped, 5-toothed; petals 5; stamens 5–10; female flowers sessile, in several-flowered clusters; stigma stout, terete, recurved. Trees polygamo-dioecious. Insect-pollinated.

Fruit. Drupe; October; borne at end of a long peduncle in clusters of 1–3, fleshy, ovoid, bluish black, 0.8–1.2 cm long, sour.

Distribution. Locally frequent in the southern half of the Lower Peninsula, north to Midland Co. A species of very wide distribution, reaching a portion of its northernmost range in southern Michigan.

Habitat. Characteristic of wet-mesic beech-maple forests, swamp borders, and generally low-lying sites with high water tables. In the Appalachian Mountains it grows on relatively dry mountain slopes. Tolerates upland conditions if planted. Associates include American elm, red maple, beech, basswood, pin oak, alternate-leaf dogwood, spicebush.

Notes. Shade-tolerant; slow-growing; moderately long-lived. Sprouts from the root collar and the roots; forms small clones. Wild trees difficult to transplant. Other common names include black tupelo, sourgum, and pepperidge. Of considerable ornamental value due to its wide site tolerance, very lustrous foliage, and bright red foliage in autumn. Noted for its strong trunk and its horizontal, narrow branches.

176

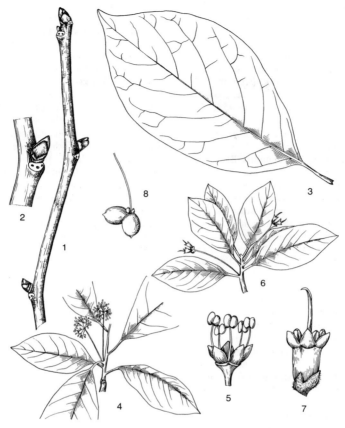

1. Winter twig, × 1.
2. Portion of twig, enlarged.
3. Leaf, × ¾.
4. Male flowering shoot, × ½.
5. Male flower, enlarged.
6. Female flowering shoot, × ½.
7. Female flower, enlarged.
8. Fruit, drupes, × ½.

Key Characters

- leaves very lustrous, typically obovate, entire; bright scarlet in autumn
- strongly excurrent habit with horizontal, narrow branches
- bark thick, blocky, often like alligator hide on mature trees
- lowland sites, often flat topography and a high water table

SIMARUBACEAE
Ailanthus altissima (Miller) Swingle

Ailanthus Tree-of-heaven

Size and Form. Medium-sized tree, 12–18 m high and 60–120 cm in diameter. Trunk often crooked and sometimes dividing 2–3 m above the ground; branches stout, crooked, spreading, forming an open, very wide crown, even on small trees. Michigan Big Tree: girth 3.9 m, diameter 125 cm, height 23 m, St. Clair Co.

Bark. Thin, dark gray, shallow fissures on old trunks appearing as pale lines.

Leaves. Alternate, pinnately compound, 30–90 cm long. Leaflets 11–41, 5–15 cm long, about ⅓ as wide; ovate-lanceolate; entire with the exception of 2 or more coarse, gland-tipped (undersurface) teeth at the base; dark green above, paler beneath, turning a clear yellow in autumn or falling without change; glabrous; odor disagreeable. Petiole smooth, terete, swollen at base. Leaves appear late in spring and leaflets drop quickly at the first hard frost.

Twigs. Very stout, yellowish to reddish brown, downy to smooth; leaf scars very large with 9 or more bundle scars in a U-shaped pattern.

Winter Buds. Terminal bud absent; lateral buds about 3 mm long, subglobose, brownish, downy.

Wood. Soft, weak, coarse- and open-grained, pale yellow, satiny, with thick, lighter-colored sapwood.

Flowers. June, when the leaves are full grown; small, yellowish green; borne in upright panicles, 15–30 cm or more long; calyx 5-lobed; petals 5, greenish, hairy, stamens 10; ovary 3–5 parted; male flowers ill-scented, female flowers almost free from odor. Trees polygamodioecious. Insect-pollinated.

Fruit. Samara; October; large, 4–5 cm long, 1-celled, 1-seeded, seed wing spirally twisted, reddish or yellowish green turning pale brown at maturity, borne in crowded clusters.

Distribution. Native in China; planted and naturalized in the United States; formerly planted widely in towns and cities of southern Michigan.

Habitat. Urban environments and warm microsites; becomes established near houses and other structures that provide warmth from reradiation; rarely colonizing natural habitats; grows in virtually all upland soils.

Notes. Shade-intolerant; very fast-growing; short-lived. Hardy in the southern half of the Lower Peninsula. Sprouts vigorously from roots and stumps; difficult to eliminate once established. If cut at the base, sprout growth may reach 2–3 m in one growing season, providing "instant shade." Generally free from insect and disease pests; resistant to city smoke and pollutants. Roots may clog drains, buckle sidewalks and foundations; not recommended for lawn or ornamental planting but may be useful where quick shade is needed and drawbacks can be tolerated. Originally introduced to provide food for silkworms as it had in China.

178

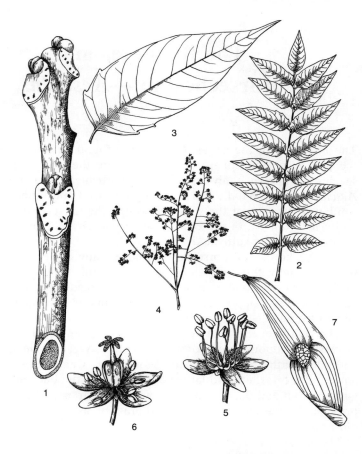

1. Winter twig, × 1.
2. Leaf, × ⅛.
3. Leaflet, × ½.
4. Male inflorescence, × ¼.

5. Male flower, enlarged.
6. Female flower, enlarged.
7. Fruit, samara, × 1.

Key Characters

- leaves very large, pinnately compound; leaflets with gland-tipped teeth at the base on undersurface
- twigs very stout
- bark smooth, dark gray with pale fissure lines
- crown very wide-spreading, branchy

179

The Buckeyes and Horsechestnut—*Aesculus*

The members of the genus *Aesculus* are found on most continents in the Northern Hemisphere but nowhere are they abundant. Some 13 species are known. Only one is native to Michigan, the Ohio Buckeye, *Aesculus glabra* Willd., and it is very localized and found only in the southernmost part of the state. However, the horsechestnut, *Aesculus hippocastanum* L., of the Balkan peninsula, Greece, and southeastern Europe, is widely cultivated.

The buckeyes and horsechestnut have many distinctive characteristics—especially the fruit and leaves. The fruit consists of a leathery capsule enclosing one or more large brown seeds. The leaves are also distinctive, being opposite and palmately compound with large, pinnately-veined leaflets.

The yellow buckeye, *Aesculus octandra* Marsh., is a large forest tree of mesic deciduous forests of southern Ohio, West Virginia, Kentucky, and the southern Appalachian Mountains. Characteristically it has leaves with 5 leaflets and large yellow flowers; the buds are ovoid, not gummy, dull and dusty orange brown in appearance; the capsule is not prickly; and the bark is smooth and gray, breaking into large plates on old trees.

The striking red horsechestnut, *Aesculus* ×*carnea* Hayne, is a hybrid between the European horsechestnut and the red buckeye, a small tree or shrub of the southern United States, *Aesculus pavia* L. The leaflets are usually 5, and the flowers are some shade of red. The capsule has small prickles, and the winter buds are resinous-sticky. It is occasionally planted as an ornamental in North America but is much more common in English and European gardens, streets, and parks.

Summer Key to Species of *Aesculus*

1. Leaflets usually 5; foliage ill-smelling when bruised; bark broken into thick plates; fruit 3–4 cm in diameter .... *A. glabra*, p. 182
1. Leaflets usually 7–9; foliage not ill-smelling when bruised; bark broken into thin plates; fruit about 5 cm in diameter .... *A. hippocastanum*, p. 184

180

Winter Key to Species of *Aesculus*

1. Terminal bud 1.5–1.8 cm long; bud scales covered with a glaucous bloom, not conspicuously resinous; bark broken into thick plates; fruit 2–3 cm in diameter .... *A. glabra*, p. 182
1. Terminal bud 2–4 cm long; bud scales conspicuously sticky-resinous, glistening; bark broken into thin plates; fruit about 5 cm in diameter .... *A. hippocastanum*, p. 184

HIPPOCASTANACEAE
Aesculus glabra Willdenow

Ohio Buckeye

Size and Form. Small to medium-sized tree, 8–12 m high and 15–30 cm in diameter. Slender, spreading branches forming a broad, rounded crown. Michigan Big Tree: girth 2.3 m, diameter 88 cm, height 21 m, Sanilac Co.

Bark. Thin, relatively smooth to scaly, yellowish brown; old trunks dark brown, densely furrowed, and broken into short, flat ridges or thick plates; ill-smelling when bruised; reported to be poisonous.

Leaves. Opposite, palmately compound. Leaflets usually 5, rarely 7, blades 7–15 cm long, 3–6 cm wide; oblanceolate, gradually narrowed to the entire base; irregularly and finely serrate; yellowish green above, paler beneath, turning yellow in autumn; glabrous. Petioles 10–15 cm long, slender, enlarged at the base; foliage ill-smelling when bruised. Leaves appear early in the spring.

Twigs. Stout, smooth, reddish brown, becoming ashy gray.

Winter Buds. Terminal buds 1.5–1.8 cm long, acute, resinous, brownish, covered with a glaucous bloom; inner scales yellowish green, becoming 3–5 cm long in spring and remaining until the leaves are nearly half-grown.

Wood. Light, soft, close-grained, weak, whitish, with thin, light brown sapwood. Uses include boxes, crates, woodenware, artificial limbs, furniture.

Flowers. April-May, after the leaves; medium-sized, yellowish green, numerous; in terminal panicles, 12–15 cm long and 5–7 cm wide, more or less downy; lateral branches 4–6-flowered; calyx campanulate, 5-lobed; petals 4, pale yellow, hairy, clawed; stamens 7, protruding, with long filaments, hairy below. Insect-pollinated. Trees polygamomonoecious.

Fruit. Capsule; October; thick, leathery, prickly, rusty-colored, 2–3 cm in diameter, containing a single (rarely 2–3) large, smooth, lustrous, brown seed, marked by a large, pale, circular scar, not edible, reported to be poisonous and containing a narcotic alkaloid.

Distribution. Very rare in the southernmost counties of the Lower Peninsula. A midwestern species reaching the northernmost limit of its range in southern Michigan.

Habitat. Scattered in deciduous forests on mesic and wet-mesic sites—river floodplains, bottomlands, stream banks. Associates include American elm, sugar maple, beech, black walnut, northern hackberry, honeylocust, Kentucky coffeetree, red mulberry.

Notes. Moderately shade-tolerant; moderately fast-growing; moderately long-lived. Slow-growing in dry soils. Relatively free from insect and disease pests. Although the seeds are thought to be poisonous to livestock they are a food of the fox squirrel. An old superstition is that carrying a buckeye in one's pocket wards off rheumatism. The flowers are attractive to ruby-throated hummingbirds. State tree of Ohio.

182

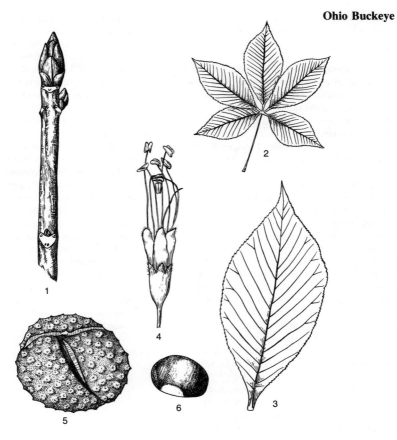

1. Winter twig, × 1.
2. Leaf, × ⅙.
3. Leaflet, × ½.
4. Flower, × 2.
5. Fruit, capsule, × ½.
6. Seed, × ½.

Key Characters
- leaves palmately compound, 5 leaflets
- winter buds resinous, brown
- fruit a leathery capsule containing a large, lustrous, brown seed

183

HIPPOCASTANACEAE
Aesculus hippocastanum Linnaeus

Horsechestnut

Size and Form. Medium-sized tree, 10–18 m high and 30–60 cm in diameter. Regularly occurring branches ascend from the trunk at first, gradually bend downward as they lengthen, and end in coarse, upturning sprays that form a broad, dome-shaped or conical crown. Michigan Big Tree: girth 4.6 m, diameter 147 cm, height 22 m, Washtenaw Co.

Bark. Moderately thick, dark brown and broken into thin, irregular plates by shallow fissures; rich in tannin, bitter.

Leaves. Opposite, palmately compound. Leaflets usually 7–9, rarely 5, blade 12–18 cm long, 3–6 cm wide; obovate, wedge-shaped at the base; irregularly and bluntly serrate; thick; rough, glabrous, dark green above, paler beneath, turning rusty yellow in autumn, sometimes drying out and turning brown at the edges; glabrous. Petioles long, grooved, swollen at the base.

Twigs. Very stout, smooth, reddish brown, with large, white lenticels; leaf scar large, like an inverted horseshoe, the bundle scars appearing as "nail holes."

Winter Buds. Terminal buds large, 2–4 cm long, acute, purplish brown, covered with glistening, resinous gum; inner scales yellowish, becoming 4–5 cm long in spring, remaining until the leaves are nearly half-grown.

Wood. Light, soft, close-grained, weak, whitish, with thin, light brown sapwood. Easily worked; uses in Europe include food containers, kitchen utensils, carvings, turned objects.

Flowers. June, after the leaves; large, whitish, numerous; in showy, upright, terminal panicles, 20–30 cm long, 10–20 cm wide; lateral branches jointed, 4–6-flowered; calyx campanulate, 5-lobed; petals 5, white, spotted with yellow and red, clawed; stamens 7, protruding, threadlike, longer than the petals. Insect-pollinated.

Fruit. Capsule; October; leathery, globular, about 5 cm in diameter, roughened with short, flexible prickles, containing 1–3 large, smooth, lustrous, mahogany brown seeds, each marked by a large, pale circular area; bitter, not edible, potentially poisonous.

Distribution. A native in the Balkan peninsula, Greece, southeastern Europe, and the Himalayan area of Asia. Introduced into England in 1616 and widely cultivated in European parks, gardens, and along streets. Formerly cultivated widely in North America; planted mainly in the Lower Peninsula; frequent in southern Michigan.

Habitat. Grows on a variety of soils, preferably in warm and protected sites.

Notes. Moderately shade-tolerant; moderately fast-growing; moderately long-lived. Showy flowers are abundant every year. Relatively free from insect and disease pests. Needs much space as an ornamental tree because of its large, wide-spreading crown. Heavy seed crops nearly every year make it undesirable for street and lawn planting. Its hybrid, the red horsechestnut (*A. ×carnea* Hayne), is sometimes planted as an ornamental because of its red flowers. Horsechestnut should not be mistaken for true chestnut, see p. 258.

184

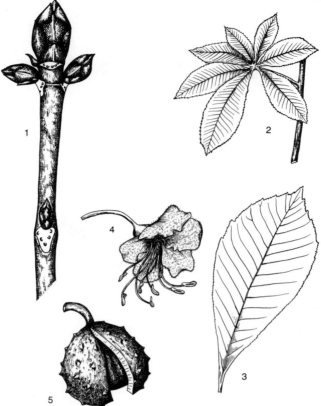

1. Winter twig, × ¾.
2. Leaf, × ⅙.
3. Leaflet, × ½.
4. Flower, × 1.
5. Fruit, capsule, × ½.

Key Characters
- leaves opposite, palmately compound; leaflets 7–9, large
- winter buds large, highly resinous, purplish brown
- fruit a leathery capsule with flexible prickles, enclosing 1–3 large, mahogany brown seeds
- large, showy clusters of white flowers in late spring

185

The Maples—*Acer*

The maple family is large, including 200 or more species. Maples are widely distributed over the Northern Hemisphere, with only one species extending south of the equator in Java. Of the 13 maples found in North America, 7 are native to Michigan, and 5 of these are medium- or large-sized trees; the others are small or shrublike. The leaves of maples are opposite, and all are simple except those of the boxelder, which are compound. The time at which the flowers bloom aids in identifying the different species, and the maples as a group are distinguished easily from all other trees by their peculiar winged fruit or "key," termed the *samara*, which is dispersed chiefly by the wind. The maples are primarily wind-pollinated although some insects are also pollinators.

Maples typically occupy mesic sites, cool, moist habitats usually well supplied with nutrients. They are not usually found on extremely hot and dry sites. Maples are very sensitive to fire injury because of relatively thin bark near the base of the trunk and shallow roots; they are typically replaced by more fire-tolerant species. With one exception, the boxelder, native maples thrive in shaded understories, often for many years. The sugar and black maples tolerate heavy shade and in turn come to control their environments by casting heavy shade. The boxelder is an aggressive pioneer species, requiring full sunlight in youth to compete in the moist, fertile river floodplains and bottomlands.

Several introduced maples are planted in Michigan, particularly the Norway maple which is described below. The sycamore maple, *Acer pseudoplatanus* L., was formerly cultivated locally but because of its susceptibility to borer injury and lesser adaptability to climatic and soil conditions it has not proved as valuable as Norway maple for a street tree. Sycamore maple has dark, leathery, 5-lobed leaves, the lobes of which are coarsely and irregularly blunt-serrate; the winter buds are bright green. It was named "sycamore" because when it was first introduced into England it was thought to be the "sycomorus" or "fig-mulberry" mentioned in the Bible.

The Amur maple, *Acer ginnala* Maxim., is a small, shrubby tree which is good for grouping or for planting singly on small lawns. It is hardy and attains a height of 5–6 meters. The 3-lobed leaves are small,

3–10 cm long, and have the terminal lobe much elongated, the margin is doubly serrate to the petiole, and they are glabrous on both sides. In autumn, the leaves turn bright red before they fall. The yellowish white flowers are fragrant, followed by paniculate clusters of paired samaras with nearly parallel wings.

The Japanese maple, *Acer palmatum* Thunb., a small broad-crowned tree or shrub, is somewhat less hardy. The leaves are 5–10 cm wide, deeply 5–9-lobed or -parted, the lobes narrow, acuminate at the apex, and doubly serrate at the margin. The flowers are small, purple, in erect corymbs. The paired samaras are less than 2 cm long with widely spreading wings. There are numerous varieties, exhibiting every possible gradation in shape, dissection, and coloration of the leaves. The leaves of the green forms turn bright red in autumn. Introduced from Korea and Japan, it is one of the most beautiful of our foreign trees.

Summer Key to Species of *Acer*

1. Leaves pinnately compound; twigs usually with whitish bloom .. *A. negundo,* p. 204
1. Leaves simple, palmately lobed; twigs without whitish bloom.
  2. Leaf sinuses acute at the base.
    3. Leaf lobes long and narrow, the sides of the terminal lobe diverging; inner bark of twigs rank-smelling . . . . *A. saccharinum,* p. 196
    3. Leaf lobes short and broad, the sides of the terminal lobe parallel or converging; inner bark of twigs not rank-smelling.
      4. Leaves distinctly white-downy beneath; twigs appressed-hairy, at least near the tip; buds more or less tomentose, short-stalked; fruit hanging in pendulous racemes, persistent on the tree until autumn; seed portion indented on one side; usually a shrub or bushy tree . . . . *A. spicatum,* p. 198
      4. Leaves not distinctly white-downy beneath; twigs glabrous; buds reddish, not stalked; fruit hanging in fascicles, falling in spring or early summer; seed portion not indented on one side; medium-sized tree .... *A. rubrum,* p. 194
  2. Leaf sinuses rounded at the base.
    5. Lower sides of leaves and petioles distinctly downy, the lobes undulate or entire; blades drooping at the sides, petiole base with stipules ..... *A. nigrum,* p. 190
    5. Lower sides of leaves and petioles essentially glabrous, the lobes serrate or coarsely toothed; blades not drooping at the sides; petiole base without stipules.
      6. Leaf blades large, finely and abundantly doubly-serrate; bark vertically white-striped; a small, bushy tree or shrub . . . . *A. pensylvanicum,* p. 200
      6. Leaf blades medium-sized, coarsely and sparsely toothed or notched; bark not vertically white-striped; medium-sized to large trees.
        7. Twigs stout; petioles exuding a milky sap when cut; wings of samara diverging by nearly 180°; bark of trunk closely fissured, not scaly . . . . *A. platanoides,* p. 202
        7. Twigs slender; petioles not exuding a milky sap when cut; wings of samara only somewhat divergent; bark of trunk deeply furrowed, often cleaving or curling in long, thick plates . . . . *A. saccharum,* p. 192

Winter Key to Species of *Acer*

1. Bud scales 2, valvate.
   2. Buds more or less tomentose, slender, 3–5 mm long, short-stalked; bark not white-striped .... *A. spicatum*, p. 198
   2. Buds glabrous, thick, 0.8–1 cm long, conspicuously stalked; bark vertically white-striped .... *A. pensylvanicum*, p. 200
1. Bud scales more than 2.
   3. Buds white-woolly; twigs green, usually with a whitish bloom; opposite leaf scars meeting; fruit often persistent until spring .... *A. negundo*, p. 204
   3. Buds not white-woolly; twigs not green, without whitish bloom; opposite leaf scars not meeting; fruit not persistent in winter.
      4. Terminal buds usually 6 mm or more long; sap milky ... *A. platanoides*, p. 202
      4. Terminal buds usually less than 6 mm; sap clear.
         5. Buds reddish or greenish; twigs red.
            6. Twigs bright chestnut brown, inner bark rank-smelling; tip of outer bud scales often apiculate; tips of branches curving upward .... *A. saccharinum*, p. 196
            6. Twigs red and lustrous, inner bark not rank-smelling; tip of outer bud scales rounded; tips of branches not conspicuously curving upward .... *A. rubrum*, p. 194
         5. Buds brownish; twigs brownish or grayish.
            7. Buds glabrous, or somewhat pubescent at the apex only; twigs glossy buff or reddish brown, glabrous .... *A. saccharum*, p. 192
            7. Buds hoary-pubescent; twigs dull straw-colored, usually hairy .... *A. nigrum*, p. 190

189

ACERACEAE
Acer nigrum Michaux f.

Black Maple

Size and Form. Large tree, 18–24 m high and 50–100 cm in diameter. Branches stout, forming a broad, rounded, symmetrical crown. Michigan Big Tree: girth 4.9 m, diameter 156 cm, height 35 m, Allegan Co.

Bark. Becoming moderately thick, deeply furrowed into long, narrow, blackish ridges; often appearing corrugated.

Leaves. Opposite, simple, concave, the sides of the larger leaves drooping, blades 10–16 cm across, usually wider than long; usually 3-lobed, occasionally 5-lobed, with the two additional lower lobes being small, often reduced to a mere curve in the outline, the pointed lobes undulate or entire and narrowed from the broad, shallow sinuses; thick and firm; glabrous, dark green above, yellowish green beneath, with dense, velvety hairs, turning yellow to brownish yellow in autumn; petioles stout, usually pendent, tomentose, 8–12 cm long, with stipules, these sometimes leafy.

Twigs. Moderately stout, usually hairy, dull straw-colored, smooth, with somewhat prominent lenticels.

Winter Buds. Small, ovoid, acute, with dark reddish brown, acute scales, hoary-pubescent on the outer surface.

Wood. Hard, heavy, strong, close-grained, creamy white, with thin, lighter-colored sapwood. Uses the same as sugar maple.

Flowers. April-May, with the leaves; in nearly sessile corymbs; about 6 mm long, yellow; on slender hairy pedicels, 5–7 cm long; calyx campanulate, pilose, 5-lobed; corolla 0; stamens 7–8; ovary hairy. Trees polygamous.

Fruit. Samara; October; glabrous, samaras paired, clustered on drooping pedicels; wings set wide apart, but only slightly diverging.

Distribution. Occasional in the southern third of the Lower Peninsula, north to Midland Co.

Habitat. Characteristic of river floodplains, bottomlands, terraces, with moist, fertile soil; occasionally found on upland soils. Associates include sugar and silver maples, bur, red, and white oaks, basswood, red ash, elms.

Notes. Highly shade-tolerant; slow-growing; long-lived. Variable in foliage and pubescence so that there is a continuum of forms intergrading with sugar maple, from which many botanists do not consider black maple distinct. Hybridization with sugar maple is likely. Reported to produce more and a better grade of maple syrup than sugar maple.

190

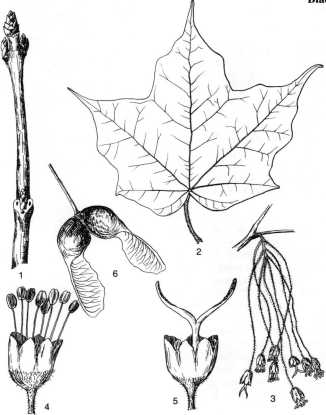

1. Winter twig, × 2.
2. Leaf, × ½.
3. Flowering twig, × ½.
4. Male flower, enlarged.
5. Female flower, enlarged.
6. Fruit, samaras, × 1.

Key Characters

• leaves opposite; leaf blades large, with 3 lobes, the side lobes drooping, the sinuses broad and rounded
• pubescent on the leaf undersurface and petiole
• stipules at the base of the petiole
• bark black, corrugated in long, narrow ridges

Distinguished from sugar maple by drooping leaves with 3 major lobes; pubescent on leaf undersurface and petiole; stipules at the base of the petiole; bark darker and more corrugated.

191

ACERACEAE
Acer saccharum Marshall

Sugar Maple   Hard Maple

Size and Form. Large tree, 18–30 m high and 60–120 cm in diameter. Open-grown trees forming stout, upright branches near the ground; in forest stands the trunk relatively straight and free of branches for many meters, supporting a broad, round-topped crown. Roots relatively shallow. Michigan Big Tree: girth 5.5 m, diameter 175 cm, height 38 m, Washtenaw Co.

Bark. Dark gray, deeply furrowed, often cleaving or curling outward at one edge in long, thick, irregular plates; often somewhat scaly.

Leaves. Opposite, simple, blades 7–13 cm long and wide; usually 5-lobed (sometimes 3-lobed), the lobes sparingly wavy-toothed, the sinuses broad and rounded at the base, the end lobe squarish with nearly parallel, entire sides; thin and firm; opaque, dark yellowish green above, lighter beneath, turning yellow, orange, or red in autumn; glabrous; petioles long, slender, glabrous.

Twigs. Smooth, lustrous, glossy buff or reddish brown, becoming gray, glabrous.

Winter Buds. Terminal buds small, about 5 mm long, acute, conical, reddish brown, many scales, glabrous or somewhat pubescent toward the apex; lateral buds smaller, appressed.

Wood. Heavy, hard, strong, close-grained, tough, durable, light brown, with thin, lighter-colored sapwood. Uses include furniture, flooring, cabinet work, veneer, plywood, tool handles, musical instruments.

Flowers. April-May, with the leaves; on threadlike, hairy pedicels in nearly sessile corymbs; greenish yellow; calyx pilose, campanulate, 5-lobed; corolla 0; stamens 7–8; ovary hairy. Trees monoecious or dioecious.

Fruit. Samara; September-October, germinating the following spring; paired samaras, glabrous, with parallel or slightly divergent wings, 2–3 cm long.

Distribution. Common to abundant throughout the state.

Habitat. Characteristic of mesic deciduous forests with moist, well to somewhat poorly drained, fertile soils of nearly all textures. Associates include beech, yellow birch, basswood, red maple, hemlock, red and white oaks, white ash, black cherry, American elm, black walnut, bitternut hickory.

Notes. Highly shade-tolerant; slow-growing; long-lived. Often the major dominant of beech-maple forest communities. Produces large seed crops at 2–5-year intervals; sprouts from stump when tree is cut. Principal source of maple sugar; trees are tapped very early in the spring. A widely planted and important ornamental species for its shade and extremely showy fall coloration.

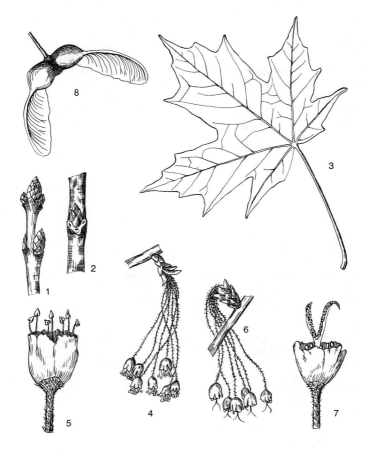

1. Winter twig, × 2.
2. Portion of twig, enlarged.
3. Leaf, × ½.
4. Male flowering twig, × ½.

5. Male flower, enlarged.
6. Female flowering twig, × ½.
7. Female flower, enlarged.
8. Fruit, samaras, × 1.

Key Characters

• leaves opposite, 5-lobed, the sinuses broad and rounded at the bases; end lobe almost square with entire, nearly parallel sides
• terminal bud sharp-pointed, conical
• fruit a samara, borne in pairs on a long pedicel; wings parallel or slightly diverging

Distinguished from black maple by the smaller, nondrooping leaves with 5 rather than 3 lobes; petiole base lacking stipules; lack of pubescence on the leaf undersurface and petiole.

193

ACERACEAE
Acer rubrum Linnaeus

Red Maple

Size and Form. Medium-sized tree, 15–21 m high and 50–80 cm in diameter. Trunk often free of branches for half its length in forest stands; upright branches form a low, dense, rather narrow, rounded crown. Root system shallow and spreading. Michigan Big Tree: girth 5.0 m, diameter 160 cm, height 39 m, Macomb Co.

Bark. Young trunks thin, smooth, light gray, often with horizontal lines on the east side of the stem; old trunks dark gray, rough-ridged, separating into long, narrow platelike scales.

Leaves. Opposite, simple, blades 7–12 cm long, equally wide; 3–5-lobed (usually 3-lobed) by broad, shallow, acute sinuses, the lobes irregularly doubly serrate or toothed, sides of end lobe usually convergent, serrate; glabrous green above, whitish and generally glabrous beneath, turning bright scarlet, orange, or yellow in autumn; petioles long, slender.

Twigs. Bright red, lustrous, becoming smooth and light gray on the branches; inner bark not rank-smelling; pith pink.

Winter Buds. Dark red, blunt; terminal bud 3–4 mm long, bud scales rounded at the apex; flower buds clustered on side shoots.

Wood. Heavy, close-grained, not strong, light brown, with thick, lighter-colored sapwood. Uses include boxes, crates, railroad ties, veneer, furniture, pulpwood, plywood, woodenware.

Flowers. March-May, conspicuous before the leaves; in compact, few-flowered fascicles on shoots of the previous year, the female red, the male orange; sepals 4–5; petals 4–5; stamens 5–8; ovary smooth. Trees polygamo-monoecious or dioecious.

Fruit. Samara; May-June, germinating soon after reaching the ground; samaras small, paired, on drooping pedicels, 5–10 cm long; wings 2–3 cm long, diverging slightly.

Distribution. Common throughout the state.

Habitat. Occupies a very broad range of site conditions. In the southern half of the Lower Peninsula, characteristic of lowland, very poorly drained deciduous swamps (associated with black ash, American elm, yellow birch) and colonizes adjacent disturbed, upland slopes (associated with oaks, hickories, white ash, black cherry, maples). In the northern half of the Lower Peninsula common in lowland areas but also occurs on upland sites such as mesic beech-maple forests and dry-mesic pine-oak forests. In the Upper Peninsula it occurs in the mesic northern hardwood forests (associated with sugar maple, beech, yellow birch, basswood, American elm, hemlock), becoming more abundant as moisture increases; very common in conifer and conifer-hardwood swamps (associated with white and black spruces, balsam fir, yellow birch, black ash, speckled alder). Not typical of stream banks and river floodplains.

Notes. Shade-tolerant; relatively fast-growing; moderately long-lived. A preferred deer food and subject to considerable damage if deer populations are high. Sprouts vigorously after injury by fire, cutting, or browsing. Among the first trees to flower in the spring. An aggressive colonizer of upland sites from its primary habitats in swampy, lowland sites; its abundance has been markedly increased due to disturbance of pre-settlement forests by humans and by subsequent fire exclusion. Often used in ornamental plantings because of its red twigs, buds, and fruits, and its brilliant fall colors.

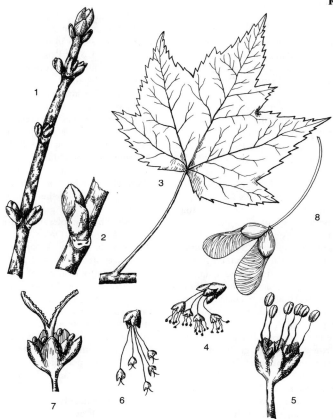

1. Winter twig, × 1.
2. Portion of twig, enlarged.
3. Leaf, × 1.
4. Male flowers, × 1.

5. Male flower, enlarged.
6. Female flowers, × 1.
7. Female flower, enlarged.
8. Fruit, samaras, × 1.

Key Characters

• leaves opposite; blades with 3 main lobes with broad, acute sinuses; sides of middle lobe usually convergent, with serrate margins
• twigs red, lustrous
• buds small, blunt, red; flower buds clustered on side shoots
• samaras small, wings slightly divergent; disseminated in late spring
• frequent in lowland, swampy habitats and adjacent uplands

Distinguished from silver maple by leaves with broader sinuses not approaching the midrib, not conspicuously silvery white on undersurface; sides of middle lobe convergent, not divergent; samaras smaller, wings not as divergent; twigs lustrous red; habitat of poorly drained swamps and adjacent uplands, not as frequent along streams.

195

ACERACEAE
Acer saccharinum Linnaeus

Silver Maple

Size and Form. Large tree, 18–24 m high and 60–120 cm in diameter. Trunk sometimes separating near the ground into 3–4 upright stems which are branch free for a considerable distance; the long, slender branches bend downward, but with their tips ascending in a graceful curve. Crown broad, especially in the upper portion. Roots typically very shallow. Michigan Big Tree: girth 7.0 m, diameter 223 cm, height 38 m, Oakland Co.

Bark. Young trunks thin, gray, smooth; old trunks dark gray, more or less furrowed, separating into thin, loose, scaly plates that are free at both sides and often flake off.

Leaves. Opposite, simple, blades 8–15 cm long, about as wide; usually 5-lobed, with narrow, acute sinuses which extend nearly to the midrib, the lobes often lobed again, sides of the lobes diverging, sharply toothed; light green above, silvery white beneath, turning pale yellow in autumn; glabrous; petioles long, slender, drooping.

Twigs. Slender, smooth, bright chestnut brown, lustrous, inner bark giving off a markedly rank, fetid odor when broken or bruised; pith pink.

Winter Buds. Blunt, dark red; the terminal bud about 6 mm long, smooth, lustrous, with bud scales often apiculate at the apex; flower buds clustered on side shoots.

Wood. Hard, strong, close-grained, rather brittle, perishable, pale brown, with thick, lighter-colored sapwood. Uses include furniture, veneer, pulpwood, woodenware, boxes, crates.

Flowers. March-April, before the leaves; small, yellowish green; in crowded, sessile umbels; calyx 5-lobed (sometimes each lobe again divided); corolla 0; stamens 3–7; ovary hairy. Trees polygamomonoecious or dioecious.

Fruit. Samara; May, germinating soon after it reaches the ground; samaras paired, large, 3–6 cm long, glabrous; wings widely diverging, forming nearly a 90° angle; one samara often aborted and only one seed maturing.

Distribution. Common in the southern half of the Lower Peninsula, north to Clare Co; rare or occasional in the northern Lower Peninsula and Upper Peninsula. A southern species reaching one segment of its northern limit in Michigan.

Habitat. Characteristic of alluvial floodplains of large rivers and moist bottomland sites of small rivers and creeks; occasionally found in deciduous swamps where adequate water movement occurs; tolerates periodic flooding and silting during the dormant season. Associates include eastern cottonwood, black willow, American elm, red ash, boxelder, sycamore, northern hackberry, red maple.

Notes. Shade-intolerant; fast-growing; moderately long-lived. One of the first trees to flower in the spring. A popular shade tree because of its foliage, fast growth, and adaptability to a variety of soils, including clay. However, the branches are rather brittle and break off in storms, and the roots often clog drains and sewers so its use as a street tree has diminished. Sprouts vigorously after cutting or fire. Shade leaves of the lower crown are less dissected than the sun leaves of the upper crown, and such shade leaves may be mistaken for leaves of red maple.

Trees with deeply cut leaves are often planted, such as cut-leaved maple and Wier's maple. The name *A. saccharinum* 'Laciniatum' (or 'Wieri') is generally applied to these cut-leaved forms. Their leaves are variable, but are deeply cleft, with the lobes much-dissected. Some cultivars have pendulous branches that give the tree a weeping habit.

196

1. Winter twig, × 1.
2. Portion of twig, enlarged.
3. Leaf, × ½.
4. Male flowering twig, × 1.

5. Male flower, enlarged.
6. Female flowering twig, × 1.
7. Female flower, enlarged.
8. Fruit, samaras, × ½.

Key Characters

- leaves opposite, blade 5-lobed with narrow, acute sinuses that extend nearly to the midrib; lobes sharply serrate, sides of the middle lobe diverging
- samaras large, with wings diverging at about a right angle
- twigs bright chestnut brown; inner bark rank-smelling
- bark silvery gray, with narrow, thin, scaly plates
- typically restricted to river floodplains, stream banks, and deciduous swamps with adequate moving water

Distinguished from red maple by leaves with long, more dissected lobes, sides of middle lobe diverging, more silvery white lower surface; larger samaras with more divergent wings; inner bark rank-smelling; habitat typically stream banks and river floodplains, not dry-mesic upland sites.

197

ACERACEAE
Acer spicatum Lamarck

Mountain Maple

Size and Form. Tall shrub or bushy small tree, 6–9 m high and 8–18 cm in diameter. Trunk short, crooked, giving rise to several small, upright branches that form a small, irregularly rounded crown. More often a straggling shrub. Root system very shallow. Michigan Big Tree: girth 0.4 m, diameter 13 cm, height 15 m, Leelanau Co.

Bark. Thin, dull, reddish brown, smooth or slightly furrowed.

Leaves. Opposite, simple, blades 10–13 cm long and ⅔ as wide; 3-lobed above the middle, the lobes coarsely and irregularly crenate-serrate with pointed teeth, the sinuses usually wide-angled and acute at the base; thin; dark green above, covered with a whitish down beneath, turning scarlet and orange in autumn; veins prominent; glabrous; petioles long, slender, with enlarged base.

Twigs. Slender, yellowish green to reddish, slightly hairy with short, gray hairs especially near the tip; pith brown.

Winter Buds. Small, flattish, acute, bright red, more or less tomentose; the terminal bud slightly stalked, 3–5 mm long, containing the flowers; bud scales 2, valvate.

Wood. Light, soft, close-grained, light brown, with thick, lighter-colored sapwood. Not commercially important.

Flowers. June, after the leaves are full grown; small, yellowish green; in erect, slightly compound, many-flowered, long-stemmed, terminal panicles; calyx downy, 5-lobed; petals 5; stamens 7–8; ovary tomentose. Trees polygamomonoecious.

Fruit. Samara; July-August; bright red, turning brown in late autumn; samaras small, glabrous, paired, in pendulous, paniculate clusters; samara wing 1–1.5 cm long, divergent; seed cavity indented.

Distribution. Common in the Upper Peninsula; occasional in the northern half of the Lower Peninsula, south and east to Oakland Co.

Habitat. Characteristic of cool, moist soils and sites of high humidity; along streams and adjacent ravines; protected, moist, rocky hillsides. Associates include spruces, black ash, northern white-cedar, red maple, Canada yew.

Notes. Shade-tolerant; slow-growing; short-lived. Sprouts vigorously following injury by fire and browsing. Reproduces vegetatively by layering. Not commonly used as an ornamental, but it has promise for use in moist, shaded sites.

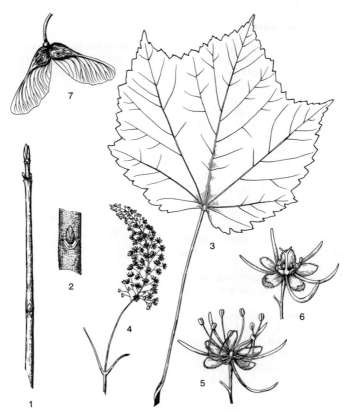

1. Winter twig, × 1.
2. Portion of twig, enlarged.
3. Leaf, × ½.
4. Flowering panicle, × ½.
5. Male flower, enlarged.
6. Female flower, enlarged.
7. Fruit, samaras, × 1.

Key Characters
- small understory tree or shrub
- leaves opposite; blades 3-lobed above the middle; coarsely and irregularly serrate; thin with prominent veins; soft, white pubescence on undersurface
- bud scales 2, valvate
- twigs velvety pubescent

199

ACERACEAE
Acer pensylvanicum Linnaeus

Striped Maple   Moosewood

Size and Form. Small tree or more often a large understory shrub, seldom more than 6–9 m high and 12–20 cm in diameter. Striped, upright branches form a broad, uneven, rounded crown. Roots shallow and wide-spreading. Michigan Big Tree: girth 1.1 m, diameter 36 cm, height 18 m, Marquette Co.

Bark. Thin, smooth, greenish brown, marked vertically by greenish white stripes.

Leaves. Opposite, simple, large, blades 12–18 cm long and nearly as wide; 3-lobed above the middle with short, tapering lobes, the end lobe broadly triangular, sinuses rounded at base, base rounded or heart-shaped; sharply doubly serrate; yellowish green above, paler beneath, turning pale yellow in autumn; palmately 3-nerved; glabrous; petioles stout, grooved.

Twigs. Moderately stout, light green, with small white lines developing the second season.

Winter Buds. Bright red; terminal bud 0.8–1 cm long, conspicuously stalked; 2 visible, valvate bud scales, keeled; lateral buds smaller, appressed.

Wood. Light, soft, close-grained, pinkish brown, with thick, lighter-colored sapwood. Not commercially important.

Flowers. May-June, when the leaves are nearly full grown; large, bright yellow, bell-shaped, in slender, drooping racemes 10–15 cm long; calyx 5-parted; petals 5; stamens 7–8; ovary downy. Trees usually monoecious.

Fruit. Samara; summer; glabrous, about 2 cm long; wings widely divergent; seed portion indented on one side; borne in long, drooping racemose clusters.

Distribution. Occasional to common in the eastern Upper Peninsula (west to eastern Baraga Co.) and northern third of the Lower Peninsula (south to Leelanau and Alcona Co.).

Habitat. Characteristic of the understory of mesic deciduous forests; associates include sugar and red maples, beech, basswood, yellow birch, red oak. Occasionally in dry-mesic, pine-oak forests.

Notes. Highly shade-tolerant; slow-growing; short-lived. Reproducing vegetatively by layering. An attractive understory species, especially in autumn because of its large, pale yellow leaves. A favorite food for moose and deer. Has potential as an ornamental tree or shrub in shaded places.

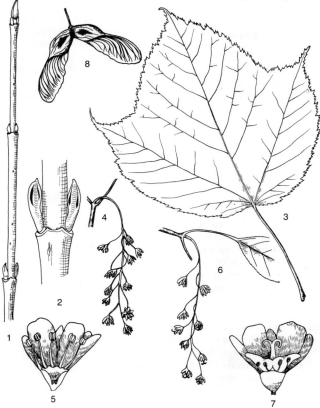

1. Winter twig, × ½.
2. Portion of twig, × 1½.
3. Leaf, × ½.
4. Male flowering raceme, × ½.
5. Vertical section of male flower, enlarged.
6. Female flowering raceme, × ½.
7. Vertical section of female flower, enlarged.
8. Fruit, samaras, × ¾.

Key Characters

- small understory tree or large shrub
- leaves opposite; blades large, 3-lobed above the middle, lobes short, doubly serrate
- bark with conspicuous long, vertical, greenish white stripes
- terminal buds conspicuously stalked; 2 visible scales, valvate
- samaras with widely diverging wings; seed cavities indented on one side

201

ACERACEAE
Acer platanoides Linnaeus

Norway Maple

Size and Form. Medium-sized tree, 12–18 m high and 30–60 cm in diameter. Forming a round, dense, spreading crown of stout branches, resembling sugar maple. Roots relatively deep and spreading. Michigan Big Tree: girth 3.4 m, diameter 109 cm, height 31 m, Wayne Co.

Bark. Moderately thin, dark gray; becoming closely fissured with shallow, interlacing ridges.

Leaves. Opposite, simple, blades 12–18 cm wide and almost as long; 5-lobed, the lobes remotely coarse-toothed with the teeth narrow tipped, separated by rounded, scalloplike sinuses; thin and firm; bright green both sides, remaining green after other native maples turn color, turning pale yellow or orange brown; glabrous; retaining leaves 2 or more weeks longer than native maples; petioles long, slender, exuding a milky sap when cut.

Twigs. Stout, shiny, light brown to greenish.

Winter Buds. Terminal bud yellowish green, red, or dull reddish brown, 6 mm or more long, broad, blunt, short-stalked; bud scales 2–3 pairs, strongly keeled; lateral buds small, appressed; buds exuding a milky sap when cut.

Wood. Moderately heavy, hard, close-grained, whitish or brownish, with white sapwood.

Flowers. May-June, before or with the leaves; mainly perfect; large, yellowish green; in erect, short, flat racemes; sepals 5; petals 5; stamens 8. Trees dioecious.

Fruit. Samara; autumn, germinating the following spring; pendent on long stalks; large, glabrous, paired samaras, with wings 4–5 cm long, diverging by nearly 180°; seed cavity flattened.

Distribution. Native in Europe and western Asia; extensively planted in cities for its dense crown, abundant shade, and adaptability to urban conditions.

Habitat. Grows well in fertile, well drained soils, but adapts itself to almost any soil and situation.

Notes. Shade-tolerant; moderately slow-growing; moderately long-lived. Termed Norway maple because it was first introduced into England from Norway. Relatively free from insect and disease pests. Becoming naturalized in disturbed areas in and around urban areas. Probably the best maple for street plantings because of its tolerance of urban planting sites and pollutants, particularly the cultivar 'Emerald Queen' with a more upright than rounded crown. Various cultivars with red, greenish purple, or purple leaves are popular lawn and park trees, such as 'Schwedleri' and 'Crimson King'.

202

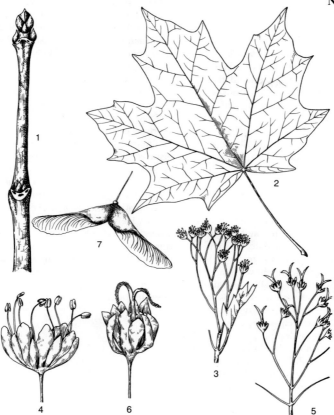

1. Winter twig, × 1.
2. Leaf, × ½.
3. Raceme of staminate flowers, × ½.
4. Male flower, enlarged.
5. Raceme of female flowers, × ½.
6. Female flower, enlarged.
7. Fruit, samaras, × ½.

Key Characters
- leaves opposite; blades 5-lobed with narrow-tipped teeth
- petioles and buds exuding milky sap when cut
- terminal buds broad, blunt, with yellowish green, red to reddish brown, strongly-keeled scales
- large samaras with widely diverging wings

Distinguished from sugar maple by darker green leaves with narrow-tipped teeth; petioles exuding white sap; terminal buds broader, more blunt, not sharp-pointed, more greenish or red in color; samaras with wider and much more widely diverging wings, seed cavity flatter; bark darker with more regular, narrow, interlacing ridges, not scaly.

ACERACEAE
Acer negundo Linnaeus

Boxelder   Ash-leaf Maple

Size and Form. Small to medium-sized tree, 12–15 m high and 30–80 cm in diameter. Trunk often dividing near the ground into several stout, wide-spreading, often crooked branches, forming a broad, unsymmetrical, open crown. Roots shallow and wide-spreading. Michigan Big Tree: girth 5.2 m, diameter 164 cm, height 34 m, Washtenaw Co.

Bark. Pale gray or light brown, becoming dark brown with age, deeply cleft into narrow, interlacing ridges.

Leaves. Opposite, pinnately compound. Leaflets 3–5 (rarely 7–9), blades 5–10 cm long, 2.5–6 cm wide, short-petioled; ovate or oval; nearly entire, irregularly and remotely coarse-toothed above the middle, or sometimes 3-lobed (often giving the leaflet a jagged outline); light green above, light grayish green beneath, turning yellow in autumn; glabrous or somewhat pubescent; veins prominent. Petiole slender, enlarged base leaving prominent crescent-shaped scars surrounding the winter buds.

Twigs. Stout, greenish, becoming purple or brownish, shiny or polished or with a waxy, glaucous bloom that rubs off easily.

Winter Buds. Terminal bud 3–6 mm long, acute, 2–4 dull red scales, hoary or minutely white-pubescent; lateral buds obtuse, appressed; opposite leaf scars meeting.

Wood. Light, soft, close-grained, weak, creamy white, with thick, hardly distinguishable sapwood. Uses include rough construction, pulpwood, boxes, furniture.

Flowers. April-May, before or with the leaves; male flowers in clusters on long, threadlike, hairy pedicels; small, yellowish green; calyx hairy, 5-lobed; corolla 0; stamens 3–6; female flowers in narrow, drooping racemes; ovary glabrous. Trees dioecious. Flowering is discussed in detail by Wagner (1975).

Fruit. Samara; autumn, and may hang on until early spring; samaras narrow, flat, in V-shaped pairs, 3–4 cm long; seed portion narrow and pointed, wrinkled; samaras clustered in drooping racemes.

Distribution. Occasional to frequent in the southern half of the Lower Peninsula; occasional to rare northward to Houghton Co.

Habitat. Characteristic of stream banks, river floodplains, bottomlands, margins of swamps, with moist, alluvial, fertile soils; associates include eastern cottonwood, willows, sycamore, silver maple, red ash, northern hackberry. Also disturbed sites.

Notes. Shade-intolerant; fast-growing; short-lived. Sprouts readily following injury by fire or cutting. Aggressive colonizer of disturbed, open sites: fence rows, roadside ditches, around houses, in gardens. Bright red boxelder bugs (*Leptocoris trivittatus*) feed on the leaves, cause no serious damage but become a nuisance to householders. Formerly widely planted along streets and around homesteads because of its ease of transplanting, rapid growth, resistance to drought, and adaptability to nearly all urban conditions. However, it is not especially attractive, sheds branches readily, and attracts boxelder bugs.

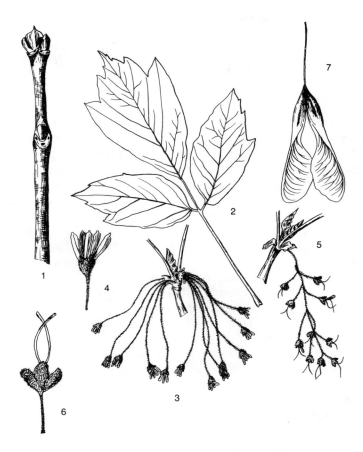

1. Winter twig, × 1.
2. Leaf, × ½.
3. Male flowering shoot, × ½.
4. Male flower, enlarged.

5. Female flowering shoot, × ½.
6. Female flower, enlarged.
7. Fruit, samaras, × 1.

Key Characters
- leaves opposite, pinnately compound, leaflets 3–5
- twigs stout, green becoming purplish, with a whitish bloom
- samaras narrow, flat, in V-shaped pairs, borne on drooping racemes, often present in winter

205

The Walnuts—*Juglans*

About 15 species of walnuts are known; 6 occur in the United States, and 2 are native to Michigan. The walnuts have pinnately compound leaves that are arranged alternately on the branches. The male flowers appear in Michigan in May and are borne on the shoots of the preceding season, while the female flowers are borne on the shoots of the current season and also appear in May. The fruit matures in the autumn and consists of a sculptured nut enclosed in a fleshy husk that does not split open into segments. The convoluted nut meat is 2–4-lobed, large, and oily. The nuts are dispersed mainly by squirrels, which bury them for food, and by rivers and creeks which carry them downstream. The pith of the twigs is a never-failing means of identification, being chambered. In black walnut it is cream colored, whereas in butternut it is chocolate brown. Both walnuts are particular in their site preferences. They require relatively high amounts of nutrients and a warm climate.

In addition to these native species, an introduction from Europe (native in southeastern Europe and Asia), the English walnut, *Juglans regia* L., is widely planted in the United States as an ornamental tree and occasionally is grown in the southernmost part of Michigan, where it is subject to winter injury, especially in youth. The English walnut has pinnately compound leaves, consisting of 7–9 glabrous and almost entire leaflets, 5–13 cm long. The twigs and buds are glabrous also, and there is no downy pad above the leaf scar. The pith is coarsely chambered and light brown. The bark is gray and smooth for many years. The thin-shelled nuts are familiar in stores, and the wood is used extensively in the manufacture of furniture, under the name Circassian Walnut.

Summer Key to Species of *Juglans*

1. Leaflets 11–17, the terminal usually present; pith of twigs chocolate brown; bark of trunk rather smooth, or fissured with broad, flat-topped, ash gray ridges; fruit elongated, sticky-downy .... *J. cinerea*, p. 208
1. Leaflets 13–23, the terminal often lacking; pith of twigs cream colored; bark of trunk rough, brownish or blackish; deeply furrowed by numerous vertical, broad, rounded ridges; fruit globose, not sticky-downy .... *J. nigra*, p. 210

Winter Key to Species of *Juglans*

1. Pith chocolate brown; leaf scar with downy pad above; fruit elongated, sticky-downy; terminal bud 1–2 cm long; bark rather smooth, or fissured, with broad, flat-topped, ash gray ridges .... *J. cinerea*, p. 208
1. Pith cream colored; leaf scar without downy pad above; fruit globose, not sticky-downy; terminal bud 6–8 mm long; bark rough, brownish or blackish, deeply furrowed by numerous vertical, broad, rounded ridges .... *J. nigra*, p. 210

JUGLANDACEAE
Juglans cinerea Linnaeus

Butternut White Walnut

Size and Form. Medium-sized tree, 12–18 m high and 60–100 cm in diameter. Trunk short; forming an open, wide-spreading, irregular, round-topped crown of few, large, horizontal branches and stout, stiff branchlets. Tap root present in youth; deeply set, spreading lateral roots; windfirm. Michigan Big Tree: girth 4.0 m, diameter 126 cm, height 24 m, Sanilac Co.

Bark. Thin, light gray, and smoothish on young trunks; becoming separated on old trunks into broad, flat and smooth-topped, vertical, interlacing ridges.

Leaves. Alternate, pinnately compound, 40–75 cm long. Leaflets 11–17, 8–10 cm long and nearly half as wide; nearly sessile except the terminal which is usually present; oblong-lanceolate; finely serrate; thin; yellowish green and rough, finely pubescent above, pale and soft-pubescent beneath. Petioles stout, hairy.

Twigs. Stout, rusty-pubescent, orange brown or bright green, becoming smooth and light gray. Leaf scar conspicuous, upper margin straight or rounded, not notched, often bordered by a downy pad, 3 U-shaped groups of bundle scars. Pith chambered, dark chocolate brown.

Winter Buds. Terminal bud 1.2–2 cm long, oblong-conical, obliquely blunt, somewhat flattened, brownish, pubescent. Lateral buds much smaller, rounded, pubescent, superposed (flower bud below vegetative bud) above the leaf scar.

Flowers. May (June in the Upper Peninsula), with the leaves; male catkins greenish, drooping, 8–12 cm long; calyx 6-lobed, borne on a hairy bract; corolla 0, stamens 8–12 with brown anthers; female flowers solitary or several on a common peduncle, about 8 mm long, their bracts and bractlets sticky-hairy; calyx 4-lobed, hairy; corolla 0; styles 2; stigmas 2, fringed, spreading, bright red. Trees monoecious. Wind-pollinated.

Fruit. Nut; October; about 6 cm long and half as wide, ovoid-oblong, pointed, greenish, sticky-downy, solitary or borne in drooping clusters of 3–5; nuts with jagged shells, enclosing a sweet, but oily, edible kernel.

Wood. Light, soft, weak, coarse-grained, light brown, with thin, lighter-colored sapwood; ring-porous. Uses include furniture, cabinet work, interior trim, woodenware.

Distribution. Rare in the southern half of the Lower Peninsula, as far north as Arenac Co; planted in northern lower Michigan; rare in Menominee and Delta Co. of the Upper Peninsula. Reaches the northern limit of its range in the western Great Lakes region in these Upper Peninsula counties.

Habitat. Characteristic of moist, fertile soils of lower slopes, coves, and river banks and floodplains; also grows on dry, rocky soils derived from limestone. Occurs singly in mesic hardwood forests with basswood, sugar maple, red oak, white oak, beech, American elm, black cherry, hackberry, bur oak, bluebeech.

Notes. Shade-intolerant; fast-growing; moderately long-lived. Leaves appear late in spring and are shed early in autumn. Squirrels and other rodents disseminate seeds, bury them, sometimes forget or lose them, thus facilitating reproduction. Husk contains an orange-yellow dye once used for coloring homespun clothing. A sweet syrup can be made by boiling down the sap. Young trees not easily transplanted because of the tap root.

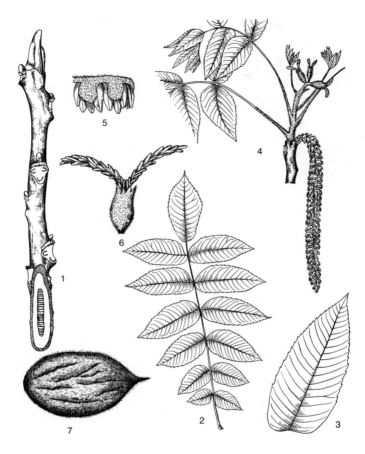

1. Winter twig, × 1.
2. Leaf, × ⅙.
3. Leaflet, × ½.
4. Flowering shoot, × ½.

5. Male flower, enlarged.
6. Female flower, enlarged.
7. Fruit, nut, × ½.

Key Characters

• alternate, pinnately compound leaves with many leaflets; terminal leaflet usually present, leaflets not stalked
• twigs with dark chocolate brown chambered pith; upper margin of leaf scar not deeply notched, with a downy pad
• fruit large, oblong-cylindrical, lemon-shaped, sticky-downy
• bark ash gray with broad, smooth, flat-topped, interlacing ridges

209

JUGLANDACEAE
Juglans nigra Linnaeus

Black Walnut

Size and Form. Large tree, 18–27 m high and 60–120 cm in diameter. Trunk massive; forming an open, wide-spreading crown of few, heavy branches and coarse branchlets. Forest-grown trees have straight, little-tapering stems and a rounded crown; trunks of open-grown trees often fork 2–4 m above the ground, developing large branches and a very broad crown. Tap root prominent in youth; lateral roots deeply set and spreading; windfirm. Michigan Big Tree: girth 5.9 m, diameter 188 cm, height 36 m, Macomb Co. (tallest tree 41.5 m, Macomb Co.).

Bark. Young bark scaly, light brown; becoming thick, dark brown or black, and deeply furrowed by broad, rounded, intersecting, vertical ridges.

Leaves. Alternate, pinnately compound, 30–60 cm long. Leaflets 13–23, short-stalked, the terminal smaller than the laterals, often absent, 5–10 cm long and less than half as wide; ovate-lanceolate, taper-pointed; sharp-serrate; thin; yellowish green and glabrous above, lighter and soft-pubescent beneath. Petioles stout, pubescent. Foliage aromatic when crushed.

Twigs. Stout, brownish and hairy, becoming darker and smooth. Leaf scar conspicuous, deeply notched on upper margin, 3 U-shaped groups of bundle scars. Pith chambered, cream colored.

Winter Buds. Terminal bud stout, 6–8 mm long and equally wide, ovoid, obliquely blunt, slightly flattened, silky-tomentose; lateral buds much smaller, often superposed (flower bud below vegetative bud above the leaf scar).

Wood. Heavy, hard, strong, close-grained, very durable in contact with soil, rich dark brown, with thin, lighter-colored sapwood. Uses include veneer, furniture, cabinet work, interior trim, paneling, caskets, gunstocks, woodenware.

Flowers. May, with the leaves; male catkins greenish, drooping, 8–12 cm long; calyx 6-lobed, borne on a hairy bract; corolla 0; stamens numerous, with purple anthers; fe-male flowers solitary or several on a common peduncle, about 6 mm long, their bracts and bractlets hairy; calyx 4-lobed, pubescent; corolla 0; styles and stigmas 2. Trees monoecious. Wind-pollinated.

Fruit. Nut; October; globose, 4–5 cm in diameter, smooth, pubescent, not sticky, solitary or borne in clusters of 2–3; husk green, thick, very aromatic; nut with irregularly grooved shell enclosing a sweet, edible kernel.

Distribution. Common in the southern half of the Lower Peninsula; except for planted trees, not found in northern lower Michigan or the Upper Peninsula. A southern species reaching the northern limit of its range in southern Michigan.

Habitat. Very sensitive to site conditions, especially soil moisture and fertility; does not tolerate very dry, acid, or wet sites; attains best development on warm, deep, fertile, moist, well drained alluvial soils. Occurs individually or in small groups in mesic and dry-mesic forests with white ash, sugar maple, black cherry, beech, basswood, white oak, red oak.

Notes. Shade-intolerant; fast-growing; moderately long-lived. Leaves appear late in spring, and are shed early in autumn. Squirrels and other rodents disseminate seeds, bury them, and sometimes forget or lose them, thus facilitating reproduction. Roots exude a chemical substance, known as juglone, that inhibits growth of many plants under or near a walnut tree (including walnut seedlings, fruit trees, and garden vegetables, especially tomatoes). Husk contains a brown dye, stains the hands, and permanently stains cloth. Pieces of walnut shell used to polish metal. The most valuable timber tree, per board foot, of eastern North America. Of significant ornamental value but may not be a desirable lawn tree. Young trees not easily transplanted because of deep taproot. A major caterpillar food of the beautiful, green, long-tailed luna moth *(Actias luna)*.

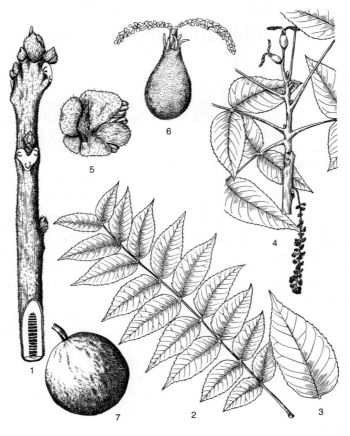

1. Winter twig, × 1.
2. Leaf, × ⅙.
3. Leaflet, × ½.
4. Flowering shoot, × ½.

5. Male flower, back view, enlarged.
6. Female flower, enlarged.
7. Fruit, nut, × ½.

Key Characters

- alternate, pinnately compound leaves with many leaflets; leaflets stalked, terminal leaflet smaller than laterals, often absent
- twigs with cream-colored chambered pith; upper margin of leaf scar deeply notched, without hairy pad
- fruit large, spherical, with thick aromatic husk

211

The Hickories—*Carya*

The hickories belong to the same family as the walnuts. Previous to the appearance of the Pleistocene Ice Age, forests of hickory existed in Europe and Greenland. Today Europe has no native hickories. Eleven of the existing 25 species are found in North America; 2 each occur in Mexico and mainland China. Four species are native to Michigan; 3 of these belong to the subgenus *Carya*, or true hickories: shagbark, shellbark, and pignut; 1 species, bitternut, belongs to the subgenus *Apocarya*, or the pecan hickories.

The hickories are important hardwood timber trees. This is not because they produce large quantities of wood, but because they yield an exceptional quality of wood. It is used in the manufacture of furniture, paneling, athletic equipment (baseball bats, hockey sticks, etc.), and tool handles of all kinds; in places where strength and elasticity are required it is almost unrivaled.

The hickories are large, long-lived trees with very deep root systems, and they are characterized by bark that is extremely hard and compact. The leaves are compound but composed of fewer leaflets than the walnuts, and they are of a firm, somewhat leathery texture. The flowers, arranged in male catkins, and small female spikes, appear in the late spring after the unfolding of the leaves. They are wind-pollinated. All species are monoecious.

The fruit matures in the autumn of the first season and consists of a nut enclosed in a husk that is 4-valved. A hard frost brings the nuts down in profusion. In most of the species, the dried husk splits open at least to the middle, but in some it separates very little. Squirrels and other rodents disseminate and bury the nuts, providing ideal conditions for germination and establishment. The nut of shagbark hickory is highly sought for its edible quality. All hickories are difficult to transplant when young because of their deep tap root. Hickories occupy markedly different habitats, ranging from moist bottomlands to xeric oak-hickory forests.

Summer and Winter Key to Species of *Carya*

1. Bud scales leaflike, valvate, appearing naked, bright sulfur yellow; bark of trunk smooth or only shallowly ridged; leaflets usually 7–9 .... *C. cordiformis,* p. 214
1. Bud scales curved plates, imbricate, not appearing naked, not sulfur yellow; bark furrowed or shaggy; leaflets usually 5–7 (rarely 9).
   2. Terminal bud small, usually less than 1 cm long; fruit husk thin .... *C. glabra,* p. 216
   2. Terminal bud large, 1.6–3.2 cm long; fruit husk thick.
      3. Leaflets 5; blades glabrous beneath, with minute, dense tufts of white hair on most of the serrations; twigs glabrate or glabrous, dark reddish brown; fruit 2–4 (rarely 4.5) cm long; nut light brown, not strongly compressed .... *C. ovata,* p. 120
      3. Leaflets 7; blades soft-pubescent beneath, without tufts of white hair on the serrations; twigs puberulent, light olive brown; fruit 4.5–7 cm long; nut brown, strongly compressed .... *C. laciniosa,* p. 218

JUGLANDACEAE
Carya cordiformis (Wangenheim) K. Koch

Bitternut Hickory

Size and Form. Medium-sized to large tree, 15–25 m high and 30–80 cm in diameter. Slender trunk; forming a broad crown of slender, stiff, upright branches, widest near the top. Prominent tap root; windfirm. Michigan Big Tree: girth 3.7 m, diameter 117 cm, height 40 m, Cass Co.

Bark. Thin, gray and smooth for many years, gradually separating into shallow line-like fissures and narrow, interlacing ridges, always tight, not shaggy.

Leaves. Alternate, pinnately compound, 15–25 cm long. Leaflets slender, 7–9, the terminal 10–15 cm long and about ¼ as wide; sessile or nearly sessile; lanceolate to oblong-lanceolate, long-pointed; finely toothed; thin and firm; shiny, bright green above, paler and pubescent on veins beneath; bright golden in autumn; glabrous. Foliage fragrant when crushed. Petioles slender, hairy.

Twigs. Slender, smooth, minutely hairy, greenish becoming brownish and finally grayish.

Winter Buds. Terminal bud 1–2 cm long, valvate, appearing naked, long-pointed, flattish, granular or scurfy, sulfur yellow; lateral buds more or less 4-angled, sometimes appearing stalked.

Wood. Heavy, very hard, strong, tough, close-grained, dark brown, with thick, lighter-colored sapwood. Not as tough or shock resistant as shagbark hickory. Uses include tool handles, furniture, dowel pins, ladders, skis and sporting goods, fuel for smoking meats.

Flowers. May or early June, with the leaves; male catkins in 3s, slightly pubescent, pendulous, 8–10 cm long; on a common peduncle 2–3 cm long; scales 3-lobed, hairy; stamens 4, with bearded yellow anthers; female flowers in 2–5-flowered short spikes, 1.3 cm long, scurfy-tomentose; involucre 4-lobed, pubescent; corolla 0; stigmas 2, greenish. Wind-pollinated.

Fruit. Nut enclosed in husk; October; obovoid to globular, 2–3 cm long, coated with yellow scurfy pubescence, with very thin husk, 4-winged to about the middle, splitting halfway to the base; nut quite smooth, with very thin shell and small, very bitter kernel.

Distribution. Occasional in the southern half of the Lower Peninsula, as far north as Gladwin and Ogemaw Co. Little (1971) shows it occurring in Menominee Co. in the Upper Peninsula. Widely distributed to the south of Michigan and reaching one edge of its northern limit in southern Michigan.

Habitat. Characteristic of mesic hardwood forests with low-lying, moist, cool, fertile, deep soils; also stream borders, lower upland slopes, especially north and east aspects. Associated with red oak, sugar maple, basswood, beech, white ash, shagbark hickory, black ash, silver maple.

Notes. Relatively shade-tolerant, especially as a seedling; moderately slow-growing; moderately long-lived (shorter-lived than other hickories). Reported to sprout more vigorously than other hickories. Reported to be the best fuel for giving meats the true "hickory smoked" flavor.

214

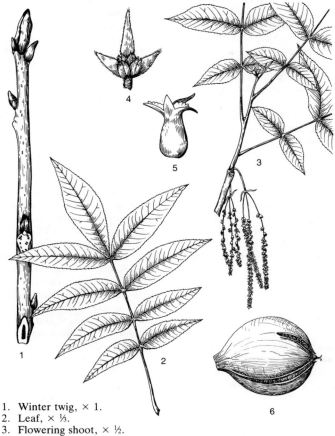

1. Winter twig, × 1.
2. Leaf, × ⅓.
3. Flowering shoot, × ½.
4. Male flower, enlarged.
5. Female flower, enlarged.
6. Fruit, nut enclosed in husk, × 1.

Key Characters

- buds sulfur yellow, granular-scurfy, valvate and appearing naked
- leaves pinnately compound, usually 9 relatively narrow leaflets
- fruit 4-winged to about the middle; husk splitting halfway to the base
- bark tight, smooth or with narrow, interlacing ridges and shallow fissures, not shaggy in appearance
- characteristic of fertile, moist, cool sites and mesic hardwood forests

215

JUGLANDACEAE
Carya glabra (Miller) Sweet

Pignut Hickory

Size and Form. Medium-sized tree, 15–20 m high and 30–80 cm in diameter. Forming a rather narrow, cylindrical, open crown of slender, often contorted branches. Prominent tap root with few laterals. Michigan Big Tree: girth 3.7 m, diameter 116 cm, height 21 m, Ingham Co.

Bark. Relatively thin, hard and grayish, with a firm, tight surface divided by small fissures and interlacing ridges, occasionally separating into small loose strips.

Leaves. Alternate, pinnately compound, 20–30 cm long. Leaflets rather narrow, 5–7 (rarely 9, usually 5), the terminal 8–15 cm long, 5–6 cm wide; nearly sessile, except the terminal; oblong, ovate, or lanceolate, taper-pointed; sharply serrate, not fringed with hairs; thick and firm; lustrous, dark yellowish green above, paler beneath, pubescent on larger veins and midrib, glabrous. Petioles long, slender, glabrous or pubescent. Foliage fragrant when crushed.

Twigs. Slender, lustrous, greenish, glabrous or nearly so, becoming reddish, and finally grayish.

Winter Buds. Terminal bud small, 0.6–1.2 cm long, dome-shaped, greenish or grayish, finely downy; outer bud scales shed in early autumn leaving the small, stout bud; laterals smaller, broad and blunt-tipped.

Wood. Heavy, hard, very strong, tough, close-grained, elastic, dark brown, with thick, whitish sapwood. Uses include tool handles, furniture, sports equipment.

Flowers. May-June, with the leaves; male catkins in 3s, pendulous, 8–18 cm long, slender, yellowish green, tomentose; scales 3-lobed, nearly glabrous; stamens 4–6, with orange anthers; female flowers in crowded, 2–5-flowered spikes, 6 mm long; involucre 4-toothed, hairy, corolla 0; stigmas 2, yellow. Wind-pollinated.

Fruit. Nut enclosed in husk; October; variable in size and shape, pear-shaped, oval, or rounded, 1.6–3.2 cm long, with a thin husk that may split only at the apex, split along one suture to the base, or split along 3–4 su-tures to the base; nut 4-ribbed or not, with thin or thick, hard shell and small, sweet or slightly bitter kernel that is hard to remove.

Distribution. Common in the southern part of the Lower Peninsula, north to Isabella Co.; reaching the northernmost limit of its midwestern range in southern Michigan.

Habitat. Characteristic of xeric to dry-mesic, oak-hickory forests, with well drained, droughty, upland soils. Associated with black, white, and red oaks, white ash, shag-bark hickory, black cherry, hop-hornbeam. Infrequent on mesic sites with sugar maple, beech, basswood.

Notes. Moderately shade-tolerant as a seedling, requiring considerable light to reach the overstory; slow-growing; long-lived. Sprouting profusely following fire, cutting, or browsing. Apparently named pignut for the bitter nuts which were considered fit only for pigs.

Closely related and distinguished with difficulty from *C. ovalis* (Wangenheim) Sargent, the false shagbark, red, or oval pignut hickory. Characters reported to distinguish *C. ovalis* from *C. glabra* are: more leaflets, usually 7; more ovate or obovate leaflets; more rounded, less pear-shaped fruit; fruit husk splitting freely along 3–4 sutures to the base; nut ridged, thin shelled (not unridged and thick shelled); and bark scaly or shaggy, not tight. In Michigan these characters are not consistently found occurring together on the same tree. No site or geographic differences are observed among trees with different leaf, bark, and fruit morphology. See Manning (1950) for more on characters of *C. glabra* and *C. ovalis*. Rather than describe these two closely related species with many overlapping characters, we have elected to describe one species in a way that incorporates the traits of both. In our experience, a clear-cut distinction between the two has not yet been compellingly demonstrated in Michigan.

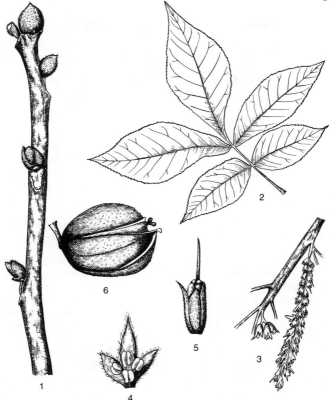

1. Winter twig, × 1.
2. Leaf, × ¼.
3. Flowering twig, × 1.
4. Male flower, enlarged.
5. Female flower, enlarged.
6. Fruit, nut enclosed in husk, × ⅔.

**Key
Characters**
- bark tight, shallowly fissured, or not markedly shaggy
- twigs slender, more or less glabrous
- fruit pear-shaped or rounded with usually thin husk; husk often not splitting completely to the base
- terminal bud small, downy, dome-shaped
- typical of dry-mesic, upland, oak-hickory forests

JUGLANDACEAE
Carya laciniosa (Michaux f.) G. Don

Shellbark Hickory

Size and Form. Medium-sized to large tree, 18–22 m high and 60–80 cm in diameter. Forming a narrow, oblong-cylindrical crown of spreading branches. Prominent tap root; windfirm. Michigan Big Tree: previous record is of *C. ovata;* new record proposed: girth 2.3 m, diameter 74 cm, height 31 m. Washtenaw Co.

Bark. Thin and smooth on young trees; soon separating into narrow, dark gray strips, 1–1.2 m long, free on lower end or on both ends that curve away from the trunk.

Leaves. Alternate, pinnately compound, 25–50 cm long. Leaflets almost always 7, the terminal 13–22 cm long, 8–12 cm wide, usually larger than the laterals; subsessile; oblong-lanceolate to obovate, taper-pointed; finely serrate, ciliate, without tufts of white hair; thick and firm; lustrous, dark green above, paler and soft-pubescent beneath. Fragrant when crushed. Petioles stout, glabrous or pubescent, often persistent on branches during the winter.

Twigs. Very stout, buff or light olive brown, usually puberulent becoming darker in the first winter, finally grayish.

Winter Buds. Terminal bud large, 2–3 cm long, ovoid, obtuse, dark brown; outer scales pointed, puberulent, loosely spreading; inner scales silky-pubescent below and minutely glandular-puberulent above, yellowish or purplish, persistent; lateral buds smaller, ovoid-oblong, divergent.

Wood. Heavy, very hard, strong, tough, close-grained, very elastic, dark brown, with thin, whitish sapwood; ring-porous. Uses similar to those of shagbark hickory.

Flowers. May and early June, with the leaves; male catkins in 3s, pendulous, 12–20 cm long; scales 3-lobed, tomentose; stamens 4–6, with yellow, hairy anthers; female flowers in 2–5-flowered spikes, involucre of 4 fused bracts with free tips, the bract opposite the longest bract often bilobed, yellow glands few, densely white-pubescent, fusion lines of bracts red pubescent; corolla 0; stigmas 2, light green. Wind-pollinated.

Fruit. Nut enclosed in husk; October; oblong to subglobose; 4.5–7 cm long, usually longer than wide, with very thick, woody husk, splitting to the base; nut 4–6 ribbed, strongly compressed, with thick, brown, hard shell and large, sweet kernel; fruit largest of all hickories.

Distribution. Rare. Occurs in the southernmost 2 tiers of counties of the Lower Peninsula; reaches its northernmost midwestern limit in southern Michigan.

Habitat. Characteristic of river floodplains and moist woodland soils that are deep, fertile, neutral or slightly alkaline, and of a loam or silt loam texture. Requires moister, more fertile soils than shagbark or pignut hickories. Associated with American elm, slippery elm, bur oak, swamp white oak, butternut, white ash, shagbark hickory, red maple, red ash, eastern cottonwood, pawpaw.

Notes. Similar to shagbark hickory in many characters—a somewhat larger version of shagbark hickory adapted to moist, fertile bottomlands. Shade-tolerant as a seedling, may persist in the understory many years; needs considerable light to reach the overstory. Moderately fast-growing; fastest of all Michigan hickories; long-lived. Sprouts vigorously following fire, cutting, or browsing.

218

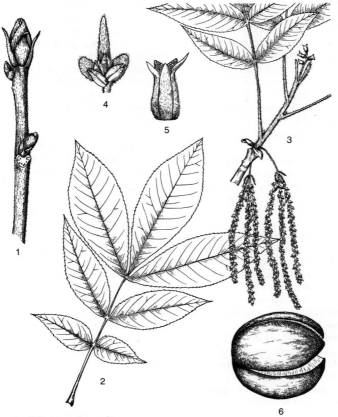

1. Winter twig, × ½.
2. Leaf, × ¼.
3. Flowering shoot, × ½.
4. Male flower, enlarged.
5. Female flower, enlarged.
6. Fruit, nut enclosed in husk, × ½.

Key Characters

- leaves pinnately compound, 7 leaflets, soft-pubescent beneath
- fruit very large, husk very thick; nut large, brown, strongly compressed
- twigs very stout, puberulent, light olive brown
- occurs in mesic, floodplain, and fertile woodland sites

Distinguished from shagbark hickory by 7 instead of 5 leaflets; leaflets soft-pubescent beneath; nut larger, longer than wide, darker, more compressed; lighter colored twigs; longer male catkins; and not occurring in dry-mesic, upland forests.

219

JUGLANDACEAE
Carya ovata (Miller) K. Koch

Shagbark Hickory

Size and Form. Medium-sized to large tree, 18–22 m high and 30–80 cm in diameter. Trunk straight, slender, little-tapering; forming a narrow, somewhat open crown of few, stout, slightly spreading limbs and stout branchlets. Prominent tap root extending as much as 1 m the first year. Michigan Big Tree: girth 3.5 m, diameter 110 cm, height 23 m, Calhoun Co.

Bark. Thin, smooth, gray on young trunks; soon separating into rough plates 30–90 cm long, free at one or both ends that curve away from the trunk, giving a characteristic shaggy appearance.

Leaves. Alternate, pinnately compound, 20–25 cm long. Leaflets almost always 5, long-pointed at both ends, the terminal 13–18 cm long and 5–8 cm wide, larger than the lateral leaflets; subsessile, except the terminal; obovate to oblong-lanceolate; finely serrate, fringed with minute, dense tufts of white hair upon most of the serrations; thick and firm; glabrous, dark yellowish green above, paler beneath and usually glabrous; golden yellow in autumn. Fragrant when crushed. Petioles stout, glabrous or hairy, almost never persisting over winter.

Twigs. Stout, dark reddish brown, glabrate, becoming glabrous and grayish.

Winter Buds. Terminal bud 1.3–2 cm long, broadly ovoid, obtuse, brown; outer bud scales large, dark brown, pointed, loosely spreading; inner scales silky-pubescent below and minutely glandular-puberulent above, not persistent over winter; lateral buds smaller, divergent.

Wood. Heavy, very hard and strong, tough, close-grained, elastic, light brown, with thin, whitish sapwood; ring-porous. Uses include tool handles, furniture, ladders, sporting equipment.

Flowers. May and early June, with the leaves; male catkins in 3s, greenish, hairy, pendulous, 10–13 cm long, on a common peduncle 2–3 cm long; scales 3-parted, bristle-tipped; stamens 4–6, with bearded, yellow anthers; female flowers in 2–5-flowered spikes, involucre of 4 fused bracts with free tips, the bract opposite the longest bract not bilobed, yellow, densely glandular, sparsely pubescent, fusion lines of bracts strongly ridged; corolla 0; stigmas 2, large, fringed. Wind-pollinated.

Fruit. Nut enclosed in husk; October; globular, 2–4 (rarely 4.5) cm long, shorter than wide, thick husk separating completely; nut usually 4-ribbed, light yellowish brown with thick shell and large, sweet, edible kernel.

Distribution. Common in the Lower Peninsula as far north as Roscommon and Missaukee Co.; primary range south of Michigan, reaching its northernmost midwestern limit in the southern half of the Lower Peninsula.

Habitat. Characteristic of dry-mesic, oak-hickory forests; associated with black, red, and white oaks, pignut hickory, white ash, black cherry. Occasional on mesic sites; associated with sugar maple, beech, basswood, red oak, bitternut hickory. Also occurs in the drier parts of river floodplains. Tolerant of drought but not of prolonged high water table.

Notes. Seedlings relatively shade-tolerant, existing in the understory many years until they die or a disturbance to the overstory makes a gap for them to reach the overstory. Slow-growing; long-lived. Susceptible to fire when young but marked ability to sprout from root collar following fire, cutting, or browsing. Root suckers may be produced, especially by older trees; not forming multi-stemmed clones. Produces the major hickory nut of commerce. Wood smoke used to cure meat; excellent firewood. Relatively free of insect and disease pests.

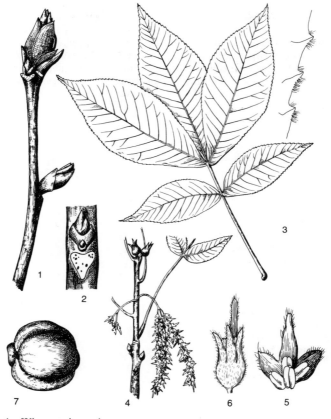

1. Winter twig, × 1.
2. Portion of twig, enlarged.
3. Leaf, × ⅓.
4. Flowering shoot, × ½.
5. Male flower, enlarged.
6. Female flower, enlarged.
7. Fruit, nut, × ½.

Key Characters

- leaves pinnately compound, 5 leaflets; leaflets fringed with minute tufts of white hair
- bark in long plates, free at one or both ends and curving outward, giving a shaggy appearance
- terminal buds large, with loosely spreading outer scales
- nut light yellowish brown, wider than long, thick husk splitting freely to the base and separating completely; kernel sweet

Distinguished from shellbark hickory by 5 instead of 7 leaflets; leaflets glabrate or glabrous beneath; nut smaller, wider than long, lighter colored, less compressed; darker colored twigs; shorter male catkins; often found on dry-mesic, upland sites.

221

HAMAMELIDACEAE
Hamamelis virginiana Linnaeus

Witch-hazel

Size and Form. Low-spreading shrub or small tree to 8 m. Several large, crooked trunks typically grow together in a clump, forming an irregular, open crown. Michigan Big Tree: girth 0.4 m, diameter 14 cm, height 13 m, Muskegon Co.

Bark. Thin, smooth, becoming scaly, light brown with conspicuous lenticels; inner bark reddish purple.

Leaves. Alternate, simple, blade 10–15 cm long; oval-obovate, base strongly asymmetrical; sinuate-dentate; thin; dark green to yellowish green; glabrous; petioles short, 0.5–1.5 cm.

Twigs. Slender, zigzag, scurfy-pubescent or glabrous, reddish brown to light orange.

Winter Buds. Terminal bud naked, elongate, stalked, scurfy, yellowish brown; lateral buds smaller, appressed.

Wood. Hard, heavy, light brown with whitish sapwood.

Flowers. October-November, during and after leaf fall; perfect; showy, in clusters of 3; calyx 4-parted; petals 4, very narrow, bright yellow, twisted; 1.5–2 cm long. Insect-pollinated.

Fruit. Capsule; broad-obovoid, 1–1.5 cm long, tan; ripening and discharging 2 lustrous black seeds the autumn following flowering; capsule opening and mechanically discharging the seeds some distance.

Distribution. Common in the southern half of the Lower Peninsula; occasional in the northern half of the Lower Peninsula; rare in the Upper Peninsula (only known from Ontonagon, Baraga, and Menominee Co.).

Habitat. Characteristic of the understory of dry-mesic oak-hickory forests (especially those toward the mesic end of the spectrum). Associates include black, white, and red oaks, pignut and shagbark hickories, black cherry, white ash, black walnut, hop-hornbeam.

Notes. Shade-tolerant; slow-growing; short-lived. Forked twigs used by the water diviner or "well witcher" to seek water. Witch-hazel astringent is obtained from the leaves, twigs, and bark; used in lotions and medicinal extracts. Occasionally used ornamentally as a shrub border for its abundant flowering in late autumn, the flowers remaining after the leaves have dropped. Other species, native both of North America and Asia, flower in the spring. The common name is said to be applied due to the hazellike straight veins of the leaves.

222

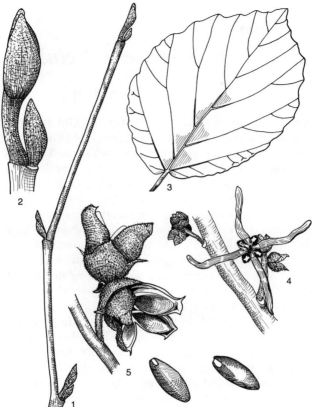

1. Winter twig, × 1.
2. Portion of twig, × 3½.
3. Leaf, × ½.
4. Flowering twig, with 1 flower, × 1½.
5. Fruit, capsule open with seeds disseminated, × 1½.

Key Characters
- leaf blade oval, wavy-dentate, base strongly asymmetrical
- buds naked, stalked, yellowish brown, pubescent
- flowers appearing in late autumn, petals narrow, bright yellow
- fruit a woody capsule, persisting on branches
- shrub or small tree with several, large, spreading trunks

223

The Birches—*Betula*

The birches are distributed widely over the Old and the New Worlds, being most abundant in the high latitudes. About 15 species occur in North America. Two tree birches (white and yellow birch), the shrubby bog birch, *B. pumila* L., and three hybrids occur in Michigan. The birches are graceful trees with slender, flexible branches and delicate foliage. The bark is characterized by horizontally elongated lenticels, and in some species it peels off in thin, papery layers. The papery curls of outer bark make good tinder. The Native Americans cut off the bark of the white birch to use in the construction of canoes and wigwams. It furnished cups, pails, pots, pans, and many other useful articles for the early settler. The wood, being dense and hard, is used for interior finish, veneer, furniture, pulpwood, and numerous small articles. It also has a high fuel value.

The leaves of the Michigan tree birches are doubly serrate on the margin and arranged alternately on the branches. Often they appear in clusters of 2 or 3 on the short, spurlike branchlets of the older branches. The flowers appear in the spring before or with the developing leaves and are wind-pollinated. They are unisexual, borne in separate clusters, but both kinds are found on the same tree (monoecious). The male catkins are produced early in the preceding season, appearing short and rigid on the twigs during the winter but becoming long and pendulous when they open the following spring. The female flowers appear below the male flowers from buds of the preceding season, in small slender catkins. The fruit is a small winged nut or samara borne on a catkin which consists of a central axis to which the numerous bracts and samaras are attached. The samaras are light and are easily scattered long distances by the wind.

The European white birch, *Betula pendula* Roth, is often planted for shade and ornament in North America. It is a small to medium-sized tree of graceful habit that may grow to a height of 9–12 m. The branches ascend, but the very slender branchlets are more or less drooping, forming a rather open, ovoid crown. The young twigs are reddish and glandular-dotted, while the bark of the trunk is silvery white, peeling off in papery layers, finally becoming furrowed and almost black near the ground. The leaves are 3–7 cm long, acuminate at the apex, doubly serrate to somewhat lobed, and have long, slender petioles. They resemble leaves of the gray birch, *Betula populifolia* Marshall, of northeastern North America. The catkins of the European white birch are cylindrical, 2–3 cm long, and the samaras have rather wide wings. Unfortunately this species is short-lived, apparently due to a combination of factors; it is not hardy in our climate, has a weak and shallow root system, and is subject to attack by stem borers. The cut-leaf weeping birch, 'Dalecarlica' (L.) Schneider f., is the type of European white birch most frequently planted; a number of other varieties and cultivars differing in form of leaf and habit are also planted. *Betula pendula* and some of its forms may become established and reproduce spontaneously, especially in southwestern Michigan, where it has become confused with the eastern *B. populifolia.*

Summer and Winter Key to Species of *Betula*

1. Bark of trunk white, separating freely into thin, papery layers; twigs without wintergreen odor or taste; leaves solitary on long shoots or in clusters of three on short, spurlike shoots .... *B. papyrifera*, p. 228
1. Bark of trunk not white, usually yellowish gray, not separating into papery layers, but exfoliating in strips curled at the edges; twigs with wintergreen odor and taste; leaves solitary on long shoots or in clusters of two on short, spurlike shoots .... *B. alleghaniensis*, p. 226

BETULACEAE
Betula alleghaniensis Britton

Yellow Birch

Size and Form. Medium-sized to large tree, 15–25 m high and 60–100 cm in diameter. Numerous slender, pendulous branches form a broad, open, rounded crown. Shallow, wide-spreading root system; not windfirm. Michigan Big Tree: girth 4.5 m, diameter 144 cm, height 35 m, Mackinac Co. (tree 151 cm in diameter in Marquette Co.).

Bark. Thin, smooth, dark on young stems; becoming silvery yellowish gray as the trunk expands, usually breaking into narrow strips curled at the edges; highly variable in degree of exfoliation (Dancik and Barnes 1971). Old trunks becoming gray or blackish, dull, deeply and irregularly fissured into large, thin plates. Lenticels conspicuous, horizontally elongated.

Leaves. Alternate, simple, solitary on long shoots, in pairs on short, spur shoots of older branches, blades 7–12 cm long and half as wide; oval, apex acuminate; sharply doubly serrate; thin and firm; dull, dark green above, yellowish green beneath; glabrous; 8–12 or more pairs of veins; petioles short, slender, grooved, hairy; slightly aromatic.

Twigs. Slender, greenish, pubescent when young, becoming glabrous, very lustrous, silvery gray or light orange; slightly aromatic with wintergreen taste and odor.

Winter Buds. Terminal bud absent; end and lateral buds 5–7 mm long, conical, acute, chestnut brown, more or less appressed; bud scales 3–5, more or less pubescent.

Wood. Heavy, very strong and hard, close-grained, light brown tinged with red, with thin, whitish sapwood. Uses include veneer, furniture, paneling, cabinet work, interior trim, flooring, plywood.

Flowers. April-May, before the leaves; male catkins 7–10 cm long, slender, pendent, purplish yellow; female catkins sessile or nearly so, erect, 2 cm long, greenish. Wind-pollinated.

Fruit. Samara; autumn; borne in sessile or short-stalked, erect, oval catkins 2–4 cm long, bracts slowly deciduous, catkins often remaining on the tree over winter; bracts with 3 ascending lobes, pubescent on the back and edges; samara with narrow wings, shed throughout late autumn and winter.

Distribution. Common throughout the state, but more abundant and of larger size in the northern half of the Lower Peninsula and in the Upper Peninsula.

Habitat. Characteristic of various sites and communities: in mesic, northern, mixed hardwood forests associated with sugar maple, beech, eastern hemlock, basswood, red maple, red oak; in poorly drained northern swamps associated with red maple, black ash, white and black spruces, speckled alder; in poorly drained microsites with eastern hemlock; also found along lake and stream margins. In southern Michigan, typically restricted to deciduous swamps, associated with American elm, red maple, black ash, tamarack. Thrives on a variety of sites and soil conditions including both basic and acid soils.

Notes. Intermediate in shade tolerance; moderately fast-growing; long-lived. Rarely forms pure stands. Seedlings establish in mineral soil, also on rotting logs, stumps, and in moss on rocks. Logs and stumps decay leaving the tree perched on stilt roots. Hybridizes with white birch (Barnes et al. 1974) and bog birch (Dancik and Barnes 1972). Dark, tight-barked trunks are common in swamps of southern Michigan (Dancik 1969) and have been confused with the sweet or black birch, *B. lenta* L. of eastern North America.

Hybrid with bog birch (*B. pumila*), *B. ×purpusii* Schneid., occasionally found in swamps of southern Michigan (Dancik and Barnes 1972). It is a small tree, the largest known being 46 cm in girth, 14.6 cm in diameter, 9 m tall (Jackson Co.). Its morphological characteristics are intermediate between those of the parents; distinguished from *B. ×sandbergii* by wintergreen taste and odor of bark of twigs and branches, ascending lateral lobes of bracts of female catkins, and more veins in the leaves.

226

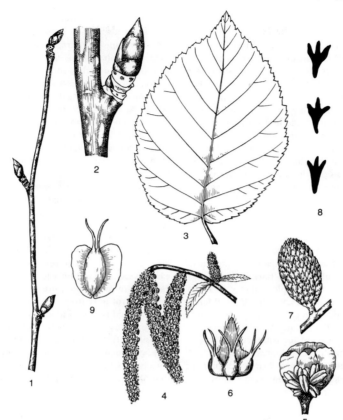

1. Winter twig, × 1.
2. Portion of twig, enlarged.
3. Leaf, × ½.
4. Flowering twig, × ½.
5. Male flower, enlarged.
6. Bract with female flowers, enlarged.
7. Fruiting catkin, × ½.
8. Silhouettes of female bracts, in winter, from three trees, × 1.
9. Fruit, samara, × 5.

Key Characters

- leaves of short, spur shoots in 2s; 12 or more pairs of veins
- bark yellowish gray, exfoliating in horizontal strips, curled at edges
- fruit bracts with 3 ascending lobes, pubescent on back and edges
- twigs and buds with wintergreen taste and odor

227

BETULACEAE
Betula papyrifera Marshall

White Birch   Paper Birch

Size and Form. Medium-sized tree, 12–20 m high and 30–50 cm in diameter. Forming in youth a compact, pyramidal or oval crown of many slender branches ending in very fine branchlets; becoming in old age a long, branchless trunk with a broad, open crown, composed of a few large limbs ascending to an acute angle, with almost horizontal branches. Michigan Big Tree: girth 3.7 m, diameter 118 cm, height 24 m, Schoolcraft Co.

Bark. Thin; smooth and often reddish brown on young trunks, becoming creamy white on outer surface of the trunk and large branches, bright orange on the inner surface, separating freely into thin, papery layers; highly flammable; becoming furrowed and almost black near the ground. Lenticels conspicuous, horizontally elongated. Trunk turns dark brownish black when bark is removed.

Leaves. Alternate, simple, solitary on long shoots, in 3s on short, spur shoots of older branches, blades 5–8 cm long, 3–5 cm wide; ovate or triangular; coarsely, more or less doubly serrate except for rounded, entire base; thick and firm; dark green above, lighter beneath; glabrous; 9 or fewer pairs of veins; petioles stout, yellow, glabrous or pubescent.

Twigs. Slender, dull red, becoming lustrous, orange brown; no wintergreen taste or odor.

Winter Buds. Terminal bud absent; end and lateral buds 5–7 mm long, narrow-ovoid, acute, flattish, often gummy, usually divergent.

Wood. Light, hard, strong, tough, very close-grained, light brown tinged with red, with thick, whitish sapwood. Uses include turned products (bobbins, spools, handles, dowels, woodenware), pulpwood, veneer stock, fireplace wood.

Flowers. April-May, before or with the leaves; male catkins clustered or in pairs, 7–10 cm long, slender, pendent, brownish; female catkins 3–4 cm long, slender, erect or spreading, greenish; styles bright red. Wind-pollinated.

Fruit. Samara; August-September; borne in long-stalked, cylindrical, glabrous, drooping catkins, 3–4 cm long, disintegrating rapidly when ripe; bracts cross-shaped with 2 lobes pointing away from the short middle lobe, hairy on margin; samara with wide wings, shed in early autumn.

Distribution. Rare in the southernmost tier of counties, becoming abundant northward. A Boreal Forest tree reaching one part of its southernmost limit in southern Michigan.

Habitat. Characteristic of burned-over and cutover areas of a great variety of soils, and with water-table conditions from well drained to somewhat poorly drained: margins of lakes, streams, seepages, swamps, and on drier microsites in swamps. Associated with a great variety of species; among the most common are pines, oaks, and aspens.

Notes. Very shade-intolerant; fast-growing; short-lived. Highly variable; many varieties have been described. Fire-dependent—fire exposes mineral soil on which seedlings may establish in profusion; pure stands common. Sprouts profusely from the base of the trunk of fire-killed stems. Native Americans used the bark for canoes, wigwam coverings, and utensils. Often planted as an ornamental tree, although less common than the cut-leaf variety of European white birch. More hardy than the European birch, but still short-lived and highly susceptible to the bronze birch borer (*Agrilus anxius*).

Hybrid with bog birch (*B. pumila*), *B. ×sandbergii* Britt., occasionally found in bogs, swamps, and disturbed areas of the Upper Peninsula and as far south as Livingston and Oakland Co. It is a small tree whose morphological characteristics are intermediate between those of the parents; distinguished from *B. ×purpusii* by cruciform lateral lobes of bracts of female catkins; lack of wintergreen taste and odor of twigs and branches; and fewer veins of the leaf.

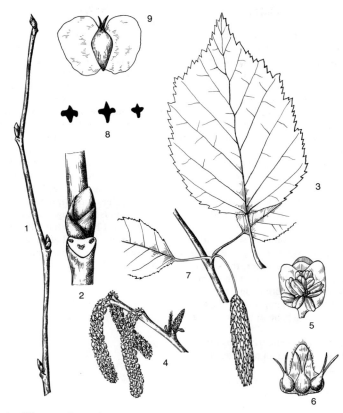

1. Winter twig, × 1.
2. Portion of twig, enlarged.
3. Leaf, × 1.
4. Flowering twig, × ½.
5. Male flower, enlarged.
6. Bract with female flowers, enlarged.
7. Fruiting shoot with catkin, × ½.
8. Silhouettes of female bracts, in winter, from three trees, × 1.
9. Fruit, samara, × 5.

Key Characters

- leaves of short, spur shoots in 3s; 9 or less pairs of veins
- bark creamy-white, peeling readily in large, thin sheets
- fruit bracts cross-shaped with 2 lobes pointing away from the short middle lobe; samara with wide wings
- twigs with no wintergreen taste or odor

229

BETULACEAE
Alnus rugosa (Du Roi) Sprengel

Speckled Alder

Size and Form. Shrub or small tree, 2–8 m high and 3–6 cm in diameter. Usually a wide-spreading shrub. Several crooked stems rising from the root collar form an open, irregular, sparsely branched crown; trunks are typically bent or curved at the base due to a phototrophic response toward light and to snow pressure that flattens young stems to the ground. Clone-forming by sprouting from the root collar; thickets often dense with contorted stems. Roots very shallow. Michigan Big Tree: girth 84 cm, diameter 27 cm, height 17 m. Ottawa Co.

Bark. Thin, rough, reddish brown, many horizontal, whitish or light orange lenticels up to 7 mm long.

Leaves. Alternate, simple, blades 5–10 cm long, half as wide; oval to obovate, rounded at base; doubly and finely serrate; thick; glabrous, dull green above, pale to hoary beneath, pubescent or glabrous on veins beneath; veins straight, impressed above, conspicuously projecting beneath; petioles 1–2 cm long.

Twigs. Moderately slender, reddish brown, glabrous; pith triangular in cross section; leaf scars half-round, raised.

Winter Buds. Terminal bud absent; lateral and end buds distinctly stalked, 2–3 scales, reddish brown, 5–8 mm long.

Flowers. March-May, before the leaves; male catkins clustered, 5–10 cm long, slender, pendent, brownish; female catkins 1.5–3 cm long, borne at right angles to the male catkins, becoming woody. Trees monoecious. Wind-pollinated.

Fruit. A tiny nut; autumn; fruiting body oval, conelike, woody, long-stalked, drooping, persistent into the next growing season, 1–1.5 cm long; nut with narrow wings.

Distribution. Abundant in the Upper Peninsula and the upper half of the Lower Peninsula, occasional or rare south to Berrien, St. Joseph, Ingham, and Monroe Co.

Habitat. Wet, open sites along streams; also in depressions and open swamps with moving water. Tolerates neutral, acid, or basic conditions, not stagnant swamps. Associates include willows, yellow birch, red maple, white spruce, black spruce, white pine, mountain-holly.

Notes. Very shade-intolerant; moderately fast-growing; short-lived. Often forming dense thickets along small streams, bending out over streams; very difficult to walk through. Named for the speckled appearance of lenticels on the bark.

A related species that has been long cultivated in eastern North America and is becoming naturalized in Michigan, is the black alder of Europe, *A. glutinosa* (L.) Gaertner. Black alder is a shade-intolerant, fast-growing tree, reaching 20 m high. Leaves notched at the apex; dark green, lustrous above, paler beneath; remaining green until late autumn, abscising green or brown. Tolerant of wet habitats but will grow well on upland soils. Like all alder species it has the ability to fix atmospheric nitrogen. Hardy in the Lower Peninsula.

230

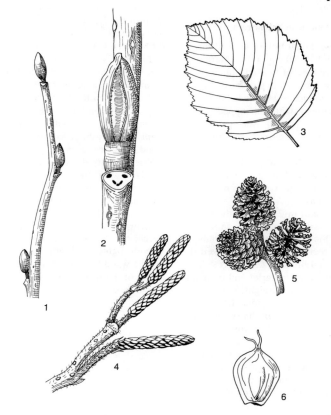

1. Winter twig, × 1.
2. Portion of twig, × 4.
3. Leaf, × ½.
4. Male catkins, × 1.
5. Female catkins, × 1.
6. Fruit, nut, × 5.

Key Characters

- leaves ovate-obovate; veins straight, impressed above, prominently projecting beneath
- buds distinctly stalked
- bark smooth, lenticels conspicuous
- fruit-bearing body conelike, woody, persistent into next growing season
- typically a many-stemmed shrub growing along streams and in swamps

BETULACEAE
Carpinus caroliniana Walter

Blue-beech   American Hornbeam

Size and Form. Small tree or large shrub, 3–10 m high and 15–30 cm in diameter. Trunk short, crooked or twisted, fluted or with musclelike ridges, wavy in cross section; slender, zigzag branches with fine shoots in flat sprays forming a tight, flat-topped crown. Shallow root system. Michigan Big Tree: girth 1.1 m, diameter 36 cm, height 14 m, Wayne Co.

Bark. Thin, smooth, tight, dark bluish gray, often mottled with lighter or darker patches; bark conspicuous because of muscle-like ridges on trunk.

Leaves. Alternate, in 2 rows on the shoots, simple, blades 5–10 cm long, 2–4 cm wide; ovate to oval, long-pointed; sharply doubly serrate, larger teeth at ends of major veins; thin and firm; dull bluish green above, lighter beneath, turning scarlet and orange in autumn; glabrous; veins straight, not branched; petioles short, slender, hairy.

Twigs. Slender, pale green, hairy, becoming lustrous, dark red the first winter, glabrous or nearly so.

Winter Buds. Terminal bud absent; end and lateral buds 3 mm long, narrow-ovoid, slightly angled, blunt, puberulent, brownish; bud scales with a whitish margin, appressed against the shoots.

Wood. Heavy, hard, tough, very strong, close-grained, light brown, with thick, whitish sapwood. Uses include tool handles, wedges.

Flowers. April-May, with the leaves; apetalous; male catkins not visible until spring, 2.5–4 cm long, scales greenish, boat-shaped, each bearing 3–20 stamens; female catkins 1.2–1.9 cm long, scales hairy, greenish, each bearing 2 pistils with long, scarlet styles. Trees monoecious. Wind-pollinated.

Fruit. A small nut; midsummer, often remains on the tree long after the leaves have fallen; in loose, terminal clusters; bract leaf-like, 3-lobed, the central lobe the largest, 2 cm long, enclosing a small, ovoid, brownish, ribbed nut. The nuts remain attached to the bract which behaves like a large, wind-borne samara.

Distribution. Common in the lower ⅔ of the Lower Peninsula; absent in the upper third of the Lower Peninsula and the eastern half of the Upper Peninsula; occasional in the western Upper Peninsula.

Habitat. Characteristic of moist, low, fertile, somewhat poorly drained to poorly drained sites along the borders of swamps and streams; in the wetter parts of beech-maple forests and drier areas of deciduous swamps. Associated with American elm, red maple, black ash, yellow birch, beech, basswood, tuliptree, sugar maple.

Notes. Highly shade-tolerant; slow-growing; relatively short-lived. An important subdominant tree of moist, fertile deciduous forests, but smaller in size and occupying a different site than hop-hornbeam. Attractive as an ornamental tree but rarely planted. Not a true beech; common name derived from the smooth, tight, bluish gray bark; also called muscle-wood because of the musclelike ridges of the trunk. Sometimes called ironwood because of its hard, tough wood.

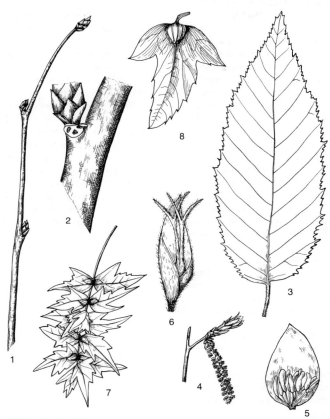

1. Winter twig, × 1.
2. Portion of twig, enlarged.
3. Leaf, × 1.
4. Flowering twig, × ½.
5. Male flower, enlarged.
6. Female flower, enlarged.
7. Fruiting twig, × ½.
8. Fruit bract with nut, × 1.

Key Characters
- leaves with straight, unbranched veins
- fruit a small nut at the base of a 3-lobed, leaflike bract
- bark smooth, thin, tight, bluish gray
- trunk with musclelike ridges, wavy in cross section

Distinguished from hop-hornbeam when young by leaves with straight, un-branched veins; easily distinguished as an adult by bark and fruit.

233

BETULACEAE
Ostrya virginiana (Miller) K. Koch

Hop-hornbeam

Size and Form. Small to medium-sized tree, 9–16 m high and 20–30 cm in diameter. Forming a broad, rounded or conical crown of many long, slender branches; trunk extends nearly to top. Prominent tap root; windfirm. Michigan Big Tree: girth 2.8 m, diameter 91 cm, height 22 m, Grand Traverse Co.

Bark. Thin, soft, grayish brown, broken into narrow longitudinal strips loose at the ends, giving a shreddy appearance; bark of saplings smooth, tight, chestnut brown.

Leaves. Alternate, simple, 7–12 cm long, 3–5 cm wide; borne singly on shoots, not on short, spur shoots; sharply doubly serrate, larger teeth at ends of major veins; thin and very tough; dull, dark yellowish green and glabrous above, paler and finely pubescent beneath, turning dull yellow in autumn; some veins (especially near base of blade) branch near the margin; petioles short, slender, pubescent, the hairs usually gland-tipped.

Twigs. Slender, at first light brown, becoming lustrous, reddish brown, finally dull dark brown.

Winter Buds. Terminal bud absent; end bud and lateral buds 3–6 cm long, ovoid, acute, greenish brown to pale brown; bud scales striated.

Wood. Heavy, very strong and hard, tough, close-grained, durable, light reddish brown, with thick, whitish sapwood. Uses include fence posts, tool handles, wedges.

Flowers. April-May, with the leaves; male catkins drooping, cylindrical, usually in 3s, visible in winter; stamens 3–14, crowded on a hairy receptacle; female catkins erect, usually in pairs, each flower enclosed in a hairy saclike bract. Trees monoecious. Wind-pollinated.

Fruit. Nut; September; fruits in clusters, 3–6 cm long, borne on slender, hairy stems; nut small, 6 mm long, flat, enclosed by an oval, flattened saclike bract, 1.5–2 cm long, in clusters of 4–10, resembling hops.

Distribution. Common throughout the state.

Habitat. Characteristic of the understory of dry-mesic, oak-hickory forests on well-drained, upland sites; associated with black, white, and red oaks, shagbark and pignut hickories, white ash, black cherry. Also occurs in mesic beech-maple forests on moist, fertile slopes; associated with sugar maple, beech, basswood, red oak. Not found on poorly drained sites.

Notes. Shade-tolerant; very slow-growing; moderately long-lived. One of the few trees in northern deciduous forests that occupies a subdominant position. Handsome foliage and form for lawn or park plantings; difficult to transplant because of deep tap root. Known as ironwood because of its exceedingly tough, hard wood; used for prying poles, levers, sleigh runners, wagon tongues, wheel rims and spokes, and many other uses in pioneer days.

234

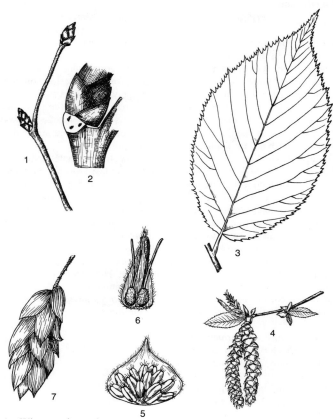

1. Winter twig, × 1.
2. Portion of twig, enlarged.
3. Leaf, × ½.
4. Flowering shoot, × ½.
5. Male flower, enlarged.
6. Female flower, enlarged.
7. Fruiting twig, × ½.

Key Characters

- leaves with several veins, especially near the blade base, that branch near the margin
- fruit, a nut, enclosed by an oval, flattened, saclike bract; fruit cluster resembling hops
- bark grayish brown, separating into narrow, longitudinal strips, loose at the ends, giving a shreddy appearance

Distinguished from blue-beech by leaves having several veins, especially near the blade base, that branch near the margin.

Distinguished from yellow birch by leaves borne singly along the shoots, not borne on short, spurlike shoots.

235

ULMACEAE
Celtis occidentalis Linnaeus

Northern Hackberry

Size and Form. Medium-sized tree, 12–18 m high and 30–60 cm in diameter. Open-grown trees may branch 3–4 m from the ground into a few large limbs and many slender, horizontal, zigzag branches, forming a broad, rounded crown. Forest-grown trees have straight, tall trunks and a more slender crown. Roots shallow on lowland sites. Michigan Big Tree: girth 6.0 m, diameter 190 cm, height 36 m, Allegan Co.

Bark. Relatively thin, light brown or silvery gray, broken into deep, short, narrow ridges or distinctive corky excrescences.

Leaves. Alternate, simple, blades 5–14 cm long and half as wide; ovate to ovate-lanceolate, base inequilateral, apex usually long-pointed; coarsely serrate above the entire base; thin; light green to bluish green above, paler beneath and hairy on the veins, turning light yellow late in autumn; glabrous or somewhat scabrous; veins conspicuous in a lacelike network, 5–8 per side; petioles short, slender, hairy.

Twigs. Slender, greenish, puberulent, becoming lustrous, reddish brown in the first winter; pith small, white, closely chambered; bundle scars 1 or 3.

Winter Buds. Terminal bud absent; end and lateral buds light brown, 3–6 mm long, ovoid, acute, flattened, the tip appressed.

Wood. Heavy, rather soft, coarse-grained, weak, light yellow, with thick, whitish sapwood. Wood of little commercial importance, uses similar to those of American elm.

Flowers. May, with or soon after the leaves; greenish; inconspicuous; on slender pedicels; male flowers in clusters at the base of the shoot; calyx greenish, deeply 5-lobed; corolla 0; stamens 5; female flowers usually solitary in the axils of the upper leaves; ovary 1-celled. Wind-pollinated.

Fruit. Drupe, September-October; slender-stalked, thin-fleshed, globular with a smooth coat, 6–8 mm in diameter, dark purple, edible, becoming deeply puckered, prunelike; pit wrinkled.

Distribution. Occasional in the southern half of the Lower Peninsula, north to Newaygo, Midland, and Arenac Co.

Habitat. Characteristic of banks of small streams, river floodplains and moist, fertile bottomlands with calcareous soils. Not typical of the often-flooded bottoms where silver maple, red ash, and American elm thrive. Also grows on limestone outcrops and on dry, gravelly or rocky slopes where the subsoil is circumneutral to basic and rich in lime. Associates include basswood, American elm, cottonwood, red ash, bur oak, sycamore.

Notes. Intermediate in shade tolerance; relatively fast-growing; moderately long-lived. Sprouts from the root collar or stump of young trees following fire or cutting. Seeds widely dispersed by birds. Highly susceptible to fire. Easily transplanted and some forms are valuable as lawn and park trees. A type of "witches'-broom," a rosettelike proliferation of shoot tips, is the most important disease. The brooming is caused by the combined action of a powdery mildew fungus, *Sphaerotheca phytophila,* and a gall mite, *Eriophyes* sp.

236

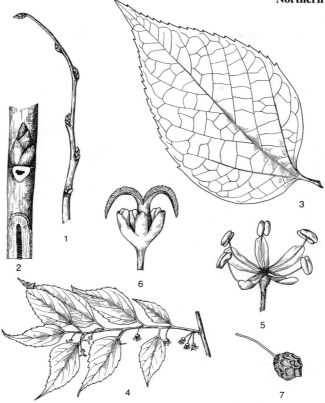

1. Winter twig, × 1.
2. Portion of twig, enlarged.
3. Leaf, × ¾.
4. Flowering shoot, × ½.
5. Male flower, enlarged.
6. Female flower, enlarged.
7. Fruit, drupe, × 1.

Key Characters

- leaf blade thin, base very inequilateral or oblique; veins prominent in a lacy pattern
- bark with corky thickenings, forming short, narrow ridges
- fruit a dark purple drupe, becoming puckered and prunelike when dried
- clusters of proliferated shoot tips, termed "witches brooms," scattered throughout the crown

Distinguished from dwarf hackberry by its much larger size; larger and long-tipped leaves; and fruits which are puckered or prunelike when dried.

237

ULMACEAE
Celtis tenuifolia Nuttall

Dwarf Hackberry

Size and Form. Small tree or shrub, 2–6 m high and 5–20 cm in diameter. Trunk commonly divided; irregular and asymmetrical crown; the branches numerous, stiff, twisted and intergrown. Michigan Big Tree: no record.

Bark. Thin, smooth, pale gray except for wartlike thickenings.

Leaves. Alternate, simple, blades 4–6 cm long, 2.5–4 cm wide; ovate, short-acuminate tip, base moderately asymmetrical; entire to irregularly shallowly toothed; thick, coriaceous; gray green; glabrous to somewhat scabrous or finely hairy; 3–5 major veins per side; petiole short, 0.5–1 cm long.

Twigs. Slender, narrow, stiff, sometimes thornlike, grayish; bundle scars 1 or 3.

Winter Buds. Similar to northern hackberry but smaller, 1–2 mm long.

Flowers. May, similar to those of northern hackberry but appearing about 10 days later. Wind-pollinated.

Fruit. Drupe, September; globular, pinkish brown, thin-fleshed, mature fruit with smooth surface, persistent on wiry stalk through the winter, sweet flavor, 5–7 mm in diameter; pit smooth.

Distribution. Rare in the southern part of the Lower Peninsula, highly localized; known from Jackson, Lenawee, Livingston, St. Joseph, and Washtenaw Co.

Habitat. Characteristic of dry-mesic to xeric sites, including wooded sand dunes, sandy, calcareous glacial deposits, and soils with limestone near the surface. Associates include dwarf chinkapin oak, pignut hickory, sassafras, black cherry, black walnut, scarlet oak, eastern redcedar, New Jersey tea, fragrant sumac.

Notes. Shade-intolerant; slow-growing; short-lived. A rare but easily overlooked species, becoming more frequent south of Michigan. Found on disturbed sites and apparently eliminated by developing oak-hickory forests. It rarely occurs together with the more common northern hackberry. First discovered in Michigan in 1971 and described in detail by Wagner (1974).

238

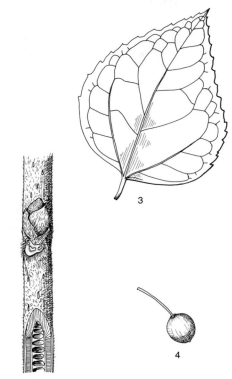

1. Winter twig, × 1.
2. Portion of twig, × 4.
3. Leaf, × 1.
4. Fruit, drupe, × 1.

Key Characters

- small, compact, irregular form
- coriaceous leaves with equal or moderately unequal bases, short-acuminate tip
- drupe smooth when mature, sweet, persistent; pit smooth
- rare, reported only from five counties in southern Michigan

Distinguished from northern hackberry by small size; smaller leaves with short acuminate tips; smooth, longer-persistent fruits.

The Elms—*Ulmus*

The elms are among the better known eastern deciduous trees. They are highly esteemed for their shade and ornamental value and are useful commercially because of their heavy, hard, and exceedingly tough wood. Some 45 species of elms are known, 6 of which are native in North America (all east of the Rocky Mountains); 3 are native in Michigan.

The elms are among the first trees to flower in the spring. The tiny, greenish, perfect flowers arise before the leaves appear. The flowers are wind-pollinated, and a profusion of fruits soon follows, maturing before the leaves are full grown. The fruits are soon dispersed and the seeds germinate not long thereafter. The fruit, a samara, has a broad wing surrounding the seed.

The leaves have a distinctive oblique, asymmetrical base, full and rounded on one side and wedge-shaped on the other. They are simple, alternate, and borne in two rows along the twig. Terminal buds are absent, one of the fully formed lateral buds forming the end bud. The buds are obliquely sessile above the leaf scars which are light brown and have three sunken bundle scars.

The native elms have been severely decimated by the Dutch elm fungus (*Ceratocystis ulmi*) in combination with another disease, phloem necrosis. Mature elms have been eliminated from mesic and lowland forests in many localities in eastern North America. However, many young elms, especially American elm, still thrive in Michigan in a variety of disturbed habitats (Barnes 1976). They become more susceptible to the disease as they mature.

Several elms have been introduced and planted in North America for shade and ornament. They are hardy in the southern half of the Lower Peninsula. Two are briefly described below and a third, the Siberian elm, is described fully in the text.

The English elm, *Ulmus procera* Salisbury, is a large tree with a massive straight trunk persisting halfway or more through the crown and bearing only a few, massive, twisting, ascending branches; sprouts are typical along the trunk and large limbs. The bark is gray and deeply fissured into rectangular flakes. The twigs are dark reddish brown, nearly glabrous or somewhat downy; winter buds are

241

small, 2–3 mm long, dark smoky brown, slightly pubescent. Some cultivars have corky ridges on the branches resembling rock elm, but several of the leaf veins fork, which is not common in rock elm. The leaf blades are smaller than those of the native elms, 4–8 cm long, very doubly-toothed, often curled or puckered, scabrous above and soft-pubescent beneath, and darker green than those of the American elm. They remain green long after those of American elm have fallen. The samara is hairless, 1.2 cm wide.

The wych elm, *Ulmus glabra* Hudson, is a medium-sized tree whose bark remains smooth and silvery gray for many years (hence *"glabra"*). Both the twigs and the blackish red winter buds are pubescent. The leaf blades are 8–16 cm long, very unequal at the base, abruptly acuminate, rough-scabrous above and pubescent beneath; petioles are very short and thick, 2–5 mm long. The samaras are larger than those of any native species. A cultivar form of one of its hybrids, known as the Camperdown or weeping elm, *U. ×vegeta* cv. Camperdownii, with pendulous branches and shoots, is commonly planted and forms a small tree 3–5 m high with a rounded crown. It is usually produced by grafting on an upright stock, which leads to a striking umbrellalike, weeping form.

Summer Key to Species of *Ulmus*

1. Leaf blades small, 3–7 cm long .... *U. pumila*, p. 250
1. Leaf blades large, 7–18 cm long.
  2. Leaf blades essentially smooth on both sides; branches with irregular, corky, winglike ridges; lowermost branches usually short and strongly drooping; main trunk usually continuous into the crown without dividing, tree outline narrow-oblong .... *U. thomasii*, p. 246
  2. Leaf blades usually rough on one or on both sides; branches without corky ridges; lowermost branches not short, not strongly drooping; main trunk usually dividing into several large limbs, tree outline more or less vase-shaped.
    3. Leaf blades usually rough above but smooth beneath; bark of trunk gray, deeply fissured into broad, scaly ridges, when broken across showing alternating whitish and brown layers; inner bark not mucilaginous .... *U. americana*, p. 244
    3. Leaf blades usually rough both sides; bark of trunk dark reddish brown, shallowly fissured into large, loose plates, when broken across showing brown without alternating whitish and brown layers; inner bark mucilaginous .... *U. rubra*, p. 248

Winter Key to Species of *Ulmus*

1. End and lateral buds small, usually less than 3 mm long; twigs very slender; outer trunk bark with orange-colored layer in fissures, more or less solid dark brown when broken across, whitish layers not conspicuous .... *U. pumila*, p. 250

242

1. End and lateral buds larger, 3–6 mm long; twigs slender to moderately stout; outer trunk bark without orange-colored layer in fissures, solid brown or with conspicuous alternating whitish and brown layers when broken across.
    2. Buds conspicuously rusty-tomentose, especially at tip; outer bark solid brown when broken across; inner bark very mucilaginous when chewed ..... *U. rubra*, p. 248
    2. Buds not conspicuously rusty-tomentose; outer bark with alternating whitish and brown layers when broken across; inner bark not mucilaginous.
        3. Bundle scars usually 3; twigs without corky ridges; outline of tree vase-shaped .... *U. americana*, p. 244
        3. Bundle scars usually 4–6 in a curved line; twigs often with irregular corky ridges; outline of tree narrow-oblong .... *U. thomasii*, p. 246

ULMACEAE
Ulmus americana Linnaeus

American Elm   White Elm

Size and Form. Large tree, 20–30 m high and 50–120 cm in diameter. Trunk commonly dividing 6–9 m above the ground into a few large branches that rise upward and outward to form a vase-shaped or umbrella-like outline; branchlets typically drooping; trunk often buttressed. Root system shallow, wide-spreading on poorly drained sites, deep on well drained sites. Michigan Big Tree: girth 4.9 m, diameter 154 cm, height 37 m, Leelanau Co.

Bark. Thick, ashy gray, deeply fissured into broad, interlacing, scaly ridges; outer bark with alternating whitish and brown layers when broken across.

Leaves. Alternate, simple, blades 10–15 cm long, half as wide; obovate-oblong to oval; base asymmetrical; coarsely, doubly serrate; thick and firm; dark green and somewhat rough above, pale and soft-pubescent or glabrous beneath; veins seldom forking; petioles short and stout.

Twigs. Slender, at first light green, glabrous, or downy, reddish brown, finally ashy gray; leaf scars covered with a corky layer, bundle scars depressed, usually 3.

Winter Buds. Terminal bud absent; end and lateral buds in two rows, ovoid, acute, flattened; scales glabrous or slightly hairy, brown, 3–6 mm long, appressed.

Wood. Heavy, hard, strong, tough, difficult to split, coarse-grained, light brown, with thick, lighter-colored sapwood. Uses include furniture, boxes, crates, barrels, veneer.

Flowers. March-April, before the leaves; mostly perfect; small, brown to red; borne on slender pedicels in loose clusters; calyx campanulate, 5–9-lobed; corolla 0; stamens 4–9, with bright red anthers; ovary 2-celled; stigmas 2, green. Wind-pollinated.

Fruit. Samara; May; ovate, 1-seeded, smooth and glabrous both sides, hairy on the margin, 1.2 cm long, deeply notched at the tip, long-stalked, in crowded clusters.

Distribution. Common throughout the state.

Habitat. In southern Michigan, characteristic of river floodplains (associates include eastern cottonwood, silver maple, red ash), poorly drained deciduous swamps (associates include red maple, black ash, yellow birch, blue-beech), and disturbed sites such as open pastures, hillsides, old fields, roadsides, ditches, and cutover mesic and dry-mesic forests. In the northern half of the Lower Peninsula and in the Upper Peninsula, occurring occasionally in mesic northern hardwood forests (associated with sugar maple, beech, basswood, yellow birch, hemlock, red maple), wet-mesic floodplains and swamp edges (associated with red maple, black ash, balsam poplar), also colonizing pastures, hillsides, old fields, roadsides, and cutover forests.

Notes. Moderately shade-tolerant; rapid-growing; long-lived. Sprouts vigorously following injury. Leaves of seedlings and young sprouts more roughly pubescent than those of mature trees; such plants are often mistaken for slippery elm. Aggressive colonizer of open, disturbed areas, especially where the site is wet in the spring. Susceptible to Dutch elm and phloem necrosis diseases; mature trees decimated in many native stands. In southeastern Michigan, seedlings still occur in deciduous swamps but are more prevalent in open fields and roadsides (Barnes 1976). Not in danger of extinction. Before the introduction of the Dutch elm disease it was an ideal street and park tree (probably the most widely planted street tree in Michigan), valued for its shade and graceful habit.

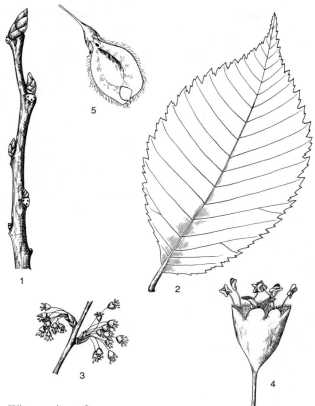

1. Winter twig, × 2.
2. Leaf, × ½.
3. Flowering twig, × ½.
4. Flower, enlarged.
5. Fruit, samara, × 2.

Key Characters

- leaf blades of mature trees somewhat rough on upper surface; veins rarely forked
- bark thick, ashy gray; outer bark layered with alternating light- and dark-colored bands in cross section
- samara with hairy margin, deeply notched at tip

Distinguished from rock elm by divided trunk and several widely arching branches; twigs without corky ridges.

ULMACEAE
Ulmus thomasii Sargent

Rock Elm   Cork Elm

Size and Form. Medium-sized tree, 15–22 m high and 30–60 cm in diameter. Central trunk pronounced, extending unbranched well into the narrow, oblong-cylindrical crown; side and lower branches short and drooping. Root system deep and wide-spreading on well drained sites. Michigan Big Tree: girth 2.3 m, diameter 73 cm, height 28 m, Grand Traverse Co.

Bark. Thick, grayish, with wide fissures separating broad, flat-topped, interlacing, scaly ridges; outer bark with alternating whitish and brown layers in cross section.

Leaves. Alternate, simple, blades 7–14 cm long, half as wide; obovate to oblong-oval, base usually asymmetrical, sometimes rounded; coarsely doubly serrate; thick and firm; dark green above, pale-pubescent beneath; many closely spaced veins that rarely fork; petioles pubescent, about 6 mm long.

Twigs. Slender, at first light brown and pubescent, becoming lustrous, reddish brown, finally grayish brown, with irregular corky, winglike ridges; branches developing thick gnarled, corky bark; leaf scars covered with a corky layer, bundle scars depressed, usually 4–6 in a curved line.

Winter Buds. Terminal bud absent; end and lateral buds in two rows, ovoid, acute to sharp-pointed, not flattened, divergent, about 6 mm long; scale margins pilose.

Wood. Heavy, very strong and tough, very difficult to split (hardest and toughest of all Michigan elms), light reddish brown, with thick, lighter-colored sapwood. Uses include hockey sticks, piano frames, boat frames, and other uses similar to those of American elm.

Flowers. April-May, before the leaves; mostly perfect; greenish; borne on slender, drooping pedicels in loose racemes; calyx campanulate, 7–8-lobed; corolla 0; stamens 7–8, with purple anthers; ovary hairy; stigmas 2, greenish. Wind-pollinated.

Fruit. Samara; May; ovate, 1-seeded, pubescent all over, 1.3–2 cm long, wings shallowly notched at the tip; seed cavity indistinct.

Distribution. Occasional in the southern third of the Lower Peninsula, north to Oscoda and Antrim Co.; absent in the Upper Peninsula. Approaching the northern limit of its range in Michigan.

Habitat. Generally less demanding of moisture than American and slippery elms. Found scattered in mesic hardwood forests on moist, well drained to somewhat poorly drained, sandy to silt loam soils; also on drier, limestone-derived soils. Associated with basswood, butternut, sugar maple, beech, white and red ashes, American elm.

Notes. Moderately shade-tolerant; moderately fast-growing; moderately long-lived. Sprouts vigorously from the root collar and stump following fire, cutting, or browsing; also sprouts from roots. Susceptible to the Dutch elm and phloem necrosis diseases.

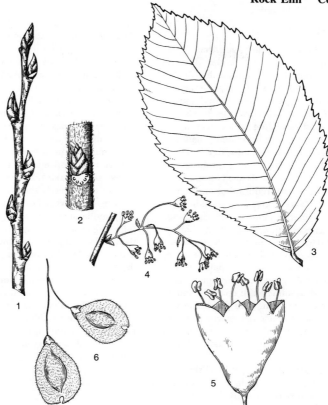

1. Winter twig, × 1.
2. Portion of twig, enlarged.
3. Leaf, × 1.
4. Flowering twig, × 1.
5. Flower, enlarged.
6. Fruit, samaras, × 1.

Key Characters

- leaf blades with many, closely spaced veins; base often rounded, nearly symmetrical
- twigs and branches with irregular, corky, winglike ridges
- samara pubescent all over, seed cavity indistinct
- unbranched trunk extending well into the upper crown

Distinguished from American elm by unbranched trunk that extends well into the relatively narrow crown, not broadly vase-shaped; twigs with irregular corky ridges; samara larger, pubescent all over, not just on margin.

247

ULMACEAE
Ulmus rubra Muhlenberg

Slippery Elm   Red Elm

Size and Form. Medium-sized tree, 15–21 m high and 30–60 cm in diameter. The trunk longer and more limb-free than that of the American elm, divides into large branches that form an irregular, open, broad and spreading, flat-topped crown; branches spreading and ascending rather than drooping. Root system wide-spreading, shallow or deep depending on soil and water table conditions. Michigan Big Tree: girth 4.0 m, diameter 129 cm, height 41 m, Ontonagon Co.

Bark. Thick, dark reddish brown, shallowly fissured into large, loose plates—more parallel than in American elm; outer bark solid brown in cross section, without alternating light and dark layers; inner bark slippery, mucilaginous, especially when chewed.

Leaves. Alternate, simple, blades 10–18 cm long, about half as wide; ovate-oblong to elliptical, base asymmetrical; coarsely doubly serrate; thick and firm; dark green and very rough-pubescent above, paler, rough to soft-hairy beneath; several lateral veins fork near the margin; fragrant; petioles short, stout, hairy.

Twigs. Moderately stout, at first bright green and pubescent, becoming light to dark brown or grayish; leaf scars covered with a corky layer, bundle scars depressed, usually 3.

Winter Buds. Terminal bud absent; end and lateral buds in two rows, ovoid, rather blunt, dark brown to black, rusty-tomentose, especially at tip, 4–6 mm long; flower buds large, globose, with rusty orange hairs at tip.

Wood. Heavy, hard, strong, very close-grained, durable, easy to split while green, dark reddish brown, with thin, lighter-colored sapwood. Uses same as American elm.

Flowers. March-April, before the leaves; mostly perfect; borne on short pedicels in crowded clusters; calyx campanulate, 5–9-lobed, green, hairy; corolla 0; stamens 5–9, with dark red anthers; stigmas 2, reddish purple. Wind-pollinated.

Fruit. Samara; May; suborbicular, 1-seeded, short-stalked in dense clusters; seed cavity brown-tomentose; wings smooth, 1.8–2 cm long, entire or nearly so at the tip, shallowly notched at the tip.

Distribution. Frequent in the southern half of the Lower Peninsula; occasional in the northern half of the Lower Peninsula; absent in the Upper Peninsula. Approaching the northern limit of its range in Michigan.

Habitat. Characteristics of mixed hardwood forests with mesic sites and moist, fertile soils: lower slopes, river terraces, bottomlands; also found on drier slopes with soils of high lime content. Associated with white, bur, and swamp white oaks, red ash, sugar maple, black walnut, butternut, basswood.

Notes. Moderately shade-tolerant; fast-growing (somewhat faster than American elm); moderately long-lived. Sprouts readily following injury. Seedlings spread vegetatively by sending out rhizomes from which shoots develop. Susceptible to Dutch elm disease and phloem necrosis. The slippery inner bark forms a mucilaginous mass when chewed and was once used as a thirst quencher. In pioneer days it was also valued medicinally for soothing sore throats and as a poultice for minor injuries; slippery elm throat lozenges are available today. Not as attractive ornamentally as the American elm.

248

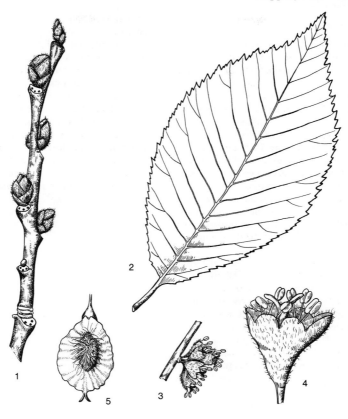

1. Winter twig, × 2.
2. Leaf, × ¾.
3. Flowering twig, × 1.
4. Perfect flower, enlarged.
5. Fruit, samara, × 1.

**Key
Characters**

- leaf blade very rough-pubescent, especially on the upper surface; several veins fork near the margin
- outer bark reddish brown, solid brown in cross section, not layered with light and dark bands
- inner bark of branches and trunk slippery, mucilaginous when chewed
- samara pubescent over the seed, slightly notched at tip
- buds dark brown to black, rusty-pubescent, especially at the tips

ULMACEAE
Ulmus pumila Linnaeus

Siberian Elm

Size and Form. Medium-sized tree, 15–22 m high and 30–60 cm in diameter. Trunk short, thick, soon dividing into several, large, wide-spreading limbs, forming an irregular, open, dome-shaped crown; when young some branchlets arranged in a herringbone pattern; many dead branchlets and branches in the interior and lower crown. Roots wide-spreading. Michigan Big Tree: girth 4.0 m, diameter 129 cm, height 37 m, Oakland Co.

Bark. Thick, dark gray, becoming deeply fissured and forming a marked network of broad interlacing ridges, orange-colored inner bark layers visible in the fissures; outer bark tough, hard, mostly solid brown in cross section, light bands inconspicuous; inner bark mucilaginous.

Leaves. Alternate, simple, small, blades 3–7 cm long, about half as wide; elliptical to elliptical-lanceolate, tip acute or acuminate, base almost symmetrical; nearly singly serrate; thin and firm; dark green, lustrous above, paler beneath, glabrous or nearly so; petioles short, 2–4 mm long.

Twigs. Very slender, at first green, becoming gray, glabrous or somewhat pubescent; leaf scars covered with a corky layer, bundle scars depressed, 3.

Winter Buds. Terminal bud absent; end and lateral buds in 2 rows, small, 1–3 mm long, narrow or broad-ovoid, dark reddish brown, somewhat pubescent; flower buds numerous, relatively large, globose.

Flowers. March-April, before the leaves; mostly perfect; very short-stalked in crowded clusters; stamens 4–5, with purple anthers. Wind-pollinated.

Fruit. Samara; April; suborbicular, 1-seeded, glabrous, 1–1.5 cm long, deeply notched at the tip.

Distribution. Native in eastern Siberia, northern China, Manchuria, Korea; introduced about 1860. Widely planted throughout the state; hardy.

Habitat. Lawns and city streets; becoming naturalized and colonizing weedy habitats in urban environments, also roadsides and fence rows.

Notes. Moderately shade-tolerant; very fast-growing; moderately long-lived. Tolerates droughty soils of light to heavy texture (sands to heavy clay). Desirable for its hardiness, fast growth, quick shade-producing quality, and high resistance to Dutch elm disease and phloem necrosis; undesirable as a lawn and street tree because dead branchlets constantly shed, highly susceptible to breakage by glaze and ice storms, and heavily attacked by the elm leaf beetle, *Pyrrhalta luteola*. Often mistakenly called the Chinese elm, *U. parvifolia* Jacq., which is a rarely cultivated but attractive, nearly evergreen, tree.

250

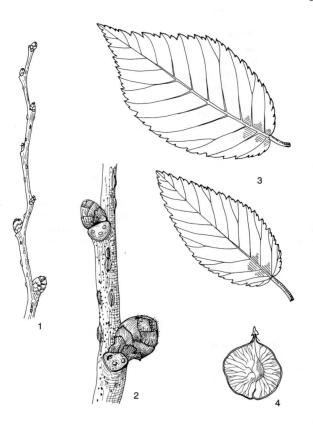

1. Winter twig, × 1.
2. Portion of twig: vegetative bud (above), flower bud (below), × 3½.
3. Leaves, × 1.
4. Fruit, samara, × 1.

Key Characters
- leaf blade small, glabrous both sides, nearly singly serrate
- samara small, glabrous, deeply notched at the tip
- trunk short, dividing into several large limbs; many dead branchlets and branches in crown
- orange-colored inner bark layers visible in fissures

251

MORACEAE
Maclura pomifera (Rafinesque) Schneider

Osage-orange

Size and Form. Small tree, 5–12 m high and 30–60 cm in diameter. Trunk short, dividing into a few large limbs with curving branches, forming a symmetrical, rounded crown. Roots deep and wide-spreading, root bark bright orange, exfoliating in papery layers. Michigan Big Tree: girth 4.3 m, diameter 136 cm, height 15 m, Berrien Co.

Bark. Thick, dark orange brown, deeply furrowed with coarse interlacing ridges; brown-shreddy on old trees.

Leaves. Alternate, simple, borne singly on new long shoots, borne in clusters on short, spur shoots of older branches; blades 6–12 cm long, 5–7 cm wide; ovate to oblong-lanceolate with a long, taper-pointed apex; entire, slightly wavy margin; thick and firm; dark glossy green above, paler beneath; glabrous; petioles slender, pubescent, 3–6 cm long.

Twigs. Stout, zigzag, at first bright green, pubescent, becoming orange brown and armed with stout, straight, axillary spines, 1–2 cm long. Short shoots form the second year and may bear 2–4 leaves.

Winter Buds. Terminal bud absent; lateral and end buds depressed-globular, partly hidden in the bark, glabrous, pale brown.

Wood. Heavy, very hard and strong, flexible, coarse-grained, very durable, bright orange, with thin, lemon-colored sapwood. Uses include archery bows, fenceposts, lumber, fuel.

Flowers. May-June, after the leaves; male flowers slender-pedicelled, borne in short racemes at the end of long, slender, drooping peduncles; calyx 4-lobed, hairy; corolla 0; stamens 4; female flowers in dense, globose heads at the end of short, stout peduncles; style covered with white, stigmatic hairs. Trees dioecious. Wind-pollinated.

Fruit. Multiple of drupes; autumn; pale green, knobby sphere, 10–14 cm in diameter, composed of numerous narrow drupes crowded and grown together, exuding a bitter, milky juice when crushed, inedible.

Distribution. Native in eastern Texas, southeastern Oklahoma, and southwestern Arkansas; formerly planted widely in eastern North America. Occasional in the southern half of the Lower Peninsula.

Habitat. Characteristic of river valleys and bottoms in its native range. Formerly planted extensively for hedge fences, thus found along roads and between fields. Hardy in the southern half of the Lower Peninsula.

Notes. Moderately shade-intolerant; fast-growing; moderately long-lived. Sprouts from roots and difficult to eradicate when once established. Rarely naturalizing by seed. Because land has become so valuable the old hedgerow fences are being dug up. Free from insect and fungus pests. A yellow dye may be extracted from the bark of the roots and the stemwood. The French named the tree bois-d'arc (wood of the bow); other common names include hedge-apple and yellowwood.

252

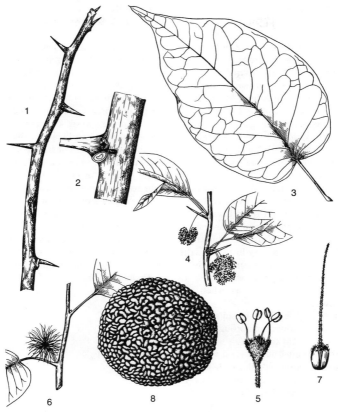

1. Winter twig, × 1.
2. Portion of twig, enlarged.
3. Leaf, × ½.
4. Male flowering shoot, × ½.
5. Male flower, enlarged.
6. Female flowering shoot, × ½.
7. Female flower, enlarged.
8. Fruit, multiple of drupes, × ¼.

Key Characters

- leaf blades with entire margins, dark, glossy green upper surface; tip long-acuminate
- young shoots with axillary spines
- bark dark, orange brown; root bark bright orange
- fruit a large (10–14 cm in diameter) knobby, greenish sphere, hard and heavy when fresh

MORACEAE
Morus alba Linnaeus

White Mulberry

Size and Form. Small tree, 6–12 m high and 20–40 cm in diameter. Trunk short, thick, separating into several stout limbs, forming a spreading, bushy crown of many fine twigs. Roots wide-spreading. Michigan Big Tree: girth 4.9 m, diameter 156 cm, height 25 m, Kalamazoo Co.

Bark. Moderately thick, light to dark gray becoming orange brown, shallowly furrowed into flat, wavy ridges; orange inner layers visible in the fissures.

Leaves. Alternate, simple, blades 5–10 cm long, nearly as wide; ovate to broadly ovate, unlobed to variously lobed (lobed blades characteristic of young trees and vigorous sprout shoots); coarsely serrate with big triangular teeth; thin; in sun very lustrous, light green above, paler beneath; glabrous both sides (except along main veins beneath); petioles smooth, exuding a milky juice when cut, 1–3 cm long.

Twigs. Slender, reddish brown and slightly pubescent at first, becoming glabrous and yellowish brown or light orange.

Winter Buds. Terminal bud absent; end and lateral buds triangular-ovoid, short, 3–4 mm long, lustrous, light brownish orange, closely appressed, offset to one side above the leaf scar; bud scales generally uniformly colored.

Wood. Similar to that of red mulberry.

Flowers. May or June, with the leaves; male flowers in dense catkins, 1–3 cm long, on short peduncles; calyx 4-lobed, corolla 0, stamens 4; female flowers in dense catkins, 1–2 cm long, on short pedicels; stigmas 2, spreading. Trees monoecious or more usually dioecious. Wind-pollinated.

Fruit. Multiple of drupes; June-July; 1–2 cm long, white to pink (rarely purple), sweet but insipid.

Distribution. Native in China, long cultivated in Europe and North America. Frequent in urban environments in the southern half of the Lower Peninsula; occasional in the northern half of the Lower Peninsula and in the Upper Peninsula. Naturalized in urban environments, rare in disturbed forest communities.

Habitat. Grows well in nearly any upland habitat.

Notes. Shade-intolerant; fast-growing; short-lived. Leaf lobing highly variable and strongly related to physiological stage of development, whether juvenile or adult. Young trees and sprout shoots from older trees bear a high proportion of many-lobed leaves. Shoots in the crowns of mature trees tend to bear mostly unlobed leaves. The leaves are the food of the silkworm, and the species was introduced to help establish the silkworm industry in America. Crown branchy, with several shoots often arising at one node. Fruits vary in sweetness among trees, from sweet to dry and barely edible; less sweet than red mulberry. Roots spread vigorously and are noted for clogging drains. Not recommended as an ornamental tree. Fruits serve as food for many birds and mammals, and seeds are disseminated widely by them.

254

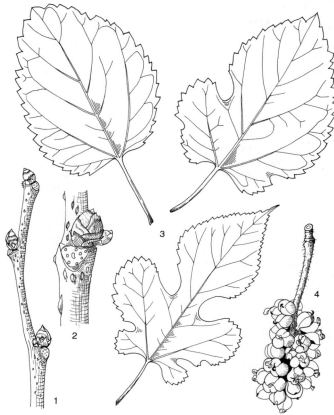

1. Winter twig, × 1.
2. Portion of twig, × 2.
3. Leaves, × ¾.
4. Fruit, multiple of drupes, × 2.

Key Characters
- leaf blades in sun very lustrous; glabrous; variously lobed
- bark orange brown, orange inner layers visible in fissures
- fruit a multiple of drupes, usually white to pink
- crown bushy, with many slender, light orange twigs
- winter buds offset to one side above the leaf scar

Distinguished from red mulberry by smaller, more lustrous leaves; lower blade surface glabrous (except along main veins); winter buds smaller, more appressed; bark and twigs with a more yellow or orange color; urban habitats rather than floodplain forests.

MORACEAE
Morus rubra Linnaeus

Red Mulberry

Size and Form. Small to medium-sized tree, 6–12 m high and 25–35 cm in diameter. Trunk short; forming a dense, round-topped crown of stout, spreading branches and more or less zigzag, slender branchlets. Michigan Big Tree: girth 5.2 m, diameter 164 cm, height 18 m, Shiawassee Co.

Bark. Thin, dark brown tinged with red or yellow, scaly and separating into long flaky plates, resembling plates of hop-hornbeam.

Leaves. Alternate, simple, blades 7–13 cm long, nearly as wide; outline variable, ovate to semiorbicular, unlobed to variously lobed (lobed blades characteristic of young trees and vigorous sprout shoots); coarsely serrate; thin; dark bluish green and smooth or rough above, pale and more or less downy beneath; petioles smooth, exuding a milky juice when cut, 2–5 cm long.

Twigs. Slender, greenish and more or less downy, becoming smooth and orange brown.

Winter Buds. Terminal bud absent; lateral buds broadly ovoid, elongated, abruptly pointed, 5–8 mm long, lustrous, light brown, somewhat divergent, offset to one side above the leaf scar; bud scales with brown margins.

Wood. Light, soft, weak, rather tough, coarse-grained, very durable, pale orange, with thick, lighter-colored sapwood. Uses include fence posts, furniture, caskets, barrels, boat-building materials.

Flowers. May or early June, with the leaves; male flowers in dense catkins, 2–5 cm long, on short, hairy peduncles; calyx 4-lobed, hairy; corolla 0; stamens 4, with green anthers; female flowers in dense catkins, about 2 cm long, on short, hairy peduncles; stigmas 2, spreading. Dioecious. Wind-pollinated.

Fruit. Multiple of drupes; July; about 2 cm long, bright red at first, finally blackish, sweet, juicy, edible.

Distribution. Rare to occasional in the southern to southwestern third of the Lower Peninsula, as far north as the Grand River. A tree of widespread distribution, reaching a segment of its northernmost range in southern lower Michigan.

Habitat. Scattered among other hardwoods in river floodplains and fertile bottomlands. Associates include American elm, silver maple, red ash, basswood, redbud, northern hackberry, tuliptree, pawpaw.

Notes. Moderately shade-tolerant; moderately fast-growing; moderately short-lived. Leaf lobing highly variable and strongly related to physiological state of development, whether juvenile or adult. Young trees and sprout shoots from older trees bear a high proportion of many-lobed leaves. Shoots in the crowns of mature trees tend to bear mostly unlobed leaves. Easily transplanted. Many species of birds and mammals eat the fruits and disseminate the seeds.

In superficial appearance easily confused with basswood, the leaves of which are about the same size. Basswood differs in the oblique leaf base, glabrous leaf undersurface, the different much darker bark, as well as numerous other characters.

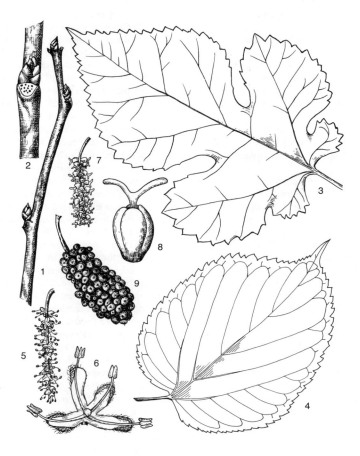

1. Winter twig, × 1.
2. Portion of twig, enlarged.
3. Leaf, lobed, × 1.
4. Leaf, unlobed, × ½.
5. Catkin of male flowers, × 1.

6. Male flower, enlarged.
7. Catkin of female flowers, × 1.
8. Female flower, enlarged.
9. Fruit, multiple of drupes, × 1.

Key Characters

- leaf blades large, unlobed to variously lobed on the same tree; undersurface downy
- buds elongated, somewhat divergent
- fruit a multiple of drupes, at first bright red, turning blackish

Distinguished from white mulberry by the larger and less lustrous upper leaf surface; lower leaf surface downy not glabrous; fruit longer, at first bright red, turning blackish, not white or pink; winter buds longer, more divergent; bark with less of an orange or yellow color; natural not urban habitats.

257

FAGACEAE
Castanea dentata (Marshall) Borkhausen

American Chestnut

Size and Form. Most large chestnuts were killed by chestnut blight; in the forest only small trees remain, usually from root-collar sprouts. Formerly a large tree, 18–25 m high and 50–100 cm in diameter; now usually less than 10 m high. Tap root prominent. Michigan Big Tree: girth 5.1 m, diameter 163 cm, height 22 m, Kent Co.

Bark. Thin, smooth, dark brown; separating into shallow fissures and broad, flat-topped ridges.

Leaves. Alternate, simple, blades 15–21 cm long, 5–7 cm wide; oblong-lanceolate, long-pointed; coarsely toothed, teeth incurved, a vein extending beyond each tooth forming a short, curved bristle; thin; dull yellowish green above, lighter beneath; glabrous; petioles short, stout, puberulent.

Twigs. Stout, lustrous, yellowish green, becoming olive green, and finally dark brown.

Winter Buds. Terminal bud usually absent; end and lateral buds 6 mm long, ovoid, acute, brownish.

Wood. Light, soft, coarse-grained, weak, easily split, very durable in contact with the soil, reddish brown, with very thin, lighter-colored sapwood; ring-porous. Formerly used for lumber, furniture, interior trim, posts, poles, and fences.

Flowers. June-July, after the leaves; male catkins, unisexual, stiff, borne near the base of the new shoots, 15–20 cm long, slender, puberulent, bearing scattered, 3–7-flowered clusters of yellowish green flowers; calyx 6-cleft, pubescent; stamens 10–20; bisexual catkins borne nearer the apex of shoot, 6–13 cm long, puberulent, bearing 2–3 prickly involucres containing female flowers near their base; calyx campanulate, 6-lobed; styles 6. Trees monoecious. Insect-pollinated.

Fruit. Nut enclosed in a globose, bristly bur with branched spines, autumn; bur 2–3 cm in diameter; 1–3 nuts in each bur, nuts somewhat flattened, dull, brownish, coated with whitish down at the apex, sweet and edible.

Distribution. Rare in southeastern Michigan; formerly native as far north as St. Clair Co. and abundant in Monroe and Wayne Co. Reaching the northwestern limit of its range in southeastern Michigan. Planted trees, more or less healthy, are widespread throughout the Lower Peninsula to Benzie and Emmet Co. and Beaver Island.

Habitat. Characteristic of dry-mesic sites and oak-hickory forests where it tolerates droughty soils and periodic fires; associated with black, white, and red oaks, pignut and shagbark hickories, white ash, black cherry.

Notes. Shade-intolerant; fast-growing; today short-lived, formerly moderately long-lived. Once a major dominant in oak forests throughout much of the eastern United States. The chestnut blight fungus, *Endothia parasitica,* was introduced about 1900 on seedlings of Asiatic chestnut and first discovered in 1904 at the New York Zoological Gardens. Within 50 years the disease had spread throughout the range of the species and eliminated it as a commercial species. Sprouts from the root collar of former trees still perpetuate chestnut today, but the disease usually kills the young trees before many seeds are produced. A plantation of chestnut trees, established in 1910 in Benzie Co., has given rise to a stand of several thousand offspring (Thompson 1969). The largest trees in the plantation are well over 100 cm in diameter. *C. mollissima* Bl., Chinese chestnut, highly resistant to the disease, has been planted widely in the eastern United States for nut production.

There has arisen an unfortunate confusion by the public between the true chestnut and horsechestnut. Horsechestnut should not be called chestnut. The fruits are fundamentally different, and the seeds of the horsechestnut are potentially poisonous.

258

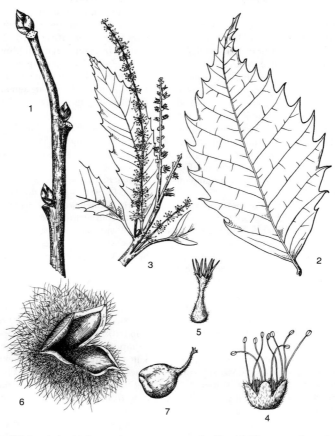

1. Winter twig, × 1.
2. Leaf, × ½.
3. Flowering shoots, × ½.
4. Male flower, enlarged.

5. Female flower, enlarged.
6. Prickly bur, opened, × ½.
7. Nut, × ½.

Key Characters
- leaves long, narrow, with pronounced teeth at the end of each major vein
- bark smooth, dark brown, separating into broad, flat-topped ridges
- fruit a large, spiny bur enclosing 1–3 brown, flattened nuts

FAGACEAE
Fagus grandifolia Ehrhart

American Beech

Size and Form. Large tree, 18–26 m high and 50–100 cm in diameter. In the forest tall and slender, with short branches forming a narrow crown; in the open with a short, thick trunk and numerous slender, crooked, spreading branches, forming a broad, compact, rounded crown. Trunk often crooked due to the highly phototropic nature of the shoots. Roots shallow and extensive. Root suckers often produced, but multistemmed clones rare. Michigan Big Tree: girth 4.2 m, diameter 135 cm, height 49 m, Berrien Co. (tree with 5.0 m girth and 158 cm diameter in Van Buren Co.).

Bark. Very characteristic: thin, smooth, tight, ashy gray or light bluish gray, often mottled by darker blotches or carved initials.

Leaves. Alternate, simple, blades 7–12 cm long, nearly half as wide; oblong-ovate, acuminate; coarsely toothed, a vein terminating in each incurved tooth; thin; dull bluish green above, light yellowish green and very lustrous beneath; glabrous; petioles short, hairy. Persistent over winter on young trees and often on the inner and lower part of open-grown mature trees.

Twigs. Slender, lustrous, olive green, finally changing through brown to ashy gray.

Winter Buds. End buds very slender, 1–2 cm long, cylindrical (cigar-shaped), gradually tapered, sharp-pointed, lustrous, brownish; many bud scales, each with a gray, hairy margin; lateral buds smaller, 2-ranked, diverging at nearly right angles to the thin twigs.

Wood. Hard, tough, strong, close-grained, not durable, difficult to season, light or dark red, with thin, whitish sapwood. Uses include flooring, furniture, tool handles, woodenware.

Flowers. April-May, with the leaves; male flowers in globose heads, 2 cm in diameter, on long, slender, hairy peduncles, yellowish green; calyx campanulate, 4–7-lobed, hairy; corolla 0; stamens 8–10; female flowers on short, hairy peduncles, usually in pairs surrounded by numerous needle-shaped, hairy bracts; calyx urn-shaped with 5–6 pointed lobes; corolla 0; ovary usually 3-celled; styles 3. Trees monoecious. Wind-pollinated.

Fruit. Nut enclosed in a bristly bur or husk; autumn; borne on a stout, hairy peduncle, persistent on the shoot after the nuts have fallen; nuts usually 2, 1–2 cm long, sharply triangular, reddish brown, sweet and edible; 3–5 years between good seed crops; nut often without a living seed. The bur of beech is unusual in being remarkably capsulelike; it splits and opens like a true capsule.

Distribution. Common in the Lower Peninsula; locally common in the eastern half of the Upper Peninsula, west to Marquette and Dickinson Co.

Habitat. Characteristic of mesic beech-maple forests with well drained to somewhat poorly drained soils of a wide range of textures, from loamy sand to clay loam. Associated with sugar maple, basswood, red oak, white ash, American elm, tuliptree, eastern hemlock. Tolerates acidic or basic conditions.

Notes. Very shade-tolerant, young trees may persist in the understory many years; very slow-growing; long-lived (300–400 years). Highly susceptible to fire because of thin bark and shallow roots. Sprouts from stump if cut or from root-collar if stem is killed by fire. Important ornamental tree because of its smooth bark and limbs, spreading form, dense canopy, and relative freedom from insect and disease pests.

The European beech, *Fagus sylvatica* L., often planted as an ornamental tree, can be distinguished from the native beech by its often-villous twigs and puberulent buds and by the leaves, which are shorter, rather blunt, and minutely toothed. The most frequently planted varieties include the copper or purple beech (*F. sylvatica* 'Atropunicea'), the cut-leaf beech (*F. sylvatica* 'Laciniata'), and the weeping beech (*F. sylvatica* 'Pendula'). The largest copper beech, in Jackson Co., has girth 3.8 m, diameter 120 cm, and height 26.2 m.

260

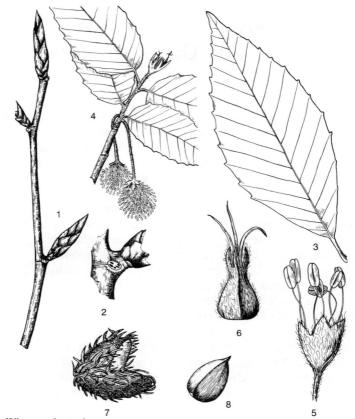

1. Winter twig, × 1.
2. Portion of twig, enlarged.
3. Leaf, × 1.
4. Flowering shoot, × ¾.
5. Male flower, enlarged.
6. Female flower, enlarged.
7. Bur, opened, × 1.
8. Nut, × 1.

Key
Characters
• bark smooth, ashy gray
• buds long, thin, sharp-pointed; lateral buds extended at nearly right angles to the thin twigs
• fruit with bristle-covered husk, enclosing 2–3 triangular nuts

261

The Oaks—*Quercus*

The oaks are noted for their massive trunks, their thick, rugged bark, and their large, deep roots. In the open, oaks have a broad, wide-spreading crown. In the forest their stems are usually straight and the crown is shorter but spreads out wherever space in the canopy permits.

The oaks are divided into two groups. The white oaks have leaves with rounded lobes, their acorns mature in the autumn of the first season, and their kernels are relatively sweet. The red oaks have leaves with bristle-tipped lobes, their acorns mature in the autumn of the second season, and their kernels are usually bitter. All oaks have several leaves and lateral buds clustered around the terminal bud. Hybridization is extensive among species within each group and creates many problems in identification.

Oaks are distinguished from all other trees by their cupped fruit. However, many who have seen these fruits have not noticed the small, scaly masses of flowers that produce them. The male and female flowers appear on different parts of the same tree (monoecious) and often on the same branch. The male flowers are small, arranged in long, slender catkins, from buds on shoots of the preceding season. The female flowers are small and inconspicuous, appearing singly or in groups in the axils of the leaves on new shoots. Pollination is by wind. Oak acorns form a very important food for squirrels, birds, and other animals. The animals carry off and bury or store many acorns. Some of these are forgotten or lost, and the seeds germinate to form a new crop of seedlings—away from the parent plant.

Acorns were once extensively used by Native Americans for bread purposes. Once leached, acorns lose their bitter, astringent properties. However, there are records of poisoning, especially of livestock, by acorns. Our descriptions of sweet versus bitter are relative; to some palates all acorns are at least somewhat bitter. The acorns of white oaks have less tannin content than acorns of red oaks and are, therefore, sweeter.

Young oaks, especially those growing in the open, retain their leaves over winter and shed them in the spring. The leaves of the lower, inner crown of mature trees are often also retained in winter. Oaks are noted for their highly variable leaf size, shape and pubescence. Much of this is related to the location of the leaf on the tree. Blades of leaves receiving full sun are typically smaller and more deeply lobed than shade leaves of the interior and lower crown or those on epicormic branches of the trunk or large limbs. Almost all oaks have more or less pubescence in the axils of the main veins on the blade undersurface. The axillary pubescence is not very useful in identification because it occurs whether the blades are elsewhere glabrous or pubescent.

The genus *Quercus* is large, comprising over 400 trees and shrubs widely distributed and very important in the Northern Hemisphere. About 70 trees and shrubs are found in North America, and 12 are native in Michigan. Ecologically, the oaks are the angiospermous equivalents of the pines. They are a group of deep-rooted, xerophytic trees that occupy dry sites from the southern edge of the Boreal Forest well into the tropics. Oak bark is thick and fire-resistant. However, if the oak stem is killed, the root system remains alive almost indefinitely, sending up generation after generation of sprouts from the root collar or stump. This vegetative propagation perpetuates both the individual trees and the dominance of oaks in the forest. Throughout much of their range oaks are the characteristic late-successional dominants on the drier sites and occur also as mid-successional species on the more mesic sites. Oaks and pines often grow together and the oaks, being more tolerant of understory conditions, follow the pines in natural succession in the absence of severe fires that bring pines again to dominance.

Summer Key to Species of *Quercus*

1. Leaves deeply cut or lobed.
   2. Leaf lobes rounded, not bristle-tipped; fruit maturing in the first season.
      3. Sun leaves near tip of shoots cut nearly to the midrib by a pair of deep sinuses near the middle of the leaf; branches frequently corky-ridged; nut 1.5–3 cm long, deeply seated in a large, conspicuously fringed cup .... *Q. macrocarpa*, p. 270
      3. Sun leaves not as above; branches not corky-ridged; nut 1.3–2 cm long, about ¼ covered by a thin, tomentose, warty cup .... *Q. alba*, p. 266
   2. Leaf lobes acute, bristle-tipped; fruit maturing in the second season.
      4. Lower surface of leaves more or less pubescent; buds hoary-tomentose; inner bark yellow or yellowish orange; cup scales of acorn silky-pubescent, spreading and squarish at the tip .... *Q. velutina*, p. 278
      4. Lower surface of leaves glabrous or nearly so; buds not as above; inner bark not as above; cup scales not as above.
         5. Cup of acorn top-shaped or cup-shaped, enclosing ⅓ to ½ of the nut.
            6. Kernel of nut yellow; buds glabrous, lustrous, only slightly angled in cross section; trunk with stubs of dead branches near the ground .... *Q. ellipsoidalis*, p. 282
            6. Kernel of nut whitish; buds pubescent above the middle, distinctly angled

in cross section; trunk without pins or stubs of branches near the ground .... *Q. coccinea*, p. 280
    5. Cup of acorn saucer-shaped, enclosing only the base of the nut.
       7. Upper surface of leaves usually lustrous, especially on the lower branches; lowermost branches of open-grown trees drooping nearly to the ground; nut about 1.3 cm or less in diameter, 1 cm or less long .... *Q. palustris*, p. 284
       7. Upper surface of leaves usually dull; lowermost branches of open-grown trees not drooping nearly to the ground; nut 1.3–2 cm in diameter, 2–3 cm long .... *Q. rubra*, p. 276
1. Leaves neither cut nor deeply lobed.
    8. Margin of leaves entire to sinuate-crenate, but not toothed; acorns on stalks 1.3–8 cm long.
      9. Margin of leaves entire or only slightly undulate; acorns on stalks about 1 cm long, the nut about 1.2–1.6 cm long; bark on branches not breaking into large, papery scales .... *Q. imbricaria*, p. 286
      9. Margin of leaves sinuate-crenate, rarely lobed; acorns on stalks 2.5–8 cm long, the nut 2–3 cm long; bark on branches breaking into large papery scales that curl back .... *Q. bicolor*, p. 268
    8. Margin of leaves coarsely toothed; acorns sessile or on stalks less than 1.3 cm long.
      10. Low clonal shrub or small tree, 1–5 m high; leaf blades with 4–8 teeth per side .... *Q. prinoides*, p. 274
      10. Erect solitary tree, 12–15 m high; leaf blades with 9–13 teeth per side .... *Q. muehlenbergii*, p. 272

Winter Key to Species of *Quercus*

1. Terminal buds usually about 3–4 mm long.
    2. Cup of acorn conspicuously fringed at the rim; branches frequently corky-ridged; young twigs thick-tomentose .... *Q. macrocarpa*,[1] p. 270
    2. Cup of acorn without fringe or only slightly fringed at the rim; branches without corky ridges; young twigs glabrous to only moderately tomentose.
      3. Bark on branches breaking into large, papery scales that curl back; buds pilose above the middle; acorns on pubescent peduncles 2.5–8 cm long .... *Q. bicolor*,[1] p. 268
      3. Bark on branches tight, buds glabrous; acorns sessile or short-stalked.
        4. Bark of trunk light to dark brown, smooth or only slightly fissured; acorns maturing in autumn of second season; kernel of nut bitter.
          5. Lateral buds widely divergent; bud scales pubescent, membranous on the margins; lowermost branches of open-grown trees not drooping nearly to the ground; leaves entire .... *Q. imbricaria*,[2] p. 286
          5. Lateral buds more or less appressed; bud scales not as above; lowermost branches of open-grown trees drooping nearly to the ground; leaves lobed .... *Q. palustris*,[2] p. 284

---

1. Acorns ripen in the autumn of the first season, hence mature acorns will not be found on mature trees but on the ground beneath the tree in a good seed year.
2. Acorns ripen in the autumn of the second season, hence immature acorns will be found on last season's twigs of mature trees, and mature acorns on the ground beneath the tree in a good seed year.

4. Bark of trunk ashy gray, flaky; acorns maturing in autumn of first season; kernel of nut relatively sweet.

  6. Low clonal shrub or small tree, 1–5 m tall .... *Q. prinoides,*[1] p. 274

  6. Erect solitary tree, 12–15 m tall.

    7. Buds conical, acute; bud scales with membranous margins; nut white-downy at apex .... *Q. muehlenbergii,* [1] p. 272

    7. Buds broadly ovoid, obtuse, often nearly globose; bud scales not as above; nut not as above .... *Q. alba,*[1] p. 266

1. Terminal buds usually 6 mm or more long (slightly shorter in *Q. ellipsoidalis*).

  8. Buds conspicuously hairy or tomentose; inner bark of trunk yellow to yellowish orange .... *Q. velutina,*[2] p. 278

  8. Buds glabrous or pubescent only above the middle; inner bark of trunk whitish, flesh-colored to reddish.

    9. Buds pale-pubescent above the middle, but usually glabrous below, not lustrous, distinctly angled .... *Q. coccinea,*[2] p. 280

    9. Buds mostly glabrous throughout, lustrous, not angled or only slightly angled.

      10. Buds obtuse at the apex; trunk with stubs of dead branches near the ground; nut 1.2–1.8 cm long, enclosed for ⅓ to ½ of its length in a top-shaped cup; kernel of nut yellow .... *Q. ellipsoidalis,*[2] p. 282

      10. Buds acute at the apex; trunk not as above; nut 2–3 cm long, enclosed only at the base by a shallow, saucer-shaped cup; kernel of nut white . *Q. rubra,*[2] p. 276

FAGACEAE
Quercus alba Linnaeus

White Oak

Size and Form. Large tree, 18–25 m high and 60–120 cm in diameter. Forming a short, thick trunk with stout, horizontal, far-reaching limbs, more or less gnarled and twisted in old age, and a broad, open crown. Tap root very deep; major lateral roots deep set and wide spreading; very windfirm. Michigan Big Tree: girth 6.0 m, diameter 191 cm, height 37 m, Allegan Co.

Bark. Thick, light gray or whitish, broken into longitudinal scaly blocks or shallowly fissured into broad, flat-topped ridges; highly variable; fire resistant.

Leaves. Alternate, simple, blades 12–20 cm long, about half as wide; obovate to oblong; 5–9 lobed, lobes rounded, some with broad lobes and shallow sinuses (shade leaves), others with narrow lobes and deep, narrow sinuses (sun leaves), the lobes usually entire; thin and firm; bright green above, pale or glaucous beneath, turning brownish purple in autumn; glabrous; persistent through the winter on open-grown young trees and often on the lower, inner part of mature trees; petioles moderately stout, short, 1–2 cm long.

Twigs. Moderately stout, at first bright green, tomentose, later reddish and finally ashy gray.

Winter Buds. Terminal bud 3–4 mm long, broadly ovoid, often nearly globose, blunt; scales glabrous, dark reddish brown; lateral buds smaller, divergent.

Wood. Very heavy, strong, hard, tough, close-grained, durable, light brown, with thin, light brown sapwood; ring-porous. Uses include furniture, flooring, interior trim, veneer, wine casks, barrels.

Flowers. May-June, with the leaves; male catkins hairy, 5–8 cm long; calyx campanulate, 6–8-lobed, yellow, hairy; corolla 0; stamens 6–8, with yellow anthers; female flowers short-peduncled, reddish, tomentose; stigmas red. Wind-pollinated.

Fruit. Acorn; autumn of first season; sessile or short-stalked; cup with small wartlike or knoblike scales, enclosing ¼ of the nut, no marginal fringe; nut oblong-ovoid, rounded at the apex, 1.3–2 cm long, light brown; kernel relatively sweet.

Distribution. Common to abundant in the Lower Peninsula, especially in the lower half; rare in the Upper Peninsula (Schoolcraft, Delta, Menominee Co.).

Habitat. Characteristic of oak-hickory forests on dry-mesic, upland sites, with drought-prone, well drained sandy loam to clay loam soils; associated with black, scarlet, and red oaks, shagbark and pignut hickories, white ash, black walnut, black cherry, hop-hornbeam. Also occurs in mesic sites with sugar maple and beech and in dry, sandy soils of the northern Lower Peninsula with white, red, and jack pines, red oak, red maple, and bigtooth aspen. Not found in poorly drained sites.

Notes. Intermediate in shade tolerance; slow-growing; long-lived (500–600 years). Acorns germinate in autumn. Desirable as a lawn or shade tree but difficult to transplant due to long tap root.

The related English oak, *Quercus robur* L., is sometimes planted. It is a large, spreading tree with dark gray or brownish bark, closely fissured into short, narrow, vertical plates. Leaves similar to white oak but sessile or nearly so with ear-shaped lobes at the blade base. Acorns borne on slender peduncles, 2–7 cm long. Twigs reddish; winter buds glabrous or nearly so, somewhat angular, with lateral buds diverging. Relatively fast-growing; various cultivars in use. Michigan Big Tree: girth 3.9 m, diameter 125 cm, height 24.7 m, Benzie Co.

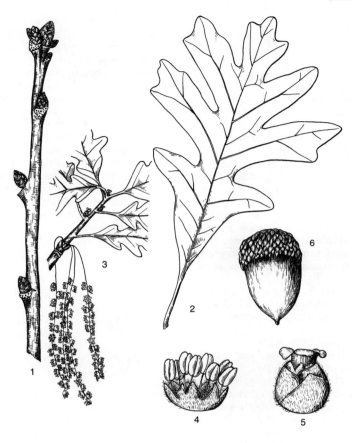

1. Winter twig, × 2.
2. Leaf, × ½.
3. Flowering shoot, × ½.

4. Male flower, enlarged.
5. Female flower, enlarged.
6. Fruit, acorn, × 1.

**Key
Characters**
• leaves completely glabrous with narrow lobes and rounded tips, often deep
sinuses
• acorn cup with warty or knoblike scales, no fringe
• bark light gray, small vertical blocky plates to broad, flat-topped ridges
   Distinguished from bur oak by acorn cup without fringe; leaf blade undersurface not pubescent; upper portion of blade not broad with shallow lobes.

267

FAGACEAE
Quercus bicolor Willdenow

Swamp White Oak

Size and Form. Medium-sized tree, 15–21 m high and 60–100 cm in diameter. Forming a rather open, rugged, rounded crown of ascending upper branches and tortuous, pendulous lower branches; foliage-spray short, stiff, bushy; lower branches are retained and droop. Roots shallow in poorly drained sites. Michigan Big Tree: girth 5.7 m, diameter 182 cm, height 38 m, Wayne Co.

Bark. Thick, grayish brown, deeply fissured into broad, flat-topped, scaly ridges.

Leaves. Alternate, simple, blades 12–18 cm long, 7–12 cm wide; obovate to oblong-obovate; coarsely wavy-toothed or sinuate-crenate, rarely lobed; thick and firm; dark green and shining above, whitish and tomentose beneath, turning yellowish brown or orange in autumn; petioles stout, about 1 cm long.

Twigs. Stout, at first lustrous green, becoming reddish brown, finally dark brown and separating into large, papery scales that curl back.

Winter Buds. Terminal bud 3 mm long, broadly ovoid to globose, blunt, light brown, pilose above the middle.

Wood. Heavy, hard, strong, tough, coarse-grained, light brown, with thin, indistinguishable sapwood; ring-porous. Uses similar to those of white oak.

Flowers. May-June, with the leaves; male catkins hairy, 7–10 cm long; calyx deeply 5–9-lobed, yellowish green, hairy; corolla 0; stamens 5–8, with yellow anthers; female flowers tomentose, on long, tomentose peduncles, in few-flowered spikes; stigmas bright red. Wind-pollinated.

Fruit. Acorn; autumn of first season; on pubescent peduncles 2.5–8 cm long, usually in pairs; cup bowl-shaped, with swollen, somewhat loose scales, rim often slightly fringed, enclosing ⅓ of the nut; nut ovoid, light brown, pubescent at the apex, 2–3 cm long; kernel white, relatively sweet.

Distribution. Occasional in the southern half of the Lower Peninsula. A species of predominantly midwestern range reaching one segment of its northern limit in southern to central Michigan.

Habitat. Characteristic of low, wet, somewhat poorly to poorly drained soils; borders of swamps and along streams; moist flats and bottomlands; associated with silver maple, American elm, bur oak, red ash, basswood, tuliptree, yellow birch. Adapted to conditions of poor aeration and high water tables but not abundant in deciduous swamps having a continually high water table.

Notes. Intermediate in shade tolerance; relatively slow-growing; long-lived (300+ years). More susceptible to fire than upland oaks because of shallow roots. Leaves flush in late spring. The name *bicolor* derived from the marked difference of the dark green upper leaf surface and the whitish lower surface.

1. Winter twig, × 2.
2. Leaf, × ½.
3. Flowering shoot, × ½.
4. Male flower, enlarged.
5. Female flower, enlarged.
6. Fruit, acorn, × 1.

Key Characters

- leaves with coarse, wavy teeth or shallow lobes, not deeply lobed; upper surface dark green, lower surface white-tomentose
- acorn borne on long peduncle
- typically occurs in low, wet sites—swamp margins, stream borders, and river floodplains

Distinguished from white and bur oaks by the absence of long leaf lobes and deep sinuses; acorn long-stalked.

269

FAGACEAE
Quercus macrocarpa Michaux

Bur Oak

Size and Form. Large tree, 18–25 m high and 60–120 cm in diameter. Spreading branches form a broad, rugged, rounded crown; epicormic branches often found on lower trunk. Tap root very deep, to 1.2 m the first year, to 4 m in 8 years; lateral roots deep and wide-spreading; very windfirm. Michigan Big Tree: girth 6.7 m, diameter 213 cm, height 32 m, Berrien Co.

Bark. Thick, grayish brown, deeply and coarsely furrowed with scaly ridges.

Leaves. Alternate, simple, blades 15–25 cm long and nearly half as wide; obovate to oblong, wedge-shaped at the base; 5–9-lobed, highly variable in lobing, but usually at least one leaf per shoot with a broad, crenately toothed upper portion separated from the lower portion by a pair of center sinuses reaching nearly to the midrib (wasp-waist shape), other leaves with several opposite, deeply cut sinuses near the middle; thick and firm; dark green and shining above, pale, finely white-pubescent beneath; petioles short, stout.

Twigs. Stout, thick-tomentose, yellowish brown, becoming ashy gray or brownish; branches often with corky ridges.

Winter Buds. Terminal bud 3–4 mm long, broadly ovoid or conical, blunt, reddish brown, pale-pubescent; lateral buds smaller, appressed.

Wood. Heavy, hard, strong, tough, close-grained, very durable, brownish, with thin pale sapwood; ring-porous. Uses include furniture, flooring, interior trim, casks and barrels, fence posts, pilings.

Flowers. May-June, with the young leaves; male catkins slender, hairy, 10–15 cm long, stamens 4–5, with yellow anthers; calyx 4–6-lobed, yellowish green, downy; corolla 0; female flowers sessile or short-stalked, reddish, tomentose; stigmas 3, bright red. Wind-pollinated.

Fruit. Acorn; autumn of first season; sessile or short-stalked; variable in size and shape; cup typically deep, cup-shaped, pale-tomentose, strongly, conspicuously fringed at the rim, enclosing ⅓ or more of the nut; nut broad-ovoid, 1.5–3 cm long, brownish, pubescent; kernel white, relatively sweet.

Distribution. Common in the southern half of the Lower Peninsula; locally in the northern half; rare and sporadic in the Upper Peninsula.

Habitat. Found on a variety of sites (particularly on limestone-derived soils and transported soils of high lime content) including (1) oak savannas of the transition zone between deciduous forest and prairie ("oak openings"), (2) ravines and bottomlands of southern Michigan; associated with red, white, and swamp white oaks, black and white walnuts, shellbark hickory, red maple, basswood, eastern cottonwood, American and slippery elms, hackberry, (3) dry-mesic upland oak forests with calcareous soils; associated with black, red, and white oaks, white ash, black cherry, shagbark and pignut hickories. Highly drought-tolerant, invades prairies and extends into the Great Plains, yet tolerant of flooding in spring and can compete in low, seasonally wet bottomlands.

Notes. Moderately shade-tolerant; slow-growing; long-lived (200–300+ years). Highly fire resistant (thick bark and deep roots). Acorns germinate in autumn. A suitable landscape tree although difficult to transplant because of deep tap root; reportedly more tolerant of city pollutants than other oaks.

270

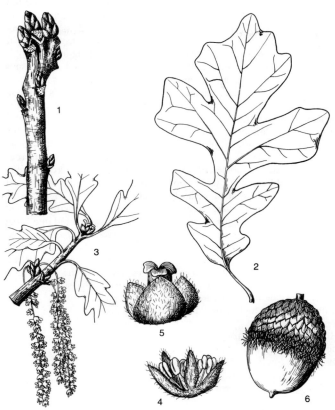

1. Winter twig, × 2.
2. Leaf, × ⅓.
3. Flowering shoot, × ½.
4. Male flower, enlarged.
5. Female flower, enlarged.
6. Fruit, acorn, × 1.

Key Characters

- leaf lobing highly variable, but usually at least one leaf per shoot with a broad, crenately toothed upper blade and a pair of opposing, very deep sinuses; other leaves with 2–3 pairs of deeply cut sinuses
- leaves finely white-pubescent beneath
- acorns seated in a massive, deep, conspicuously fringed cup

Distinguished from white oak by pubescent leaf undersurface; broader upper portion of many leaves; and strongly fringed acorn cup.

Distinguished from swamp white oak by more deeply cut leaf sinuses; sessile or short-stalked acorns; and larger, deeper, more heavily fringed cup.

FAGACEAE
Quercus muehlenbergii Engelmann

Chinkapin Oak   Yellow Oak

Size and Form. Medium-sized tree, 12–15 m high and 30–60 cm in diameter. Trunk straight, extending far into the crown, tapering, often buttressed at base; erect, somewhat short branches form a narrow, rounded crown. Michigan Big Tree: girth 5.0 m, diameter 158 cm, height 28 m, Genesee Co.

Bark. Thin, silvery gray or ash colored, shallowly fissured and flaky.

Leaves. Alternate, simple, blades 10–16 cm long, 3–8 cm wide; oblong-lanceolate to obovate, often somewhat lance-shaped; coarsely and somewhat sharp-toothed, sharp notches separate the teeth, 9–13 teeth per side; thick and firm; lustrous, yellowish green above, pale-pubescent beneath; petioles slender, 2–3.5 cm long.

Twigs. Slender, greenish at first, becoming grayish brown, finally gray or brown.

Winter Buds. Terminal bud 3 mm long, conical, acute; scales chestnut brown, thin, membranous margin.

Wood. Heavy, very hard, strong, close-grained, durable, dark brown, with thin, pale brown sapwood; ring-porous. Wood sold as white oak; uses similar.

Flowers. May-June, with the leaves; male catkins hairy, 7–10 cm long; calyx campanulate, 5–8-lobed, yellow, hairy; corolla 0; stamens 5–8, with yellow anthers; female flowers sessile or in short spikes, hoary-tomentose; stigmas red. Wind-pollinated.

Fruit. Acorn; autumn of first season; sessile or short-stalked; cup with thin, small, appressed scales, hoary-tomentose, deep, enclosing ⅓–½ of the nut; nut ovoid, 1.3–1.9 cm long, dark brown to nearly black, white-downy at apex; kernel relatively sweet.

Distribution. Occasional, confined to the southern half of the Lower Peninsula, north to Kent, Gratiot, and Saginaw Co.

Habitat. Occurs on limestone outcrops, limestone-derived soils, or transported soils with lime in the topsoil; tolerates dry sites with soils rich in lime, such as limestone outcrops and calcareous dry slopes; thrives in moist bottomlands with neutral or basic soils.

Associated with white and red oaks, basswood, beech, tuliptree, black walnut.

Notes. Intermediate in shade tolerance, becoming intolerant; relatively fast-growing; moderately long-lived.

A tree with somewhat similar characteristics, chestnut oak or rock chestnut oak, *Quercus prinus* L., is common south and east of Michigan and is known from one locality in Michigan, Waterloo State Recreation Area, Washtenaw Co. It differs from the chinkapin oak in that the leaves are broader, the teeth of the blade are rounded, the nut of the acorn is lustrous at maturity, the acorn cup is shallow, the twigs are stout, orange brown, and the bark of the trunk is dark reddish brown to nearly black and characteristically deeply fissured into broad, rounded, continuous, vertical ridges. The chestnut oak is a species of xeric and dry-mesic sites and of the oak (formerly oak-chestnut) and oak-pine forests of the Appalachian Mountains and the Southeast.

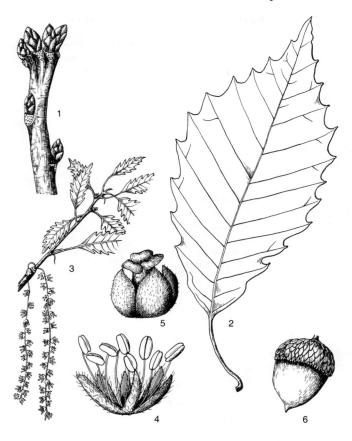

1. Winter twig, × 2.
2. Leaf, × ½.
3. Flowering shoot, × ½.

4. Male flower, enlarged.
5. Female flower, enlarged.
6. Fruit, acorn, × 1.

Key Characters

• leaves long, relatively slender, coarsely toothed, teeth sharp-pointed
• acorn cup with small, hoary-tomentose scales, not fringed, deep, enclosing ⅓–½ of the nut

Distinguished from dwarf chinkapin oak by straight stem; larger size; longer leaves with more teeth; and acorn cup with thin, appressed scales, not knobby toward the base.

FAGACEAE
Quercus prinoides Willdenow

Dwarf Chinkapin Oak

Size and Form. A low, spreading clonal shrub, 1–4 m high; rarely a slender tree to 5 m high and 8–12 cm in diameter. Trunk slender, usually crooked and leaning, supporting a thin, rounded, scraggly crown. Typically occurring in small clonal groups. Deep-rooting. Michigan Big Tree: no record.

Bark. Smooth and thin, ashy gray; becoming roughened and flaky with age.

Leaves. Alternate, simple, blades 6–12 cm long and 4–7 cm wide; oblong-lanceolate to obovate, often somewhat lance-shaped, apex acute; margin wavy and coarsely toothed with 4–8 rounded teeth; thick and firm; yellow green above, pale-pubescent beneath; petioles short, 1–2 cm long.

Twigs. Slender, rusty-pubescent on new growth, becoming reddish brown, lenticels inconspicuous.

Winter Buds. Terminal bud 2–3 mm long, ovate, rounded at the apex, light brown.

Wood. Similar to that of chinkapin oak; stems too small to be commercially important.

Flowers. May, with the leaves; male catkins hairy, 2.5–7 cm long; female flowers solitary or in pairs, sessile, stigmas yellowish red. Tree monoecious. Wind-pollinated.

Fruit. Acorn, ripening in autumn of first season; sessile or short-stalked; cup with small, appressed, somewhat swollen scales, becoming knobby toward the base, pale woolly outside, downy inside, thin, deep, enclosing about ½ of the nut; nut ovoid to ellipsoid, 1.2–2 cm long, chestnut brown, pale-downy at apex, blunt-pointed; kernel relatively sweet.

Distribution. Occasional in the southern portion of the Lower Peninsula.

Habitat. Characteristic of open or thinly forested xeric sites with calcareous soils, including sandy-gravelly hillsides, knobs, kames, and eskers; associated with black and white oaks, eastern redcedar, pignut hickory, smooth, staghorn, and fragrant sumacs.

Notes. Intolerant of shade; slow-growing. Develops small clones by vigorous sprouting around the root cellar of the dead parent tree whose roots remain alive. In addition, small suckers arise from underground axes. Sometimes, what appears to be a single colony is clusters of root-collar sprouts, each cluster circling what appears to be the core of a former tree.

The leaves of dwarf chinkapin oak in Michigan are notably variable in size, shape, and margins. The teeth vary from long and and pointed to extremely shallow and rounded.

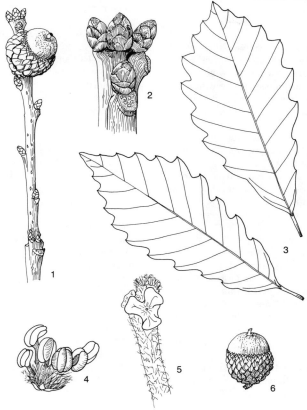

1. Winter twig, × 1.
2. Terminal portion of twig, × 3½.
3. Leaves, × ½.
4. Male flower, enlarged.
5. Female flower on stalk, enlarged.
6. Fruit, acorn, × 1.

Key Characters

- low shrub or scraggly small tree, usually forming a small clone, trunk crooked, leaning
- leaves with coarse, rounded teeth
- acorn cup thin, deep, with knobby scales toward the base
- Distinguished from chinkapin oak by shrub or small tree form, crooked trunk, and scraggly crown; smaller leaves with fewer, more rounded teeth; acorn cup with knobby scales toward the base.

275

FAGACEAE
Quercus rubra Linnaeus

Red Oak

Size and Form. Large tree, 20–30 m high and 40–100 cm in diameter. Forming a broad, rounded crown of a few large wide-spreading limbs and slender branches; dead branches usually not persistent on lower trunk. Tap root prominent in young trees; major lateral roots deep-set and wide-spreading. Michigan Big Tree: girth 7.1 m, diameter 226 cm, height 36 m, Berrien Co.

Bark. Moderately thick, young trunks smooth, grayish brown; old trunks darker, thicker, shallowly fissured into long, broad, flat and smooth-topped ridges (as if "ironed out") inner bark pink to flesh-colored, not bitter but gritty.

Leaves. Alternate, simple, blades 13–23 cm long, 9–15 cm wide; oval to obovate; 5–11-lobed with coarse-toothed, bristle-tipped lobes tapering from broad bases and wide, oblique, rounded sinuses; thin and firm; usually dull dark green above, paler beneath, pinkish red when flushing in spring, leaves of young seedlings and sprouts turning red in autumn; glabrous; petioles stout, 2–4 cm long.

Twigs. Moderately stout, lustrous, green, becoming reddish, finally dark brown.

Winter Buds. Terminal bud 6 mm long, ovoid, acute, only slightly angled, reddish brown, smooth, tip often hairy.

Wood. Heavy, hard, strong, coarse-grained, pale reddish brown, with thin, lighter-colored sapwood; ring-porous. Uses include furniture, flooring, veneer, interior trim, posts, pilings, crates, boxes.

Flowers. May-June, when the leaves are half-grown; male catkins hairy, 10–13 cm long; calyx 4–5-lobed, greenish; corolla 0; stamens 4–5, with yellow anthers; female flowers on short, glabrous peduncles; stigmas long, spreading, bright green. Wind-pollinated.

Fruit. Acorn; autumn of second season; sessile or short-stalked; cup shallow, saucer-shaped, usually enclosing only the base of the nut, rarely to ⅓ of the nut; scales closely appressed, more or less glossy, puberulent, bright reddish brown; nut oblong-ovoid with a broad base, 2–3 cm long, 1.3–2 cm in diameter, reddish brown; kernel white, very bitter.

Distribution. Common in the southern half of the Lower Peninsula; frequent in the northern half and the Upper Peninsula; frequent along Lakes Michigan and Superior. Most northerly distributed of Michigan oaks; approaching its northern range limit in the Upper Peninsula.

Habitat. Characteristic of mesic forests throughout the state on moist, cool, well drained sites; associated with sugar maple, beech, basswood, white ash, bitternut hickory, tuliptree, blue-beech in southern Michigan and many of these same species in the northern hardwoods forests of the northern Lower Peninsula and the Upper Peninsula. Also occurring in dry-mesic forests of southern Michigan with white and black oaks, shagbark and pignut hickories, white ash, black cherry. Found on sandy, well drained soils of the northern Lower Peninsula and Upper Peninsula with white and red pines, aspens, and red maple; locally frequent near the shores of the Great Lakes and on rock outcrops. More demanding of moisture than black and white oaks; tolerating a colder climate than black or white oaks.

Notes. Intermediate in shade tolerance; relatively fast-growing; long-lived (300+ years). Acorn size is related to latitude and to site conditions; smaller acorns are found in the more northerly localities and on the poorer (lower fertility) sites (Overlease 1975). An important landscape tree for parks and spacious lawns. Relatively free of insect and disease pests, the most threatening being the gypsy moth (*Porthetria dispar*) and oak wilt (*Ceratocystis fagacearum*).

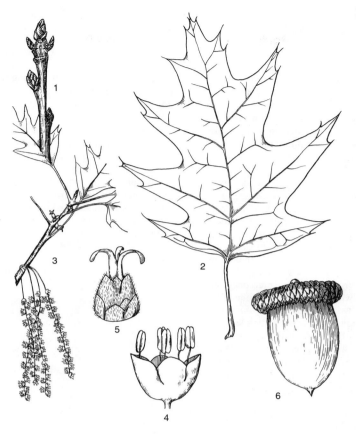

1. Winter twig, × 1.
2. Leaf, × ½.
3. Flowering shoot, × ½.
4. Male flower, enlarged.
5. Female flower, enlarged.
6. Fruit, acorn, × 1.

Key Characters

- leaves usually with dull green upper surface
- acorn with shallow cup, enclosing just the base of the nut
- terminal bud lustrous, reddish brown
- inner bark not bitter, pink or flesh-colored

Distinguished from scarlet oak by less deeply cut sinuses; duller upper leaf surface; shallow acorn cup, enclosing just the base of the nut; typically found in a more mesic habitat.

Distinguished from northern pin oak by larger, broader, less deeply cleft leaves; shallow acorn cup; lower trunk well pruned of dead branches.

277

FAGACEAE
Quercus velutina Lamarck

Black Oak

Size and Form. Large tree, 18–24 m high and 40–120 cm in diameter. Slender branches and stout branchlets form a wide-spreading, often irregular, rounded crown; dead lower branches usually not persistent on lower trunk. Tap root prominent; lateral roots wide-spreading and deeply set; wind-firm. Michigan Big Tree: girth 6.0 m, diameter 191 cm, height 35 m, St. Clair Co.

Bark. Thick and nearly black, deeply furrowed with many horizontal cracks, forming irregular, short, rounded ridges having a squarish-blocky appearance; inner bark thick, bright yellow or orange, very bitter.

Leaves. Alternate, simple, blades 10–20 cm long, 10–15 cm wide; ovate to oblong; usually 7-lobed, shade leaves with shallow sinuses and broad, rounded, mucronate lobes, sun leaves with wide, rounded sinuses extending halfway or more to the midrib and narrow-oblong or triangular, bristle-tipped lobes, the lobes more or less coarse-toothed, each tooth bristle-tipped; thick and leathery; lustrous, dark green above, yellow green, roughened and scurfy to pubescent beneath, with conspicuous axillary tufts; petioles stout, yellow, 3.5–6 cm long.

Twigs. Stout, at first scurfy-pubescent, later glabrous, reddish brown, finally mottled gray.

Winter Buds. Terminal bud 6 mm long, ovoid to conical, obtuse, strongly angled, hoary-tomentose.

Wood. Heavy, hard, strong, coarse-grained, bright reddish brown, with thin, paler sapwood; ring-porous. Uses similar to those of red oak.

Flowers. May, when the leaves are half-grown; male catkins pubescent, 10–15 cm long; calyx acutely 3–4-lobed, reddish, hairy; corolla 0; stamens usually 4–5, with acute, yellow anthers; female flowers reddish, on short, tomentose peduncles; stigmas 3, divergent, red. Wind-pollinated.

Fruit. Acorn; autumn of second season; sessile or short-stalked; cup deep and bowl-shaped, enclosing ⅓–½ of the nut; scales thin, loosely fitting and overlapping, squarish at the ends, forming a slightly fringed cup, dull light brown, satiny pubescent; nut ovoid, 1.2–1.8 cm long, reddish brown, often pubescent; kernel yellow, bitter.

Distribution. Common in the southern half of the Lower Peninsula, occasional in the northern half; not known from the Upper Peninsula.

Habitat. Characteristic of xeric and dry-mesic oak-hickory forests and oak-pine forests with well to very well drained, upland soils, especially sandy to gravelly textures; intolerant of high water tables; associated with white, red, northern pin, and scarlet oaks, pignut and shagbark hickories, white ash, black cherry, bigtooth aspen, white and red pines, red maple.

Notes. Shade-intolerant; moderately fast-growing; long-lived. A good indicator of dry to xeric site conditions. Not an important ornamental tree.

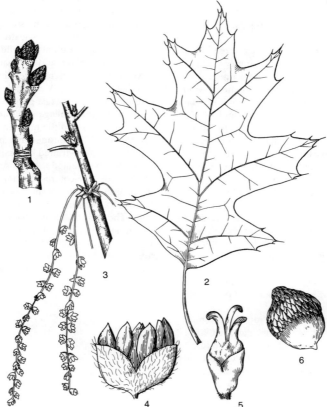

1. Winter twig, × 1.
2. Leaf, × ½.
3. Flowering shoot, × ½.
4. Male flower, enlarged.
5. Female flower, enlarged.
6. Fruit, acorn, × 1.

Key Characters

- leaves very shiny, dark green above and yellow green beneath, lower surface scurfy-pubescent
- inner bark bright yellow or orange, very bitter
- acorn cup deep, bowl-shaped, with dull, light brown, loosely fitting scales, squarish at the tips, forming a slightly fringed cup
- dry, upland habitats

Distinguished from northern pin and scarlet oaks by bitter, bright yellow or orange inner bark; loosely fitting cup scales, cup often fringed; lower dead branches not persistent.

FAGACEAE

Quercus coccinea Muenchhausen

Scarlet Oak

Size and Form. Medium-sized tree, 15–21 m high and 30–60 cm in diameter. Long, slender branches form a rather open, rounded crown. Tap root prominent; windfirm. Michigan Big Tree: girth 4.2 m, diameter 133 cm, height 34 m, Calhoun Co.

Bark. Moderately thick, dark gray or brown on old trunks, shallowly fissured, scaly; inner bark pink to red, not bitter.

Leaves. Alternate, simple, blades 8–15 cm long, 7–13 cm wide; broadly obovate to oval; 5–9-lobed by deep, wide, rounded sinuses that extend halfway or further toward the midrib, the lobes toothed and bristle-tipped; thin and firm; lustrous, bright green above, paler beneath, turning scarlet in autumn, strongly persistent in winter; glabrous; petioles slender, 2–5 cm long.

Twigs. Slender, at first scurfy-pubescent, later lustrous, green, finally smooth, light brown.

Winter Buds. Terminal bud about 6 mm long, broadly ovoid, acute, dark reddish brown, pale-pubescent above the middle.

Wood. Heavy, hard, strong, coarse-grained, light reddish brown, with thick, darker brown sapwood; ring-porous. Uses same as those of red oak.

Flowers. May, with the leaves; male catkins glabrous, 7–10 cm long; calyx 4–5-lobed, reddish, pubescent; corolla 0; stamens usually 4, with yellow anthers; female flowers on pubescent peduncles 12 cm long, bright red, pubescent; stigmas long, spreading, bright red. Wind-pollinated.

Fruit. Acorn; autumn of second season; sessile or short-stalked; cup mainly cup-shaped, deep, with closely appressed, slightly puberulent, reddish brown or orange scales, enclosing about half the nut; nut usually short-ovoid, 1.3–2.2 cm long, light reddish brown, often with concentric rings near the apex, dropped late in autumn; kernel whitish, bitter.

Distribution. Frequent in the southern third of the Lower Peninsula.

Habitat. Characteristic of open, xeric, and dry-mesic oak and oak-hickory forests with dry, very well drained sandy soils; also found on sites that are wet in the spring due to high water table and then become droughty in summer. Associated with black, white, and northern pin oaks, pignut and shagbark hickories.

Notes. Shade-intolerant; relatively fast-growing; long-lived. A desirable ornamental tree for its relatively fast growth, attractive form, and scarlet foliage in autumn.

Closely related to the northern pin oak; Overlease (1977) considers northern pin oak a northern, small-fruited expression of scarlet oak. We have treated the two separately to allow readers to contrast the features said to distinguish the species and to encourage readers to examine these characters in the field. The fruit characters become quite different and distinctive at the extremes of distribution of these species. Thus their major area of overlap, in southern Michigan, is an extremely important area for study.

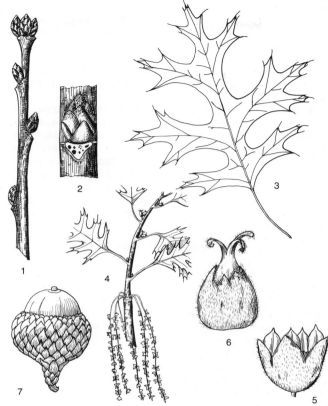

1. Winter twig, × 1.
2. Portion of twig, enlarged.
3. Leaf, × ⅔.
4. Flowering shoot, × ½.

5. Male flower, enlarged.
6. Female flower, enlarged.
7. Fruit, acorn, × 1.

Key Characters

• shiny leaves with deeply cut, nearly round sinuses, glabrous beneath
• acorn cup deep, enclosing about half the nut, cup scales closely appressed, reddish brown or orange
• scarlet foliage in autumn

Distinguished from black oak by pinkish inner bark (not bright yellow or orange), not bitter; glabrous lower blade surface, more deeply cut sinuses; scales of cup more closely appressed and lustrous, cup not fringed.

Distinguished from red oak by shinier leaves and more deeply cut sinuses; acorn cup deeper, enclosing half the nut.

Distinguished from northern pin oak by slightly larger leaf blade, leaf blade not as deeply cleft; acorn cup larger, cup scales more reddish brown to orange; nut larger, not ellipsoidal; kernel of nut whitish; dead branches usually not as persistent on lower trunk.

281

FAGACEAE
Quercus ellipsoidalis E. J. Hill

Northern Pin Oak   Upland Pin Oak

Size and Form. Medium-sized tree, 15–18 m high and 30–60 cm in diameter. Forming a rather narrow, oblong-cylindrical crown of upright and horizontal branches; many small, drooping branches or stubs of dead branches occurring on lower trunk, persistent when dead. Tap root prominent; windfirm. Michigan Big Tree: girth 3.5 m, diameter 112 cm, height 26 m, Oakland Co.

Bark. Thin, dull gray to dark brown, rather smooth or closely ribbed; inner bark flesh-colored, not bitter.

Leaves. Alternate, simple, blades 7–13 cm long and about as wide; oval to nearly orbicular; narrowly 5–7-lobed by very deep, wide, rounded sinuses, the lobes few-toothed, bristle-tipped; thin and firm; lustrous, bright green above, paler beneath; glabrous; petioles slender, glabrous.

Twigs. Slender, bright reddish brown, covered with matted, pale hairs.

Winter Buds. Terminal bud 3–6 mm long, ovoid, rather obtuse, slightly angular, lustrous, reddish brown, usually glabrous.

Wood. Heavy, hard, strong, coarse-grained, reddish brown, with thin, paler sapwood; ring-porous. Uses same as those of red oak.

Flowers. May, with the leaves; male catkins puberulent, 2.5–7 cm long; calyx 4–5-lobed or parted, glabrous except at the apex, which is fringed with long, twisted hairs; corolla 0; stamens 2–5, with short filaments; female flowers red, tomentose, borne on stout, tomentose peduncles; stigmas 3, recurved, dark red. Wind-pollinated.

Fruit. Acorn; autumn of second season; short-stalked or nearly sessile; cup top-shaped, ashy gray to brownish, with scales thin, appressed, puberulent, enclosing ⅓–½ of the nut; nut ellipsoid or rounded, 1.2–1.8 cm long, light brown, puberulent; kernel yellow, bitter.

Distribution. Occasional in the southern part of the Lower Peninsula, locally common in the northern half of the Lower Peninsula; rare in the Upper Peninsula (Menominee, Iron Co.).

Habitat. Characteristic of open, xeric, and dry-mesic oak and oak-pine forests with very well drained sites, especially on deep sands and sandy to gravelly soils (outwash plains, kames, and some other glacial features). Associated with black and scarlet oaks in southern lower Michigan and jack and red pines and bigtooth aspen in northern lower Michigan.

Notes. Shade-intolerant; moderately fast-growing; relatively short-lived. Also known as Hill's oak. The nut, not always ellipsoidal, is often rounded or bullet-shaped; more like that of black oak than pin oak.

Closely related to scarlet oak; Overlease (1977) considers it a northern, small-fruited expression of scarlet oak. See discussion under notes of scarlet oak, p. 280.

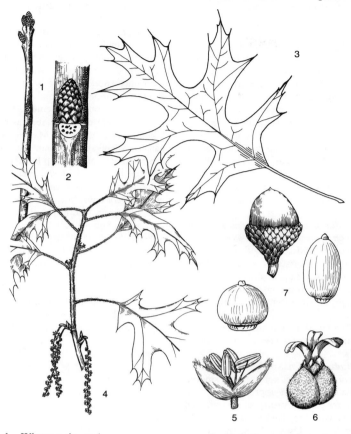

1. Winter twig, × 1.
2. Portion of twig, enlarged.
3. Leaf, × ½.
4. Flowering shoot, × ½.

5. Male flower, enlarged.
6. Female flower, enlarged.
7. Fruit, acorn, shape variations
    illustrated, × 1.

**Key
Characters**

• relatively small leaves with deep sinuses, glabrous both sides
• acorn cup scales appressed; cup deep, top-shaped, enclosing ⅓–½ of the nut;
  nut rounded or ellipsoidal
• many drooping branches on lower trunk, persistent even when dead
• dry, upland, sandy to gravelly sites

Distinguished from black oak by smaller, glabrous leaves; inner bark not
bright yellow or orange, not bitter; cup with more appressed scales, no marginal
fringe; branches more persistent on lower trunk.

Distinguished from scarlet oak by slightly smaller leaf blade, blade more
deeply cut; smaller cup, not as reddish brown or orange; nut smaller, often
ellipsoidal; kernel of nut yellow; dead branches more persistent on lower trunk.

Distinguished from pin oak by the deeper cup, enclosing up to half the nut;
larger nut, often ellipsoidal.

283

FAGACEAE
Quercus palustris Muenchhausen

Pin Oak

Size and Form. Medium-sized tree, 12–20 m high and 30–60 cm in diameter. Straight trunk, reaching high into the crown, strongly excurrent form; forming an oblong-cylindrical or pyramidal crown of many upright spreading, slender branches, with short, spurlike or pin-like laterals, the lowermost branches drooping nearly to the ground and, when dead, persisting on the trunk. Root system shallow. Michigan Big Tree: girth 4.0 m, diameter 129 cm, height 32 m, Wayne Co.

Bark. Relatively thin, grayish brown, smooth in youth, checking into shallow narrow ridges.

Leaves. Alternate, simple, blades 8–15 cm long, 5–10 cm wide; obovate to ovate; 5–7-lobed by deep, wide, rounded, U-shaped sinuses, the lobes horizontal, wide-spreading, few-toothed, bristle-tipped; thin and firm; very shiny, dark green above, paler beneath, turning bright red in autumn; glabrous; petioles slender.

Twigs. Slender, dark red and tomentose at first, becoming lustrous, green, finally grayish brown.

Winter Buds. Terminal bud 3 mm long, ovoid or conical, acute, light brown, smooth; lateral buds more or less appressed.

Wood. Heavy, hard, strong, coarse-grained, light brown, with thin, darker-colored sapwood; ring-porous. Uses same as those for red oak.

Flowers. May, with the leaves; male catkins hairy, 5–10 cm long; calyx 4–5-lobed, hairy; corolla 0; stamens 4–5, with yellow anthers; female flowers tomentose, borne on short, tomentose peduncles; stigmas recurved, bright red. Wind-pollinated.

Fruit. Acorn; autumn of second season; sessile or short-stalked; cup saucer-shaped with scales closely appressed, dark reddish brown, enclosing only the base of the nut; nut nearly round, very small, 1.3 cm or less in diameter, light brown; kernel bitter.

Distribution. Locally frequent in the southern two tiers of counties and in southeastern lower Michigan, north to St. Clair Co.; outliers in Gratiot, Montcalm, and Muskegon Co. Reaching the northern limit of its range in southern Michigan.

Habitat. Characteristic of sites that are flat and seasonally wet and then dry, i.e., excessively wet in late winter and spring and excessively dry in summer; including upland river flats where ponding of surface water in shallow depressions is common, bottomland soils of poor internal drainage, areas with high spring water tables (such as the former lake bed of glacial Lake Maumee in southeastern Michigan, sand dunes in southwestern Michigan, and swamp borders); not adapted to continually wet sites such as deciduous swamps. Associated with American and slippery elms, bur oak, swamp white oak, blackgum, red ash, red maple, northern hackberry, honeylocust.

Notes. Shade-intolerant; moderately fast-growing; moderately long-lived. The tiny branchlets at a distance give the impression of the tree being full of pins. The common name is apparently derived from the many pin-knots in the lumber caused by the many persistent branches. An attractive and important tree in landscaping, easily transplanted.

284

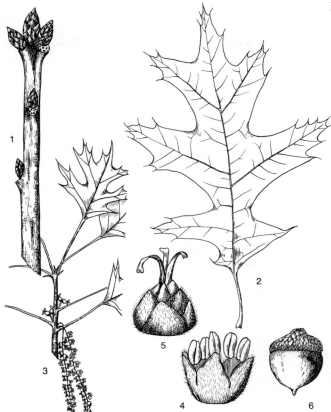

1. Winter twig, × 3.
2. Leaf, × ½.
3. Flowering shoot, × ½.
4. Male flower, enlarged.
5. Female flower, enlarged.
6. Fruit, acorn, × 1.

Key Characters

- small leaves with wide-spreading, narrow, horizontal lobes and very deeply cut, U-shaped sinuses
- acorn cup shallow, enclosing just the base of the nut, scales appressed; nut very small, nearly spherical
- lower live branches drooping and dead lower branches persistent
- occurs in flat, seasonally wet areas, riverbottoms

Distinguished from northern pin and scarlet oaks by shallower cup; smaller, more spherical, and flatter nuts; occurrence in seasonally wet sites in southern Lower Peninsula.

285

FAGACEAE

Quercus imbricaria Michaux

Shingle Oak

Size and Form. Medium-sized tree, 10–18 m high and 30–60 cm in diameter. Forming a rather open, rounded crown of slender, horizontal branches. Michigan Big Tree: girth 3.8 m, diameter 120 cm, height 27 m, Branch Co.

Bark. Thin, smooth, and gray on young trunks; becoming moderately thick, light grayish brown with very shallow, wide fissures and broad, low ridges.

Leaves. Alternate, simple, blades 13–18 cm long, 4–7 cm wide; oblong-lanceolate to oblong-obovate; entire or somewhat undulate, crinkled, spine-tipped; thin; very lustrous, dark green above, paler and pubescent beneath, persistent over winter on open-grown young trees; petioles stout, short, pubescent, 0.5–1.5 cm long.

Twigs. Slender, lustrous, dark green, becoming brown.

Winter Buds. Terminal bud 3–4 mm long, ovoid, acute, shiny brown; lateral buds widely divergent, but scales pubescent, membranous on the margin.

Wood. Heavy, hard, coarse-grained, light reddish brown, with thin, lighter-colored sapwood. Uses similar to those of red oak.

Flowers. May, with the leaves; male catkins slender, hoary-tomentose, 5–7 cm long; calyx 4-lobed, yellow, downy; corolla 0; stamens 4–5, with yellow anthers; female flowers on slender, tomentose peduncles; stigmas short, recurved, greenish yellow. Wind-pollinated.

Fruit. Acorn; autumn of second season; on stout peduncles, about 1 cm long; cup thin, bowl-shaped, with appressed, reddish brown, downy scales, enclosing ⅓–½ of the nut; nut subglobose, 1.2–1.6 cm long, dark brown, often striate; kernel very bitter.

Distribution. Rare in the southernmost Lower Peninsula; reaching the northern limit of its distribution in southern Michigan.

Habitat. Characteristic of moist, fertile lower slopes and river floodplains and bottomlands. Typically colonizing roadsides and hedgerows near rivers and creeks. Associates include American elm, red ash, red maple, eastern cottonwood, black cherry, red oak, shagbark hickory.

Notes. Shade-intolerant; moderately fast-growing; moderately long-lived. In disturbed habitats hybrids with black oak (*Q.* ×*leana* Nutt.) and red oak (*Q.* ×*runcinata* (A.DC.) Engelm.) are relatively common, whereas the hybrid with scarlet oak is rare. The occurrence and morphology of shingle oak in southern Michigan together with its hybridization with other oaks is described by Wagner and Schoen (1976). The common name derives from the use of this wood by pioneers for split shingles or shakes. Also known as northern laurel oak. It is attractive as an ornamental tree.

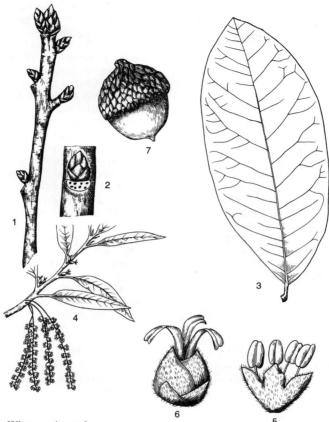

1. Winter twig, × 2.
2. Portion of twig, enlarged.
3. Leaf, × ½.
4. Flowering shoot, × ½.
5. Male flower, enlarged.
6. Female flower, enlarged.
7. Fruit, acorn, × 1.

Key   • leaf blade with entire margin
Characters • acorn cup thin, bowl-shaped; scales appressed, reddish brown; nut nearly
              globular

287

PLATANACEAE
Platanus occidentalis Linnaeus

Sycamore   American Planetree

Size and Form. Large tree, 18–30 m high and 100–200 cm in diameter. Central trunk strong, forming a broad, open, irregular crown of massive, crooked, spreading branches; occasionally dividing near the ground into several large, secondary trunks. Roots shallow and wide-spreading on wet soils of lowland habitats but penetrating much deeper when planted on upland soils. Michigan Big Tree: girth 7.4 m, diameter 236 cm, height 49 m, Lenawee Co.

Bark. Thin, but forming thick plates on the lower trunk; reddish brown on the lower trunk and broken into oblong, platelike scales; separating higher up into large, thin, irregular plates which flake off readily, exposing the thin, greenish or cream colored inner layers and producing the mottled appearance.

Leaves. Alternate, simple, blades 10–20 cm long, slightly wider; broadly ovate; more or less 3–5-lobed by broad, shallow sinuses, the lobes sinuate-toothed; thin and firm; bright green above, paler beneath; glabrous; petioles stout, puberulous, hollow at base and completely enclosing the bud, 2–5 cm long.

Twigs. Moderately slender, zigzag, pale green and tomentose, becoming smooth, dark green, finally grayish.

Winter Buds. Terminal bud absent; end and lateral buds 6–9 mm long, conical, blunt, lustrous, pale brown; forming in summer within the petiole of the leaf.

Wood. Heavy, tough, hard, rather weak, coarse-grained, difficult to split, light reddish brown, with thick, darker-colored sapwood. Uses include butcher's blocks, interior finish, boxes, crates, veneer, furniture.

Flowers. May, with the leaves; borne in dense heads; male flowers dark red, extremely reduced, numerous, on short, axillary peduncles; stamens 3–6; female flowers greenish on long, slender, terminal peduncles; sepals 3–6, minute; petals 3–6, minute; styles long, red. Trees monoecious. Wind-pollinated.

Fruit. Multiple of achenes; October; persistent on the shoots throughout the winter, solitary in occurrence (rarely 2), dense brown heads 2–3 cm in diameter, on slender, glabrous stems, 7–15 cm long; achenes late-ripening, dispersed in winter and spring.

Distribution. Occasional in the Lower Peninsula, rare north to Newaygo and Midland Co. Primarily a midwestern and southern species, reaching a portion of its northernmost range in Michigan.

Habitat. Characteristic of river floodplains and bottomland forests with moist, alluvial soils; also lake shores. Tolerates flooding, silting, high water tables, and soils with slow drainage. Associates include willows, eastern cottonwood, silver maple, red ash, American elm, swamp white oak. Also, open, moist upland sites, old fields and ditches.

Notes. Shade-intolerant; fast-growing; relatively long-lived. Very susceptible to fire injury and along rivers suffers damage from ice floes; decay soon follows such injuries and hollow old sycamores were common in old-growth forests. Pioneers used the hollow logs to smoke meat and store grain. Sprouts vigorously from the root collar and may be propagated easily by stem cuttings. Often used for street and lawn plantings. Desirable due to good survival, deep rooting, fast growth, and the moderate shade it casts. Undesirable due to coarse leaves, wide-spreading crown, and lack of tolerance to pollutants and anthracnose (*Gnomonia platani*), a fungus infection which defoliates trees in the early spring. Probably named sycamore by early settlers for the English sycamore maple (*Acer pseudoplatanus* L.) because its leaves resemble those of this European maple.

A similar tree, the London planetree, *Platanus ×acerifolia* (Ait.) Willd. (a hybrid between the American planetree, *P. occidentalis,* and the Oriental planetree, *P. orientalis*) has been planted extensively in American cities as well as in Europe. The London planetree apparently originated in Spain or southern France about 1650 and was first planted in England about 1680. Clones of this hybrid are vigorous and more resistant than the native sycamore to anthracnose. This tree may be distinguished from the sycamore by the occurrence of 2 or more fruit heads (instead of 1) on each stem and the more distinct, middle blade lobe (typically as long as or longer than it is wide).

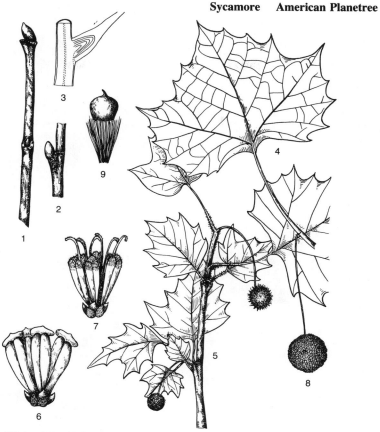

1. Winter twig, × 1.
2. Portion of twig, side view, × 1.
3. Vertical section of twig, summer bud, and leaf petiole, enlarged.
4. Leaf, × ⅜.
5. Flowering shoots, × ½.
6. Male flower, enlarged.
7. Female flower, enlarged.
8. Fruit, multiple of achenes, × ⅜.
9. Achene, enlarged.

Key Characters

- leaf blades large, broad, with 3–5 wavy-toothed lobes with shallow sinuses
- buds conical, completely enclosed by the leaves
- mottled bark on upper trunk (brown, gray, green, white) due to flaking off of irregular thin pieces
- fruit heads dense, brown, borne singly on the shoots

289

The Catalpas—*Catalpa*

The genus *Catalpa* comprises about 11 species distributed in relatively warm climates of eastern North America, eastern Asia, and the West Indies. Because they are adapted to warm climates they are not particularly hardy in far northern regions. The two species described, southern catalpa, *Catalpa bignonioides,* and northern catalpa, *Catalpa speciosa,* were planted in Michigan, have become naturalized, and are hardy in the Lower Peninsula. The catalpas were introduced as ornamental trees because of their large, showy flowers and were widely planted for fence posts because of their durable wood.

The catalpas are trees of rapid growth with stout, pithy twigs. The leaves are large, simple, usually entire, opposite or whorled in arrangement, mostly ill-smelling when bruised. Very showy flowers, in large, terminal panicles, are insect-pollinated, and appear in profusion after the leaves are fully grown. They are followed by long, cylindrical capsules filled with small winged seeds, and the trees in some parts of the United States are known as cigartrees from these distinctive fruits that hang on the trees all winter.

Key to Species of *Catalpa*

1. Leaves 12–20 cm long, thin; flowers 3–4 cm across, prominently yellow-spotted; fruiting capsules about 1 cm in diameter; seeds with pointed, fringed wings at each end; branches rather crooked and straggling; bark thin, separating into thin scales on the trunk .... *C. bignonioides,* p. 292
1. Leaves 20–30 cm long, thick; flowers 5–6 cm across, not prominently yellow-spotted; fruiting capsules about 1.5 cm in diameter; seeds with rounded, wide-fringed wings at each end; branches not as above; bark thick, separating into thick, longitudinal, platelike ridges .... *C. speciosa,* p. 294

BIGNONIACEAE
Catalpa bignonioides Walter

Southern Catalpa

Size and Form. Medium-sized tree, 8–12 m
high and 50–100 cm in diameter. Trunk
short, thick, supporting a broad, irregular
crown of long, crooked branches and coarse,
upright twigs. Michigan Big Tree: girth 5.1
m, diameter 163 cm, height 23 m, Kent Co.

Bark. Thin, reddish brown, separating into
large, thin irregular scales.

Leaves. Opposite or whorled, simple,
blades 12–20 cm long, 10–12 cm wide; heart-
shaped, short-acuminate apex; entire or
sometimes slightly lobed; thin and firm; glabrous, bright light green above, downy beneath, with dark, nectariferous glands in the
axils of the primary veins, turning black and
falling with the first severe frost; strong-
scented; petioles long, stout, flattened, glabrous. Leafing-out very late in the spring.

Twigs. Stout, greenish purple, becoming
reddish brown and marked by a network of
thin, flat ridges; leaf scars large, nearly circular.

Winter Buds. Terminal bud absent; lateral
buds orange brown, globose, inconspicuous.

Wood. Light, soft, weak, coarse-grained,
light brown, with very thin, whitish sapwood;
very durable in contact with the soil. Uses
similar to those of northern catalpa.

Flowers. June-July, after the leaves are
fully grown; perfect; borne on slender, hairy
pedicels in compact, many-flowered panicles
20–30 cm long; calyx 2-lobed, green or
purple; corolla very showy with prominent
yellow spots and dark lines in the throat, apically 2-lipped and basally tubular, 5-lobed,
3–4 cm across; stamens 2, staminodia 3;
ovary 2-celled. Insect-pollinated.

Fruit. Capsule; early autumn; slender,
2-celled, cylindrical, 15–40 cm long and 0.8–
1.2 cm in diameter, hangs on tree all winter,
opening in spring before falling; seeds silvery
gray, 2–3 cm long, with pointed, fringed
wings at each end.

Distribution. Native in central Mississippi,
Alabama, eastern Georgia, and northwestern
Florida; planted in southern Michigan; rare.

Habitat. Native habitats are river floodplains and bottomlands; will survive and
grow in most mineral soils in southern Michigan, including dry, upland sites.

Notes. Shade-intolerant; fast-growing; moderately long-lived. A smaller tree than the
northern catalpa and less hardy. Sometimes
known as Indian-bean tree. Planted for its
showy and fragrant flowers; not desirable as
a street tree.

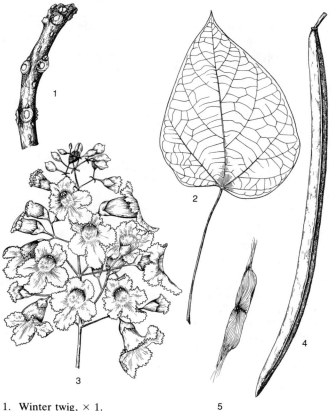

1. Winter twig, × 1.
2. Leaf, × ⅜.
3. Panicle of flowers, × ⅓.
4. Fruit, capsule, × ½.
5. Seed, × 1.

Key Characters
- leaves opposite or whorled; blades very large, heart-shaped, apex short-acuminate, entire
- fruit capsules long, thin, cigar-shaped
- twigs with large, opposite or whorled leaf scars
- seeds with pointed, hair-tipped wings

293

BIGNONIACEAE
Catalpa speciosa Warder

Northern Catalpa   Hardy Catalpa

Size and Form. Medium-sized tree, 10–15 m high and 20–40 cm in diameter. Trunk short, often crooked, supporting a broad, conical or rounded crown of slender, spreading branches and thick twigs. Michigan Big Tree: girth 5.9 m, diameter 187 cm, height 30 m, Ingham Co.

Bark. Thick, reddish brown, deeply fissured into thick, scaly, longitudinal ridges.

Leaves. Opposite or whorled, simple, blades 20–30 cm long, 15–20 cm wide; heart-shaped, apex long-acuminate; entire or sometimes slightly lobed; thick and firm; glabrous, dark green above, downy beneath, with clusters of dark, nectariferous glands in the axils of the primary veins, turning black and falling with the first severe frost; scentless; petioles long, stout, terete, yellow, finely pubescent at first. Leafing-out late in the spring.

Twigs. Stout, greenish, often with a purple tinge, becoming orange or reddish brown and covered with a slight bloom the first winter, finally darker with age; leaf scars large, nearly circular, the upper margin flattened.

Winter Buds. Terminal bud absent; lateral buds brownish, globose, slightly hairy, inconspicuous.

Wood. Light, soft, weak, coarse-grained, light brown, with very thin, almost white sapwood; very durable in contact with the soil. Uses include fence posts, interior trim, picture frames, cabinetwork, lumber.

Flowers. June-July, after the leaves are full grown; perfect; borne on slender, purplish pedicels in open, few-flowered panicles 12–20 cm long; calyx 2-lobed, purple; corolla very showy, white with inconspicuous yellow spots and dark lines in the throat, apically 2-lipped and basally tubular, 5-lobed, 5–6 cm across; stamens 2, staminodia 3; ovary 2-celled. Insect-pollinated.

Fruit. Capsule; early autumn; slender, 2-celled, cylindrical, 25–50 cm long, about 1.5 cm in diameter, hangs on tree all winter, opening in spring before falling; seeds light brown, 2–3 cm long, with rounded, wide-fringed wings at each end.

Distribution. Native in the Mississippi and Ohio River valleys (Indiana, Illinois; as far south as western Tennessee and northeastern Missouri). Much planted in the Lower Peninsula and naturalized in urban environments; rarely found in cutover forests or field habitats.

Habitat. Native habitats are river floodplains and bottomlands. Grows on most mineral soils, including dry upland sites, but growth is slow there and the trees grow proportionally more in diameter than in height.

Notes. Shade-intolerant; fast-growing; moderately long-lived. Sprouts readily from the stump. A larger and hardier tree than the southern catalpa. Also known as western catalpa. Widely planted for fence posts because of its fast growth and durable wood; typically grown at a regular spacing in small plantations to promote natural pruning of lateral branches. In some areas, large caterpillars, the catalpa sphinx (*Ceratomia catalpae*), that feed on catalpa leaves, were once highly sought as fish bait.

294

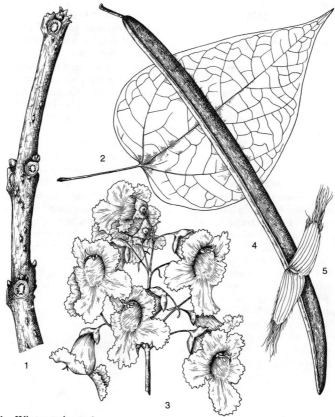

1. Winter twig, × 1.
2. Leaf, × ¼.
3. Panicle of flowers, × ⅜.
4. Fruit, capsule, × ½.
5. Seed, × 1.

Key Characters

- leaves opposite or whorled; blades very large, heart-shaped, apex long-acuminate, entire
- fruit capsules long, thin, cigar-shaped
- twigs with large, opposite or whorled leaf scars
- seeds with rounded hair-tipped wings

CAPRIFOLIACEAE
Viburnum lentago Linnaeus

Nannyberry

Size and Form. Tall shrub or small tree, 4–7 m high and 10–20 cm in diameter. Trunks usually several, slender, often crooked; numerous tortuous branches form a wide, irregular, open, rounded crown. Shallow root system giving rise to root suckers. Michigan Big Tree: girth 0.8 m, diameter 26 cm, height 12 m, Oakland Co.

Bark. Thin, grayish brown; becoming reddish brown on old trunks and broken into small, thick plates.

Leaves. Opposite, simple, blades 5–10 cm long, half as wide; ovate to suborbicular, apex long-acuminate; serrations fine, sharp, incurved; thick and firm; lustrous, bright green above, pale and marked with tiny black dots beneath; petioles broad, grooved, more or less winged, 2–3 cm long.

Twigs. Slender, at first light green, rusty-pubescent, becoming glabrous and dark reddish brown; lenticels round.

Winter Buds. Vegetative buds slender, acute, 1–1.5 cm long; bud scales 2, closely valvate, scurfy; flower buds swollen at the base, apex spirelike, grayish with scurfy pubescence, 1.5–2 cm long.

Wood. Heavy, hard, close-grained, ill-smelling, dark orange brown, with thin, whitish sapwood.

Flowers. May-June, after the leaves; perfect; small, cream white; borne in stout-branched, scurfy, flat, terminal cymes 7–12 cm across; calyx tubular, 5-toothed; corolla 5-lobed, cream color or white, 6 mm across; stamens 5, with yellow anthers; ovary 1-celled, with short, thick, green style and broad stigma. Insect-pollinated.

Fruit. Drupe; September; fleshy, 1–1.5 cm long, ovoid, flattened, bluish black, borne in few-fruited, reddish-stemmed clusters; stone oval, flat, rough; flesh sweet, edible.

Distribution. Frequent in the Lower Peninsula; locally frequent in the eastern portion of the Upper Peninsula; known from Houghton Co. in the western Upper Peninsula.

Habitat. Characteristic of mesic and wet-mesic sites: river floodplains, stream banks, swamp margins, bottomlands with basic soils; open and disturbed areas such as roadsides, stream banks, lake margins. Associates include American elm, eastern cottonwood, red ash, maples, ashes, beech.

Notes. Moderately shade-tolerant; moderately fast-growing; short-lived. Fruits are food for many birds and mammals; often planted to improve wildlife habitat. Sometimes used as an ornamental for its attractive flowers; the tendency to form suckers in lawns and gardens makes it somewhat undesirable for domestication.

Two closely related species occur in Michigan. The wild-raisin, *V. cassinoides* L., is frequent northward and differs in its lack of a wing on the petiole. A much rarer plant, found only sporadically in southern Michigan, is the black-haw, *V. prunifolium* L. Its leaves are only about ⅓ the size of those in *V. lentago*, and the petiole lacks wings.

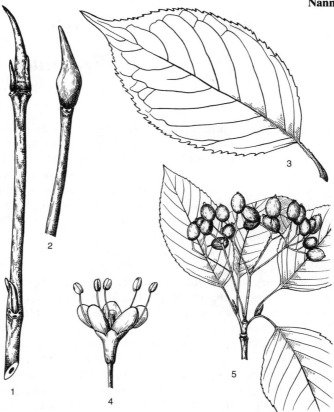

1. Winter twig, with leaf buds, × 1.
2. Winter twig, with flower bud, × 1.
3. Leaf, × ¾.
4. Flower, enlarged.
5. Fruiting shoot with drupes, × ½.

Key Characters

- leaves opposite; blades ovate, apex long-acuminate; tiny black dots on the undersurface; petiole more or less winged
- vegetative buds long, slender; bud scales 2, valvate, scurfy-pubescent; flower buds swollen at the base, apex spirelike
- fruit a bluish black drupe, born on a red pedicel
- tall shrub or small tree in moist to wet habitats

The Ashes—*Fraxinus*

The olive family takes its name from the olive tree (*Olea europaea* L.) of Eurasia. The only representatives among our native trees are the ashes; but several of the commonly planted ornamental shrubs, the lilacs (*Syringa*), privets (*Ligustrum*), and the beautiful forsythia (*Forsythia*) belong to this family. The genus *Fraxinus* includes about 70 species distributed throughout the northern hemisphere and in Cuba, Mexico, northern Africa, southern Asia, and Java. Twelve species occur in North America, four of which are native to Michigan.

Possessing opposite, pinnately compound leaves, the ashes are not likely to be confused with many other trees. The individual flowers of the ashes are small, but coming as they do before the late-flushing leaves and appearing in crowded clusters, they are quite conspicuous. They are wind-pollinated. In all but one species (black ash), the male and female flowers are borne mostly on separate trees, i.e., dioecious. The ashes, like the maples, have prominently winged fruits, the samaras, but those of the ashes are single, whereas the maple samaras are always in pairs. Both wind and water disseminate the samaras.

The ashes are among the most distinctive of tree groups in having markedly different native habitats of the respective species. However, their occurrences have been somewhat blurred by major disturbances associated with human settlement such as land clearing, logging, and drainage of low-lying areas. Nevertheless, habitat is an excellent supplementary character in distinguishing the ash species.

The European ash, *Fraxinus excelsior* L., is sometimes planted in parks and in private gardens. In many characteristics it resembles the native white ash, and since it is not superior to white ash, it has not been planted extensively.

Summary Key to Species of *Fraxinus*

1. Lateral leaflets sessile or nearly so .... *F. nigra*, p. 302
1. Lateral leaflets short-stalked.
   2. Twigs, petioles, and lower sides of leaves pubescent .... *F. pennsylvanica*, p. 304
   2. Twigs, petioles, and lower sides of leaves essentially glabrous.
      3. Twigs prominently 4-angled .... *F. quadrangulata*, p. 306

3. Twigs round in cross section.
  4. Lower sides of the leaflets conspicuously paler than the upper; epidermis of twigs (except current shoot) flaking or peeling .... *F. americana*, p. 300
  4. Lower sides of the leaflets not as above; epidermis of twigs not flaking or peeling .... *F. pennsylvanica*, p. 304

Winter Key to Species of *Fraxinus*

1. Twigs prominently 4-angled; fruit falling in early autumn .... *F. quadrangulata*, p. 306
1. Twigs round in cross section; fruit often persistent on the tree until midwinter or the following spring.
  2. Twigs downy .... *F. pennsylvanica*, p. 304
  2. Twigs not downy.
    3. Buds bluish black; twigs with uppermost pairs of lateral buds usually some distance (often 0.3–1 cm) below the base of the terminal bud; samaras with broad wings, extending to the base of the flattish seed cavity; bark flaky, the surface rubbing off easily .... *F. nigra*, p. 302
    3. Buds brown or reddish brown; twigs with uppermost pair of lateral buds adjacent to the terminal at nearly the same level; samaras with narrow wings; bark ridged, surface not flaky or rubbed off easily.
      4. Epidermis of twigs (except current shoot) flaking or peeling; seed cavity relatively large .... *F. americana*, p. 300
      4. Epidermis of twigs not flaking or peeling; seed cavity narrow .... *F. pennsylvanica*, p. 304

OLEACEAE
Fraxinus americana Linnaeus

White Ash

Size and Form. Large tree, 15–24 m high and 60–100 cm in diameter. Trunk straight, extending well into the upper crown, in forest stands free of branches for a considerable length; forming an open, pyramidal crown of long, slender lateral branches. Roots shallow, becoming moderately deep. Michigan Big Tree: girth 6.2 m, diameter 198 cm, height 35 m, Lenawee Co.

Bark. Thick, gray, deeply furrowed into firm, narrow, regular, flattened interlacing ridges giving a diamond-shaped pattern.

Leaves. Opposite; pinnately compound, 20–38 cm long. Leaflets usually 7–9, 7–13 cm long, 2.5–5 cm wide; short-stalked; ovate to oblong-lanceolate; entire or obscurely serrate; thick and firm; dark green above, conspicuously paler or whitish beneath, turning purple or yellow in autumn; glabrous. Petioles glabrous, stout, grooved.

Twigs. Stout, glabrous, at first dark green, becoming gray or light brown; leaf scars raised at an angle giving the twigs a knobby appearance; epidermis flaking or peeling (except on current shoot) and forming a loose, waxy covering or membranous strips; leaf scars sometimes deeply notched at the top, bundle scars many, forming a U-shaped line.

Winter Buds. Terminal bud short, blunt; bud scales somewhat apiculate, keeled, 4 pairs, rusty or dark reddish brown, finely scurfy; uppermost pair of lateral buds adjacent to the terminal at nearly the same level, not set down 3–6 mm.

Wood. Heavy, hard, strong, close-grained, tough, brown, with thick, lighter-colored sapwood; ring-porous. Uses include furniture, interior trim, sporting goods, tool handles, and dairy, poultry, and apiary supplies.

Flowers. May, before the leaves; borne in loose panicles on shoots of the previous season; calyx campanulate, 4-lobed; corolla 0; male flowers with 2 stamens, rarely 3; female flowers with 2-celled ovary. Trees dioecious. Wind-pollinated.

Fruit. Samara; August-September, persistent on the branches until midwinter or the following spring; 2.5–5 cm long, in crowded, drooping, paniculate clusters; seed cavity relatively large, plump-cylindrical; wing gradually narrowed at the seed cavity.

Distribution. Common in the southern half of the Lower Peninsula; occasional in the northern half of the Lower Peninsula and the eastern half of the Upper Peninsula; rare in the western half of the Upper Peninsula.

Habitat. Characteristic of upland sites, dry-mesic oak-hickory forests (associated with black, red, and white oaks, pignut and shagbark hickories, black cherry, black walnut, hop-hornbeam); less frequent in the mesic beech-maple forests (associated with sugar maple, beech, basswood, yellow birch, hemlock, eastern white pine, American elm); not tolerant of poorly drained sites such as swamps and frequently flooded river banks and floodplains.

Notes. Moderately shade-tolerant; moderately fast-growing; moderately long-lived. Leaves flush late in the spring and are among the first to drop in autumn. Sprouts readily following injury by fire, cutting, or browsing. In youth it exhibits a strong central trunk and an excurrent growth form, with a rapidly growing terminal shoot and short lateral branches. Relatively free of major insect and disease pests; small mites (*Aceria fraxinivorus*) attack the male flowers and cause irregular galls that dry out and form black clusters that are persistent over winter.

300

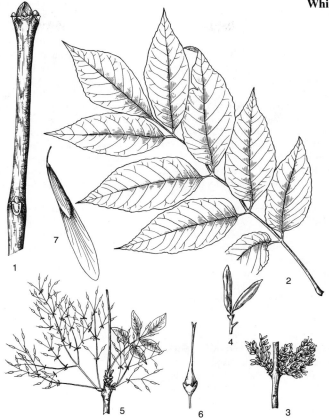

1. Winter twig, × 1.
2. Leaf, × ¼.
3. Male flowering twig, × ½.
4. Male flower, enlarged.

5. Female flowering shoot, × ½.
6. Female flower, enlarged.
7. Fruit, samara, × 1.

Key Characters

- leaves opposite, pinnately compound with short-stalked leaflets; leaflets pale or whitish on undersurface
- epidermis of twigs (except current year) separating from the shoot and giving a flaky, scaly, or peeling appearance
- leaf scars raised at an angle such that the stout, glabrous twigs appear knobby
- seed cavity relatively large and cylindrical; wing gradually narrowed at the seed cavity, not extending to the base of the seed

Distinguished from red ash by peeling or flaking epidermis on older twigs; twigs more knobby with raised leaf scars; samara with a larger seed cavity; twigs gray not reddish; upland habitat, not usually along stream banks or wet sites; crown with dominant terminal shoots and less lateral branch development.

301

OLEACEAE
Fraxinus nigra Marshall

Black Ash

Size and Form. Medium-sized tree, 12–18
m high and 30–60 cm in diameter. Trunk
often leaning or crooked, extending to the
top of the crown; coarse, upright branches
form an open, narrow crown in the forest
stand, when open-grown a rounded, ovoid
crown. Roots very shallow. Michigan Big
Tree: girth 2.4 m, diameter 75 cm, height 20
m, Ontonagon Co.

Bark. Thin, soft, ashy gray, scaly; surface
of bark flakes off when rubbed with the
hand.

Leaves. Opposite, pinnately compound,
25–40 cm long. Leaflets 7–11, 7–13 cm
long, 2.5–5 cm wide; sessile, except the terminal; oblong to oblong-lanceolate, long-
pointed; remotely but sharply serrate; thin
and firm; dark green above, paler beneath;
glabrous. Petioles stout, grooved, glabrous.

Twigs. Stout, glabrous, at first dark green,
becoming ashy gray or orange, finally dark
gray and warty; bundle scars many, forming
a U-shaped line.

Winter Buds. Terminal bud ovoid, pointed;
bud scales rounded on the back, 3 pairs, bluish black; uppermost pair of lateral buds
typically set down 0.3–1 cm below the base
of the terminal bud.

Wood. Heavy, tough, coarse-grained,
weak, rather soft, dark brown, with thin,
lighter-colored sapwood; ring-porous. Uses
include interior finish, cabinet work, furniture, baskets.

Flowers. May, before the leaves; borne in
loose panicles on shoots of the preceding
season; calyx 0, corolla 0; male flowers with
2 stamens; female flowers with 2-celled
ovary. Trees polygamodioecious. Wind-
pollinated.

Fruit. Samara; August-September, falling
early, or sometimes hanging on the tree until
the following spring; 2.5–4.5 cm long, in
open, paniculate clusters; seed cavity flattened; wing broad, often twisted and extending to the base of the seed cavity.

Distribution. Locally common throughout
most of the state.

Habitat. Characteristic of poorly drained
sites with organic soils: deciduous swamps in
the southern half of the Lower Peninsula (associated with red maple, yellow birch,
American elm) and deciduous-conifer
swamps in northern lower Michigan and the
Upper Peninsula (associated with red maple,
American elm, yellow birch, balsam poplar,
speckled alder, northern white-cedar, white
and black spruces, tamarack); not typically
found on upland sites.

Notes. Moderately shade-tolerant; relatively slow-growing; short-lived. Sprouts vigorously following damage by cutting, browsing, or fire. Leaves flush late in spring and
drop early in autumn. Native American basket weavers used the wood, which was pre-
pared by pounding fresh, green wood until it
separated into sheets along the annual
growth rings; strips were then cut for
weaving.

1. Winter twig, × 1.
2. Leaf, × ⅓.
3. Male flowering twig, × ½.
4. Male flower, enlarged.
5. Female flowering twig, × ½.
6. Female flowers, enlarged.
7. Fruit, samara, × 1.

Key Characters
• opposite, pinnately compound leaves with sessile leaflets
• twigs with the uppermost pair of lateral buds set 0.3–1 cm below the base of the terminal bud
• bark thin, soft, ashy gray, scaly
• samara wing broad and twisted, extending to the base of the seed cavity
• occurs in poorly drained swamps

Distinguished from all other ashes by the sessile leaflets; twigs with the uppermost pair of lateral buds set below the base of the terminal bud; occurs primarily in poorly drained swamps.

303

OLEACEAE
Fraxinus pennsylvanica Marshall

Red Ash

Size and Form. Medium-sized tree, 12–16 m high, and 30–60 cm in diameter. Trunk sometimes crooked; stout upright branches and many slender lateral branches form a compact, irregular crown. Roots shallow. Michigan Big Tree: girth 4.8 m, diameter 154 cm, height 31 m, Oakland Co.

Bark. Thick, brown or dark gray, with many irregular, vertical, shallow furrows and interlacing ridges; somewhat scaly.

Leaves. Opposite, pinnately compound, 25–30 cm long. Leaflets 7–9, 7–13 cm long, 2.5–4.5 cm wide; short-stalked; oblong-lanceolate to ovate; slightly serrate or entire; thin and firm; glabrous, yellowish green both sides or only slightly paler beneath, glabrous to downy beneath. Petioles stout, glabrous or pubescent.

Twigs. Stout, current shoots glabrous, or densely pubescent at first, the pubescence lasting 1–3 years, finally ashy gray or reddish brown, turning conspicuously reddish in the upper crown in early spring; epidermis of older twigs not peeling or flaking; leaf scars sometimes straight across at the top, bundle scars many, forming a U- or V-shaped line.

Winter Buds. Terminal bud small, rounded; bud scales rounded on the back, 3 pairs, dark rusty brown, finely scurfy; uppermost pair of lateral buds adjacent to the terminal at nearly the same level.

Wood. Heavy, hard, strong, brittle, coarse-grained, light brown, with thick, yellow-streaked sapwood; ring-porous. Uses similar to those of white ash.

Flowers. May, before or with the leaves; borne in compact, downy panicles on shoots of the previous season; calyx cup-shaped, 4-toothed; corolla 0; male flowers with 2 stamens, rarely 3; female flowers with 2-celled ovary. Trees dioecious. Wind-pollinated.

Fruit. Samara; September, persistent on the branches throughout the winter; 2.5–5 cm long, in open, paniculate clusters; seed cavity narrow-cylindrical.

Distribution. Common to occasional throughout the state.

Habitat. Characteristic of sites that are poorly drained or flooded during the spring (such as stream and lake borders, river floodplains, and bottomlands) but not under continuing high water tables such as in deciduous or deciduous-conifer swamps where black ash is dominant; associated with eastern cottonwood, black willow, silver maple, American elm, boxelder, trembling aspen. Also occurs on disturbed sites with periodically high water tables, such as in roadside ditches, highway median strips, and old fields.

Notes. Shade-intolerant; fast-growing; moderately long-lived. Leaves flush out late in spring and drop early in autumn. Sprouts readily following injury by fire, cutting, or browsing. Crown usually more branchy than white ash because of weaker terminal shoot growth and greater lateral branch development. Has both glabrous and pubescent forms (twigs, rachis, leaf undersurface) that are not consistent in other morphological traits. Thus all ashes with pubescent twigs are red ash, but those with glabrous twigs may or may not be red ash. The proportion of pubescent trees (about 50 percent in southeastern Michigan) declines toward the west until virtually all trees are glabrous in the western part of the species' range. The glabrous form, often called green ash, is widely planted as a shade and ornamental tree and is widely and successfully used as a shelterbelt tree.

1. Winter twig, × 1.
2. Leaf, × ⅓.
3. Male flowering twig, × ½.
4. Male flower, enlarged.

5. Female flowering twig, × ½.
6. Female flower, enlarged.
7. Fruit, samara, × 1.

**Key
Characters**
• opposite, pinnately compound leaves; leaflets short-stalked
• current shoots of some trees densely pubescent, trees with glabrous shoots do not exhibit flaking or peeling of the epidermis
• seed cavity narrow, slender; not extending to the base of the seed
   Distinguished from white ash by pubescent twigs on some trees, trees without pubescent shoots do not exhibit flaking or peeling of epidermis on older twigs; leaf blades not so pale beneath; twigs not as knobby with raised leaf scars; narrower seed cavity; mature crowns with more lateral branching, terminal shoots not as vigorous as in white ash; habitat of periodically high water tables (river floodplains), not typically upland forests.

OLEACEAE
Fraxinus quadrangulata Michaux

Blue Ash

Size and Form. Medium-sized tree, 12–15 m high and 30–50 cm in diameter. Small, spreading branches and stout, more or less 4-winged branchlets form a narrow crown. Michigan Big Tree: girth 1.7 m, diameter 55 cm, Washtenaw Co.

Bark. Moderately thin, light gray tinged with red, irregularly divided into large, plate-like scales, often with the shaggy appearance of a shagbark hickory; a mucilaginous substance of the inner bark turns blue when exposed.

Leaves. Opposite, pinnately compound, 20–38 cm long. Leaflets 5–9, usually 7, 7–13 cm long, 2.5–5 cm wide; short-stalked; ovate-oblong to lanceolate, long-pointed; coarsely serrate; thick and firm; yellowish green above, paler beneath; glabrous. Petioles slender, glabrous.

Twigs. Stout, orange, rusty-pubescent, becoming brownish or grayish; conspicuously 4-sided between the nodes with low corky ridges or wings; bundle scars many, forming a U-shaped line.

Winter Buds. Terminal bud short, rather blunt; bud scales rounded on the back, 3 pairs, dark reddish brown, somewhat pubescent; uppermost pair of lateral buds adjacent to the terminal at nearly the same level.

Wood. Heavy, hard, close-grained, brittle, light yellow streaked with brown, with thick, light yellow sapwood; ring-porous. Uses similar to those of white ash.

Flowers. April, before the leaves; perfect; borne in loose panicles on shoots of the previous season; calyx reduced to a ring; corolla 0; male flowers with 2 stamens; female flowers with 2-celled ovary. Wind-pollinated.

Fruit. Samara; September-October, falling soon after; 2.5–5 cm long, in long, loose paniculate clusters; seed cavity flat; wing broad, often twisted and extending to the base of the seed cavity and surrounding it.

Distribution. Rare in the southernmost part of the Lower Peninsula.

Habitat. Characteristic of lime-rich bottomlands, beaches, mesic slopes and ravines; also on drier hills of limestone-derived soils. Associates include white ash, chinkapin oak, black walnut, rock elm, redbud.

Notes. Moderately shade-tolerant; moderately fast-growing; moderately short-lived. Sprouts readily following injury by fire, cutting, or browsing. Formerly a blue dye was made by macerating the inner bark in water and concentrating the color by boiling.

306

1. Winter twig, × 1.
2. Leaf, × ½.
3. Flowering twig, × 1.
4. Flower, enlarged.
5. Fruits, samaras, × ½.

Key Characters

- opposite, pinnately compound leaves; leaflets short-stalked
- twigs conspicuously 4-sided with low, corky ridges extending between the nodes
- bark with scaly plates, shaggy
- samara with flat seed cavity; wing broad, twisted and extending to the base of the seed cavity and surrounding it

307

Selected Shrubs and Woody Vines

In the following section we briefly describe shrubs, woody vines, and a few small trees that are frequently found in Michigan and the western Great Lakes region. Some nonnative species that are often planted around homes, in gardens and parks, and for wildlife habitat improvement also are included. Many of the native species grow in highly disturbed habitats—roadsides, old fields, fence rows—in open, well-lighted sites where competition is or has been low or lacking. Some shrubs are typical of cutover forests and are good indicators of xeric, mesic, or hydric habitat conditions.

Typically a shrub is a low, usually several-stemmed, woody plant, but shrubs are not clearly set apart from trees. Some may be taller than trees, and some may have a single main trunk. Moreover, trees may sometimes be multiple stemmed. Nevertheless, the arbitrary classification is useful, and shrubs constitute important members of forest communities, especially in dry-mesic oak forests and in swamps and bogs. They provide food and cover for wildlife in a variety of habitats. Some of the shrubs that may also occur as small trees include *Cotinus coggygria, Elaeagnus angustifolia, Ptelea trifoliata, Rhamnus cathartica, R. frangula, Rhus glabra, R. typhina, Staphylea trifolia,* and *Toxicodendron vernix.*

A key to the species described is provided. The key is designed for use in the field, and vegetative characters are stressed. Unless one is certain that the plant is a shrub or a woody vine, one should first use the summer (p. 53) or winter (p. 57) key to tree genera.

The descriptions are arranged by families within each subclass (Magnoliidae, Dilleniidae, etc.) in clusters according to their affinities. Within families, arrangement of the genera and species is alphabetical within natural clusters.

Key to Selected Shrubs and Woody Vines[1]

1. Leaves or leaf scars opposite, opposite *and* alternate, or whorled.
    2. Leaves needlelike or scalelike, evergreen . . . . *Juniperus communis,* p. 318
    2. Leaves broad, with flattened blade, deciduous.
        3. Plants low creepers (growing along ground, no higher than 40 cm),
        twigs green . . . . *Euonymus obovata,* p. 337
        3. Plants upright shrubs, usually over 50 cm tall, twigs various.
            4. Leaves compound, with 3, 5, or more leaflets.
                5. Twigs slender, lacking wartlike lenticels; leaves with 3 leaflets; pith small;
                fruits large, 3–4 cm long, inflated capsules,
                persistent . . . . *Staphylea trifolia,* p. 348
                5. Twigs stout, with conspicuous wartlike lenticels, leaves with 5–7 or more
                leaflets; pith large; fruits small and fleshy, deciduous.
                    6. Pith white; flowers June-July, inflorescences flat; fruit purplish black;
                    buds conical, light brown or green . . . . *Sambucus canadensis,* p. 353
                    6. Pith brown; flowers April-May, inflorescences pyramidal; fruit red; buds
                    globular, red . . . . *Sambucus pubens,* p. 353
            4. Leaves simple.
                7. Leaves and leaf scars both opposite and whorled; buds small, often sunken
                in the bark . . . . *Cephalanthus occidentalis,* p. 351
                7. Leaves and leaf scars all opposite (except *Rhamnus cathartica* which has
                both opposite *and* alternate leaves and leaf scars on the same plant).
                    8. Twigs tipped with narrow, sharp thorns; bark
                    blackish . . . . *Rhamnus cathartica,* p. 339
                    8. Twigs without spines; bark brown, reddish, green, or paler.
                        9. Leaves and twigs covered with delicate, flat, silver and rusty snowflake-
                        like scales . . . . *Shepherdia canadensis,* p. 341
                        9. Leaves and twigs lacking snowflakelike scales.
                            10. Twigs 4-sided with 4 low, longitudinal ridges; fruit rounded, rough-
                            surfaced, pinkish red, containing seeds with fleshy scarlet
                            arils . . . . *Euonymus atropurpurea,* p. 336
                            10. Stems round, lacking 4 low ridges; fruit otherwise, the seeds lacking
                            arils.
                                11. Fruit capsules, opening to release seeds, or samaras.
                                    12. Fruit samaras; bud scales 2, valvate.
                                        13. Terminal buds glabrous, thick, 0.8–1 cm long, conspicuously
                                        stalked; bark vertically
                                        white-striped . . . . *Acer pensylvanicum,* p. 200

----

1. Some small trees are also included. Unless one is certain that the plant is a shrub use
the summer (p. 53) or winter (p. 57) key to tree genera. The shrub and vine key may
key out certain species not included here. To check whether this has happened,
compare your specimen with the description. If it does not fit, then use Billington
(1949) or Symonds (1963).

13. Terminal buds puberulent, slender, 0.3–0.5 cm long, only short stalked; bark without white stripes .... *Acer spicatum,* p. 198

12. Fruit capsules; bud scales imbricate.

14. Shrub less than 1 m high; twigs with 2 hairy ridges below the nodes; leaves serrate; capsules 0.7–1 cm long, beaked with shriveled calyx .... *Diervilla lonicera,* p. 352

14. Shrub 1–4 m high; twigs lacking hairy ridges; leaves entire; capsules 1–1.5 cm long, lacking beak or calyx.

15. Twigs slender 0.1–0.3 cm thick; capsules oblong to cylindrical; leaves narrowly oblong, 3–8 cm long, with translucent dots .... *Hypericum prolificum,* p. 326

15. Twigs moderately stout, 0.6 cm or more thick; capsules ovoid; leaves ovate, 5–12 cm long, lacking transparent dots .... *Syringa vulgaris,* p. 350

11. Fruit fleshy, seeds retained.

16. Leaf buds with 1 pair of scales visible, valvate.

17. Leaves 3-lobed; fruit scarlet, persistent .... *Viburnum trilobum,* p. 354

17. Leaves unlobed; fruit whitish, bluish, or black, deciduous.

18. Leaf blades entire, veins arcuate .... *Cornus* (see p. 334 for key to species)

18. Leaf blades finely serrate, veins pinnate .... *Viburnum lentago,* p. 296

16. Leaf buds with 2 or more pairs of scales, imbricate.

19. Leaves 3-lobed, maplelike ... *Viburnum acerifolium,* p. 354

19. Leaves not 3-lobed.

20. Leaf blades dentate, teeth large, 2–4 mm wide, pubescent when mature .... *Viburnum rafinesquianum,* p. 354

20. Leaf blades entire, glabrous when mature.

21. Shrub less than 1.5 m high; fruit elongate, 1–1.5 cm long; native plant .... *Lonicera canadensis,* p. 352

21. Shrub 2–4 m high (if not pruned); fruit rounded; introduced plant, becoming naturalized.

22. Leaf blades dark green, moderately thick in texture; fruits borne in terminal panicels, blackish; pith white (plants commonly pruned as hedges) .... *Ligustrum vulgare,* p. 350

22. Leaf blades green, thinner; fruits stalked in pairs in leaf axils, red; pith brown (plants usually grown solitary) .... *Lonicera tatarica,* p. 352

1. Leaves and leaf scars alternate.

23. Plants climbing or creeping.

24. Plants climbing.

25. Attaching by spiralling around, leaning on, or growing among and over host stems, without tendril, disk, or root holdfasts.

26. Plants armed; fruits achenes contained within a hip .... *Rosa,* p. 327

26. Plants unarmed; fruits berries or capsules.

27. Leaf blades mostly coarsely 1–4-lobed, broadly lanceolate, texture thin; climbing by leaning on and growing among and over host stems; fruit a berry with many small seeds .... *Solanum dulcamara,* p. 351

27. Leaf blades finely serrate, ovate, thickish; climbing by spiralling around host stems; fruit a capsule with 3–6 large seeds, covered with a fleshy red aril .... *Celastris scandens,* p. 336
25. Attaching with tendrils, discs, or roots.
    28. Support by large tendrils; berries blue or black.
        29. Twigs green, armed; leaf blades rough-margined or with a few, minute bristle-tipped teeth; veins arcuate .... *Smilax tamnoides,* p. 335
        29. Twigs not green, unarmed; leaf blades coarsely toothed; veins pinnate.
            30. Tendrils very long, to 20 cm long, not ending in flat discs .... *Vitis riparia,* p. 340
            30. Tendrils shorter, 1.5–10 cm long, ending in flat adhesive discs.
                31. Leaves compound, leaflets 5; tendrils long (5–10 cm) .... *Parthenocissus quinquefolia,* p. 339
                31. Leaves mostly simple, 3-lobed; tendrils short (1.5–3 cm) .... *Parthenocissus tricuspidata,* p. 340
    28. Support by clusters of tiny aerial roots; leaflets 3; drupes whitish or yellowish; PLANT POISONOUS TO TOUCH .. *Toxicodendron radicans,* p. 345
24. Plants creeping or trailing.
    32. Leaves compound.
        33. Stems unarmed; fruit individual whitish or yellowish drupes; PLANT POISONOUS TO TOUCH .... *Toxicodendron radicans,* p. 345
        33. Stems prickly or bristly; fruit achenes contained within a red hip or an aggregate of purple to black drupes.
            34. Fruit achenes contained within a red hip, somewhat persistent; stipules fused to, and running up, petiole base .... *Rosa,* p. 327
            34. Fruit an aggregate of purple to black drupes, soon deciduous; stipules free.
                35. Armed with abundant, straight or slightly recurved, bristles; fruit small, reddish purple; moist to wet, usually shaded habitats .... *Rubus hispidus,* p. 329
                35. Armed with narrow scattered, recurved, prickles; fruit large, black; dry, open habitats .... *Rubus flagellaris,* p. 329
    32. Leaves simple.
        36. Leaves usually more than 10 mm wide.
            37. Leaves, twigs, and buds aromatic; leaves ovate to elliptic, shallowly crenate-serrate with short bristles ...... *Gaultheria procumbens,* p. 321
            37. Leaves, twigs, and buds not aromatic; leaves obovate to spatulate, entire .... *Arctostaphylos uva-ursi,* p. 320
        36. Leaves usually 3–8 mm wide.
            38. Leaves 3–8 mm long, strongly revolute, conspicuously glaucous beneath; flower or fruit pedicels with two lanceolate bracts near or below the middle .... *Vaccinium oxycoccos,* p. 325
            38. Leaves 0.6–1.8 cm long, only slightly revolute, somewhat paler below; flower and fruit pedicels with two lanceolate bracts borne above the middle .... *Vaccinium macrocarpon,* p. 325
23. Plants erect or upright, not climbing or creeping.
    39. Leaves linear, evergreen.
        40. Leaves usually 3–6 cm long, undersurface densely white-pubescent, margin strongly revolute; seeds borne in a capsule .... *Andromeda glaucophylla,* p. 320

312

40. Leaves 1–3 cm long, undersurface yellowish green, margin flat; seeds borne singly and surrounded by a reddish aril.
    41. Shrub typically 2–4 m high; planted around houses and in other urban environments .... *Taxus cuspidata*, p. 318
    41. Shrub typically less than 2 m high, occurring as a native plant in mesic forests and along streams .... *Taxus canadensis*, p. 318
39. Leaves broader, deciduous or evergreen.
  42. Leaves compound.
    43. Stems armed with bristles, prickles, or thorns.
      44. Stems armed with spines paired at the nodes; tall shrub; wood very hard and yellow .... *Zanthoxylum americanum*, p. 347
      44. Stems with bristles or prickles scattered; tall or short shrubs; wood otherwise.
        45. Few-branched, very thick-stemmed shrub or small tree; leaves 2–3 times pinnately compound, leaflets numerous; leaf scars nearly encircling the twig .... *Aralia spinosa*, p. 347
        45. Habit not as above; leaflets 3–11; leaf scars not encircling the twig.
          46. Fruit a red persistent hip; stipules fused lengthwise to petiole base; stems round, green .... *Rosa*, p. 327
          46. Fruit a red or black deciduous aggregate of drupes; stipules free from petiole base; stems round or angled, green, red, or brown .... *Rubus* (see p. 328 for species key)
    43. Stems unarmed.
      47. Plants short, usually less than 1 m high; leaflets 5, 1–2 cm long, clustered on a short (3–5 mm) rachis; fruits clusters of achenes surrounded by 5 dry sepals; flowers bright yellow, 2–3 cm across .... *Potentilla fruticosa*, p. 326
      47. Plants usually taller than 1 m; leaflets 3, or 7–31, more than 3 cm long, spread out on a long (2–30 cm) rachis; fruits samaras or clusters of drupes; flowers greenish or whitish.
        48. Leaves with 3 leaflets.
          49. Leaflets entire; rachis unwinged; fruits light yellowish gray, glabrous drupes borne in loose, open panicles; PLANT POISONOUS TO THE TOUCH .... *Toxicodendron vernix*, p. 346
          49. Leaflets serrate, or if not, rachis winged; fruits reddish, hairy drupes, usually borne in dense terminal panicles .... *Rhus* (see p. 343 for key to species)
        48. Leaves with 7–31 leaflets.
          50. Plants normally 3–5 m high; fruit a large, waferlike samara; leaves dotted with translucent glands .... *Ptelea trifoliata*, p. 346
          50. Plants rarely more than 2 m high; fruits small, fleshy drupes; leaves without translucent glands.
            51. Terminal leaflet stalked; fruits whitish or yellowish, glabrous drupes borne in open panicles; catkins not present; POISONOUS TO THE TOUCH .... *Toxicodendron radicans*, p. 345
            51. Terminal leaflet not stalked; fruits reddish, hairy drupes borne in compact clusters; small catkins present in fall and winter .... *Rhus aromatica*, p. 344
42. Leaves simple.
  52. Leaves thick and leathery, evergreen.

313

53. Leaf blades flat or margin only slightly rolled, dull green and silvery-scaly above, scurfy below, not rusty-woolly below .... *Chamaedaphne calyculata*, p. 320

53. Leaf blades strongly rolled along margins, bright green above, densely rusty-woolly below .... *Ledum groenlandicum*, p. 322

52. Leaves thinner, deciduous.

  54. Stems armed with prickles, spines, or thorns.

    55. Leaves, shoots, and buds covered with fine silvery scales .... *Elaeagnus angustifolia*, p. 341

    55. Leaves, shoots, and buds lacking such scales.

      56. Small trees; thorns sparse, only terminating twigs .... *Rhamnus cathartica*, p. 339

      56. Shrubs; spines and prickles abundant, borne laterally.

        57. Leaf blades medium-sized, 2–6 cm long, 3–5-lobed, crenate-dentate; mature fruits reddish purple, prickly, globose; native plant .... *Ribes cynosbati*, p. 332

        57. Leaf blades small, 1–3 cm long, not lobed, spatulate, entire; mature fruits red, unarmed, narrowly ellipsoidal; nonnative, cultivated .... *Berberis thunbergii*, p. 319

  54. Stems unarmed.

    58. Leaf blade margin entire or nearly so, wavy, or very coarsely crenate.

      59. Twigs with swollen nodes; leaf scars encircling the bud; bark extremely pliable .... *Dirca palustris*, p. 340

      59. Twigs without swollen nodes; leaf scars not encircling the bud; bark not extremely pliable.

        60. Short shrubs, less than 1 m high.

          61. Twigs brownish; lower surface of leaf blade covered with resinous dots .... *Gaylussacia baccata*, p. 321

          61. Twigs greenish; lower surface of leaf blade without resinous dots .... *Vaccinium* (see p. 323 for key to species)

        60. Tall shrubs or small trees, to 7 m high.

          62. Leaves, buds, and twigs aromatic when crushed.

            63. Leaves very large, 10–25 cm long; fruit a very large berry, 5–12 cm long .... *Asimina triloba*, p. 102

            63. Leaves smaller, 3–15 cm long; fruit a small drupe, less than 2 cm long.

              64. Leaf blades oval to obovate; introduced, showy shrub, widely planted around homes and in gardens; fruit a small, brown, dry drupe, surrounded by finely plumose branches .... *Cotinus coggygria*, p. 342

              64. Leaf blades obovate or elliptic; native species of moist to wet habitats; fruit a fleshy, bright red drupe, no plumose branches .... *Lindera benzoin*, p. 319

          62. Leaves, buds, and twigs not aromatic.

            65. Buds stalked; leaf blade margin sinuate-dentate; fruits persistent capsules .... *Hamamelis virginiana*, p. 222

            65. Buds not stalked; leaf margin entire or nearly so; fruits fleshy, deciduous.

              66. Buds naked .... *Rhamnus frangula*, p. 339

              66. Buds with scales.

67. Leaves and leaf scars crowded at ends of upswept twigs; leaf blades 7–12 cm long, petioles 2–5 cm long, veins arcuate .... *Cornus alternifolia*, p. 172

67. Leaves and leaf scars scattered along straight twigs; leaf blades 2–8 cm long, petioles short, 2 cm or less long, veins pinnate.

    68. Blade apex mucronate; petioles purplish; bark smooth .... *Nemopanthus mucronata*, p. 338

    68. Blade apex acute; petioles not purplish; bark roughened or scaly ...... *Vaccinium corymbosum*, p. 324

58. Leaf margin serrate, toothed, cleft, or lobed, not coarsely crenate or entire.

  69. Buds prominently stalked; fruiting body conelike .... *Alnus rugosa*, p. 230

  69. Buds not prominently stalked; fruiting body not conelike.

    70. Leaves lobed.

      71. Leaves linear-lanceolate with 10–12 shallow lobes per side, like the leaflets of some ferns; aromatic .... *Comptonia peregrina*, p. 349

      71. Leaves ovate, with 3–5 lobes; not aromatic.

        72. Bark of larger branches not strongly exfoliating; leaf blade surfaces with yellow glands ..... *Ribes americanum*, p. 332

        72. Bark of larger branches strongly exfoliating; blades without glands.

          73. Leaves 3–8 cm wide; flowers 0.4–0.6 cm across in dense umbellike clusters; dense, much-branched shrub .... *Physocarpus opulifolius*, p. 331

          73. Leaves 6–20 cm wide; flowers 3–5 cm across in few-flowered clusters; open, few-branched shrub .... *Rubus parviflorus*, p. 330

    70. Leaves not lobed.

      74. Leaves doubly serrate.

        75. Twigs and petioles distinctly glandular or bristly-hairy; male catkins stalked; bracts around fruit not extended into a tubular beak .... *Corylus americana*, p. 349

        75. Twigs and petioles glabrous or merely fine-hairy; male catkins not stalked; bracts around fruit extended into a tubular beak .... *Corylus cornuta*, p. 349

      74. Leaves not doubly serrate.

        76. Buds with 1 visible scale; fruit a small capsule .... *Salix interior*, p. 326

        76. Buds with more than 1 visible scale; fruit not a capsule.

          77. Twigs aromatic when crushed.

            78. Twigs with bitter almond scent and taste when crushed; whole blade margin finely serrate .... *Prunus* (see p. 152 for key to species)

            78. Twigs, buds, and leaves fragrant when crushed; blade more coarsely serrate and only toward apex .... *Myrica gale*, p. 350

          77. Leaves, buds, and twigs not aromatic when crushed.

79. Leaf blades with small blackish scales on the
midrib .... *Aronia melanocarpa,* p. 332
79. Leaf blades without such scales.
    80. Leaf blades narrow, oblong or oblanceolate; fruit a
follicle .... *Spiraea alba,* p. 331
    80. Leaf blades broader; fruit not a follicle.
        81. Fruit a samara borne in catkins; male catkins pre-
sent in fall and winter ..... *Betula pumila,* p. 348
        81. Fruit never in catkins.
            82. Teeth extremely small or absent;
fruit a berry with calyx at
apex .. *Vaccinium* (see p. 323 for key to species)
            82. Teeth larger, obvious; fruit fleshy or dry, with-
out distinct apical calyx.
                83. Shrub 2–4 m high; leaves obovate to oblan-
ceolate; teeth with short bristle-tips that point
up (perpendicular to blade surface);
fruits red .... *Ilex verticillata,* p. 337
                83. Shrub less than 1 m high; leaves ovate to ellip-
tic; teeth pointed or rounded; tips parallel to
blade surface; fruits otherwise.
                    84. Fruit a dry capsule, falling in autumn leav-
ing a saucer-shaped silvery-lined base, per-
sistent; leaf blades with 3 prominent veins
from the base; many-branched; dry
habitats .... *Ceanothus americanus,* p. 338
                    84. Fruit a black drupe, deciduous; leaf blades
with 5–7 pinnate veins; few-branched;
wet habitats .... *Rhamnus alnifolia,* p. 338

Shrub and Woody Vine Descriptions

CUPRESSACEAE
Juniperus communis Linnaeus var. *depressa*
Pursh

Ground Juniper

Spreading evergreen, to 1.5 m high; numerous stems ascending from a prostrate base;
forming broad saucer-shaped patches to 3 m
or more across. Michigan Big Shrub: girth
0.4 m, diameter 14 cm, height 5 m, Leelanau
Co. *Bark* thin, dark reddish brown, scaly or
exfoliating in papery strips. *Leaves* in whorls
of 3, all needlelike, not decurrent at base;
sharp-pointed, straight or somewhat curved
inward, 0.8–2 cm long, 1–1.5 mm wide;
grayish or green, concave above with a broad
white stomatal band. *Seed cones* subglobose,
0.6–1 cm in diameter; dark blue, covered
with a bloom; fleshy, scales imbricate; aromatic; seeds usually 3.

Occasional to locally common. Especially
common on dunes and sandy areas near the
Great Lakes and also in old fields in southern Michigan. Shade-intolerant; slow-
growing. Characteristic of open disturbed
habitats, including cutover forests. Birds
spread the seeds widely. Upright plants exceedingly rare.

Distinguished from *J. virginiana* by its low
spreading habit; absence of scalelike leaves;
and needles with a single white band on the
upper surface.

TAXACEAE
Taxus canadensis Marshall

Canada Yew   Ground-hemlock

Erect, spreading, sometimes prostrate, straggly shrub, to 2 m high. *Bark* very thin, scaly,
reddish. *Leaves* spirally arranged, twisted at
the base to appear 2-ranked; evergreen; linear, sharp-pointed, 1.2–3 cm long, 2–3 mm
wide; dark green above, yellowish green below. *Winter buds* minute, rounded. *Seed* surrounded by a cup-shaped, fleshy aril about 6
mm long nearly covering the dark-colored
seed. Plants monoecious. Wind-pollinated.

Occasional to locally common in the northern Lower Peninsula and the Upper Peninsula. Associates include sugar maple, yellow
birch, beech, hemlock, balsam fir. Very

shade-tolerant; slow-growing; long-lived;
very hardy. Wood is exceedingly heavy,
strong, hard, resilient, and decay-resistant.
When present in large numbers in the shrub
layer of the forest, it is reported to inhibit
the development of the typical dense sugar
maple seedling layer in the understory. However, yew is severely browsed by deer and is
a rare occurrence in many places where it
once was frequent. The seed and the green
foliage contain the poisonous alkaloid taxine.

Sensitive to hot, dry conditions; limited in
landscaping to ground cover in cool, shaded
places.

TAXACEAE
Taxus cuspidata Siebold and Zuccarini

Japanese Yew

Hardy, evergreen shrub, typically not over
4–6 m high but some clones reach 12–15 m
high; branches spreading or upright. *Bark*
reddish brown, scaly. *Leaves* spirally arranged and appearing 2-ranked, often somewhat upright and forming a V-shaped trough;
evergreen; linear, sharp-pointed, 2–3 cm
long, 2–3 mm wide; dull dark green above,
yellowish green below with 2 broad, yellow
bands of stomata; narrowing to a distinctly
yellowish petiole. *Winter buds* ovoid-oblong,
chestnut brown. *Seed* surrounded by a pale
scarlet fleshy cup (aril), open at the apex,
surrounding a nutlike seed. Plants dioecious.
Wind-pollinated.

An evergreen shrub of considerable
beauty, especially the new foliage which has
a yellow green color that may last for about
a month. There are many cultivars—dwarf,
vase-shaped, pyramidal, wide-spreading, and
yellow-needled forms. Easily transplanted
when balled and burlapped; cuttings of most
clones root readily. Versatile in light response—very shade-tolerant but also thrives
in full sunlight. Very sensitive to wet sites—
must have well drained sites. Foliage is poisonous to humans and livestock, but aril not
poisonous when ripe. Tolerates urban smoke
and dust, sensitive to salt. Slow-growing.
Easily pruned and shaped. Excellent for
many landscaping purposes.

318

Closely related to the native Canada Yew, *Taxus canadensis*. Japanese Yew has hybridized with *Taxus baccata* (the Common Yew of Europe) to produce the hybrid named *Taxus ×media* Rehder. Of the many clones of this hybrid the columnar cultivar 'Hicksii' is commonly grown in gardens and around houses.

LAURACEAE
Lindera benzoin (Linnaeus) Blume

Spicebush

Tall, aromatic shrub, to 5 m high; several stems arise from a common base, their arching branches forming a wide-spreading, open, rounded or flat-topped crown. Roots shallow. Michigan Big Shrub: girth 25 cm, diameter 8 cm, height 7 m, Wayne Co. *Bark* thin, dark gray, slightly roughened by corky lenticels. *Leaves* alternate, simple, blades 5–15 cm long and about half as wide, shoots often bearing leaves markedly different in size; obovate to oval or elliptic, acute or short-acuminate; entire; thin; glabrous, light green above, paler and sometimes pubescent on veins beneath, turning yellow in autumn; veins prominent; pleasantly aromatic when crushed; petioles 0.5–2 cm long. *Twigs* slender, green or olive brown with pale corky lenticels, aromatic, spicy to taste. *Winter buds* small, superposed, ovoid, green, aromatic; terminal bud absent; flower buds conspicuous in clusters in autumn and winter. *Flowers* March-May, before the leaves; insect-pollinated; borne in dense clusters; 0.5–1 cm across; yellow; fragrant; plants dioecious or polygamous. *Fruit* a drupe; July-September; subglobose-oblong, bright red, spicy-aromatic, 0.6–1.2 cm long.

Common in the southern half of the Lower Peninsula; outlier reported in Leelanau Co. Characteristic of cool, moist to wet, fertile, moderately shaded habitats, including beech-sugar maple forests and deciduous swamps. Best growth in muck soil of deciduous swamps on slight rises above the water table. Shade-tolerant; moderately slow-growing; tolerant of high water tables. Associates include beech, basswood, sugar maple, black maple, tuliptree, blue-beech, yellow birch, black ash, red maple, American elm, winterberry, highbush-cranberry, alternate-leaf dogwood, black currant. All parts of the plant aromatic; the species name *benzoin* refers to the similarity in odor to the resin of the Asiatic tree *Styrax benzoin*. The aromatic oil was used by pioneers in making a medicinal tea, and the bark is reported to be pleasant to chew, a tonic, astringent, and a stimulant. The fruits, dried and powdered, were reportedly used in the Revolutionary War as a substitute for allspice.

The genus name is after John Linder, a Swedish physician (1676–1723). Common names include wild allspice, spicewood, fever-bush, snap-bush, and Benjamin-bush. It is an excellent native ornamental for its early, conspicuous, yellow flowers, yellow foliage in autumn, and bright red fruits remaining after the leaves fall. The caterpillars of the lovely promethea moth and the green-clouded swallowtail feed on spicebush and the related sassafras. Grows well in moist or dry situations when planted.

BERBERIDACEAE
Berberis thunbergii DeCandolle

Japanese Barberry

Erect, compact, spiny shrub, usually wider than tall, 0.5–1.5 m high; much-branched, branches stiff, low, sometimes spreading. *Leaves* alternate, simple, blades 1–3 cm long; borne singly on long shoots or in clusters on short shoots in axils of spines; highly variable in size and shape; spatulate to narrowly obovate, obtuse, rarely acute; entire; bright green above, and paler with slight bloom beneath, turning reddish to dark purple in autumn; glabrous; petioles 0.2–1 cm long. *Twigs* slender, conspicuously grooved, yellow to purplish red turning purplish brown the second year; spines usually simple; pith relatively large, continuous; pith and wood yellow. *Winter buds* small, ovoid. *Flowers* April; insect-pollinated; perfect; borne solitary or 2–4 in umbels under the foliage; small; yellowish; sepals and petals 6; stamens 6. *Fruit* a berry; September-

October, persistent into winter; bright red, narrowly ellipsoid, about 1 cm long.

Native in Japan, introduced about 1864 and widely planted for hedges. Becoming naturalized in open places and disturbed forests; seeds widely disseminated by birds. The flowers are sensitive; if the sex organs are touched the whole flower snaps closed. Extremely adaptable; moderately shade-tolerant but does best in full sun; withstands dry conditions. Easily transplanted, even as a bare-rooted plant; easily rooted from soft-wood cuttings. Many cultivars provide a variety of habits and leaf colors.

ERICACEAE
Andromeda glaucophylla Link

Bog Rosemary

Low-branching, creeping to upright, ever-green, bog shrub, 5–40 cm high; little-branched, branches very slender, spreading, ascending from a creeping stem. *Leaves* alternate, simple, evergreen, blades 2–6 cm long, 3–8 mm wide; linear to narrowly oblong, abruptly acute, mucronate; entire, strongly, often completely revolute; thick and leathery; glabrous, lustrous, dark bluish green above, very finely and densely white-pubescent beneath; petioles very short, 1–2 mm long. *Twigs* very slender, somewhat 3-sided, glaucous. *Winter buds* small, ovoid, subglobose, or conical. *Flowers* May-June; insect-pollinated; perfect; borne in small, terminal, 5–10-flowered, umbellike clusters; pedicels recurved, less than 1 cm long, not more than twice as long as the corolla; small, about 6 mm long; white to pinkish; calyx whitish, usually spreading; corolla globose, bell-shaped, with 5 short, recurved lobes; stamens 10. *Fruit* a capsule; August-September; 5-celled, glaucous, turban-shaped, 4–5 mm across, persistent in winter; seeds numerous, lustrous, light brown.

Common in acid bogs throughout the state. Characteristically growing in sphagnum moss where it is deep and wet. Shade-intolerant. The closely related northern and Old World wild rosemary, *A. polifolia* L., is distinguished by the glabrous lower surface of the leaves; reddish calyx; and longer flower pedicels, 1–2 cm long and 2–4 times as long as the corolla.

ERICACEAE
Arctostaphylos uva-ursi (Linnaeus) Sprengel

Bearberry

Trailing, evergreen shrub, to 30 cm high and 1 m long; branches flexible; rooting at the nodes; clone-forming, often in large mats. *Bark* reddish brown to ashy, exfoliating and appearing papery or flaky. *Leaves* alternate, simple, evergreen, 1–3 cm long and about half as wide; obovate to spatulate, apex rounded to obtuse; entire; coriaceous; bright green above, paler beneath, becoming bronze to reddish in autumn; glabrous; petioles short, 2–4 mm long, often pubescent. *Twigs* slender, erect becoming trailing, 3–5-sided, minutely tomentose-viscid, becoming glabrate. *Winter buds* ovoid, sessile. *Flowers* May-June; insect-pollinated; perfect; borne in 1–6-flowered racemes or panicles; pedicels 2–4 mm long; white to pale pink; calyx 4–5 parted; corolla urn- or bell-shaped with very short, rounded lobes, 4–6 mm long; stamens 8–10. *Fruit* a drupe; July-September; globose, lustrous, bright red, 6–8 mm across, persistent through winter; pit 3–7 mm across, composed of 5–10 wholly or partially fused nutlets.

Frequent in open, sandy and rocky habitats through much of the state, increasing northward; sandy lake shores, beach and dune areas; grows well in sandy, infertile, acid soils. Shade-intolerant. Difficult to transplant but may make a superb ground cover in landscape plantings.

ERICACEAE
Chamaedaphne calyculata (Linnaeus) Moench

Leatherleaf   Cassandra

Upright, evergreen, bog shrub, 0.3–1 m high; many slender branches. *Leaves* alternate, simple, evergreen, blades 1–4 cm long, 0.5–1.5 cm wide; oblong, elliptic, or oblanceolate, acute or rounded; entire or obscurely finely toothed, slightly revolute; thick and leathery; dull green, dotted with silvery scales above, brownish, coriaceous and scurfy beneath, turning brownish or reddish in winter; petioles pubescent, short, about 2 mm long. *Twigs* slender, puberulent and scurfy at first, becoming gray and shreddy, finally smooth and dark reddish brown. *Winter buds* small, globose. *Flowers* April-June; insect-pollinated; perfect; borne in many-flowered terminal, leafy racemes, 4–12 cm long; occurring singly in axils of the small leaves; small, 5–7 mm long; white; calyx 5-lobed; corolla oblong, bell-shaped, with 5 short lobes; stamens 10. *Fruit* a capsule; September; roundish, somewhat flattened, 5-celled, 3–5 mm across; seeds small, 1–2 mm long, wingless, numerous.

Common to abundant in very acid bogs throughout the state; associates are typical sphagnum bog plants. Also found in boggy lake and marsh borders and in acid depressions between dunes. Occurs in single clumps or in huge beds in pure stands. Shade-intolerant.

ERICACEAE
Gaultheria procumbens Linnaeus

Teaberry   Wintergreen

Low, creeping, evergreen shrub, 5–15 cm high; stems trailing on the ground or below the ground surface. *Leaves* alternate, simple, evergreen, blades 2–5 cm long, 1–3 cm wide; ovate, elliptic to narrowly obovate, apiculate and rounded; shallowly crenate-serrate with short bristles; thick and leathery; lustrous, dark green above, paler beneath, sometimes turning red with cold weather; glabrous; emitting a wintergreen odor when crushed; petioles 2–5 mm long, more or less pubescent. *Twigs* slender, arising from stems that are usually below ground, aromatic when crushed. *Winter buds* minute, ovoid, sessile. *Flowers* June-September; insect-pollinated; perfect; most commonly solitary in the axils of the leaves, on pedicels 4–8 mm long; small; white to pinkish; calyx 5-parted; corolla cylindric-ovoid to urn-shaped, 5-toothed, 6–7 mm long; stamens 5.

Fruit a capsule surrounded by a fleshy, berry-like expanded calyx; October, persistent through winter into spring; bright red, 0.8–1 cm across, aromatic when crushed, edible, mealy, spicy.

Locally frequent to common throughout the state. Characteristic of moist or dry, acid, sandy soils with well-developed humus; oak and pine forests; associated with blueberries. Moderately shade-tolerant. All parts contain oil of wintergreen, and it was formerly produced from the plant.

ERICACEAE
Gaylussacia baccata (Wang.) K. Koch

Black Huckleberry

Low, erect, much-branched shrub, 0.3–1.5 m high; clone-forming. *Leaves* alternate, simple, 2–5 cm long and about half as wide; oval or oblong-ovate, apex acute, obtuse, or rounded; entire, ciliate; moderately thick and leathery; yellowish green above, paler beneath; pubescent on both sides at first, becoming glabrous; lower surface densely covered with shiny, yellow, resinous dots or globules; petioles short, 2 mm long, pubescent. *Twigs* slender, brownish, more or less pubescent. *Winter buds* small, ovoid; terminal bud lacking. *Flowers* May-June; insect-pollinated; perfect; 1–7 flowers borne on short, dense, drooping, 1-sided racemes; calyx 5-lobed; corolla tubular-campanulate, 5-lobed, reddish; stamens 10. *Fruit* a drupe; August-September, globose, 6–8 mm across, black, lustrous, edible; with 10 1-seeded pits about 2 mm long.

Frequent to locally common in the Lower Peninsula; frequent to rare in the Upper Peninsula. Characteristic of dry, acid, sandy-gravelly sites such as dry-mesic oak-hickory and oak-pine forests; less common in low, acid, moist to wet areas and swamps. Moderately shade-tolerant. Associates include oaks, hickories, pines, cherries, blueberries, gray dogwood. Fruit edible but not as delicious as that of most blueberries and very seedy.

321

ERICACEAE
Ledum groenlandicum Oeder

Labrador Tea

Upright, evergreen, bog shrub, to 1 m high.
Bark of larger branches gray. *Leaves* alternate, simple, evergreen, blades 2–5 cm long
and about ¼ as wide; oblong to narrowly- or
linear-oblong, obtuse; entire, strongly revolute; thick and leathery; bright green above,
white at first, later densely rusty-woolly beneath; fragrant when crushed; petioles short,
2 mm long. *Twigs* moderately slender, rusty-
woolly the first year, becoming gray. *Winter
buds* small, ovoid, somewhat compressed.
Flowers May-June; insect-pollinated; perfect;
borne on slender, puberulent pedicels in umbellike terminal clusters; small, 6–7 mm
across; white; calyx very small, 5-toothed;
petals 5, obovate, spreading; stamens 5–7.
Fruit a capsule; August-September; narrowly
oblong, 5-parted, splitting from the base;
many seeded.

Common to abundant in acid bogs in the
northern half of the Lower Peninsula and the
Upper Peninsula; rare or absent in bogs of
the southern half of the Lower Peninsula.
Also found in open, boggy lake and swamp
margins. Shade-intolerant. Once called mus-
keg tea; northern travellers used it as a substitute for the tea of commerce.

Key to Species of Blueberries and Cranberries—*Vaccinium*[1]

1. Leaves deciduous; stems upright.
   2. Tall shrub, 1–4 m high .... *V. corymbosum*, p. 324
   2. Low shrub, to 0.5 m high.
      3. Leaves downy-pubescent beneath; twigs very hairy ..... *V. myrtilloides*, p. 324
      3. Leaves glabrous or nearly so beneath; twigs not as
         above .... *V. angustifolium*, p. 324
1. Leaves evergreen; stems creeping or trailing.
   4. Leaves very small, 3–8 mm long, strongly revolute; bracts of flower (fruit) pedicel
      borne near or below the middle .... *V. oxycoccos*, p. 325
   4. Leaves larger, 6–18 mm long, flat or only slightly revolute; bracts of flower (fruit)
      pedicel borne above the middle .... *V. macrocarpon*, p. 325

---

1. Of the many low-shrub blueberry species reported in Michigan we describe two of the
   most widely distributed species; for details of other species see Billington (1949) and
   Fernald (1950).

ERICACEAE
Vaccinium corymbosum Linnaeus

Highbush Blueberry

Erect shrub, 1–4 m high; multiple branches spreading, forming open or sometimes compact clumps. Michigan Big Shrub: girth 10 cm, diameter 3 cm, height 4 m, Oakland Co. *Bark* roughened, grayish, mottled. *Leaves* alternate, simple, 3–8 cm long and about half as wide; ovate to elliptic-lanceolate, acute; entire or obscurely serrulate; dark green above, slightly pubescent and paler beneath, becoming orange or reddish in autumn; petioles very short, 1–2 mm long. *Twigs* slender, angled, warty, greenish brown, becoming reddish on exposed sides in autumn, glabrous or pubescent in lines. *Winter buds* small, ovoid or oblong. *Flowers* May-June; insect-pollinated; perfect; borne on short racemes of 3–8 flowers; calyx 5-lobed, glaucous; corolla cylindric, urn-shaped, 0.6–1.2 cm long, white to pinkish, 5-toothed; stamens 10. *Fruit* a many-seeded berry; July-August; bluish black, with more or less bloom, 0.7–1.2 cm across, sweet, edible.

Frequent to common in the southern Lower Peninsula; occasional or absent northward. Characteristic of low, acid, wet areas; swamps, around lakes, bogs, marshes, low areas between dunes; extremely rare in dry uplands. In circumneutral to basic deciduous swamps of the Lower Peninsula, occurring on acid mounds. Associates include red maple, yellow birch, black ash, American elm, tamarack, spicebush, elders, wild black currant. Cultivars of this species furnish some of the blueberries of commerce. It is cultivated extensively in southwestern Michigan.

ERICACEAE
Vaccinium angustifolium Aiton

Low Sweet Blueberry

Low, upright shrub, to 0.5 m high; straggly, open-growing; clone-forming. *Leaves* alternate, simple, blades 1–3 cm long, 0.5–1.6 cm wide; lanceolate or oblong-lanceolate, acute, base narrowed (pointed at both ends); dis-

tinctly but very finely serrulate with bristle-pointed teeth; thin; bright green both sides; glabrous or nearly so; petioles very short, 0.5–1 mm long. *Twigs* very slender, glabrous or with finely pubescent new shoots, yellowish green, grooved above the buds or angular. *Winter buds* small, ovoid or oblong, glabrous. *Flowers* May-June; insect-pollinated; perfect; borne on few-flowered (usually not more than 5) racemes; calyx 5-toothed, greenish bordered with red; corolla cylindric, urn-shaped, 6–7 mm long; white and pink tinged, 5-toothed; stamens 10. *Fruit* a many-seeded berry; July-August; depressed-globose, color varies by clone from blue to bluish black, bloom may be light or heavy; 0.9–1.5 cm across, very sweet, edible.

Common throughout the state. Characteristic of dry, acid sites, usually sandy-gravelly soils. Associates include oaks, pines, hickories, white birch, black huckleberry. Earliest flowered of the blueberries. Moderately shade-tolerant. Different clones exhibit slight differences in various characteristics, for example leaf shape and berry shape and color. Important commercial wild blueberry.

Distinguished from the low blueberry (dryland blueberry), *V. vacillans* Torr., by lanceolate leaves (rather than oval or elliptic leaves); distinctly serrulate leaves (rather than entire or serrulate-dentate leaves, especially near the apex); and smooth twigs (rather than distinctly warty twigs). Distinguished from velvetleaf blueberry, *V. myrtilloides* Michx., by glabrous leaves and twigs (rather than very hairy leaves and twigs) and serrulate blade margin (rather than an entire blade margin).

ERICACEAE
Vaccinium myrtilloides Michaux

Velvetleaf Blueberry

Low, upright shrub, to 0.5 m high; much-branched, straggly; clone-forming. *Leaves* alternate, simple, blades 1.5–4 cm long, 0.5–1.5 cm wide; narrow-elliptic to oblong-lanceolate, acute; entire; thin; more or less pubescent, green above, downy beneath;

petioles very short, about 1 mm long. *Twigs* very slender, very hairy, nearly round, smooth, greenish brown. *Winter buds* small, ovoid or oblong, more or less pubescent. *Flowers* May-June; insect-pollinated; perfect; borne in small racemose clusters (usually not more than 5–6 per cluster); calyx 5-toothed, glabrous; corolla oblong-campanulate, 4–6 mm long, greenish white and pink tinged, 5-toothed; stamens 10. *Fruit* a many-seeded berry; July-August; depressed-globose, bluish black with much bloom, 6–8 mm across, sour to sweet, edible.

Occasional in the southern half of the Lower Peninsula; common to locally abundant in the northern half of the Lower Peninsula and the Upper Peninsula. Characteristic of dry, acid sites, usually sandy to gravelly soils. Associates include oaks, pines, white birch. Moderately shade-tolerant. Fruit often sour and not as palatable as that of the low sweet blueberry. Also called sourtop. Distinguished from the low sweet blueberry by densely pubescent leaf blade undersurface; very hairy twigs; and leaf blades with entire margins.

ERICACEAE
Vaccinium macrocarpon Aiton

Large Cranberry

Trailing or creeping, evergreen shrub, to 1 m long; branches slender, 10–25 cm long, some erect or ascending; rooting at the nodes; forming clones. *Leaves* alternate, simple, evergreen, blades 0.6–1.8 cm long, 2.5–6 mm wide; oblong-elliptic, obtuse or rounded; entire, flat or only slightly revolute; leathery; dark green above, glaucous beneath; glabrous; petioles very small, about 1 mm long. *Twigs* extremely slender, more or less pubescent, light brown becoming reddish brown in autumn. *Winter buds* small, sessile. *Flowers* June-July; insect-pollinated; perfect; 1–8-flowered in terminal racemes, pedicels usually 2–4 cm long, erect, pubescent, with 2 lanceolate bracts borne above the middle, bracts 3–5 mm long, 2–4 mm wide; calyx 4-cleft; corolla pinkish, deeply 4-cleft, lobes reflexed, 0.5–1 cm long; stamens 8. *Fruit* a many-seeded berry; September-October;

globose, red, 1–2 cm across, sour, edible.

Locally common in acid sphagnum bogs throughout the state. Associates similar to those of the small cranberry. Shade-intolerant. The cranberry of commerce, cultivated in New England and other areas for commercial production. Distinguished from small cranberry by larger leaves and fruits; flat or only slightly revolute blade margins; and bracts above the middle of the pedicel. Found in low coniferous woods in northern Michigan is the somewhat similar creeping snowberry, *Gaultheria hispidula* (L.) Bigel., that differs from cranberries in its densely hairy stems; broadly ovate, apiculate leaves; and white berries.

ERICACEAE
Vaccinium oxycoccos Linnaeus

Small Cranberry

Trailing or creeping, evergreen shrub; branches very slender, 10–15 cm long, some ascending; rooting at the nodes; forming clones. *Leaves* alternate, simple, evergreen, blades 3–8 mm long, 1–3 mm wide; ovate-oblong to triangular, acute or obtuse; entire, strongly revolute; leathery; dark green above, glaucous beneath; glabrous; petioles very short, 0.5–1 mm long. *Twigs* extremely slender, more or less pubescent, light brown. *Winter buds* very small, sessile. *Flowers* May-June; insect-pollinated; perfect; 1–6-flowered in terminal racemes, pedicels usually 1.5–5 mm long, erect, pubescent, with two lanceolate bracts near or below the middle, bracts 2–3 mm long and less than 1 mm wide; calyx 4-cleft; corolla pinkish, deeply 4-cleft, reflexed segments 5–6 mm long; stamens 8. *Fruit* a many-seeded berry; August-September; globose, red, 6–8 mm across, sour, edible.

Locally common in sphagnum bogs throughout the state. Associated with bog trees and shrubs such as tamarack, black spruce, bog birch, large cranberry, bog rosemary, leatherleaf, among others. Shade-intolerant. Distinguished from the large cranberry by smaller leaves and fruits; strongly revolute blade margins; and bracts near or below the middle of the pedicel.

HYPERICACEAE
Hypericum prolificum Linnaeus

Shrubby St. John's-wort

Upright, very bushy shrub with stout branches, to 1.5 m high. *Bark* thin, light brown, flaking or shredding. *Leaves* opposite, simple, 3–8 cm long, 0.3–1.5 cm wide; narrowly oblong to oblanceolate, apex obtuse and often mucronate; entire; lustrous green above with numerous small translucent dots; glabrous; petioles 1–5 mm long. *Twigs* slender, 1–3 mm thick, 2-edged; pith relatively large, somewhat porous, finely excavated in older stems; leaf scars small, triangular, bundle scar 1. *Winter buds* sessile, minute. *Flowers* July-September; insect-pollinated; borne in terminal and axillary few- to several-flowered cymes; about 2 cm across; brilliant yellow; sepals and petals 5; stamens numerous, distinct. *Fruit* a capsule; autumn, persistent; oblong to cylindrical, 1–1.5 cm long, 3–5 mm in diameter, 3(rarely 4)-celled; seeds many, oblong, pitted in longitudinal lines.

Common in the southern half of the Lower Peninsula and northward along Lake Michigan; less common inland and northward. Characteristic of moist to wet habitats; shade-intolerant. Appears in marshy areas, dry, open hillsides, and in second-growth situations where the soil is fairly sterile. The majority of St. John's-worts are herbaceous. The term wort is an Anglo-Saxon word which was used to distinguish low-growing plants or herbs from trees. The name St. John's is said to come from the custom of country people in England of gathering plants of this genus on St. John's Day (August 1) to protect them from evil spirits.

The much smaller Kalm's St. John's-wort, *H. kalmianum* L., is rarely over ⅔ of a meter tall. The flowers are borne only terminally and the capsules are ovoid, 4–7 mm in diameter, with 4–5 cells. Common in sandy or rocky habitats, mostly near lakes in the northern Lower Peninsula and the Upper Peninsula.

SALICACEAE
Salix interior Rowlee

Sandbar Willow

Tall, slender shrub or small tree, to 8 m high; many stems arise in clusters from roots or rooted branches to form large, dense clones. Root system very shallow and widespreading. Michigan Big Tree: girth 56 cm, diameter 18 cm, height 12 m, Macomb Co. *Bark* thin, smooth, lenticels large and conspicuous; green to brown or gray; older trunks furrowed. *Leaves* alternate, simple, blades 3–15 cm long; linear-lanceolate, acuminate; irregular, teeth sharp, widely spaced, and outward pointing; thin; glabrous, dark green above, pubescent and paler beneath when young, later usually glabrous; petioles short, 3–5 mm long. *Twigs* slender, reddish brown, glabrous or puberulent. *Winter buds* very small, appressed, terminal bud absent; with 1 visible scale. *Flowers* April-June, after the leaves; wind- and insect-pollinated; male and female flowers borne on catkins, 2–6 cm long; catkins borne on leafy shoots, small, yellow. *Fruit* a capsule; June-July; seeds minute, attached to long white hairs.

Common throughout the state. Characteristic of stream and river sandbars and banks, sand dunes, roadside ditches, lake and pond margins; in any open area subject to annual flooding or a very high water table. Plants with densely silky leaves occur on sand dunes. Associates include black willow, buttonbush, red-osier dogwood, silky dogwood, eastern cottonwood. Shade-intolerant; tolerant of high water, flooding, and silting. Stem cuttings root easily. Species name refers to its inland distribution along water courses. Important as a protector and binder of stream margins and sandbars.

Upland willow, *Salix humilis* Marsh., is a shrub up to 3 m tall that is unusual in its genus for occurring in apparently dry woodlands and prairies. The leaves are narrowly obovate or oblanceolate and 3–12 cm long. Of other well-known shrubby willows, the pussy willow, *Salix discolor* Muhl., is a much larger plant, up to 7 m tall. It grows in the more typical willow habitats of marshes and swamps. The leaves are finely veiny, some-

326

what glossy above, and broader than those of the upland willow, being more nearly elliptical in outline. This is the classical pussy willow of outdoor gardens and the florist trade.

ROSACEAE
Potentilla fruticosa Linnaeus

Shrubby Cinquefoil

Upright, bushy shrub, 0.2–1 m high. *Bark* pale reddish brown, shreddy. *Leaves* alternate, pinnately compound with a very short (3–5 mm) midrib, 1–3 cm long; leaflets usually 5 (rarely 7), sessile, narrowly oblong to lanceolate, 1–2 cm long, 2–9 mm wide; entire and revolute; silky pubescent on both sides; petioles 0.5–1 cm long. *Twigs* very slender, bark exfoliating; pith small, brown. *Winter buds* relatively large, sessile; leaf scars very small, bundle scar 1. *Flowers* June-September; borne solitary or few on slender stalk; 2–3 cm across; bright yellow to orange; sepals and petals 5; stamens numerous, carpels numerous. *Fruit* a head of many achenes, surrounded by 5 dry sepals; July-October; about 1.5 cm long, covered with long hairs.

Common in swamps, bogs, marshes, and lowland edges throughout the state; typical of rocky sites in the north. Highly shade-intolerant. One of the few species of shrubs that flowers more or less constantly throughout the summer. Some of its varieties make fine garden plants. It is a very characteristic element in calcareous bogs or fens. Most species of cinquefoils are small or medium-sized herbs, some of which are weeds.

ROSACEAE
Rosa (various species)

Roses

Upright, spreading, climbing or creeping shrubs, to 2 m high; branches usually armed with prickles. *Leaves* alternate, compound, odd-pinnate; stipules fused with the petiole base; leaflets 3–11, variable in shape, serrate or toothed; thin and firm; green; glabrous or pubescent. *Twigs* slender, usually green, smooth or in most species armed with bristles or single or paired prickles; pith relatively large, brown. *Winter buds* small, ovoid. *Flowers* June-July; insect-pollinated; perfect; solitary or in corymbose clusters; sepals and petals 5, petals showy; stamens and carpels numerous, enclosed in a bell-shaped receptacle (hip) which becomes fleshy. *Fruit* a red hip containing several to many bony achenes; autumn.

Common throughout the state in disturbed and undisturbed, dry or wet habitats: oak openings, old fields, fence rows, roadsides, cutover woods, sand dunes, swamps. Members of the genus are highly variable and hybridize widely. *Rosa palustris* Marsh. is the most common rose of swamps and many other wet habitats. Roses are easily propagated by cuttings or seed, and commercial cultivars are widely used in ornamental plantings. Past and present, among the most popular of all decorative garden plants because of their showy, fragrant flowers. Rose societies have been organized in many parts of the Great Lakes area. Most cultivar roses are "doubled," i.e., the flowers have many, rather than only 5 petals, many of the stamens having been partially or completely transformed into petals.

327

Key to Species of Blackberries and Raspberries—*Rubus*[1]

1. Plants unarmed; leaves simple, 3–5-lobed .... *R. parviflorus*, p. 330
1. Plants armed; leaflets 3–7.
  2. Canes mostly prostrate, trailing on the ground; bristly, hispid, or weakly prickly.
    3. Fruit small, reddish purple; armed with bristles, abundant; moist to wet, partially shaded habitats .... *R. hispidus*, p. 329
    3. Fruit large, black; armed with narrow prickles, scattered; dry, open habitats .... *R. flagellaris*, p. 329
  2. Canes upright; bristly or prickly.
    4. Canes weakly armed, bristly; largest leaves (those with 5 or more leaflets) pinnately constructed .... *R. idaeus*, p. 330
    4. Canes strongly armed with sharp prickles; largest leaves (those with 5 or more leaflets) palmately constructed.
      5. Young canes purplish with whitish bloom, round in cross section; leaves white-tomentose beneath .... *R. occidentalis*, p. 330
      5. Young canes green to tan, lacking bloom, angled in cross section; leaves green both sides .... *R. alleghaniensis*, p. 329

---

1. The genus *Rubus* is highly variable in morphology, and hundreds of alleged species have been recognized, although many are actually interspecific hybrids. Several of the more important species representing the dewberries, raspberries, and blackberries are described. Most are characteristic of relatively open or moderately shaded, disturbed habitats.

ROSACEAE
Rubus alleghaniensis Porter

Highbush Blackberry

Ascending, high-arching shrub, 1–2 m high; old canes with stout, usually straight prickles, brownish purple, the lower stem rounded in cross section, the upper stem angled. *Leaves* alternate, palmately compound, leaflets 3–7, usually 5 (if 5–7, palmate), 3 leaflets on flowering shoots, short-stalked except the terminal; 4–15 cm long, 3–7 cm wide; broadly ovate to ovate-lanceolate, acute or acuminate; irregularly coarsely serrate to doubly serrate; green both sides; slightly pubescent above, soft pubescent beneath; petioles and petiolules densely pubescent, glandular-hispid, with stout prickles, 5–12 cm long. *Twigs* green to tan, glabrous, becoming angled in cross section. *Flowers* May-June; insect-pollinated; perfect; borne on few- to many-flowered glandular-pubescent racemes, 10–20 cm long; white; 2.5–3.5 cm across; calyx 5-lobed, persistent; petals 5, 1–2 cm long; stamens and carpels many. *Fruit* an aggregate of drupes; July-September; not separating from the receptacle, breaking from the stalk together with the receptacle, black, hemispherical to elongate, 1–1.5 cm long, edible.

Locally frequent to common throughout the state. Characteristic of open, disturbed habitats, especially roadsides, clearings, fence rows; found on all but the wettest soils. Shade-intolerant. Stems highly prickly, dense colonies painful to walk through. Cultivars derived from this and related species provide the blackberries of commerce.

ROSACEAE
Rubus flagellaris Willdenow

Northern Dewberry

Prostrate, trailing, or low-arching shrub, 3 m or more long; stems slender, glabrous, armed with scattered, stout, recurved prickles, 1–3 mm long; young stems ascending, 10–30 cm long, soon prostrate, more or less prickly and glandular, sometimes pubescent; forming clones. *Leaves* mostly deciduous; alternate,

compound; leaflets 3–5, 4–10 cm long, terminal leaflet short-stalked, ovate to rhombic-elliptic, abruptly acuminate to acute (0.5–2 cm long), laterals nearly sessile, ovate, acute to short-acuminate; coarsely doubly serrate above the middle, teeth pointed; somewhat pubescent and green both sides, midrib prickly beneath; petioles prickly beneath, 3–5 cm long. *Flowers* May-June; insect-pollinated; perfect; solitary or borne on 2–4-flowered cymes; white; 2.5 cm across; calyx 5-parted; petals 5, 1–1.5 cm long; stamens and carpels numerous. *Fruit* an aggregate of drupes; July-August; not separating from the receptacle, breaking from the stalk together with the receptacle, short-cylindric to thimble-shaped, 1–1.5 cm long, black, juicy, edible.

Frequent to common throughout most of the state. Characteristic of open, dry, often sandy and sterile, disturbed habitats: old fields, edges of woods, roadsides, banks, heavily cutover forests. Shade-intolerant.

ROSACEAE
Rubus hispidus Linnaeus

Dwarf Blackberry   Swamp Dewberry

Trailing, creeping, or low-arching shrub, to 1.5 m long; forming wide-spreading clonal ground cover; stems very slender with abundant, very thin, slightly recurved or straight bristles, 1–2 mm long, bristle bases expanded; young branches erect, 6–20 cm long. *Leaves* mostly evergreen; alternate; compound; leaflets 3, rarely 5, 2–5 cm long, terminal leaflet short-stalked, obovate to rhombic-ovate, obtuse or acute, laterals nearly sessile, broad ovate, obtuse; coarsely and doubly serrate above the middle, teeth blunt, lower margin often entire; firm and persistent through winter; glabrous and glossy dark green above, green and glabrous or with pubescence on veins beneath; petioles with bristles similar to those on stems. *Flowers* June-July; insect-pollinated; perfect; borne on 2–6-flowered corymbs; white; 1.5–2 cm across; calyx 5-parted; petals 5, about 8 mm long; stamens and carpels numerous. *Fruit* an aggregate of drupes; August; not

329

separating from the receptacle, breaking from the stalk together with the receptacle, reddish purple, sour, edible.

Frequent throughout the state in moist, often acid, woods and swamps where the canopy is relatively open; also wet meadows. Moderately shade-tolerant.

ROSACEAE
Rubus idaeus Linnaeus

Wild Red Raspberry

Upright shrub, 0.5–2 m high; branches arching, new branches very bristly with weak, glandular bristles, older stems with small, hooked prickles. *Leaves* alternate, pinnately compound; leaflets 3–5, if 5 usually 2 pairs of lateral leaflets and a terminal leaflet, 3–8 cm long, sessile except the terminal, terminal often 3-lobed, broadly ovate, laterals smaller, ovate-oblong to lanceolate, short acuminate; coarsely doubly serrate; mostly glabrous, yellowish green above, white-tomentose beneath; petioles with small bristles and prickles, 4–7 cm long. *Winter buds* oblong-ovoid, sessile. *Flowers* May-June; insect-pollinated; perfect; borne on few-flowered, pubescent, slightly prickly, short racemes; white; about 1 cm across; calyx deeply 5-parted, often bristly; petals 5; stamens and carpels numerous. *Fruit* an aggregate of drupes; July-August; separating easily when ripe from the white receptacle which remains on the stalk, red, elongate-hemispherical, about 1 cm across, edible.

Locally frequent to common throughout the state. Characteristic of open, disturbed habitats, especially nutrient-rich, moist to wet soils. Shade-intolerant. *R. idaeus* is a species complex that ranges throughout the Northern Hemisphere. The North American representative is often treated as *R. idaeus* var. *strigosus* (Michx.) Maxim., and some authors recognize it as a distinct species. Many cultivars supply the red raspberries of commerce.

ROSACEAE
Rubus occidentalis Linnaeus

Black Raspberry

Erect shrub to 2 m high; branches arching, 1–2 m long, sometimes rooting at the tips; clone-forming; new canes conspicuously glaucous, old canes purple; sparingly armed with slightly hooked prickles. *Leaves* alternate, palmately compound; leaflets 3 (if 5 palmate), 5–8 cm long, short-stalked except the terminal, ovate (the lower 2 narrowly ovate), acuminate; doubly serrate; more or less pubescent, dull green above, white-tomentose beneath; petioles glabrous or slightly pubescent, sparsely prickly. *Twigs* slender becoming stout, prickly, new canes whitish with bloom. *Winter buds* oblong-ovoid, sessile. *Flowers* May-June; insect-pollinated; perfect; borne on few-flowered, tomentose, very prickly corymbs, pedicels 1–2.5 cm long; white; about 1 cm across; calyx 5-parted; petals 5; stamens and carpels numerous. Only second-year canes bear flowers. *Fruit* an aggregate of drupes; July; separating easily when ripe from the white receptacle which remains on the stalk, purplish black, hemispherical, 0.8–1.5 cm across, sweet, juicy, edible.

Locally frequent to common in the Lower Peninsula; infrequent in the Upper Peninsula. Characteristic of open, disturbed habitats, moist or dry soils. Moderately shade-tolerant. Many cultivars have been developed and produce the black raspberries of commerce.

ROSACEAE
Rubus parviflorus Nuttall

Thimbleberry

Upright shrub, 1–2 m high; older branches stout with grayish, exfoliating, shredding bark; unarmed; forming clones. *Leaves* alternate, simple, blades 6–20 cm long and equally as wide; reniform to orbicular, base cordate; 3–5 lobed. The lobes triangular, about the same length, acute; coarsely serrate to toothed; bright green above, paler beneath; lightly pilose both sides; petioles glandular-hispid, 5–12 cm long. *Twigs* slender, at first green becoming light brown, densely covered with brownish hairs. *Winter buds* elongate, light brown, pubescent, appressed. *Flowers* June-July; insect-pollinated; perfect; borne in few-flowered corymbs; white; 3–5 cm across; calyx 5-lobed, long-tipped; petals 5, oval, 1.5–3 cm long; stamens and carpels numerous. *Fruit* an aggregate of drupes; August-September; separating easily when ripe from the white receptacle which remains on the stalk, red, broad, low-hemispherical or thimble-shaped, edible but sour, rather dry and insipid.

Occasional in the northern tip of the Lower Peninsula; frequent to locally common on disturbed, burned-over sites in the Upper Peninsula, especially the Porcupine Mountains, Keweenaw Peninsula, and Isle Royale. Moderately shade-tolerant. The specific epithet is a misnomer; the flower is the largest among our species of *Rubus*.

ROSACEAE
Physocarpus opulifolius (Linnaeus)
   Maximowicz

Ninebark

Much-branched, erect, spreading shrub, 1–3 m high; loosely branched with stiff recurved branches forming a rounded, densely foliated crown; branches dense, tangled, giving a coarse, irregular appearance in winter. *Bark* of larger branches exfoliating in numerous, long, very thin strips or layers, exposing brown inner bark. *Leaves* alternate, simple, blades 3–8 cm long and about as wide; ovate-orbicular, 3-lobed (sometimes 5-lobed), usually smaller and unlobed on flowering branchlets, acute; irregularly crenate-dentate; glabrous, medium green above, more or less pubescent beneath, yellowish to bronze in autumn; petioles slender, 1–2 cm long. *Twigs* slender, brownish, glabrous, round, 5-lined at the nodes; pith large, brownish. *Winter buds* small, conical-oblong or ovoid, pointed, sessile; lateral buds appressed. *Flowers* June-July; insect-pollinated; perfect; borne in many-flowered (usually more than 25), umbellike corymbs; white to pinkish; 4–6 mm across; sepals 5, pubescent; petals 5, more or less pubescent;

carpels 5; stamens numerous. *Fruit* an aggregate of 5 or fewer follicles; August-September; ovoid, longer than broad, united at the base, splitting along both margins, acute to very sharp-pointed, 0.7–1 cm long, lustrous, light brown, persistent in winter; seeds 2–4 per capsule, about 2 mm long, very light brown.

Frequent in the Lower Peninsula; occasional in the Upper Peninsula. Characteristic of stream banks, lake shores, open floodplains, rocky areas; tolerant of limestone-derived soils. Shade-intolerant. Easily transplanted; easily propagated by stem cuttings. Often used in landscape plantings because of showy flowers, but due to coarse winter habit usually recommended for borders and screens.

ROSACEAE
Spiraea alba Du Roi

Meadowsweet

Erect shrub, 0.3–2 m high; often in spreading clones; stems upright, stiff, wandlike, single or branched, tough, narrow, more or less pubescent. *Leaves* alternate, simple, blades 4–7 cm long, 1–2 cm wide; narrowly oblong to narrowly oblanceolate, acute; sharply and finely serrate; firm; green; glabrous to sparingly pubescent above and beneath; petioles short, nearly sessile to 5 mm long. *Twigs* slender, yellowish brown, more or less angled, pubescent when young. *Winter buds* small, sessile, globose to fusiform. *Flowers* July-August; insect-pollinated; perfect; borne in a dense terminal panicle, persistent through the winter; peduncles and pedicels densely pubescent; white; 6–8 mm in diameter; calyx short-campanulate, 5-lobed; petals 5; stamens numerous. *Fruit* an aggregate of follicles, usually 5; September; smooth, about 3 mm long, containing 2–5 seeds; seeds linear, 1–2 mm long.

Common in the Lower Peninsula; frequent to occasional in the Upper Peninsula. Characteristic of low, wet, open places—old lake beds, marshes, low places between dunes, roadside ditches. Shade-intolerant. Also known as wild spiraea, pipestem, queen-of-the-meadow, Quaker lady, willowleaf spiraea.

ROSACEAE

Aronia melanocarpa (Michaux) Elliott

Black Chokeberry

Erect, often weakly spreading shrub, 0.5–2 m high; multistemmed, open and round-topped; forming clones by rhizomes. Michigan Big Shrub: girth 13 cm, diameter 4 cm, height 5 m, Oakland Co. *Bark* smooth to somewhat roughened, grayish brown. *Leaves* alternate, simple, 2–8 cm long, 2–2.5 cm wide; elliptic-obovate to oval or oblanceolate, acuminate or abruptly pointed; finely crenate-serrate, serrations incurved; glabrous, bright green above with small, reddish or blackish glands on the midrib, glabrous or soon glabrate and paler beneath; petioles short, glabrous, 0.2–1 cm long. *Twigs* slender, rounded, smooth, glabrous, brownish. *Winter buds* oblong, sessile, flattened, appressed. *Flowers* June; insect-pollinated; perfect; borne in compound cymes, 12 or fewer per cyme; rachis and pedicels glabrous or nearly so; white; about 1 cm across; calyx urn-shaped, 5-lobed, glabrous; petals 5; styles 5; stamens numerous. *Fruit* a small pome; September-October; lustrous black or blackish purple, globose, 6–8 mm across, persistent into winter.

Occasional to locally frequent throughout the state. Characteristic of low, wet areas, including flats with high water tables (old lake basins), swamps; usually in acid soils. Sometimes associated with pin oak and swamp white oak. Moderately shade-tolerant. Closely related to the purple chokeberry, *A. prunifolia* (Marsh.) Rehd. and virtually indistinguishable from it. Purple chokeberry has more pubescent parts, including lower sides of leaves, twigs, and flower parts (calyx, rachis and pedicels of cymes). The related red chokeberry, *A. arbutifolia* (L.) Ell., is sometimes used in landscape plantings because of its adaptability and the brilliant red fruit display in autumn and winter.

SAXIFRAGACEAE

Ribes americanum Miller

Wild Black Currant

Erect, unarmed shrub, to 1.5 m high; branches slender and spreading; roots very shallow. *Bark* thin, smooth, dark brown. *Leaves* alternate, simple, borne several to a short shoot or separately on a long shoot, blades 3–8 cm long and equally as wide; palmately 3-lobed, sometimes 5-lobed when the lower lobes are deeply cleft, lobes acute, nearly orbicular, subcordate to nearly truncate; dentate to doubly serrate; thin; glabrous, yellowish green above, pubescent beneath, yellow resin dots above and beneath; petioles pubescent, 2–4 cm long. *Twigs* slender, slightly pubescent, with large, conspicuous resin glands; leaf scar broad. *Winter buds* ovoid; bud scales with occasional hairs, with conspicuous resin glands. *Flowers* April-May; insect-pollinated; perfect; borne in racemes 2–6 cm long, 5–16 flowers per raceme; greenish to yellowish white; about 1 cm long, on peduncles 2–5 cm long; calyx tubular, 5-lobed; petals 5; stamens 5; ovary glabrous, inferior. *Fruit* a many-seeded berry; July-August; black, smooth, globose, 0.6–1 cm across, palatable when cooked.

Frequent in the Lower Peninsula; occasional in the Upper Peninsula. Characteristic of wet places in swamps, bottomlands, wet depressions, swampy borders of lakes and streams; not found in upland forests. Associates include black ash, red maple, yellow birch, common elder, spicebush, poison sumac. Moderately shade-tolerant; tolerant of high water tables. An alternate host for the eastern white pine blister rust disease organism (*Cronartium ribicola*).

332

SAXIFRAGACEAE
Ribes cynosbati Linnaeus

Prickly Gooseberry

Erect or spreading, low shrub, to 1.5 m high; solitary or forming small clones by layering; branches with 1–3 slender spines 0.5–1 cm long at each node; lower stems often very prickly along internodes. *Leaves* alternate, simple, borne several to a short shoot or separately on long shoots; blades 2–6 cm long and equally as wide; palmately 3–5-lobed, lobes acute or obtuse; crenate-dentate, often sharply cleft; glabrescent, green above, pubescent and paler beneath; petioles pubescent, 1–4 cm long. *Twigs* slender, light brown. *Winter buds* elongate, 5–6 mm long. *Flowers* April-June; insect-pollinated; perfect; borne in small clusters, 1–3 flowers on each peduncle; greenish yellow or greenish white; floral tube 3–6 mm long, 5-lobed; petals 5, shorter than the reflexed calyx lobes; stamens 5; ovary inferior. *Fruit* a many-seeded berry; July-September, not persistent in winter; globose, dark reddish purple, with long prickles, 0.8–1.7 cm across, edible.

Common in the Lower Peninsula; frequent in the Upper Peninsula. Occurs in virtually all habitats; especially in dry-mesic oak forests, also in mesic beech-sugar maple forests, floodplains; occasionally in swamps. Seeds widely disseminated by birds. Moderately shade-tolerant. An alternate host for the eastern white pine blister rust disease organism (*Cronartium ribicola*). Fruit sometimes used for jellies and pies.

Key to Species of Shrub Dogwoods—*Cornus*

1. Leaves large, broadly ovate to suborbicular; 7–10 pairs of veins .. *C. rugosa,* p. 335
1. Leaves smaller, ovate to elliptic-lanceolate; main veins fewer.
  2. Pith of 2–3-year-old twigs white; stems (3 years old and older) bright to deep red .... *C. stolonifera,* p. 336
  2. Pith of 2–3-year-old twigs brownish; stems gray, reddish, or purplish.
    3. Twigs glabrous; bark of main stems (3 years old and older) gray; fruits white (rarely bluish); inflorescence pyramidal .... *C. racemosa,* p. 335
    3. Twigs with fine, silky-downy pubescence; bark of main stems reddish or purplish with distinct fissures; fruit blue to bluish white; inflorescence flat-topped .... *C. amomum,* p. 335

CORNACEAE
Cornus amomum Miller

Silky Dogwood

Ascending or spreading shrub, 1–3 m high; branches spreading; clone-forming. *Bark* reddish, purplish, to grayish (on 3-year-old and older stems), with conspicuous, narrow, corky fissures. *Leaves* opposite, simple, blades 4–10 cm long, 2–6 cm wide; broadly ovate or elliptic, short-acuminate, base rounded; entire; nearly glabrous or with appressed pubescence and dark green to yellowish green above, lighter green to glaucous and with appressed pubescence beneath; veins 4–6, parallel-arcuate; petioles 0.5–1.5 cm long. *Twigs* slender, greenish becoming purplish, with fine silky-downy pubescence, pith of 2–3-year-old twigs brown. *Winter buds* small, oblong, nearly sessile, scales valvate. *Flowers* May-June; insect-pollinated; perfect; borne in flat to convex, dense cymes 3–6 cm across, peduncles silky-pilose; small; yellowish white; calyx minute, lobes lanceolate; petals 4, 4–5 mm long; stamens 4. *Fruit* a drupe; August-September; globose, blue to bluish white or with white areas, 6–8 mm across, cyme resembling a corymb.

Occasional to locally frequent in open, wet habitats throughout the Lower Peninsula (known only from Menominee Co. in the Upper Peninsula); marshes, swamps, lake shores, along streams. Shade-intolerant. Easily transplanted. Good for landscape plantings on wet sites but not widely used.

CORNACEAE
Cornus racemosa Lamarck

Gray Dogwood

Upright shrub, 1–4 m high; often in large, dense, many-stemmed clones. *Bark* smooth, light gray (3-year-old stems and older). *Leaves* opposite, simple, blades 2–10 cm long and half as wide; ovate to lanceolate, long-acuminate; entire; grayish green above, glaucous beneath, becoming reddish or purplish in autumn; appressed-pubescent both sides; veins 3–4, parallel-arcuate; petioles 0.5–1.5 cm long. *Twigs* slender, light red-

dish brown becoming gray, glabrous, lenticels prominent; pith of young twigs often white becoming light brown on 2–3-year-old twigs. *Winter buds* small, oblong, scales valvate. *Flowers* May-June; insect-pollinated; perfect; borne in pyramidal, loose cymose panicles 3–6 cm across, peduncles pubescent becoming reddish, 2–2.5 cm long; small and strongly convex; white; calyx minute, petals 4, recurved; stamens 4. *Fruit* a drupe; July-September; globose, white (rarely bluish), 4–5 mm across, on red pedicels.

Common to locally abundant in the Lower Peninsula; occasional to locally frequent in the Upper Peninsula. Characteristic of dry to wet-mesic, open sites: roadsides, fence rows, lake shores, river banks, open woods, edges of swamps and marshes. Moderately shade-tolerant. Forming large clones with rounded profiles. Easily transplanted. Effective ornamental plant for wide soil moisture tolerance, dense, massed growth, and red infructescences; sometimes used for hedges.

CORNACEAE
Cornus rugosa Lamarck

Roundleaf Dogwood

Coarse, upright shrub, 2–3 m high; branches loose, spreading; forming large clones. *Bark* greenish to grayish, warty. *Leaves* opposite, simple, blades 5–12 cm long, 4–10 cm wide; broadly ovate to suborbicular, short-acuminate; entire; green with appressed pubescence above, densely villous beneath; veins 7–10 pairs, parallel-arcuate; petioles 1–2 cm long. *Twigs* slender, greenish becoming pink in winter, streaked with purple, sparsely to densely pubescent, pith of 2–3-year-old twigs white. *Winter buds* small, oblong. *Flowers* May-June; insect-pollinated; perfect; borne in dense, flat-topped cymes, 5–7 cm across, peduncles stout, usually pubescent, 1–4 cm long; moderately large; white; calyx minute, 4-toothed; petals 4; stamens 4. *Fruit* a drupe; September; globose, pale blue, rarely greenish white, 5–6 mm across.

Occasional to locally common throughout the state. Characteristic of lightly shaded woods, especially on sandy soils; wooded

335

lake shores and dunes; stream banks. Moderately shade-tolerant. Attractive for planting because of its white flowers in dense clusters but rarely used in landscaping.

CORNACEAE
Cornus stolonifera Michaux

Red-osier Dogwood

Erect shrub with some branches arching, 1–3 m high; branches loose, broad-spreading, some prostrate, strongly stoloniferous; forming clones. *Bark* smooth, in open bright to deep red, greenish in shade. *Leaves* opposite, simple, blades 4–10 cm long and about half as wide; ovate to ovate-lanceolate, acuminate; entire; glabrous or appressed pubescent and dark green above, glabrous or appressed-pilose and glaucous beneath; usually 5 pairs of veins, parallel-arcuate; petioles 1–2 cm long. *Twigs* slender, green to reddish and slightly pubescent on young twigs, soon becoming glabrous and red to purplish red, lenticels prominent; pith of 2–3-year-old twigs white, large. *Winter buds* small, oblong. *Flowers* June; insect-pollinated; perfect; borne in flat-topped terminal cymes 3–5 cm across; small; dull white; calyx minute, 4-toothed; petals 4, 3–4 mm long; stamens 4. *Fruit* a drupe; August-October; globose, whitish; pits dark brown, about 5 mm long.

Common throughout the state in open, wet places; lake shores, stream banks, swamps, marshes; also on sand dunes. Shade-intolerant. Degree of stem redness directly related to amount of exposure to sunlight; shade-grown plants tend to have greenish stems. Easily transplanted and propagated. Valuable as a landscape plant because of its showy red stems during winter and spreading form; various cultivars in use.

CELASTRACEAE
Celastrus scandens Linnaeus

American Bittersweet

High-climbing, twining vine, to 12 m or more high; stems to 3.5 cm in diameter; climbing on other vegetation and sometimes trailing on the ground, attaching by spiralling around host stems; forming clones by suckering. *Bark* of large branches smooth, grayish or brownish. *Leaves* alternate, simple, blades 5–10 cm long and about half as wide; ovate to oblong-ovate, acuminate or acute; finely serrate; moderately thick; deep glossy green above in summer, becoming greenish yellow in autumn; glabrous; petioles short, 0.5–1.5 cm long. *Twigs* slender, round, glabrous, at first green becoming brownish gray; pith large, white, continuous. *Winter buds* small, subglobose, glabrous, brownish gray. *Flowers* April-May; insect-pollinated; borne in terminal panicles, 3–5 cm long; small; greenish or whitish; male flowers with 5 stamens and a rudimentary pistil, female flowers with 1 compound pistil and rudimentary stamens or flowers perfect; plants polygamodioecious. *Fruit* a capsule; September-October; orange, splitting and displaying scarlet arils covering the seeds, 1–1.2 cm across, persistent all winter; seeds 3–6, reddish brown, about 3 mm long.

Rare to locally frequent in the Lower Peninsula; rare in the Upper Peninsula. Characteristic of stream banks, lake shores, open disturbed forests, fence rows, sand dunes, roadsides; grows well on all kinds of upland soils as long as adequate light is available. Moderately shade-tolerant; tolerates basic soils. Widely planted as an ornamental vine because of its yellowish green leaves and orange scarlet fruits. Highly valued for winter bouquets and decorations. The bark was formerly used in medicine. The closely related Oriental bittersweet, *C. orbiculatus* Thunb., has become locally naturalized in southern Michigan. Its flowers and fruits are borne in small clusters in the axils of broadly ovate leaves with rounded teeth.

CELASTRACEAE
Euonymus atropurpurea Jacquin

Burningbush   Wahoo

Small shrub or small tree to 4 m high. Michigan Big Tree: girth 30 cm, diameter 10 cm, height 5.5 m, Oakland Co. *Leaves* opposite, simple, blades 4–12 cm long, 1–4 cm wide;

336

oval-elliptic, acuminate; finely serrate; thin; glabrous, dull green above, pubescent beneath, turning scarlet in autumn; petioles 1–2 cm long. *Twigs* slender, green, rounded but often 4-sided with 4 corky lines or ridges below the nodes; leaf scars half-elliptic, small, with 1 bundle scar. *Winter buds* small, oblong, green tinged with red. *Flowers* June; insect-pollinated; perfect; borne in small axillary cymes; purple. *Fruit* a capsule, September; fleshy, rough-surfaced, glabrous, rounded and deeply 4-lobed, pinkish red when ripe; seed light brown with a scarlet aril.

Occasional in the lower half of the Lower Peninsula. Especially characteristic of river banks, moist bottomlands, and floodplains. Shade-tolerant. Sometimes cultivated as an ornamental for its showy scarlet foliage in autumn. Often planted is the closely related European strawberry-bush, *E. europaea* L., with smaller leaves, and pale flowers. More highly prized as an ornamental is the winged wahoo, *E. alata* (Thunb.) Siebold, native from northeastern Asia to central China. The latter is a tall shrub to 7 m high with leaves obovate-elliptic, turning brilliant red in autumn. It is noted for its stiff, spreading twigs with 4 conspicuous, flat, corky wings.

CELASTRACEAE
Euonymus obovata Nuttall

Creeping Strawberry-bush

Trailing vine or small, creeping shrub, with upright branches to 30–40 cm high; stems taking root at the nodes in moist soil. *Leaves* opposite, simple, 3–8 cm long and 1.5–4 cm wide; obovate, cuneate, obtuse; crenate-serrate; thin; dull light green above, paler beneath; glabrous; petioles short, 2–5 mm long. *Twigs* green, erect or reclining, 4-sided, sometimes slightly winged. *Flowers* April-May; insect-pollinated; perfect; borne 1–3-flowered on long pedicelled cymes; very flat, about 6 mm across; greenish yellow with shiny nectary. *Fruit* a capsule; September; 3-lobed, rough-warty, pink; seeds with scarlet aril.

Common in the southern half of the Lower

Peninsula in rich, mesic beech-sugar maple forests, moist bottomlands, and floodplains. Shade-tolerant. Useful as ground cover under tree plantings.

AQUIFOLIACEAE
Ilex verticillata (Linnaeus) Gray

Winterberry   Michigan Holly

Erect shrub or small, slender tree, to 4 m high; slender, densely branched stems forming a round or oval crown; roots shallow. Michigan Big Tree: girth 25 cm, diameter 8 cm, height 5 m, Washtenaw Co. *Bark* thin, smooth, olive green with warty lenticels. *Leaves* alternate, simple, blades 3–10 cm long and nearly half as wide; obovate, oblanceolate, or oblong, acute or acuminate; sharply serrate or sometimes doubly serrate, teeth shallow with short bristle-tips that point up (perpendicular to blade surface); thin- to firm-coriaceous; glabrous and dull, dark green above, paler and sometimes pubescent on veins beneath, turning black after frost; veins conspicuously impressed or sunken above, strongly protruding beneath; petioles purplish, more or less pubescent, about 1 cm long. *Twigs* slender, gray to dark olive, smooth becoming roughened by lenticels. *Winter buds* dark brown with scattered white hairs along upper part of scales, superposed. *Flowers* May-July; insect-pollinated; 1–3 crowded together on short peduncles; small; greenish or yellowish white; 4–6 parted; calyx toothed; corolla with separate petals; plants dioecious or polygamodioecious. *Fruit* a drupe; September-October; bright red, persisting into mid-winter, 6–8 mm across.

Common throughout the state. Characteristic of deciduous swamps, wet woods, lake, marsh, and pond margins; found in low, moist, cool, basic or acidic habitats with high water tables. Associates include yellow birch, black ash, red maple, American elm, blue-beech, tamarack, mountain-holly, highbush blueberry, common elder, poison sumac. Moderately shade-tolerant; tolerant of high water tables. The species name *verticillata* refers to the axillary clusters of flowers. The showy red fruits make it a potentially important native landscape species for mass plantings and shrub borders, especially in wet soils.

AQUIFOLIACEAE
Nemopanthus mucronata (Linnaeus) Trelease

Mountain-holly

Slender shrub, to 4 m high; often forming clonal thickets. Michigan Big Shrub: girth 33 cm, diameter 11 cm, height 6 m, Oakland Co. *Bark* thin, smooth, gray. *Leaves* alternate, simple, blades 2–5 cm long and about ⅓ as wide, often clustered on short shoots, falling early in autumn; elliptic-oblong, often with nearly parallel sides, acute or abruptly blunt with mucronate tip; entire or rarely with a few teeth; dark green above, paler, grayish green beneath; glabrous; petioles very slender, purplish, 0.5–2 cm long. *Twigs* slender, smooth, purplish, becoming maroon or gray. *Winter buds* small, ovoid; upper bud scale thickened and slightly extending. *Flowers* May; insect-pollinated; small; greenish white; plants polygamodioecious. *Fruit* a drupe; July-August; subglobose, crimson red, 0.5–1 cm long; 4 seeds.

Frequent throughout the state. Characteristic of cool, open, acid, moist to wet habitats, especially along the margins of lakes, marshes, bogs, swamps, and small streams. Associated with tamarack, yellow birch, speckled alder, winterberry, highbush blueberry, poison sumac, highbush-cranberry. Moderately shade-tolerant; tolerant of high water tables.

RHAMNACEAE
Ceanothus americanus Linnaeus

New Jersey Tea

Low, erect shrub, to 1 m high; many-branched, branches typically upright, often dense and spreading, usually many stems arising from large, deep, dark red roots. *Bark* thin, grayish. *Leaves* alternate, simple, blades 3–10 cm long, 2–6 cm wide; ovate to ovate-oblong, acute or acuminate; irregularly serrate; glabrous or slightly pubescent, dull green above, somewhat hairy beneath; 3 prominent veins from the base; petioles short, 0.6–1.2 cm long. *Twigs* slender, rounded, greenish to brownish, puberulent; pith large, white, continuous. *Winter buds* small, ovoid, sessile. *Flowers* June-July; insect-pollinated; perfect; borne in dense clusters on long, terminal or axillary, slender peduncles; small, about 4 mm across; white; calyx 5-lobed; petals 5; stamens 5. *Fruit* a capsule; September-October; 3-celled, about 3 mm long; one seed per capsule; fruit falling and leaving a cup-shaped, silvery-lined base, persisting into winter.

Locally frequent in the southern half of the Lower Peninsula. Occasional in the northern half of the Lower Peninsula and in the Upper Peninsula. Characteristic of dry habitats: xeric, dry-mesic, open oak and oak-hickory forests, with sandy, gravelly, or loamy soils; also roadsides. Moderately shade-tolerant. Associates include black and dwarf chinkapin oaks, pignut and shagbark hickories, jack pine, fragrant sumac, gray dogwood, downy arrowwood. Leaves considered a good substitute for tea during the American Revolutionary War. The distinctive treelike fruit clusters are used for decoration. Two other species of *Ceanothus* are known from northern Michigan.

RHAMNACEAE
Rhamnus alnifolia L'Héritier

Alder Buckthorn

Low, erect, spreading shrub to 1 m high; stems upright, few-branched. *Bark* thin, reddish brown, smooth. *Leaves* alternate, simple, blades 4–10 cm long, 2–5 cm wide; ovate to elliptic; serrate, the teeth rounded; glabrous above, slightly pubescent on veins beneath; veins pinnate, 5–7 per side; petioles 0.5–1.2 cm long. *Twigs* minutely downy, becoming glabrous and gray. *Winter buds* small, less than 5 mm long. *Flowers* May-June; borne in axils of lower leaves; insect-pollinated; solitary or 2–3 together; small, 2–3 mm across; apetalous; calyx lobes 5, greenish yellow. *Fruit* a drupe; August-September; subglobose, black, 6–8 mm in diameter; seeds usually 3.

338

Occasional to common in swamps, bogs, and wet, low-lying woodlands throughout the state. Moderately shade-tolerant. Not a very distinctive or conspicuous shrub and often overlooked in its habitats.

RHAMNACEAE
Rhamnus cathartica Linnaeus

Common Buckthorn

Large shrub or small tree to 6 m high; trunk crooked, low-branching, supporting a rounded, bushy crown of crooked, stout branches. Michigan Big Tree: girth 1.1 m, diameter 36 cm, height 19 m, Washtenaw Co. *Bark* thin, dark brown or blackish, smooth, becoming rough and scaly. *Leaves* alternate, subopposite, and opposite, simple, blades 4–9 cm long and about half as wide; elliptic to ovate, acute; crenate-serrate; thin and firm; dull green above, paler, yellowish green beneath; glabrous; 3–5 veins, parallel-arcuate; petioles 3–4 cm long. *Twigs* gray, glabrous, lenticels prominent, tipped with a sharp, stout thorn as long as or slightly longer than the end lateral bud. *Winter buds* lack terminal bud (replaced by a thorn); lateral buds brownish black, appressed, with several glabrous bud scales; leaf crescent-shaped with 3 bundle scars. *Flowers* May; insect-pollinated; borne in 2–5-flowered umbels; small, inconspicuous; yellowish green; fragrant; plants polygamous or dioecious. *Fruit* a drupe; August-September; black, round, about 6 mm across; containing 2–3 nutlike pits, each enclosing a seed.

Native in Europe, western and northern Asia; naturalized in eastern North America. Unusual for its variable leaf arrangement. Common in the Lower Peninsula; hardy throughout the state. Shade-tolerant, moderately fast-growing; grows on any upland soil. Fruit nauseating. Sap capable of producing dyes. Seeds widely dispersed by birds; seedlings spreading widely in urban environments and nearby woodlands. A tough, durable tree adapted to urban environments; of low landscape value except as a hedge.

RHAMNACEAE
Rhamnus frangula Linnaeus

Glossy Buckthorn

Tall shrub or small tree to 6 m high; trunk low-branching, supporting an open crown; forming dense clones. Michigan Big Tree: girth 33 cm, diameter 10 cm, height 10 m, Oakland Co. *Leaves* alternate, simple, blades 3–7 cm long; oval or obovate to obovate-oblong, acute; entire; glabrous, dark lustrous green above, lighter and sometimes slightly pubescent beneath; 8–9 pairs of veins; petioles 0.6–1.2 cm long. *Twigs* at first pubescent, becoming glabrous; leaf scars half-elliptical, small, somewhat raised, with 3 bundle scars. *Winter buds* naked, pubescent, brown. *Flowers* May-June; insect-pollinated; inconspicuous; borne in axillary clusters; pale yellow; plants polygamous or dioecious. *Fruit* a drupe; July-September; enclosing 2–3 nutlike pits that contain the seeds.

Native in Europe, western Asia, North Africa; long introduced and naturalized in North America. Frequent in the Lower Peninsula and hardy throughout the state. Shade-tolerant; moderately fast-growing; grows on almost any site. A weedy species, widely spread by birds. A very serious pest with a notorious history of invading swamps and fens and smothering the native vegetation. Not recommended for landscape use.

VITACEAE
Parthenocissus quinquefolia (Linnaeus) Planchon

Virginia Creeper

High-climbing or trailing woody vine, the stem up to 6 cm or more in diameter. *Leaves* alternate, palmately compound; leaflets 5, stalked, 4–12 cm long and nearly half as wide; elliptic or obovate-oblong, acuminate to acute; coarsely sharp-serrate, lower portion entire; green above, paler beneath, turning red to reddish purple in late summer or early autumn; glabrous to pubescent; leaflets falling early in autumn; petioles 20 or more cm long. *Twigs* moderately stout, nearly round, usually pubescent, nodes swollen;

pith large, continuous; tendrils with 5–12 rather long branches (5–10 cm long) ending in adhesive disks; leaf scars concave on top, bundle scars in an ellipse. *Winter buds* round-conical, light brown; terminal bud absent. *Flowers* June-July; insect-pollinated; perfect; borne in cymes or panicles, 6–12 cm long, with usually 50–150 flowers, opposite the leaves; small, about 6 mm across; greenish white; calyx minute; petals 5 (rarely 4), spreading; stamens 5 (rarely 4). *Fruit* a berry; September-October; pedicels in sunlight turning red; subglobose, dark blue to bluish black with slight bloom, 5–8 mm across; seeds 1–4.

Common to abundant in the southern half of the Lower Peninsula; occasional to rare northward. Characteristic of open places, roadsides, banks, stream and lake shores, fence rows; also in many forest communities. Not habitat-specific. Moderately shade-tolerant. Widely used in landscaping for its creeping and climbing abilities, its attractive summer foliage, and its brilliant red autumnal coloration. Also called five-fingered ivy and woodbine. The adhesive disks attach tightly to surfaces, and it is reported that a tendril with 5 disk-bearing branches would stand a force of 4.5 kg (10 lbs.) without separating from the surface.

Another species, *P. inserta* (Kerner) K. Fritsch lacks adhesive disks on the tendrils, usually has fewer flowers per cluster, and has dark green, lustrous leaves. Its generally more northerly range overlaps that of *P. quinquefolia*. The nonnative Boston ivy, *P. tricuspidata* (Sieb. and Zucc.) Planchon, is also widely used in landscape plantings. Boston ivy has simple, lustrous, 3-lobed leaves (or somtimes three leaflets), short tendrils (1.5–3 cm long), and glabrous twigs that are channeled or grooved (not almost round).

VITACEAE
Vitis riparia Michaux

River Bank Grape

Large, vigorous, high-climbing or trailing vine, attaching by tendrils, the stem up to 10 cm in diameter, rarely more. *Bark* dark brown, shredding in strips. *Leaves* alternate,

simple, blades 6–15 cm long and equally wide; usually 3-lobed, lobes short-acuminate, sinuses acute; unequally, coarsely, sharply toothed, mucronate; glabrous, lustrous bright green above, more or less pubescent beneath; stipules 4–6 mm long, often persistent until fruit is formed; petioles more or less pubescent, 3–5 cm long. *Twigs* slender to stout, green or dull red when young, becoming brownish, glabrous; nodal diaphragms very thin, 0.8–2 mm thick; tendrils long (to 20 cm long), intermittent on stem and usually lacking at each third node, not ending in flat discs. *Winter buds* subglobose; bud scales 2; terminal bud lacking. *Flowers* May-June; insect-pollinated; borne in panicles, 8–18 cm long, opposite the leaves; small; greenish; calyx minute; petals 5, coherent at apex, falling without expanding; fragrant; stamens 5, nectaries alternate with the stamens; plants polygamodioecious. *Fruit* a berry; August-October; clusters compact to loose, 4–12 cm long, bluish black, with bloom; 0.9–1.2 cm in diameter, tart, edible; seeds 1–4, about 5 mm long; panicle axes and withered fruits persist through winter.

Frequent to abundant in the Lower Peninsula; occasional to frequent in the Upper Peninsula. Characteristic of open habitats; river banks, lake shores, fence rows, roadsides; also in forests with relatively open canopies, especially oak forests. Moderately shade-tolerant. Most common of the several grape species in Michigan. Fruits make excellent juice, jelly, and jam.

THYMELEACEAE
Dirca palustris Linnaeus

Leatherwood

Erect shrub, to 2 m high; low and widely branching from a crooked stem, forming a dense, rounded crown. *Bark* smooth, gray, leathery, exceedingly pliable. *Leaves* alternate, simple, blades 4–8 cm long and about half as wide; oval to obovate, obtuse; entire; light green above, somewhat glaucous beneath; pubescent when young, becoming glabrous; petioles very short, covering the buds. *Twigs* slender, smooth, light brown, becom-

340

ing darker, with conspicuous white lenticels, prominently jointed with swollen nodes; leaf scars raised and encircling the stem. *Winter buds* small, conical, covered by petiole; terminal bud absent. *Flowers* April-May, before the leaves; insect-pollinated; perfect; borne in clusters of 3; bud scales densely brown-hairy; light yellow. *Fruit* a drupe; June, falling early; pale green, oval, 1–1.2 cm long.

Occasional to locally frequent throughout the state. Characteristic of shaded understories of nutrient-rich, mesic, beech-sugar maple forests where moisture is plentiful; also on moist stream banks and alluvial soils. Associates include sugar maple, beech, red oak, alternate-leaf dogwood, creeping strawberry-bush. Excellent indicator of moist, fresh, fertile sites that are usually associated with beech-sugar maple forests and excellent displays of wild flowers in spring. Shade-tolerant; slow-growing. Common name from the leathery, pliable bark of stems and branches; very difficult to break; used by Native Americans in basket weaving and for bowstrings and fish lines. One of the earliest shrubs to flower in spring. Potentially valuable in landscaping for shady, moist situations.

ELAEAGNACEAE
Elaeagnus angustifolia Linnaeus

Russian-olive   Oleaster

Tall shrub or small tree, 5–8 m high; erect or commonly leaning or twisted and distorted, branching low to form an open crown with a number of erect or pendulous, often thorny branches. Michigan Big Tree: girth 120 cm, diameter 40 cm, height 12 m, Oakland Co. *Leaves* alternate, simple, blades 5–8 cm long; lanceolate or oblong-lanceolate, acute to obtuse; entire; light green above, silvery-scaly beneath; petioles 5–8 mm long. *Twigs* at first silvery-scaly, becoming glabrous, lustrous brown, often thorny; leaf scars semicircular, minute, more or less raised, with 1 bundle scar. *Winter buds* small, round or conical, grayish brown with silvery scales. *Flowers* June; insect-pollinated; borne in the axils of the leaves; apetalous; calyx tube campanulate, 4-lobed, silvery gray outside, yellow within; stamens 4; very fragrant and rich in honey; flowers perfect or plants polygamous. *Fruit* a drupe; olive-shaped, silvery gray to yellowish, coated with silvery snowflakelike scales, about 1 cm long, persisting on the branches into late autumn or the next spring.

The native home of Russian-olive is Europe and western Asia; hardy throughout the state. An excellent low windbreak; used for wildlife cover and food; planted to prevent erosion. Important in landscaping for its silvery foliage. Moderately shade-tolerant; fast-growing; short-lived. Thrives in sandy soils; tolerant of drought, salt, and soils with high concentrations of lime. Propagated either from seed or by cuttings; easily transplanted.

Autumn-olive, *Elaeagnus umbellata* Thunb., (a native of Asia) is a tall shrub much used for wildlife cover and now becoming naturalized in southern Michigan. It has a more shrubby growth than Russian-olive, and the leaves are broadly ovate. Not recommended for home landscaping.

ELAEAGNACEAE
Shepherdia canadensis (Linnaeus) Nuttall

Soapberry   Canada Buffaloberry

Upright, spreading, unarmed shrub, to 3 m high. *Leaves* opposite, simple, blades 2–4 cm long; elliptic to ovate, obtuse; entire; dark green and sparingly scurfy above, densely stellate-scurfy beneath and silvery brown with snowflakelike scales; petioles short, 4–6 mm long. *Twigs* slender, reddish brown, scurfy, not thorny. *Winter buds* small, oblong, stalked, with 2–4 valvate scales, appearing naked; leaf scars half-round, minute, 1 bundle scar. *Flowers* April-May; insect-pollinated; borne in short spikes; small, about 4 mm across; yellowish; plants dioecious. *Fruit* a drupe; July-August; ovoid, yellowish red, insipid.

Hardy throughout the state, especially northward; cold- and drought-tolerant. Common on lake shores, calcareous sands, and limestone rocks and banks. Difficult to transplant and rarely used in cultivation.

The related silver buffaloberry, *S. argentea* Nutt., is a tall, thorny shrub or small tree of more northern and western distribution. It is distinguished from our native species by leaves silvery on both sides; thorns on branches; and scarlet fruit. Very hardy; sometimes used as a hedge plant.

ANACARDIACEAE
Cotinus coggygria Scopoli

Smoketree

Many-stemmed, tall, rounded shrub or small tree, to 5 m high, often broader than high; branches thick, often crooked and twisted, spreading. Michigan Big Tree: girth 58 cm, diameter 19 cm, height 9 m, Oakland Co. *Bark* dark gray, scaly, lighter-colored inner layers often visible, soon splitting into longitudinal ridges. *Leaves* alternate, simple, blades 3–8 cm long and nearly as wide; oval to obovate, apex rounded or slightly emarginate; entire; bluish green above, paler below, turning yellowish red to purple in autumn; glabrous; strongly aromatic when crushed; petioles 1–4 cm long. *Twigs* stout, greenish brown or purplish, glabrous, aromatic, lenticels prominent; pith yellow to orange brown; leaf scars crescent-shaped, raised, with 3 bundle scars. *Winter buds* small, acute, dark reddish brown, aromatic. *Flowers* June-July; insect-pollinated; tiny, yellowish; borne in large, terminal, densely plumose panicles, becoming billowy masses of green, yellow, and red, suggesting puffs of smoke ("nonsmoking" trees are sometimes cut down—nonsmoking being hazardous to their health); plants dioecious or polygamous. *Fruit* a small, brown, dry drupe, surrounded by finely plumose branches.

Introduced from southern Europe and western Asia and long cultivated. Hardy in the Lower Peninsula. Various cultivars used in landscaping, especially one pendulous form and one with purple leaves and flowers. Extremely showy, and used for borders and in groups; easily transplanted.

342

Key to Species of *Rhus*

1. Low, erect or spreading shrub; leaflets usually 3, crenate-serrate; leaves, twigs, and buds aromatic when crushed .... *R. aromatica,* p. 344
1. Tall, erect shrub or small tree; leaflets many (7–31), serrate or entire; leaves, twigs, and buds not aromatic.
  2. Leaf rachis winged between leaflets .... *R. copallina,* p. 344
  2. Leaf rachis not winged.
    3. Twigs glabrous .... *R. glabra,* p. 344
    3. Twigs densely pubescent .... *R. typhina,* p. 345

343

ANACARDIACEAE
Rhus aromatica Aiton

Fragrant Sumac

Low, erect, spreading or prostrate shrub, to 2 m high; many branches sprout from underground parts to form a shrub of irregular habit. *Bark* thin, smooth, brownish to gray. *Leaves* alternate, compound, 5–12 cm long; leaflets usually 3, subsessile, the terminal not stalked, 2.5–7 cm long; ovate, terminal sometimes 3-lobed; crenate-serrate; thin and soft; green, becoming orange to red in autumn; pubescent both sides, becoming glabrate; aromatic when crushed. Petioles slender, 1–3 cm long. *Twigs* slender, pubescent, brown to reddish brown, aromatic when bruised; leaf scars circular, raised. *Winter buds* small (terminal bud absent), pubescent, yellow, hidden by leaf scars. *Flowers* April-May, before the leaves; insect-pollinated; yellow; male flowers borne in short catkins; female flowers borne on short spikelike branches of small terminal panicles; plants dioecious or polygamous. *Fruit* a drupe; July-August, persistent; produced sparingly, clustered in compact panicles, subglobose, reddish, hairy, 6–8 mm across.

Frequent in the understory of open, oak-hickory forests on dry, sandy calcareous soils in the southern part of the Lower Peninsula; rare in the northern half of the Lower Peninsula and in the Upper Peninsula (known in Chippewa Co.). Associates include black oak, white oak, dwarf chestnut oak, pignut hickory, shagbark hickory, white ash, black cherry, New Jersey tea. Moderately shade-tolerant; relatively slow-growing. Sprouting vigorously following fire. Drought- and lime-tolerant. An excellent indicator of dry-mesic to xeric habitats. Similar to poison ivy, but distinguished by smaller, prominently crenate-serrate leaflets; terminal leaflet not stalked; fruits pubescent and reddish not white and glabrous.

ANACARDIACEAE
Rhus copallina Linnaeus

Winged Sumac   Shining Sumac

Clonal shrub or small tree, to 8 m high; similar to smooth and staghorn sumacs in form and clonal habit but often smaller. Michigan Big Shrub: girth 46 cm, diameter 15 cm, height 10 m, Kalamazoo Co. *Bark* thin, smooth, greenish brown. *Leaves* alternate, pinnately compound, 15–40 cm long; rachis winged between leaflets, pubescent; leaflets 7–21, laterals subsessile, 4–10 cm long; lanceolate to ovate, acute or acuminate, base often asymmetrical to oblique; entire or few-toothed near the apex; very lustrous, dark green above, usually pubescent, paler beneath, turning red, crimson, scarlet, or reddish purple in autumn; glabrous. *Twigs* stout, reddish-pubescent, sometimes becoming glabrous, green to reddish brown; leaf scars horseshoe-shaped. *Winter buds* pubescent, reddish brown. *Flowers* similar to smooth sumac but appear later—July to August. *Fruit* a drupe; September; borne in dense erect or drooping panicles, subglobose, red, glandular-hairy, 3–4 mm across.

Frequent in sandy, open habitats in the southern half of the Lower Peninsula north to Manistee and Grand Traverse Co. Tolerant of high spring water tables; common on old lake plains in the southeastern Lower Peninsula. Shade-intolerant; fast-growing. Sprouting from a wide-spreading root system following fire. Desirable ornamentally because of its very lustrous foliage and autumn colors, but rarely cultivated. Species name *copallina* means "copal gum."

ANACARDIACEAE
Rhus glabra Linnaeus

Smooth Sumac

Clonal shrub or small tree, to 7 m high; many crooked stems, sprouting from a shallow, wide-spreading root system, form an open or dense clone; often crowns of many stems merge, giving a dense, rounded or flat-topped appearance. Michigan Big Shrub: girth 38 cm, diameter 12 cm, height 9.1 m,

Washtenaw Co. *Bark* thin, smooth, brownish to gray. *Leaves* alternate, pinnately compound, 20–50 cm long; leaflets 11–31, laterals subsessile, middle leaflets larger than those at both ends, 5–12 cm long; lanceolate to oblong, acuminate; serrate; dark green above, paler to conspicuously white beneath, turning orange, scarlet, crimson, or purple in autumn; glabrous; petioles glabrous, 3–10 cm long. *Twigs* stout, glabrous, glaucous, somewhat 3-sided, light brown; leaf scars horseshoe-shaped. *Winter buds* ovoid, pubescent. *Flowers* June; insect-pollinated; borne in large terminal panicles, 10–25 cm long; small; greenish yellow; plants dioecious. *Fruit* a drupe; August, persistent most of the winter; globose, densely clustered, 3–4 mm across, scarlet, covered with dense, sticky, short hairs, sour-lemony to taste.

Abundant in old fields, fence rows, roadsides, swamp margins, and openings of forests throughout the Lower Peninsula; common in the Upper Peninsula. Characteristic of open areas and xeric and dry-mesic forests, but will grow in almost any environment except bogs and swamps. Shade-intolerant; fast-growing; individuals are short-lived but clones may be long-lived. Tolerant of droughty and calcareous soils. Sprouting from roots following fire. Good for mass plantings in dry, infertile soils. Hybrids between this species and *R. typhina* are commonly encountered in the state. They can be recognized by their finely hairy twigs and by the intermediate nature of the hairs on the fruit. The hybrids are known as *R. ×pulvinata* Greene (*R. glabra* var. *borealis* Britt.).

ANACARDIACEAE
Rhus typhina Linnaeus

Staghorn Sumac

Clonal shrub or small tree, to 10 m high; many crooked, many-branched stems, often appearing as antlers, sprouting from a shallow, wide-spreading root system, form an open or dense clone; often crowns of many stems merge, giving a dense, rounded or flat-topped appearance. Michigan Big Shrub: girth 74 cm, diameter 23.4 cm, height 15 m,

Oakland Co. *Bark* thin, smooth, gray. *Leaves* similar to those of smooth sumac except pubescent on leaflet midrib and main veins beneath; petioles and rachis pubescent. *Twigs* stout, densely velvety-pubescent with long hairs, brown, exuding a milky, yellowish sap when cut; pith thick, yellowish brown; leaf scars horseshoe-shaped. *Winter buds* small, round, velvety-pubescent. *Flowers* similar to those of smooth sumac. *Fruit* similar to that of smooth sumac except the dense cluster of fruits is more erect and the hairs are long and narrow.

Distribution, habitat, and notes are similar to those of smooth sumac.

ANACARDIACEAE
Toxicodendron radicans (Linnaeus) Kuntze

Poison Ivy

Usually a creeping or climbing vine, but may be an erect shrub; climbing tree trunks, attaching to the bark by tiny aerial rootlets, and branching outward over 1 m. *Bark* gray. *Leaves* alternate, pinnately compound, 3 leaflets, 15–30 cm long; leaflets 5–12 cm long, terminal leaflet longer-stalked than laterals; ovate to rhombic, short-acuminate; entire or sparingly or coarsely dentate or sinuate; usually more or less wrinkled; glabrous, lustrous yellowish green above, more or less pubescent beneath; not aromatic; petioles 5–10 cm long. *Twigs* slender, yellowish brown, sparingly pubescent or glabrate. *Winter buds* naked, light brown, scurfy-pubescent; terminal buds erect, fingerlike; lateral buds much smaller, appressed. *Flowers* May-June; insect-pollinated; borne in loose paniculate clusters; small; greenish white; plants polygamous. *Fruit* a drupe; August-September; borne in open clusters, whitish or yellowish, shiny, globose, 5–6 mm across, persistent into winter.

Common to locally abundant in the southern half of the Lower Peninsula. Characteristic of open areas and the understory (or climbing on tree trunks) of open woodlands on virtually any kind of soil; stream banks, lake margins, fence rows, and where birds are likely to disperse the seeds. Especially vigorous on calcareous soils and in flood-plains. On mounds in swamps and climbing swamp trees. Moderately shade-tolerant; rapid-growing; forming long-lived clones. *Toxicodendron* is from the Greek and means "poison tree." Traditionally botanists have classified this species and *T. vernix* as members of the genus *Rhus*.

A common plant in the northern Upper Great Lakes area (in Michigan roughly north of Clare Co.) and in the Lake Michigan dunes is the similar Rydberg's poison ivy, traditionally treated as *T. radicans* var. *rydbergii* Rydberg. A northerly and westerly plant, it is a shrub or subshrub; it does not climb. Its leaflets are relatively broad, rhomboid to suborbicular in outline.

The oily sap of leaves and stems is highly poisonous to the touch, producing acute irritation of the skin, accompanied by itching, swelling, and formation of watery blisters. No one should handle the plant who is supposedly immune. Persons who have come in contact with the plant should wash the affected parts with rubbing alcohol as soon after exposure as possible. Strong soap and water, with vigorous scrubbing, is an alternative treatment. Such treatments may not prevent poisoning but may reduce the spread of excess sap which has not immediately reacted with the skin and which might otherwise reach other body surfaces. If the eruption has already appeared, various commercial preparations are available to alleviate the discomfort and hasten drying up and healing.

ANACARDIACEAE
Toxicodendron vernix (Linnaeus) Kuntze

Poison Sumac

Tall, upright shrub or small tree, to 7 m high and 6–8 cm in diameter; crown open, rounded or flat-topped with stout, spreading, sparsely-foliated branches. *Bark* thin, smooth, dark gray. *Leaves* alternate, pinnately compound, 15–35 cm long, rachis unwinged; leaflets 7–13, subsessile except for the stalked terminal; 5–10 cm long; elliptic to obovate, acuminate; entire; thick and firm; glabrous, lustrous, dark green with

scarlet midribs above, slightly pubescent beneath, turning orange to scarlet in autumn; petioles stout, reddish. *Twigs* stout, greenish to brownish yellow, glabrous, lenticels numerous; leaf scars broad, shield-shaped with many bundle scars in three groups. *Winter buds* small, brown, hairy. *Flowers* June; insect-pollinated; borne in loose paniculate clusters; very small; yellowish green. *Fruit* a drupe; September; borne in loose, open panicles, persistent long into winter, light yellowish gray, glabrous, lustrous, subglobose, 4–6 mm across.

Common in swamps and marshes in the southern half of the Lower Peninsula, north to Grand Traverse Co. Associates include tamarack, bog birch, yellow birch, black ash, red maple, American elm, spicebush, red-osier dogwood. Moderately shade-tolerant; fast-growing; short-lived. All parts of the plant are poisonous; use preventive measures discussed under poison ivy. Poisoning cases are often more serious than with poison ivy because the victim has greater likelihood of facial and neck contact with the allergenic parts. Sap was once used to make a high-grade varnish. Species name *vernix* means "varnish," erroneously referring to the Japanese Lacquer Tree. Traditionally, botanists have classified this species and *T. radicans* as members of the genus *Rhus*.

RUTACEAE
Ptelea trifoliata Linnaeus

Wafer-ash   Hoptree

Tall shrub or small tree, 3–5 m (to 8 m) high; trunk short, crooked, often low-branched; crown irregular, rounded. Michigan Big Tree: girth 84 cm, diameter 27 cm, height 11 m, Kent Co. *Bark* thin, smooth, with numerous excrescences, becoming roughened, light to dark gray or brown, bitter to the taste. *Leaves* mostly alternate, compound, 3 leaflets; leaflets subsessile, 5–12 cm long, the terminal larger than the laterals; ovate-oblong to obovate, acute to acuminate; entire to crenulate; glabrous, dark green above, slightly pubescent and paler beneath, dotted with translucent glands; emit-

346

ting an unpleasant citruslike odor when crushed; petioles stout, 6–10 cm long. *Twigs* slender, glabrous or pubescent, yellowish brown to dark reddish brown, aromatic when bruised. *Winter buds* small, low-conical, closely superposed in pairs, yellow, silky-pubescent, sunken beneath petiole bases and breaking through the leaf scars; leaf scars rather large, horseshoe-shaped when torn by the buds, bundle scars 3. *Flowers* June; insect-pollinated; borne in corymbs; small; greenish white; plants polygamous. *Fruit* a samara with a conspicuous suborbicular, membranous wing surrounding the seed cavity (hence the name wafer-ash); September-October; 2-celled, 2-seeded, borne in drooping clusters, persistent.

Occasional in the southern half of the Lower Peninsula, north along Lake Michigan to Manistee Co. Characteristic of open areas, sandy beaches, dunes, river floodplains; rarely in the forest understory; particularly common near the Lake Michigan shore. Moderately shade-tolerant; limestone-tolerant. All parts when bruised produce an odor usually regarded as disagreeable, but described as pleasant by some. The fruit was once used as a substitute for hops in beer brewing. Rarely planted as an ornamental.

RUTACEAE
Zanthoxylum americanum Miller

Prickly-ash

Tall, spiney, aromatic shrub or small tree, to 3 m high; sprouting profusely from the roots and forming dense, multistemmed clones. Michigan Big Tree: girth 25 cm, diameter 8 cm, height 8 m, Oakland Co. *Bark* smooth, gray to brown. *Leaves* alternate, pinnately compound, 15–25 cm long; leaflets 5–11 with 2–5 pairs and a terminal leaflet, nearly sessile, 3–6 cm long; ovate to elliptic, acuminate; entire to crenulate; glabrous, dark green above, paler and slightly pubescent beneath; aromatic when crushed; rachis occasionally prickly, petioles 2–4 cm long. *Twigs* slender, zigzag, smooth with persistent, paired, stipular spines at the nodes, spines about 1 cm long. *Winter buds* small, super-

posed, woolly, rusty red. *Wood* yellow, hard. *Flowers* April-May, before the leaves; insect-pollinated; borne in axillary clusters; small; greenish; plants dioecious. *Fruit* a capsule; August-September; bright red, 4–6 mm long, strongly aromatic with a lemony odor, bitter to taste; seeds 2, black and lustrous.

Common throughout most of the Lower Peninsula. Characteristic of open, disturbed, moist sites or lightly shaded woods, especially stream banks and floodplains. Moderately shade-tolerant. Typical of fence rows and forest edges. Dense clones of the spiny, branchy stems are extremely difficult to penetrate. The genus name is derived from Greek *xanthos*, yellow, and *xylon*, wood. Species of the genus have been used medicinally. Powdered bark and leaves are reported to be used as a condiment and also to produce a yellow dye. Prickly-ash is the larval food plant for Michigan's largest butterfly, the handsome giant swallowtail.

ARALIACEAE
Aralia spinosa Linnaeus

Hercules-club   Devils-walkingstick

Prickly, few-branched shrub or small tree, to 15 m high and 15 cm in diameter; crown flat-topped, consisting of a few, very stout, club-like, spreading branches; trunk usually branchless; sprouting from roots, forming small clonal thickets. Michigan Big Tree: girth 48 cm, diameter 15 cm, height 11 m, Oakland Co. *Bark* dark brown, ridges irregular, armed with sharp, yellowish prickles; leaf scars many, conspicuous. *Leaves* alternate, 2–3-times pinnately compound, borne at top of trunk, 50–120 cm long, 50–100 cm wide; leaflets opposite, numerous, short-stalked, 5–8 cm long; broadly ovate to lanceolate; finely serrate; glabrous, dark green above, paler, glabrous or somewhat pubescent and often with prickles on the midribs beneath; veins curving upward before reaching the margin; petioles to 25 cm long, with enlarged, clasping bases. *Twigs* very massive, tan-gray, armed with prickles; pith large; leaf scars prominent, narrowly flattened, nearly encircling the twig, with about 20 bundle

347

scars arranged in a single, curved line. *Winter buds:* terminal buds large, ovoid-conic, few scales; lateral buds smaller, appressed. *Flowers* late July-August; insect-pollinated; perfect; borne in umbels on large, terminal panicles that occur singly or in groups, often 80–100 cm long; tiny; creamy white. *Fruit* a drupe; late August-September; black, ovoid, 5-angled, juicy, about 6 mm across.

Native south of Michigan—western Pennsylvania, southern Indiana, southeastern Missouri, south to eastern Texas and Florida. Moderately shade-tolerant; fast-growing; short-lived. Hardy in southernmost Michigan. Planted for its grotesque habit, clublike stems, and large, handsome foliage; a novelty plant for landscaping.

STAPHYLEACEAE
Staphylea trifolia Linnaeus

American Bladdernut

Erect shrub or small tree, to 6 m high. Michigan Big Tree: girth 48 cm, diameter 15 cm, height 11 m, Macomb Co. *Bark* thin, smooth, greenish gray, striped with linear, white fissures. *Leaves* opposite, pinnately compound; leaflets 3, terminal long-stalked, laterals short-stalked, 4–10 cm long; elliptic-ovate to obovate, short-acuminate; finely serrate; glabrous, green above, pubescent and paler beneath, turning dull, pale yellow in autumn; petioles 3–12 cm long. *Twigs* slender, pale green becoming gray, pubescent, lenticels white; leaf scars half-round with 3 (sometimes 5–7) bundle scars; pith small. *Winter buds* ovoid, glabrous, with 4 blunt scales; terminal bud usually lacking, pairs of lateral buds at stem tip cause the stem to fork repeatedly. *Flowers* April-May; insect-pollinated; perfect; borne in drooping racemes, 3–6 cm long; white; bell-shaped; 1 cm long. *Fruit* a membranous, inflated or bladderlike capsule resembling a pale green Japanese lantern; September; 2- or usually 3-lobed, 3–4 cm long, persistent; containing a few bony, brown, shiny seeds that break loose when mature and rattle about when the capsule is shaken.

Occasional to locally common on stream banks and bottomlands in the southern half of the Lower Peninsula, north to Midland and Charlevoix Co. Characteristic of moderately to lightly shaded understories and moist, fertile, alluvial soils. Moderately shade-tolerant. Occasionally planted ornamentally; in open situations under cultivation it develops a more densely branched and foliated habit, grows more luxuriantly, and flowers more profusely.

BETULACEAE
Betula pumila Linnaeus

Dwarf Birch   Bog Birch

Erect shrub, 0.5–3 m high; few to many ascending branches per clump. *Bark* smooth, reddish brown, light-colored lenticels prominent. *Leaves* alternate, simple, blades 1–5 cm long, 1–3 cm wide; suborbicular, obovate, or broad-elliptic, apex rounded or obtuse; coarsely crenate-dentate; dull green above, paler to whitish beneath; pubescent when young becoming more or less glabrous; veins finely reticulated, 4–6 main pairs; petioles short, 0.3–1 cm long. *Twigs* slender, reddish brown becoming grayish, pubescent, usually not resinous-glandular. *Winter buds* small, 2–4 mm long, ovoid, acute, usually divergent; terminal bud absent. *Flowers* May-June; wind-pollinated; borne in catkins; male catkins clustered or in pairs, 1.5–3 cm long, slender, brownish; female catkins erect, 1–3 cm long, slender, sessile, greenish; bracts pubescent, lateral lobes spreading. *Fruit* a small samara; August-September; wings narrow.

Frequent to common in bogs, open swamps, and marshes throughout the state. Shade-intolerant. Also called swamp birch. Hybrid with yellow birch, *B.* ×*purpusii* Schneid., more frequent in southern Michigan than in northern Michigan. See Dancik and Barnes (1972) for details of hybridization with yellow birch. Hybrid with white birch, *B.* ×*sandbergii* Britt., occasional in the state.

348

BETULACEAE
Corylus americana Walter

American Hazelnut

Erect, bushy shrub, to 3 m high; numerous stems arising from belowground parts develop spreading branches that form a low, rounded crown. *Bark* smooth, gray. *Leaves* alternate, simple, blades 6–15 cm long, 4–12 cm wide; broad-ovate to oval or orbicular, apex short-acuminate, base oblique, rounded, or subcordate; more or less irregularly, doubly-serrate; coriaceous; slightly hairy, dark green above, soft-pubescent and paler beneath; petioles glandular-bristly, 0.5–2 cm long. *Twigs* slender, glandular-pubescent with fine, bristly hairs, brown; male catkins conspicuous in fall and winter toward the twig ends, many catkins with a characteristic kink or curl due to insect attack. *Winter buds* small, globose, brown; terminal bud absent. *Flowers* March-April; wind-pollinated; male flowers in stalked catkins, 4–8 cm long; female flowers in small, budlike clusters toward the ends of twigs; plants monoecious. *Fruit* a nut; August-September; large, 2–4 in a cluster, each nut tightly enclosed by 2 leaf-like bracts about twice as long as the nut (not forming a beak); nut flattened-globose, 1–1.5 cm long, edible.

Common to abundant in the southern half of the Lower Peninsula; absent in the northern half of the Lower Peninsula; rare in the Upper Peninsula. Characteristic of open sites in dry and moist situations: roadsides, fence rows, edges of woods, old fields. Shade-intolerant. Nuts rapidly removed by animals and rarely found or collected by humans except in early autumn. Nuts about as good as the larger, imported hazelnut or filbert, from the European *C. avellana* L. Not widely used in landscaping, but a native species of potential importance in dry or moist sites.

Distinguished from the beaked hazel by twigs and petioles glandular-hairy; bracts surrounding the nut broad, distinct nearly to the base, not united into a tubular beak; male catkins stalked; absent in northern lower Michigan and rare in the Upper Peninsula.

BETULACEAE
Corylus cornuta Marshall

Beaked Hazelnut

Erect, bushy shrub, to 4 m high; form similar to American hazelnut. *Bark* smooth, gray. *Leaves* alternate, simple, blades 4–13 cm long, 3–8 cm wide; ovate or ovate-oblong, acuminate, subcordate; more or less irregularly doubly serrate or slightly lobed; mostly glabrous, dark green above, paler and pubescent on veins beneath; petioles puberulent, not bristly-hairy, 0.5–1.5 cm long. *Twigs* slender, glabrous or only slightly hairy. *Winter buds* small, globose, brown, terminal bud absent. *Flowers* April-May; wind-pollinated; male flowers in nonstalked catkins; female flowers in small, budlike clusters toward the ends of twigs. *Fruit* a nut; August-September; in clusters of 2–4, each nut tightly enclosed by a tubular involucre of united bracts, much constricted and prolonged above the nut to form a beak, 2.5–4 cm long; nut flattened-globose, edible.

Common in the Upper Peninsula and the northern half of the Lower Peninsula; found south only to Gratiot and St. Clair Co. in the Lower Peninsula. Habitat and other notes similar to that for American hazelnut.

Distinguished from American hazelnut by twigs and petioles not glandular or bristly-hairy; bracts surrounding the nut united and forming a tubular beak, much constricted and extending far beyond the nut; male catkins not stalked; rare or absent in the southern half of the Lower Peninsula.

MYRICACEAE
Comptonia peregrina (Linnaeus) Coulter

Sweet-fern

Low, erect, many-branched shrub, 30–60 cm high; branches erect or spreading; forming dense clones. *Leaves* alternate, simple, resembling a type of leaflet common in ferns, blades 5–12 cm long, 1–1.5 cm wide; linear-lanceolate, apex rounded or acute; margin cut into 10–12 rounded or obtuse, often mucronate segments or lobes per side, some sinuses nearly reaching the midrib; more or

349

less pubescent, dark green above, pubescent and paler beneath, covered with scattered yellow, shiny resin-dots; sweet-scented; petioles short, 1–5 mm long. *Twigs* slender, resin-dotted when young; leaf scars somewhat raised; fragrant when bruised. *Winter buds* ovoid, fragrant when broken. *Flowers* April-May; wind-pollinated; male flowers in catkins about 2 cm long; female flowers in catkins 1.5–2.5 cm long. *Fruit* a nut; July-August; conical, light brown, smooth, fragrant, surrounded by 8 long, linear bracts forming a bur.

Locally frequent to abundant in dry, sandy, acid, infertile sites; typically in pine and oak plains; occasionally in sandy, moist flats with pin oak. Some brown, withered leaves usually persist on the plant through winter. Heavily browsed by deer. All parts of the plant give off a fragrant, spicy odor. Leaves formerly used in tonics, home remedies, and as a substitute for tea.

MYRICACEAE
Myrica gale Linnaeus

Sweet Gale

Low, ascending shrub, 0.3–1.5 m high; branches strongly ascending, brown. *Leaves* alternate, simple, blades 3–6 cm long, 0.8–1.8 cm wide; oblanceolate, obtuse or acute; slightly toothed toward the apex; glabrous, dark green above, more or less pubescent and grayish beneath; aromatic when crushed; petioles short. *Twigs* slender, downy, resin-dotted when young, fragrant when crushed. *Winter buds* conical-ovoid, fragrant when broken. *Flowers* April-May; wind-pollinated; male flowers in catkins, 1–1.5 cm long, scales brown, lustrous, glabrous; female flowers ovoid, conelike, about 5 mm long. *Fruit* a nut; July; borne in compact catkins, 0.8–1 cm long, dry, resin-dotted, 2-winged by thick ovate scales, 2–3 mm long.

Locally frequent to common in acid swamps, fens, along streams, and on moist, sandy soils in the northern half of the Lower Peninsula and in the Upper Peninsula. Moderately shade-tolerant. All parts pleasantly fragrant when crushed. Formerly used in clothes closets to repel moths; young buds reportedly used by Native Americans for dyeing porcupine quills.

OLEACEAE
Ligustrum vulgare Linnaeus

Common Privet

Tall shrub, to 5 m high; stout, much branched. *Leaves* opposite, simple, blades 3–6 cm long; oblong-ovate to lanceolate, obtuse to acute; entire; moderately thick; dark green above, paler beneath; foliage retained long into the winter but dropping before spring; glabrous; petioles 0.3–1 cm long. *Twigs* slender, green and usually minutely puberulent when young, becoming light brown to gray; leaf scars elliptical; pith white. *Winter buds* small, ovoid, somewhat divergent; scales imbricate. *Flowers* June; insect-pollinated; perfect; borne in rather dense terminal panicles 3–6 cm long; white; heavy odor; calyx short-tubular, 4-toothed; corolla tubelike and abruptly expanded into 4 spreading lobes; stamens 2. *Fruit* a drupe; September, persisting through winter until spring; lustrous, blackish, ovoid to subglobose, 6–8 mm long; 1–4 seeded.

Native in Europe and northern Africa. Widely planted and used as a low or tall hedge. Seeds widely disseminated by birds. Becoming naturalized in urban environments and in disturbed forests where it is sometimes not identified because of its unpruned habit. Moderately shade-tolerant. Extremely popular as a hedge plant; stands pruning and shaping well. Several cultivars are in use as well as two closely related species.

OLEACEAE
Syringa vulgaris Linnaeus

Common Lilac

Tall, upright shrub or small tree to 7 m high; typically growing in dense clumps of many stems. Michigan Big Tree: girth 1.1 m, diameter 34 cm, height 9 m, Mackinac Co. *Bark* relatively thin, gray to brownish, splitting into long, narrow, scaly ridges, scales gradually flaking off. *Leaves* opposite, simple, blades 5–12 cm long; ovate or broadly ovate, apex acute, base truncate to subcordate; entire; dark green to bluish green above, paler beneath; glabrous; petioles 1.5–3 cm long. *Twigs* moderately stout, 6 mm or more thick, glabrous, lenticels prominent. *Winter buds* ovoid; terminal bud frequently absent; two lateral buds often found at end of twig; bud scales fleshy. *Flowers* May; insect-pollinated; borne in panicles 10–20 cm long; showy and very fragrant; corolla tubular, slender, about 1 cm long with wide-spreading lobes; white or light to dark purple (lilac). *Fruit* a capsule, ovoid, 1–1.5 cm long.

Native in southeastern Europe and one of the most widely planted shrubs. Numerous cultivars, over 400 (possibly 800–900), offer a variety of colors (white to reddish purple), double flowers, and variegated leaves. For best flowering the inflorescences should be removed after flowering ceases. Grows well in any upland soil. Common and hardy throughout the state. Lilac cultivars have been a major component of some of Michigan's public gardens (e.g., Fernwood, Niles).

SOLANACEAE
Solanum dulcamara Linnaeus

Nightshade   Bittersweet

Perennial climber to 2.5 m; climbing by leaning on and growing among and over host stems; branches woody and persistent; stems slightly pubescent, olive-colored. *Leaves* alternate, simple, blades 4–10 cm long, 2.5–6 cm wide; ovate to ovate-oblong; coarsely 1–4-lobed or entire, acuminate, usually cordate; thin; bright green, glabrous or slightly pubescent; rank-smelling when crushed; petioles 1–3 cm long. *Twigs* slender, olive to straw-colored; leaf scars oval and slightly flattened at top, bundle scar 1. *Winter buds* sessile, subglobose, pubescent. *Flowers* May-June; insect-pollinated; perfect; borne in long-peduncled cymes; 1–1.5 cm across; violet (rarely white); calyx 5-lobed; corolla deeply 5-cleft, the lobes reflexed; stamens 5, exserted. Fruit a berry; August-October; scarlet, ovoid or ellipsoid, 2-celled; seeds numerous.

Native in Europe, introduced and naturalized in North America. Common in the Lower Peninsula, less common in the Upper Peninsula. Shade-tolerant. The red berries are not believed to be poisonous, but the young green berries and the foliage may be poisonous. The family Solanaceae contains many poisonous members.

RUBIACEAE
Cephalanthus occidentalis Linnaeus

Buttonbush

Large, erect, spreading shrub, to 5 m high; many stems branch vigorously and form a densely foliated shrub or clonal thicket. Michigan Big Shrub: girth 84 cm, diameter 27 cm, height 9 m, Oakland Co. *Bark* dark gray or brown, furrowed with flat-topped ridges, young stems yellowish and slightly fissured. *Leaves* whorled or opposite, simple, blades 7–14 cm long and about half as wide; ovate to lanceolate, acuminate; entire; thick and leathery; glabrous, lustrous, dark green above, glabrous to somewhat pubescent and paler beneath; petioles stout, 1–2 cm long, stipules interpetiolar, occurring singly between the whorled or opposite leaf bases. *Twigs* slender, smooth, glabrous, grayish brown with prominent, vertical lenticels; pith large and yellow; leaf scars small, half-round. *Winter buds* small, brownish, often sunken and covered by a thin layer of bark; terminal bud absent. *Flowers* July-August; insect-pollinated; perfect; borne in globose heads 2–3 cm across, on peduncles 3–6 cm long, 100–200 flowers in each head; creamy white. *Fruit* a multiple of capsules; September-October; each capsule yellowish brown, conical, 7–8 mm long.

Abundant in the southern half of the Lower Peninsula; occasional in the northern Lower Peninsula; absent in the Upper Peninsula. Characteristic of open swamps, stream margins, and lake shores. Typical of small glacial depressions (kettle holes) or any low area where water stands at least half the year. Usually forming dense thickets that are very difficult to penetrate. Shade-intolerant; tolerant of high water and slow-moving and

351

stagnant water. Flowers very attractive to small butterflies. Of potential ornamental value in open, low, wet situations.

CAPRIFOLIACEAE
Diervilla lonicera Miller

Bush-honeysuckle

Low, upright shrub, 0.4–1 m high. *Bark* grayish brown, shredding on older stems. *Leaves* opposite, simple, blades 6–12 cm long, 2–5 cm wide; ovate to lanceolate, acuminate; serrate, ciliate; glabrous, green above, paler and sometimes pubescent on main veins beneath; petioles short, 3–8 mm long. *Twigs* slender, round, brownish, with 2 hairy-lined ridges decurrent from each node, otherwise glabrous. *Winter buds* oblong, sessile. *Flowers* June; insect-pollinated; perfect; usually 3-flowered on peduncled cymes; yellow; calyx 5-lobed; corolla tubular, 2-lipped; stamens 5. *Fruit* a capsule; September-October; 2-celled, 0.7–1 cm long, beaked with shriveled calyx; seeds many, minute, not winged.

Frequent in open, typically dry, disturbed habitats; lake shores, dune areas, old fields, stream banks, rocky places; frequency increasing northward. Moderately shade-tolerant. Easily distinguished from true honeysuckles (*Lonicera* spp.) by toothed leaves and capsular fruit.

CAPRIFOLIACEAE
Lonicera canadensis Marshall

American Fly Honeysuckle

Erect or semierect straggling shrub, to 1.5 m high; branches flexible, spreading, some becoming prostrate; clone-forming. *Bark* light brown, peeling or shredding in thin strips. *Leaves* opposite, simple, 4–9 cm long and about half as wide; ovate to ovate-oblong, acute or blunt; entire, ciliate; thin; green above, paler beneath; villous-pubescent when young, becoming more or less glabrous both sides; veins pinnate; petioles slender, short, about 5 mm long. *Twigs* slender, rounded, glabrous; pith white, continuous. *Winter buds* short-ovoid or nearly globose, glabrate. *Flowers* May-June; insect-pollinated; perfect; paired on long axillary stalks, 2–2.5 cm long; pale yellow to creamy white, sometimes tinged with red or purple; calyx 5-toothed; corolla tubular-funnelform, about 1.5–2 cm long, 2-lipped; stamens 5. *Fruit* a berry; July-September; elongate, 1–1.5 cm long, red to purplish, usually 2 together on a long stalk; seeds 3–4.

Frequent in open, mesic to dry-mesic habitats throughout the state. Moderately shade-tolerant. Several Eurasian honeysuckles are widely used in landscape plantings.

The Japanese honeysuckle, *L. japonica* Thunb., is a native of eastern Asia and was introduced about 1806. The stems are finely hairy and the leaves are semipersistent. The flowers are white, strongly 2-lipped, and large (3 cm or more long), with a rich fragrance, especially in the evening. The fruits are round, black, and lustrous. A semievergreen, twining vine, or creeper (2–6 m long), it has become a very serious and noxious weed in most of the midwestern and southern states. Its dense growth smothers tree, shrub, and herbaceous regeneration and kills or rides-down trees by its climbing, twining habit. It has invaded Michigan and is found sporadically in southern Michigan from Oakland to Ottawa Co. It should never be planted, and it should be eradicated wherever found. It is distinguished from the American fly honeysuckle by its twining, semievergreen habit and its hairy, reddish brown stems.

Another vining honeysuckle, *L. dioica* L., is frequently confused with the Japanese honeysuckle. It is a native species, however, differing from the latter in its glabrous, glaucous leaves which tend to fuse along their bases near the inflorescence, forming a cup.

CAPRIFOLIACEAE
Lonicera tatarica Linnaeus

Tatarian Honeysuckle

Upright to spreading shrub to 3 m high. *Bark* light gray, somewhat exfoliating. *Leaves* opposite, simple, blades 3–6 cm long,

2–4 cm wide; ovate to ovate-lanceolate, acute to rarely obtuse; entire; dark green above, paler beneath; glabrous; petiole 2–6 mm long. *Twigs* slender, brown to reddish; pith brown, excavated between the nodes. *Winter buds* oblong or ovoid; scales short-pointed, glabrous. *Flowers* May-June; insect-pollinated; perfect; paired on long axillary stalks, 1.5–2 cm long; pink to white; calyx 5-toothed; corolla tubular-funnelform, about 1.5–2 cm long, lobes unequal, widely spreading; stamens 5. *Fruit* a berry; July-September; globose, stalked in pairs in leaf axils, slightly united at base, red to orange.

Native in southern Russia and Asia. Introduced and widely used in North American landscape plantings because of its showy flowers. Naturalized and commonly found in cutover woods (becoming a pest in some places), along roadsides and railroad tracks especially near cities and towns. Hardy throughout the state.

Distinguished from the native *L. canadensis* by a much taller habit; twigs with brown pith, hollow between the nodes; leaf blades the margins of which are not usually ciliate and are not downy-pubescent when young.

The Amur or Maack's honeysuckle, *L. maackii* Maxim., is a native of Manchuria and Korea and is becoming widely naturalized in southern Michigan. It is a tall shrub, to 5 m high, and is distinguished by its relatively thick, nonexfoliating bark with conspicuously interlacing ridges, leaf blades with a distinctive long-acuminate apex, and persistent red berries that are borne on very short stalks.

CAPRIFOLIACEAE
Sambucus canadensis Linnaeus

Common Elder   American Elder

Erect, stoloniferous shrub, to 4 m high; many, few-branched stems arise from a common base to form a broad, rounded, often unkempt, irregular crown of arching branches; shallow-rooted; clone-forming by stolons and runners. Michigan Big Shrub: girth 36 cm, diameter 11 cm, height 8 m, Leelanau Co. *Bark* thin, gray, with conspicu-

ous warty lenticels. *Leaves* opposite, pinnately compound, 10–30 cm long; leaflets 5–11 (usually 7), the lowermost often 3-parted, short-stalked, 5–15 cm long, 3–6 cm wide; elliptic, lanceolate, or ovate-oblong, acute or acuminate; sharply serrate; lustrous, glabrous, bright green above, paler and glabrous or pubescent on veins beneath; rachis pubescent or glabrous, petioles 4–5 cm long. *Twigs* stout, swollen at the nodes, yellowish gray, warty with conspicuous lenticels; pith large and white; ill-smelling when crushed. *Winter buds* small, conical, light brown or green; 4–5 pairs of bud scales. *Flowers* June-July; insect-pollinated; borne in conspicuous, large, terminal, flat-topped or slightly convex cymes; small; white. *Fruit* a drupe; September-October; purplish black, with red juice, borne on rose red stalks, 4–6 mm across.

Common in deciduous swamps, floodplains, bottomlands, and stream banks throughout the state; more abundant in the Lower Peninsula. Characteristic of wet-mesic, circumneutral, fertile sites, open or shaded; rarely on drier upland sites. Shade-tolerant; slow-growing in shade; fast-growing in full sunlight. Spreading by stolons and runners and forming multistemmed clones. Although vegetative parts may cause poisoning, the fruits may be used in jellies, wines, and pies; flowers may be used to flavor candies and jellies. Fruits are excellent wildlife food, especially for birds such as quail and pheasant. Transplants well but is used rarely in landscaping.

Distinguished from red-berried elder by leaves larger, with more leaflets; pith white, not dark brown; fruits in late summer and early fall, flowers and purplish black fruits borne in large flat-topped cymes; winter buds conical, light brown or green.

CAPRIFOLIACEAE
Sambucus pubens Michaux

Red-berried Elder

Erect shrub, to 4 m high; similar to the common elder in size and form. Michigan Big Shrub: girth 46 cm, diameter 15 cm, height 8 m, Keweenaw Co. *Bark* gray and warty with conspicuous lenticels. *Leaves* opposite, pinnately compound, 10–25 cm long; leaflets 5–7 (usually 7), short-stalked, 4–10 cm long, 2–4 cm wide; ovate-oblong to ovate-lanceolate; acute or acuminate; serrate; glabrous, lustrous, bright green above, pubescent and paler beneath; rachis pubescent, petioles 2.5–5 cm long. *Twigs* stout, yellowish brown, glabrous or pubescent, warty with conspicuous lenticels; pith large and dark brown. *Winter buds* globular, red, stalked; 2–3 pairs of bud scales. *Flowers* April-May; insect-pollinated; borne in pyramidal, compound cymes; small; yellowish white. *Fruit* a drupe; June-July; bright red, 5–7 mm across.

Common in the northern half of the Lower Peninsula and the Upper Peninsula; less common in the southern half of the Lower Peninsula. Characteristic of open areas such as roadsides, fence rows, edges of woods, stream banks, and lake shores; also found in mesic sugar maple forests. Shade-tolerant; slow-growing in shade, fast-growing in full sunlight. Although vegetative parts may cause poisoning, the fruits may be used in jellies, wines, and pies.

Distinguished from common elder by leaves smaller, with fewer leaflets; pith dark brown, not white; fruits in early summer, flowers and bright red fruits borne in pyramidal cymes; winter buds globular, red.

CAPRIFOLIACEAE
Viburnum acerifolium Linnaeus

Mapleleaf Viburnum

Low, upright shrub, to 2 m high; forming large, clonal thickets. *Leaves* opposite, simple, blades 6–10 cm long and equally as wide; suborbicular to ovate, 3-lobed, lobes acute to acuminate, sinuses shallow; coarsely dentate; thin; dull green above, paler beneath; pubescent; petioles 1–3 cm long, pubescent. *Twigs* slender, finely pubescent, tan to reddish brown, becoming gray. *Winter buds* appressed, stalked; 4 bud scales, the lower scales very short. *Flowers* May-June; insect-pollinated; borne in long-stalked cymes 3–8 cm long; yellowish white. *Fruit* a drupe; September; purplish black, ellipsoid to globose, 6–8 mm long, persistent.

Common in the Lower Peninsula; occasional in the Upper Peninsula. Characteristic of dry-mesic oak-hickory and oak forests; also found in mesic beech-sugar maple forests. Shade-tolerant; slow-growing. Common and scientific names both refer to maplelike foliage.

CAPRIFOLIACEAE
Viburnum rafinesquianum Schultes

Downy Arrowwood

Upright shrub, to 2 m high; many arching stems form a moderately dense, rounded crown. *Leaves* opposite, simple, blades 3–7 cm long and about half as wide; ovate to elliptic, acute to acuminate; coarsely dentate, teeth 2–4 mm wide; light green, slightly pubescent above, more or less densely downy-pubescent beneath; petioles short, 2–5 mm long. *Twigs* slender, tan to gray, pubescent. *Winter buds* divergent, plump, often with 6 scales. *Flowers* May-June; insect-pollinated; borne on dense cymes 3–6 cm across; small; white. *Fruit* a drupe; August-September; bluish black, ellipsoid, flattened, 6–8 mm long.

Common in the southern half of the Lower Peninsula. A typical shrub of dry-mesic to xeric oak-hickory and oak forests. Characteristic of calcareous and droughty, sandy and gravelly soils. Moderately shade-tolerant; drought-tolerant. Similar to the more southerly *V. dentatum* L., arrowwood, but distinguished by the somewhat downy undersurface of the leaves and the ellipsoid (not spherical), flattened fruits.

CAPRIFOLIACEAE
Viburnum trilobum Marshall

Highbush-cranberry

Tall, spreading shrub, to 4 m high; many arching stems form a dense, round-topped crown. Michigan Big Shrub: girth 28 cm, diameter 9 cm, height 7 m, Oakland Co. *Leaves* opposite, simple, blades 4–10 cm long and equally wide; broadly ovate, strongly 3-lobed, lobes spreading, acuminate; coarsely dentate; glabrous, green, lustrous above, paler and pubescent on veins beneath or becoming glabrous; petioles 1–3 cm long, with stalked glands near blade base. *Twigs* stout, glabrous, gray. *Winter buds* plump, green, glabrous, lustrous; bud scales 2, closely valvate. *Flowers* May-June; insect-pollinated; borne in flat-topped cymes 5–10 cm long; white. *Fruit* a drupe; September; globose or short-ellipsoid, 0.8–1 cm across, scarlet, translucent, persistent, acid when fresh, palatable (to some) when cooked.

Locally frequent throughout the state along streams, in open or lightly shaded swamps and wet grounds. Moderately shade-tolerant. Fruit used as a substitute for cranberries (*Vaccinium*) in making jelly, but lose their tastiness during late fall. A potentially important ornamental because of its handsome clusters of white flowers and scarlet fruits. Seldom available in nurseries although it transplants easily. Widely planted is its close relative, *V. opulus* L., European cranberry-bush. The European species is very similar to the native one in most respects; it can be distinguished by its more compact, shrubby habit; shorter leaves that have more pronounced toothing of the lobes; as well as its fruit which is bitter whether fresh or cooked.

LILIACEAE
Smilax tamnoides Linnaeus

Bristly Greenbrier

Stout, climbing vine, to 10 m long; branches slightly spreading; clone-forming; climbing by tendrils borne in pairs on the petioles. *Leaves* alternate, simple, blades 5–12 cm long, 3–9 cm wide; broadly ovate, acute, or cuspidate; rough-margined or with few minute bristle-tipped teeth; thin; dark green, glabrous above and beneath; usually 5 primary veins, parallel-arcuate; leaves falling away above the petiole base; petioles 1–2 cm long, bearing tendrils. *Twigs* slender, round, green, glabrous, armed with straight, slender, blackish prickles, to 1.2 cm long; lower stem densely bristly, current shoots and younger branches unarmed or nearly so; pith lacking; vascular bundles scattered throughout; no definite leaf scar. *Winter*

buds 3-sided, pointed, divergent; 1 exposed scale. *Flowers* June; insect-pollinated; borne in few- to many-flowered umbels, peduncles up to 7 cm long, each branch bearing 4–12 flowers; small; greenish bronze; 3 lanceolate sepals and 3 petals; plants dioecious. *Fruit* a berry; October-November; globose, black, without bloom, 5–8 mm across; mostly 1-seeded (rarely 2), the seed shiny, reddish brown.

Common in the Lower Peninsula; rare in the Upper Peninsula. Characteristic of open, moist habitats or lightly shaded woods, stream and lake environs, dunes, roadsides, fence rows, old fields, edges of woods, banks, cutover forests. Moderately shade-tolerant. There are four or five *Smilax* species in the state that lack spines and are herbaceous. Also known as *S. hispida* Muhl.

Glossary

Abortion. Imperfect development or nondevelopment of an organ or part.

Abscise. To cut off.

Achene. A 1-seeded, dry, indehiscent fruit with seed attached to fruit wall at 1 point only, derived from a superior ovary.

Acorn. The fruit of the oak, consisting of a nut with its base enclosed in a cup of imbricated scales.

Acuminate. Gradually tapering to a long point. Page 9.

Acute. Terminating with a sharp angle; tapering to a point, but not long-pointed. Page 9.

Aggregate fruit. A group of separate fruits developed from one flower.

Alternate. Arrangement of leaves, branches, buds, etc., scattered singly along the stem; occurring one at each node; not opposite.

Angiosperm. A flowering plant.

Anther. The part of a stamen which bears the pollen. Page 18.

Apetalous. Without petals.

Apex. The top, as the tip of a bud or the end of a leaf, which is opposite the petiole.

Apiculate. Ending in a short-pointed tip.

Apophysis. The exposed portion of the cone scale of a conifer.

Appressed. Lying close and flat against; (of buds) lying flat against the stem.

Arborescent. Attaining the size or character of a tree.

Arcuate veins. Curved and arranged nearly parallel to the blade margin, as in leaves of *Cornus* and *Ceanothus.*

Aril. A fleshy outgrowth that surrounds the seed, commonly brightly colored.

Armed. Bearing thorns, spines, or prickles.

Aromatic. Fragrant; having an agreeable odor.

Ascending. Arising somewhat obliquely, or curving upward.

Astringent. Shrinking and driving the blood from the tissues; contracting.

Awl-shaped. Tapering from the base to a slender or rigid point.

Axil. The upper one of the angles formed by the juncture of a leaf with a stem.

Axillary. Situated in an axil.

Axis. The central line of support, as a stem.

Bark. The outer covering of a trunk or branch. Page 6.

Bast. Fibrous, attenuated, sharp-pointed, thick-walled cells which give strength and protection to the tissues of the stem.

357

Berry.   A juicy or fleshy fruit in which the seeds are embedded in the pulp.

Bipinnate.   Twice pinnate.

Bisexual.   Having both sex organs in the same individual.

Blade.   The expanded portion of a leaf.

Bloom.   A powdery or waxy substance that is easily rubbed off.

Board foot.   A piece of wood 12 in × 12 in × 1 in in size; a measure for determining the merchantable volume of trees.

Boreal.   Of or pertaining to Boreas (god of the north wind), hence northern.

Borer.   A beetle or other insect that bores, usually in the larval state, in wood.

Bract.   A modified leaf often subtending a flower or belonging to an inflorescence.

Branch.   A secondary division of a trunk.

Branchlet.   A small branch.

Bristle.   A flexible, pointed outgrowth from the epidermis or cortex of any organ.

Calcareous.   Said of soil containing free lime ($CaCO_3$) and having a basic pH reaction.

Calyx.   The outer part of a perianth, usually green in color.

Cambium.   A layer of cells between wood and bark, capable of producing new elements, by which the stem grows in diameter.

Campanulate.   Bell-shaped.

Cane.   The long shoots of certain shrubs, as the raspberries, blackberries, etc.

Capsule.   A dry fruit of two or more carpels which splits at maturity to release the seeds.

Carpel.   A floral organ that contains ovules in angiosperms either borne separately or as a unit of a compound pistil.

Catkin.   A spike or elongate axis bearing apetalous, unisexual flowers; falling as a unit after flowering or fruiting.

Chambered.   Said of pith when divided into small compartments separated by transverse partitions.

Ciliate.   Fringed with hairs on the margin.

Clay.   A kind of soil containing more than 40 percent clay particles, less than 45 percent sand particles, and less than 40 percent silt particles; a soil particle less than 0.002 mm in diameter.

Cleft.   Cut about halfway to the middle.

Clone.   The aggregate of stems descended asexually from one sexually produced individual.

Cluster.   A group of two or more organs (flowers, fruits, etc.) on a plant at a node or end of a stem.

Collateral.   Said of extra buds which occur on either side of an axillary bud.

Compound.   Composed of two or more similar parts united into a whole.

Compound leaf.   One divided into separate leaflets.

Compressed.   Flattened laterally.

Concentric.   One within another, with a common center.

Cone. The reproductive structure of gymnosperms, consisting of an axis to which are attached many woody, overlapping scales which bear seeds.

Confluent. Blended or flowing into one; passing by degrees one into the other.

Conifer. A gymnosperm of the order Coniferales; a cone-bearing tree.

Connate. United to another part of the same kind.

Continuous. Said of pith that is solid, not interrupted by cavities.

Cordate. Heart-shaped. Page 8.

Coriaceous. Leatherlike in texture.

Corky. Made of cork cells; corklike.

Corolla. The inner part of a perianth, composed of separate or connate petals, usually brightly colored.

Cortex. The outer tissue that lies between the epidermis and the vascular strands.

Corymb. A flower cluster in which the axis is shortened and the pedicels of the lower flowers lengthened, forming a flat or more or less round-topped inflorescence, the marginal flowers blooming first. Page 19.

Corymbose. Arranged in corymbs.

Creeping. Running at or near the surface of the ground and rooting.

Crenate. Dentate, with the teeth much rounded; scallop-toothed. Page 9.

Crenulate. Finely crenate.

Cross section. Said of a section cut at right angles to the long axis.

Crown. The upper part of a tree, including the living branches with their foliage.

Cultivar. A cultivated variety.

Cuneate. Wedge-shaped.

Cuspidate. Tipped with a firm, sharp point.

Cutting. A piece of the stem, root, or leaf which, if placed in contact with a rooting medium, will form new roots and buds, reproducing the parent plant.

Cyme. A broad and flattish inflorescence consisting of a determinate central axis bearing a number of pedicelled flowers, the central flowers blooming first. Page 19.

Cymose. Arranged in cymes.

Deciduous. Not persistent; falling away, as the leaves of a tree in autumn.

Decumbent. Stems or branches reclining, but the ends ascending.

Decurrent. Continued down the twig in a ridge or wing, as applied to leaf bases.

Dehiscent. Opening by valves or slits.

Deltoid. Delta-shaped (Δ); triangular. Page 8.

Dentate. Toothed, with the teeth usually pointed and directed outward. Page 9.

Denticulate. Finely dentate, the teeth small and shallow.

Depressed. Somewhat flattened from above.

Diaphragmed. Said of pith which is solid with transverse bars of denser tissue at short intervals.

Dichotomous. Branching regularly in pairs.

Diffuse-porous. Said of the wood of broad-leaved trees in which the pores are of practically uniform size throughout the growth ring or decrease only slightly toward the outer portion of the summer wood. See *ring-porous.*

Dioecious. Unisexual, with male and female flowers on different individuals.

Disk. A rounded, flat plate.

Dispersal. The spread of objects (e.g., pollen, fruits, seeds) from a fixed or constant source.

Dissected. Cut or divided into numerous segments.

Distribution. The geographical extent and limits of a species.

Divergent. Said of buds, cones, etc., which point away from the twig, or of pine needles, etc., which spread apart.

Divided. Cleft to the base or to the midvein.

Dormant. A term applied to whole plants or parts which are in a resting stage.

Dorsal. Pertaining to the back or outer surface of an organ.

Downy. Covered with fine hairs.

Drupe. A fleshy or pulpy fruit in which the inner portion of the ovary wall is hard or stony.

Ellipsoid. An elliptical solid.

Elliptical. Oval or oblong with regularly rounded ends. Page 8.

Emarginate. Notched at the apex. Page 9.

Entire. Blade margin smooth, lacking teeth or other protrusions.

Epicormic branches. Small branches arising from dormant buds from the trunk or large branches.

Epidermis. The outer cell layer or covering of plants.

Escape. Any plant formerly cultivated that grows wild in nature.

Esker. A long, narrow ridge chiefly composed of stratified glacial drift.

Evergreen. Having foliage which does not fall at the end of the growing season, having green leaves in winter.

Excavated. Hollowed out; hollow.

Excrescences. Warty outgrowths or protuberances.

Excurrent. With axis forming an undivided major trunk, as in conifers.

Exfoliate. To peel away, as of the outer layers of bark.

Exserted. Projecting beyond a covering.

Fascicle. A compact cluster of leaves or flowers.

Fascicled. Arranged in fascicles.

Fastigiate. Said of branches which are erect and close together.

Feather-veined. Having veins extending from the midrib to the margin, featherlike.

Fen. A grassland on a wet and springy site with an internal water flow rich in calcium and magnesium bicarbonates.

Fertile. Capable of bearing fruit; normally reproductive. Of a site, rich or well supplied with nutrients.

Fertilization. The union of a sperm (contained in pollen) and an egg (contained in ovule).

Filament. The part of a stamen which bears the anther. Page 18.

Flaccid. Without rigidity.

Flaky. With loose scales easily rubbed off, as with bark.

Fleshy. Succulent; juicy.

Flora. The plants of a particular region or area.

Flower. An axis bearing stamens or pistils or both (calyx and corolla usually accompany these). Page 18.

Fluted. Grooved longitudinally, with alternating ridges and depressions.

Foliolate. With separate leaflets.

Follicle. A dry, dehiscent fruit which opens along one side.

Forked. Divided into nearly equal branches.

Form. The general appearance of a plant; habit.

Frondlike. Shaped like the leaf of ferns.

Fruit. The matured ovary of flowering plants.

Fusiform. Thick, but tapering toward each end.

Germinate. To sprout, as a seed.

Gibbous. Swollen on one side.

Glabrate. Almost without hairs; with occasional hairs.

Glabrescent. Becoming glabrous.

Glabrous. Without hairs.

Gland. A small protuberance consisting of one or more secreting cells.

Glandular. Bearing glands.

Glaucous. Covered or whitened with bloom which may be rubbed off.

Globose. Spherical or nearly so.

Globular. Nearly globose.

Glutinous. Sticky, gluey.

Gregarious. Growing in groups or colonies.

Growth ring. The layer of wood produced in a single growing season; in a cross section of the stem these layers appear as concentric rings of growth.

Gymnospermous. Characterized by young seeds naked at the time of pollination, the mature seeds never borne in an ovary or fruit.

Habit. The general appearance of a plant, best seen from a distance.

Habitat. The place and the associated physical factors of the environment where a plant grows; site.

Hardwood. A broad-leaved, deciduous tree.

Heartwood. The dead central portion of the trunk or large branch.

Herb. A plant with no persistent live stem on or above ground; a nonwoody plant.

Hip. An aggregate of achenes surounded by an urn-shaped receptacle.

Hirsute. Covered with rather coarse or stiff, usually regularly long, hairs.

Hispid. Pubescent with bristly, rigid hairs.

Hoary.   Grayish white with a fine, close pubescence.

Homogeneous.   Uniform; composed of similar parts or elements.

Humus.   Finely decomposed organic matter; usually dark-colored organic matter in the latter stages of decomposition.

Husk.   The rough outer covering of a fruit or seed.

Hybrid.   A cross between two species, usually yielding an intermediate form.

Imbricated.   Overlapping, like the shingles on a roof.

Indehiscent.   Not opening by valves or slits; remaining persistently closed.

Indigenous.   Native and original to a region.

Inequilateral.   Unequal-sided; oblique at the base; asymmetrical.

Inflorescence.   The flowering part of a plant, and especially its arrangement; a flower cluster.

Infructescence.   A fruit cluster having the same arrangement as the inflorescence.

Internode.   The portion of a stem between two nodes.

Intolerant.   Incapable of enduring under adverse conditions, as shade, drought, etc.

Introduced.   Brought in from another region.

Involucral.   Pertaining to an involucre.

Involucre.   A circle of bracts subtending a flower or cluster of flowers.

Kame.   A moundlike hill of stratified glacial drift.

Keeled.   With a central ridge like the keel of a boat.

Kettle hole.   A basin created by the melting of a buried block of ice.

Key.   A fruit having a wing or leaflike expansion.

Laciniate.   Cut into narrow, pointed lobes.

Lanceolate.   Lance-shaped, broadest above the base and tapering to the apex, but several times longer than wide. Page 8.

Lateral.   Situated on the side.

Lax.   Loose.

Leaf.   A photosynthetic and transpiring organ; an expanded, usually green, organ borne on the stem of a plant.

Leaflet.   One of the small blades of a compound leaf.

Leaf scar.   The scar left on a twig by the falling of a leaf. Page 12.

Legume.   A simple, dry, podlike fruit composed of a solitary carpel that usually splits open along both sutures (Leguminosae).

Lenticels.   Small areas of loose, corky tissue on young bark, appearing as dots or warts, which admit air to the interior of a twig or branch.

Linear.   Long and narrow, with parallel edges (as pine needles). Page 8.

Loam.   The textural class name for soil having a moderate amount of sand, silt, and clay. Loam soils contain 7 to 27 percent of clay, 28 to 50 percent of silt, and less than 52 percent of sand.

Lobe.   Part of a blade separated by sinuses, i.e., a division of a blade that is broadly attached, not contracted or stalked at its base.

Lobed.   Provided with a lobe or lobes. Page 9.

362

Luster. Brilliancy or sheen; gloss.

Lustrous. Glossy; shiny.

Membranous. Thin, rather soft, and somewhat translucent.

Meristematic. Embryonic cells that form new tissues.

Mesic. Said of a habitat well supplied with moisture throughout the year, not overly dry or wet.

Midrib. The central vein of a leaf or leaflet.

Monoecious. Unisexual, with male and female flowers on the same individual.

Mucilaginous. Slimy; resembling or secreting mucilage or gum.

Mucronate. Tipped with a small, abrupt point. Page 9.

Multiple fruit. A cluster of ripened ovaries of separate flowers inserted on a common receptacle.

Naked. Lacking a covering, as leaves without pubescence or buds without scales.

Naturalized. Said of introduced plants which are reproducing and establishing themselves in the new environment.

Node. The region of a stem where one or more leaves arise.

Nonporous. Said of wood whose structure is homogeneous, without large pores.

Nut. A hard, indehiscent, usually 1-celled, 1-seeded fruit with a woody, leathery, bony, or papery wall; generally partly or wholly enclosed in an involucre or husk.

Nutlet. A small nut.

Oblanceolate. Lanceolate, with the broadest part toward the apex. Page 8.

Oblique. Slanting, or with unequal sides.

Oblong. Longer than broad, with sides approximately parallel. Page 8.

Obovate. Ovate, with the broadest part toward the apex. Page 8.

Obovoid. An ovate solid with the broadest part toward the apex.

Obtuse. Blunt or rounded at the apex. Page 9.

Opposite. Arrangement of leaves, branches, buds, etc., on opposite sides of a stem at a node.

Orbicular. Circular. Page 8.

Oval. Broadly elliptical. Page 8.

Ovary. The part of a pistil that contains the ovules. Page 18.

Ovate. Shaped like the longitudinal section of a hen's egg, with the broad end basal. Page 8.

Ovoid. Solid ovate or solid oval; egg-shaped.

Ovulate. Bearing ovules.

Ovule. The part of a flower which after fertilization becomes the seed.

Palmate. Radiately lobed or divided; hand-shaped.

Panicle. A loose inflorescence with two or more orders of branching and pedicellate flowers. Page 19.

Paniculate.   Arranged in panicles or resembling a panicle.

Papilionaceous.   Butterflylike, as in flowers of the Fabaceae (Leguminosae).

Pedicel.   The stalk of a single flower in a compound inflorescence.

Pedicellate.   Borne on a pedicel.

Peduncle.   A primary flower stalk, supporting either a cluster or a solitary flower.

Pendent.   Hanging downward.

Pendulous.   More or less hanging or declined.

Perfect.   Said of a flower with both stamens and pistil. Page 18.

Perianth.   The calyx and corolla of a flower considered together.

Persistent.   Staying on the plant, as leaves remaining through the winter or seed cones for years.

Petal.   One of the divisions of a corolla. Page 18.

Petiole.   The stem or stalk of a leaf.

Petiolulate.   Having a petiolule.

Petiolule.   The stem or stalk of a leaflet.

pH.   The reaction of the soil, whether basic, neutral, or acidic, based on the concentration of hydrogen ions in solution (pH value equals the logarithm of the reciprocal of the hydrogen ion concentration).

Phototrophic.   Responding toward light.

Pilose.   Hairy with long, soft hairs.

Pinnate.   Featherlike, with midrib and lateral branches or leaflets.

Pinnately compound.   With the leaflets arranged along both sides of a common midrib. Even-pinnate, without a terminal leaflet; odd-pinnate, with a terminal leaflet.

Pinnately veined.   With the lateral veins arranged along the two sides of the midvein, not arising from a single point.

Pistil.   The seed-bearing organ of a flower, normally consisting of ovary, style, and stigma. Page 18.

Pistillate.   Provided with a pistil, but usually without stamens.

Pith.   The softer central part of a twig or stem.

Platy.   Layered in flat sheets.

Plumose.   Feathery.

Pollen.   The grains (microspores, containing sperms) produced in the anther.

Polygamodioecious.   With flowers sometimes perfect, sometimes unisexual, the sexes mostly borne on different individuals.

Polygamomonoecious.   With flowers sometimes perfect, sometimes unisexual, both sexes borne on the same individual.

Polygamous.   With flowers, sometimes perfect, sometimes unisexual, the sexes borne on the same or on different individuals.

Pome.   A fleshy fruit with a papery core, derived from an inferior compound ovary and receptacle, as an apple.

Porous.   Having large pores visible to the unaided eye. See *diffuse-porous* and *ring-porous*.

Prickle.   A sharp-pointed outgrowth of the epidermis or cortex of any organ.

Prostrate. Lying flat on the ground.

Puberulent. Minutely pubescent.

Pubescence. A covering of short, soft hairs; downy.

Punctate. Dotted with translucent or colored dots or pits.

Pyramidal. Shaped like a pyramid, with the broadest part near the base.

Raceme. Usually a narrow inflorescence with only one order of branches of flowers on pedicels of about equal length at maturity, arranged on a common, elongated axis, the lowermost flowers blooming first. Page 19.

Racemose. In a raceme.

Rachis. The central axis of a spike or raceme of flowers or of a compound leaf.

Radicle. The first root formed in a seed by the embryo.

Receptacle. The more or less expanded portion of an axis which bears the organs of a flower.

Recurved. Curved downward or backward.

Reflexed. Bent sharply backward.

Remote. Scattered; not close together.

Resin ducts. Long, narrow channels between the elements of the wood, filled with resin.

Resinous. Having resin.

Reticulate. Arranged as in a network.

Revolute. Rolled backward from the edge.

Rhizome. A horizontal underground stem, usually rooting at the nodes.

Rib. A prominent vein of a leaf or the extended edge of a fruit husk, fruit, or seed.

Ring-porous. Said of the wood of broad-leaved trees in which the pores are comparatively large at the beginning of each growth ring and decrease in size more or less abruptly toward the summer wood, forming a distinct ring of large pores in the spring wood. See *diffuse-porous.*

Root. An absorbing and anchoring organ, usually initially developed from the radicle and growing downward.

Root collar. Region of the juncture of trunk base and the major roots.

Rough. Harsh to the touch.

Rugose. Wrinkled.

Rust. A fungus disease usually with orange-colored spore masses.

Samara. An indehiscent winged fruit.

Sand. A kind of soil containing at least 85 percent sand particles; a soil particle between 0.05 and 2.0 mm in diameter.

Sapwood. The outer portion of a trunk or large branch of a tree between the heartwood and the bark, containing the living elements of the wood. Page 6.

Scabrous. Rough to the touch when rubbed in at least one direction.

Scales. Small modified leaves, usually thin and scarious, seen in buds and cones; the flakes into which the outer bark often divides.

Scaly. Provided with scales.

Scarious. Thin, dry, membranous; not green.

Sculptured. Having raised or grooved contours on the surface.

Scurfy. Covered with small branlike scales.

Seed. The ripened ovule.

Segment. One of the parts of a structure that is cleft or divided.

Sepal. One of the divisions of a calyx. Page 18.

Serrate. Toothed, the teeth sharp and pointing forward. Page 9.

Serrulate. Finely serrate, the teeth small and shallow.

Sessile. Attached directly, without a stalk.

Sheath. A thin enveloping part, as of a leaf; any body enwrapping a stem.

Shoot. The repeating unit of plant construction, comprising stem, leaves, and buds.

Shrub. A woody perennial plant usually branched several times at or near the base giving a bushy appearance, usually less than 5 meters tall.

Silt. A soil textural class; soil particle between 0.05 and 0.002 mm in diameter.

Simple. Of one piece; not compound.

Sinuate. Strongly wavy. Page 9.

Sinuous. In form like the path of a snake.

Sinus. The cleft or space between two lobes of a blade.

Site. The place and associated physical factors of the environment where a plant grows; habitat.

Smooth. Lacking hairs or projections.

Soil. A dynamic natural body on the surface of the earth in which plants grow, composed of mineral and organic materials and living organisms.

Soil texture. The relative proportions of the various soil particles (sand, silt, or clay) in a soil.

Spatulate. Wide and rounded at the apex but gradually narrowed downward. Page 8.

Spike. A simple inflorescence of sessile flowers arranged on a common, elongated axis. Page 19.

Spine. A sharp-pointed stiff outgrowth from a stem derived from a leaf or part of a leaf.

Spray. The aggregate of smaller branches and branchlets.

Spring wood. That portion of a growth ring which is formed in the spring; the softer, more open wood on the inner side of the growth ring.

Spur shoot. A short, stubby branch with leaf scars greatly crowded as a result of little or no growth in length.

Stamen. The pollen-bearing organ of a flower, normally consisting of filament and anther. Page 18.

Staminate. Provided with stamens, but usually without pistils.

Staminodium. A sterile stamen.

Stellate. Star-shaped.

Stem. The organ of the plant that makes up the aerial portions (sometimes also the rhizomes) and bears the leaves and buds.

Sterigmata. The very small, woody, peglike leaf stalks of some conifers, primarily spruces.

Sterile. Nonproductive, opposite of fertile. Of a site, poor or not well-supplied with nutrients.

Stigma. The part of a pistil that receives the pollen. Page 18.

Stipules. Leaflike appendages on either side of a leaf at the base of the petiole, always in pairs.

Stipule-scar. The scar left by the fall of a stipule.

Stolon. An elongate, propagative stem with long internodes, rooting at the tip.

Stoloniferous. With stolons.

Striate. Marked with fine longitudinal stripes or ridges.

Style. The part of a pistil connecting ovary with stigma. Page 18.

Sub-. A prefix applied to many botanical terms to indicate "somewhat" or "slightly," as subcordate.

Subtend. To lie under.

Succulent. Juicy.

Sucker. A shoot arising from the base or a subterranean part of a plant.

Summer wood. That portion of a growth ring which is formed in the summer; the harder, denser wood on the outer side of the growth ring.

Superposed. Placed above, as one bud above another at a node.

Suture. A junction or line of dehiscence.

Tapering. Gradually becoming smaller in diameter or width toward one end.

Tendril. A long, slender, coiling structure serving as the organ of attachment in some climbing plants.

Terete. Circular in cross section.

Terminal. Situated at the end of a shoot or branch.

Ternate. In threes.

Thorn. A stiff, woody, sharp-pointed projection which represents a modified stem.

Tissue. A mass of cells which has a distinctive character and function, e.g., cork or wood.

Tolerant. Capable of enduring unfavorable conditions, as shade, drought, salt, etc.

Tomentose. Densely pubescent with soft, matted curled hairs; woolly.

Toothed. With teeth or short projections.

Tree. A woody perennial plant with a single trunk (typically unbranched near the base), usually exceeding 5 meters high.

Truncate. Ending abruptly, as if cut off at the end.

Trunk. The main stem of a tree.

Turbinate. Top-shaped.

Twig. The woody terminal portion of a branch.

Two-ranked. Said of leaves oriented so they appear to be on a single plane on either side of the stem, not projecting out from all sides of the stem.

Umbel. A simple inflorescence of flowers on pedicels which radiate from the same point. Page 19.

Umbellate.   Arranged in umbels.

Umbo.   A protuberance or boss, typically found on the apophysis of cone scales of conifers.

Unarmed.   Without thorns, spines, or prickles.

Undulate.   With a wavy margin or surface. Page 9.

Valvate.   Said of buds in which the scales merely meet at the edges without overlapping.

Valve.   One of the parts into which a capsule splits.

Variety.   A subdivision of a species with characteristics that separate it from other varieties of the same species, including usually a distinctive geographical range.

Vascular bundle.   A strandlike portion of the conducting system of a plant.

Veins.   Threads of vascular tissue in a leaf, petal, or other flat organ.

Vestigal.   The aborted remnant of a structure or function.

Villous.   Covered with long, soft hairs, not matted together.

Viscid.   Sticky, glutinous.

Whorl.   An arrangement of three or more similar leaves or branches arising at a single node.

Wing.   Any membranous or thin expansion bordering or surrounding an organ.

Wood.   The hard internal tissue of a perennial stem. Page 6.

Woolly.   Covered with long and matted or tangled hairs; tomentose.

Xeric.   Characterized by deficiency of moisture, or aridity. Said of a habitat that is dry or droughty.

Literature Cited

Barnes, Burton V. 1961. Hybrid aspens in the Lower Peninsula of Michigan. *Rhodora* 63:311–24.

———. 1966. The clonal growth habit of American aspens. *Ecology* 47:439–47.

———. 1969. Natural variation and delineation of clones of *Populus tremuloides* and *P. grandidentata* in northern lower Michigan. *Silvae Genetica* 18:130–42.

———. 1976. Succession in deciduous swamp communities of southeastern Michigan formerly dominated by American elm. *Canadian Journal of Botany* 54:19–24.

Barnes, Burton V.; Dancik, Bruce P.; and Sharik, Terry L. 1974. Natural hybridization of yellow birch and paper birch. *Forest Science* 15:215–21.

Bernabo, J. Christopher, and Webb, Thompson III. 1977. Changing patterns in the Holocene pollen record of northeastern North America: a mapped summary. *Quaternary Research* 8:64–96.

Billington, Cecil 1949. *Shrubs of Michigan*. Cranbrook Inst. Sci. Bull. 20, 2d ed. Bloomfield Hills, Mich.: Cranbrook Institute of Science. 339 pp.

Core, Earl L., and Ammons, Nelle P. 1973. *Woody plants in winter*. Pacific Grove, Calif.: Boxwood Press. 218 pp.

Cronquist, A. J. 1968. *The evolution and classification of flowering plants*. Boston: Houghton Mifflin Co. 396 pp.

Curtis, John T. 1959. *The vegetation of Wisconsin*. Madison: University of Wisconsin Press. 657 pp.

Dancik, Bruce P. 1969. Dark-barked birches of southern Michigan. *Michigan Botanist* 8:38–41.

Dancik, Bruce P., and Barnes, Burton V. 1971. Variability in bark morphology of yellow birch in an even-aged stand. *Michigan Botanist* 10:34–38.

———. 1972. Natural variation and hybridization of yellow birch and bog birch in southeastern Michigan. *Silvae Genetica* 21:1–9.

Daniel, Theodore; Helms, John A.; and Baker, Frederick S. 1979. *Principles of silviculture*. 2d ed. New York: McGraw-Hill.

Davis, Margaret B. 1976. Pleistocene biogeography of temperate deciduous forests. *Geoscience and Man* 13:13–26.

Dirr, Michael A. 1977. *Manual of woody landscape plants, their identification, ornamental characteristics, culture, propagation and uses*. Rev. ed. Champaign, Ill.: Stipes Publ. Co.

Dorr, John A., Jr., and Eschman, Donald F. 1970. *Geology of Michigan*. Ann Arbor, Mich.: University of Michigan Press.

Fernald, Merritt Lyndon 1950. *Gray's manual of botany.* 8th ed. New York: American Book Co. xiv plus 1632 pp.

Graham, Samuel A.; Harrison, Robert P. Jr.; and Westell, Casey E. Jr. 1963. *Aspens: phoenix trees of the Great Lakes region.* Ann Arbor, Mich.: University of Michigan Press. 272 pp.

Harlow, William M.; Harrar, Ellwood S.; and White, Fred M. 1979. *Textbook of dendrology.* 6th ed. New York: McGraw-Hill. 510 pp.

Hosie, R. C. 1969. *Native trees of Canada,* 7th ed. Ottawa, Canada: Canadian Forestry Service. 380 pp.

Hudgins, Bert. 1961. *Michigan: geographic backgrounds in the development of the commonwealth.* 4th ed. Ann Arbor, Mich.: J.W. Edwards. 116 pp.

Kapp, Ronald O. 1977. Late Pleistocene and postglacial plant communities of the Great Lakes region. In *Geobotany,* ed. Robert C. Romans. New York: Plenum.

Kemperman, Jerry A., and Barnes, Burton V. 1976. Clone size in American aspens. *Canadian Journal of Botany* 54:2603–7.

Kramer, Paul J., and Kozlowski, Theodore T. 1979. *Physiology of woody plants.* New York: Academic Press. 811 pp.

Küchler, A. W. 1964. *The potential natural vegetation of the conterminous United States.* American Geographic Society Special Publication No. 36. New York: American Geographic Society. 154 pp., map.

Li, Hui-Lin 1963. *The origin and cultivation of shade and ornamental trees.* Philadelphia: University of Pennsylvania Press. 282 pp.

Little, Elbert L., Jr. 1971. *Atlas of United States trees. Vol. 1, conifers and important hardwoods.* USDA Forest Service Miscellaneous Publication No. 1146. Washington, D.C.: Government Printing Office.

———. 1977. *Atlas of United States trees. Vol. 4, minor eastern hardwoods.* USDA Miscellaneous Publication No. 1342. Washington, D.C.: Government Printing Office. 17 pp., 230 maps.

Manning, Wayne E. 1950. A key to the hickories north of Virginia with notes on the two pignuts, *Carya glabra* and *C. ovalis. Rhodora* 52:188–99.

McKee, Russell 1979. Michigan giants. *Michigan Natural Resources Magazine* 48:41–47.

Michigan Department of Agriculture, Michigan Weather Service. 1974. *Climate of Michigan by stations.* 2d rev. ed. East Lansing, Mich: State of Michigan, Department of Agriculture.

Mirov, N. T. 1967. *The genus* Pinus. New York: Ronald Press Co. 602 pp.

Overlease, William R. 1975. Populations (six) studies of red oak (*Quercus rubra* L.) and northern red oak *(Quercus rubra* var. *borealis* (Michx. f.) Farw.). *Proc. Pennsylvania Academy of Science* 49:138–40.

———. 1977. A study of the relationship between scarlet oak (*Quercus coccinea* Muenchh.) and Hill oak (*Quercus ellipsoidalis* E. J. Hill) in Michigan and nearby states. *Proc. Pennsylvania Academy of Science* 51:47–50.

Panshin, Alexis John, and de Zeeuw, Carl 1970. *Textbook of wood technology. Vol. I, structure, identification, uses, and properties of the commercial woods of the United States.* 3d ed. New York: McGraw-Hill. 705 pp.

Pardo, Richard 1978. National register of big trees. *American Forests* 84:18–45.

Peattie, Donald Culross. 1950. *A natural history of trees of eastern and central North America.* Boston: Houghton Mifflin Co. 606 pp.

Schoenike, Roland E. 1976. *Geographical variations in jack pine* (Pinus banksiana). University of Minnesota Agricultural Experiment Station Technical Bulletin No. 304. St. Paul, Minn.: University of Minnesota. 47 pp.

Smith, Norman F. 1978. *Michigan trees worth knowing.* 5th ed. Hillsdale, Mich.: Hillsdale Educational Publishers. 88 pp.

Sommers, Lawrence M., ed. 1977. *Atlas of Michigan.* East Lansing, Mich.: Michigan State University Press. 242 pp.

Spurr, Stephen H., and Barnes, Burton V. 1980. *Forest ecology.* New York: John Wiley & Sons. 687 pp.

Symonds, George W. D. 1963. *The shrub identification book.* New York: M. Barrows and Co.

Thompson, Paul W. 1969. A unique American chestnut grove. *Michigan Academician* 1:175–78.

———. 1975. Champion trees of Michigan. *Michigan Botanist* 14:167–74.

———. 1977. *Champion trees in Michigan—the big tree state.* Ann Arbor, Mich.: Michigan Botanical Club. 7 pp.

U.S., Department of Agriculture. 1965. *Silvics of forest trees of the United States.* USDA Forest Service, Agricultural Handbook No. 271. Washington, D.C.: Government Printing Office. 762 pp.

———. 1974. *Seeds of woody plants in the United States.* USDA Forest Service, Agricultural Handbook No. 450. Washington, D.C.: Government Printing Office. 883 pp.

Van Den Brink, C.; Strommen, N. D.; and Kenworthy, A. L. 1971. *Growing degree days in Michigan.* Michigan State University Agricultural Experimental Station Research Report 131. East Lansing, Mich.: Michigan State University. 48 pp.

Voss, Edward G. 1972. *Michigan flora. Pt. I, gymnosperms and monocots.* Cranbrook Inst. Sci. Bull. 55. Bloomfield Hills, Mich.: Cranbrook Institute of Science. 488 pp.

Wagner, W. H., Jr. 1970. The Barnes hybrid aspen, *Populus ×barnesii,* Hbr. Nov. a nomenclatural case in point. *Michigan Botanist* 9:53–54.

———. 1974. Dwarf hackberry (Ulmaceae: *Celtis tenuifolia*) in the Great Lakes region. *Michigan Botanist* 13:73–99.

———. 1975. Notes on the floral biology of box-elder (*Acer negundo*). *Michigan Botanist* 14:73–82.

Wagner, W. H., Jr.; Daniel, T. F.; Beitel, J. M.; and Crispin, Sue R. 1980. Studies on *Populus heterophylla* in southern Michigan. *Michigan Botanist* 19:269–75.

Wagner, W. H., Jr., and Schoen, D. J. 1976. Shingle oak (*Quercus imbricaria*) and its hybrids in Michigan. *Michigan Botanist* 15:141–55.

Wagner, W. H., Jr.; Voss, E. G.; Beaman, J. H.; Bourdo, E. A.; Case, F. W.; Churchill, J. A.; and Thompson, P. W. 1977. Endangered, threatened, and rare vascular plants in Michigan. *Michigan Botanist* 16:99–110.

Waring, R. H., and Franklin, J. F. 1979. The evergreen coniferous forests of the Pacific Northwest. *Science* 204:1380–86.

Wearstler, Kenneth A., Jr., and Barnes, Burton V. 1977. Genetic diversity of yellow birch seedlings in Michigan. *Canadian Journal of Botany* 55:2778–88.

Wright, Jonathan W. 1972. Genetic variation patterns in Michigan's native trees. *Michigan Academician* 5:61–69.

Wright, J. W.; Pauley, S. S.; Polk, R. B.; Jokela, J. J.; and Read, R. A. 1966. Performance of Scotch pine varieties in the north central region. *Silvae Genetica* 15:101–110.

Wright, J. W.; Lemmien, W. A.; Bright, J. N.; Day, M. W.; and Sajdak, R. L. 1976. *Scotch pine varieties for Christmas tree and forest planting in Michigan*. Michigan Agricultural Experiment Station Research Report 293. East Lansing, Mich.: Michigan State University. 15 pp.

Wyman, Donald 1965. *Trees for American gardens*. New York: Macmillan Co. 502 pp.

Index

Page numbers in italic indicate a detailed description. An asterisk (*) indicates the species is illustrated. A dagger (†) indicates a description of the genus or group.

377

378

379

Redbud, 46, 49, *168**
Redcedar, eastern, 47, *98**
Red chokeberry, 332
Red elm, *248**
Red horsechestnut, 180, 184
Red maple, 24, 44, 47, 48, *194**
Red mulberry, 48, *256**
Red oak, 47, *276**
Red-osier dogwood, *336*
Red pine, 33, 38, 39, 44, 48, *90**
Red raspberry, *330*
Reproduction, 4
RHAMNACEAE, 338–39
Rhamnus
    alnifolia, *338*
    cathartica, 309, *339*
    frangula, 309, *339*
Rhus, 343
    aromatica, *344*
    copallina, *344*
    glabra, 309, *344*
    ×pulvinata, 345
    radicans, 346. *See*
        Toxicodendron
    typhina, 309, *345*
Ribes
    americanum, *332*
    cynosbati, *332*
River bank grape, *340*
Robinia, 18
    pseudoacacia, *162**
Rock chestnut oak, 272
Rock elm 47, 48, *246**
Rosa, *327*
    palustris, 327
ROSACEAE, 135–61, 326–32
Rose, 51, *327*
Rosemary
    bog, 320
    wild, 320
Roundleaf dogwood, *335*
RUBIACEAE, 351
Rubus, 328
    alleghaniensis, *329*
    flagellaris, *329*
    hispidus, *329*
    idaeus, *330*
    idaeus var. strigosus, 330
    occidentalis, *330*
    parviflorus, *330*
Russian-olive, *341*

RUTACEAE, 346–47
Rydberg's poison ivy, 346

SALICACEAE, 51, 110–33, 326
Salix, 125[†]
    alba, 128
    amygdaloides, 48, 49, *126**
    babylonica, *128**
    discolor, 326
    fragilis, *130**
    humulis, 326
    interior, *326*
    nigra, 48, 49, *132**
Sambucus
    canadensis, *353*
    pubens, *353*
Sandbar willow, *326*
Sapwood, 6, 17
Sassafras, 49, *104**
    albidum, 49, *104**
Saucer magnolia, 106
SAXIFRAGACEAE, 332
Scarlet oak, 48, *280**
Scotch pine, *86**
Scots pine, *86**
Serviceberry, 145[†]
    Allegheny, 146
    downy, 47, *146**
    smooth, 146
Shadbush, 145
Shagbark hickory, 47, *220**
Shellbark hickory, 49, *218**
Shepherdia canadensis, *341*
Shingle oak, 46, 49, *286**
Shining sumac, *344*
Shoot
    defined, 4
    types, 7, 10–11
Showy mountain-ash, 142
Shrubby cinquefoil, 21, *327*
Shrubby St. John's-wort, *326*
Shrubs, 2, 309
    key to, 310
Siberian elm, *250**
Silky dogwood, *335*
Silver buffaloberry, 342
Silver maple, 47, 48, *196**
SIMARUBACEAE, 178
Site, 23
Slippery elm, 47, 48, *248**
Small cranberry, 325

381

Conversion Factors for Selected English and Metric Units

Metric Units	English Equivalents
Length	
1 cm (centimeter)	0.393 701 inch
1 m (meter)	3.280 84 feet
1 m (meter)	1.093 61 yards
1 km (kilometer)	0.621 371 mile
Area	
1 cm^2 (square centimeter)	0.155 000 square inch
1 ha (hectare)	2.471 05 acres
1 m^2 (square meter)	10.763 9 square feet
Mass or Weight	
1 gm (gram)	0.035 274 ounce
1 kg (kilogram)	2.204 62 pounds

English Units	Metric Equivalents
Length	
1 inch	2.54 cm (exactly)
1 foot	0.304 8 (exactly)
1 yard	0.914 4 (exactly)
1 mile	1.609 34 km
Area	
1 acre	0.404 686 ha
1 square foot	0.092 903 m^2
1 square inch	6.451 6 cm^2 (exactly)
Mass or Weight	
1 ounce	28.349 5 gm
1 pound	0.453 592 kg
Temperature	
Celsius (Centigrade) degrees	$\frac{5}{9}$ (°F − 32)
Fahrenheit degrees	$\frac{9}{5}$ (°C + 32)